Phil,
This is what I
got up to in
1969 – 1975 !!
Sam.

THE ARCHAEOLOGY OF RUTLAND WATER

The Archaeology of Rutland Water:

Excavations at Empingham in the Gwash Valley, Rutland, 1967-73 and 1990

by

Nicholas J. Cooper

with contributions from:

R. Alvey, R. Bellamy, P. Blinkhorn, I. Bowden, P. Buckland, J. Buckley, B. Dickinson, A. Diver, S. M. Fraser, S. J. Glaswell, R. Head, P. Liddle, A. Monckton, G. C. Morgan, A. Morrison, M. Ponting, J. Wakely, and R. Young

Leicester Archaeology Monographs No. 6

2000

University of Leicester Archaeological Services,
School of Archaeological Studies,
University of Leicester for English Heritage

ISBN 0 953 8914 0 2

Published by
University of Leicester Archaeological Services,
School of Archaeological Studies,
University of Leicester

100370203x T

Front Cover: *Rutland Water reservoir from the air (Courtesy Leics. County Council)*
Rear Cover: *Empingham I Early Anglo-Saxon Cemetery (Site 3): Grave 5*
Frontispiece: *View north across the Gwash Valley*

Designed and produced by
The TypeFoundry, Northampton

Contents

INTRODUCTION
Nicholas J. Cooper 1

PEOPLE AND PLACES
Nicholas J. Cooper with Peter Liddle and Samantha J. Glaswell (Site 3), Josephine Buckley (Site 7), Jennifer Wakely and Rachel Bellamy (population)

MATERIAL CULTURE

PLANTS AND ANIMALS

SETTLEMENT IN THE GWASH VALLEY TO THE NORMAN CONQUEST
Nicholas J. Cooper 142

BIBLIOGRAPHY
. 156

Figures

Plates

Front Cover: Rutland Water from the air, 1991. Excavations concentrated in the area of the dam, bottom right close to the village of Empingham (refer to Fig. 1). (1:10,000 vertical shot, courtesy of Leicestershire County Council.)

Rear Cover: Empingham I Early Anglo-Saxon Cemetery (Site 3), Grave 5.

Frontispiece: View north across the Gwash valley from Site 1 *c.* .1969 prior to the reservoir's construction.

Tables

Acknowledgements

None of the excavations documented in this report could have been undertaken without the voluntary help and support given by the many individuals who took part. Special thanks must go to Sam Gorin who took over the direction of the excavations following the tragic death of Malcolm Dean in 1970. As well as discussing the excavations, Sam provided access to additional site records and finds not stored at Nottingham University or Rutland County Museum. Of the other individuals involved in the excavations, only a few are known to the writer, but I would like to thank those who have provided additional photographic evidence (Jim Neville, Valerie Nourish, and Shirley Priest) and those who have given freely of their time to discuss the sites (John Golds and Bill Thomas). During the latter years of excavation, M.J. Gleeson Group plc, contractors for Anglian Water Authority, and consultant engineers T and C Hawkesley were particularly helpful in bringing discoveries to the notice of the archaeologists and for leaving areas available for excavation.

Much of the post-excavation work was undertaken by post-graduate students on the MA course in Post-Excavation Skills in the School of Archaeological Studies, Leicester University, supervised by staff of the School among whom I would particularly like to thank Anthony Gouldwell, Annie Grant, Graham Morgan, Deirdre O'Sullivan, Jenny Wakely and Rob Young.

Additional post-excavation work was undertaken by staff of Leicestershire Museums and special thanks must go to Anthony Reed for undertaking conservation work on the finds from the 'Empingham I' Early Anglo-Saxon cemetery (Site 3) and for Richard Knox for illustrating them. Other illustration work for the report was undertaken by David Hopkins (Leicestershire Archaeology Unit), Martha de Bethune (University of Nottingham), Cain Hegarty, Deborah Miles-Williams, Lucy Farr (School of Archaeology, University of Leicester), and individual authors.

The project could not have been undertaken without the generous financial support of English Heritage throughout, and I would like to thank successive East Midlands Team inspectors Deborah Priddy and Andrew Brown for monitoring the project.

Finally, I would especially like to thank Peter Liddle, Keeper of Archaeology for Leicestershire, who initially suggested the project and has provided constant encouragement and inspiration throughout, and Richard Buckley(ULAS), Neil Christie (School of Archaeology, University of Leicester) and staff of the Type Foundry, Northampton, for steering the production through the final stages.

Note: Most of the text was prepared during the period 1991-3 and although some up dating has taken place during the final editing stages, it should be borne in mind that many of the specialist reports will not incorporate the results of fieldwork and research published since.

N. J. Cooper
September 2000

Plate 1: Excavation in progress on Site 1 1970

INTRODUCTION

Nicholas J. Cooper

Context of the Excavations

With the exception of Site 7, excavated in 1990, the excavations published in this report were undertaken between 1967 and 1973, in advance of and during, the construction of Rutland Water reservoir. The reservoir, which lies 20 miles east of Leicester, was created by damming the River Gwash immediately south-west of Empingham village (fig.1) and flooding the twin valleys formed by its upper reaches to the west. The lower reaches of the river continue to flow eastwards to join the Welland, just beyond Stamford, Lincs., which ultimately flows into the Wash. The flooding of the reservoir covered an area of 3,100 acres of farmland in a rural part of the County of Rutland, submerging in perpetuity a sizeable portion of the archaeological heritage of the East Midlands.

Today, the construction of the largest artificial lake in Western Europe would occasion a full-scale archaeological investigation in advance of its construction, but in the late 1960s there was no permanent archaeological unit in the region that might monitor the impending destruction. For this reason a great debt is owed to those individuals who undertook the excavation work described in this report, often under extreme rescue conditions. The archaeological work which took place, was

Plate 2: Construction underway in the area of the dam c.1972.

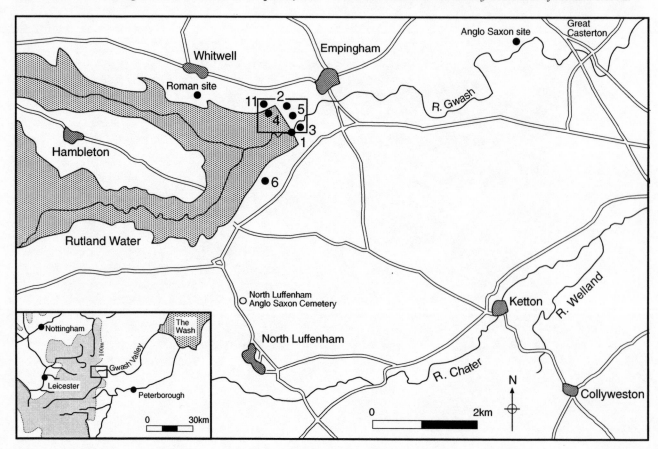

Fig. 1 a) The Gwash Valley within the East Midlands b) Rutland Water, the Gwash Valley, and Empingham

concentrated at the eastern end of the reservoir, in the area of the dam, where construction work was most intense, and so only a relatively small part of the submerged area was investigated in detail. However, the combination of the excavation of known sites with watching brief activities during the grading (topsoil removal) of the valley sides meant that a relatively complete picture of an approximately one square kilometre area (fig.2) was obtained, with two major additional sites excavated in the immediately surrounding area in subsequent years.

These two sites comprised firstly, the Empingham II Anglo-Saxon Cemetery excavated in 1974-75 (Timby 1996), and, secondly, the Iron Age and Roman settlement at Whitwell excavated in 1976-77 (Todd 1981). Neither site was actually to be submerged, but the building of car parking, administrative and leisure facilities on the north shore of the reservoir led to their discovery and dictated their partial destruction. The full publication of these two sites is now complete, and while a brief statement summarising the results of all the excavations undertaken in the area has been published (Adams *et al.* 1982), the present publication seeks to complete the outstanding record of the Prehistoric to Anglo-Saxon periods. The only other outstanding excavations are those undertaken by the Rutland Field Research Group at the medieval villages of Nether Hambleton in the south western part of the reservoir and Whitwell (Adams *et al.* 1982).

Excavations 1967-73 and 1990

The excavations undertaken between 1967 and 1973, were initially directed (Sites 1 and 3) by Malcolm Dean who was tragically killed in a car crash in May 1970. Direction (Sites 1, 2, and 3) was taken on by Sam Gorin during the summer seasons of 1970 and 1971, who then oversaw work that continued at weekends into the Autumn of 1971, and then, intermittently, under watching-brief conditions, through 1972 and 1973 (Sites 4 and 6). Site 5 was excavated in 1968 by Anthea Diver. This report also includes an account of the salvage excavations undertaken in 1990 by Leicestershire Archaeological Unit at Tickencote (Site 7), along the line of the Petrofina plc pipeline, situated three miles downstream of Empingham.

To avoid confusion when referring to the excavations by their original names, each has been given a number, and a concordance and period description are listed below.

Site 1 Known as 'Empingham Roman' (site code EPR) and excavated in 1969, 1970, and 1971. Romano-British aisled barn and farmstead (Wilson 1970, 286; 1971, 258-9, and 1972, 316).

Site 2 Known as 'Empingham North' (site code EPN) to distinguish it from EPR. Trial trenched in 1970 and excavated in 1971. Roman-British aisled villa building with middle Anglo-Saxon burials (Wilson 1972, 316).

Site 3 Known as 'Empingham I' Anglo-Saxon Cemetery to distinguish it from the cemetery at 'Empingham II'.

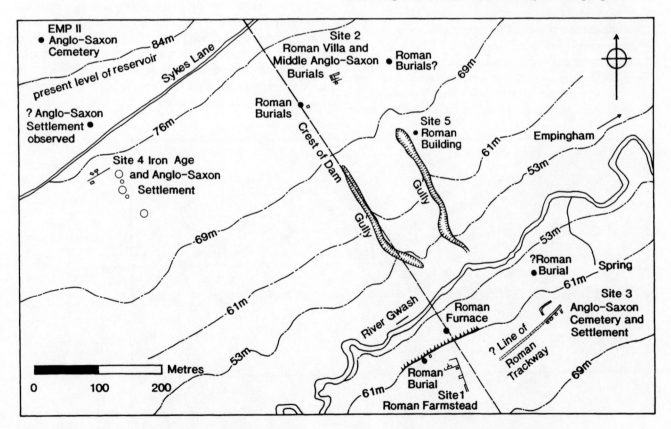

Fig. 2 The Excavations at Empingham 1967-73

Excavated in 1967 (site code EMP 67) and subsequently in 1969, 1970 and 71 when known as 'Empingham Saxon' (site code EPS) to distinguish it from Site 1. Limited early Roman evidence overlain by Early Anglo-Saxon settlement and cemetery (HMSO DoE 1968 and 1970, 68).

Site 4 Known as 'Empingham West' (site code EPW). Excavated in 1971 and 1972. Iron Age and Early Anglo-Saxon settlement.

Site 5 Known as 'Empingham 1968' (site code EMP 68). Excavated in 1968. Late Roman farm building and grain processing oven.

Site 6 Known as 'Renner's Park' or 'Empingham 73' (site code EMP 73). Excavated in 1973. Roman farmstead with well and grain processing oven.

For a number of reasons the excavations at Sites 1 to 6 remained unpublished for nearly three decades. The main reason was that the director was not a full-time archaeologist and had neither the time nor the resources to undertake the necessary post-excavation work. Additionally, the death of Malcolm Dean made the publication of the Empingham I cemetery difficult, although he had written a draft report on the 1967 excavations. The lack of published sites from Rutland, in any case, created a significant lacuna in the archaeology of Leicestershire, and the sites in the area of Rutland Water were particularly significant since nowhere else in the county had such a detailed picture of a small area of landscape been revealed by excavation, with prehistoric, Roman, and Anglo-Saxon sites in close proximity, for the simple reason that in no other instance has such a wide area been stripped of topsoil.

Discussions between the writer and Peter Liddle, now Keeper of Archaeology for Leicestershire Museums, generated a project proposal (The Rutland Water Project) to undertake the post-excavation work necessary to produce this volume within the School of Archaeological Studies at Leicester University, and English Heritage were enthusiastic in providing financial support. In addition to the post-excavation project, the needs of student fieldwork training within the School provided the opportunity to undertake a programme of fieldwalking survey in the area of the reservoir which would help place the earlier work within the context of the surrounding landscape. Twenty-five fields were walked in the parishes of Empingham and Hambleton between 1990 and 1994 and the preliminary results of this survey have been incorporated into the final discussion section of this report with a summary published elsewhere (Cooper 1998, 189-90).

Geological Background

The solid and drift geology of the Gwash valley is summarised in figure 3 with the locations of the major archaeological sites marked for comparison (map based on OS Solid and Drift Geological.Sheet 157 for Stamford, 1957). The Gwash Valley cuts through a low limestone plateau which forms the eastern side of the Vale of Catmose and, together with the twin tributaries of the Chater to the south, forms part of the northern catchment of the River Welland which flows into the fens some twelve miles to the east. The landscape produced is one of rolling country rising to 120m punctuated by broad valleys supporting rich arable farming and sheep pasture. The area of the valley near Empingham cuts through the Lincolnshire Limestone which, in the immediate area of the sites, towards the valley bottom, gives way to ironstone with liassic clay forming the base. The narrow stream itself has formed only a thin band of alluvium over this. The boundary between the clay and the base of the ironstone acted as a spring line which appears to have been an important factor in settlement location along the valley sides.

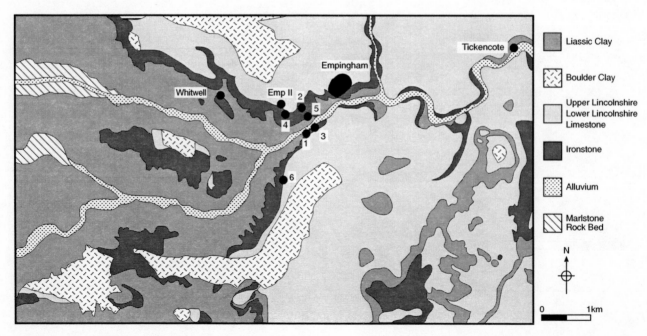

Fig. 3 The Geology of the Gwash Valley

SITE 1:
EMPINGHAM ROMANO-BRITISH FARMSTEAD

Nicholas J. Cooper

Introduction

Excavation of the site was directed successively by Malcolm Dean in 1969 and M.S. Gorin in 1970 and 1971 (Archive site code: EPR 1969-71). The site lay 80m south of the River Gwash at SK 943 077, and 150m west of Site 3, where evidence of first and second century AD occupation preceded the Early Anglo-Saxon settlement and cemetery. It was first identified during the excavation of Site 3 in 1967, when the line of the Romano-British stone trackway, recognised on that site, appeared to continue westwards into the adjacent field. Random fieldwalking detected a scatter of Roman pottery and building materials on the conjectured line of the trackway.

The site was excavated over three seasons; initially for a period of three weeks in 1969, while work continued on Site 3, and subsequently during the summers of 1970 and 1971, with work continuing at weekends during the autumn. The first season revealed the basic plan of the masonry phase aisled barn (Building 1) in the northern part of the site, and work extended southwards during the following seasons.

Note: The series of feature numbers mentioned in the following text has been created during the writing of the report in order to allow easy reference to the plans, and to avoid repeating lengthy descriptions and grid-coordinates. The on-site recording system comprised a series of two letter codes (AA, AB, AC.....ZZ) each assigned to a finds tray, or group of finds, excavated from a particular feature or area (if unstratified) at a particular time. Therefore, several codes may relate to the excavation of one feature, but do not always have stratigraphical significance within that feature. The two-letter codes are accompanied by a description of the area or feature, and site grid-coordinates in the site records. In the text the two-letter codes are pre-fixed by the year of excavation (69, 70, or 71) in order to avoid confusion between the separate series of codes.

A Summary of the Structural Sequence

The following phasing represents a suggested reconstruction of the sequence of events on the site based upon the evidence of stratification recorded, and the associated artefactual material. The contemporaneity or otherwise of structures and features is difficult to prove conclusively where stratification is shallow, and it is therefore based largely on the evidence of the pottery contained in the fills of negative features.

A series of six phases has been identified:
Phase 1: Prehistoric Activity
Phase 2A: *c.* mid-first to early second century AD.
Phase 2B: *c.* mid-first to *c.*160 AD.

Phase 3: *c.* 220 to 270/300 AD
Phase 4: *c.* 270/300 to 350 AD
Phase 5A: *c.* 350 AD
Phase 5B: *c.* 350 to 400 AD
Phase 6: Post-Roman Activity

Occupation Prior to the Masonry Farmstead (Phases 1 and 2)

Phase 1: Prehistoric Activity

This phase was represented by a general scatter of flint implements and waste across the field in which the site was located. The material was collected during random fieldwalking in 1967 and during the excavation itself, and indicated activity from the Mesolithic to the Neolithic or Early Bronze Age.

Phase 2A and B: c. mid 1st century AD to c.AD 160

This phase was represented by a group of features sealed by the Phase 3-5 masonry structures, and comprised a number of ditches, pits, post holes, sleeper beam trenches, and possible furnace structures or hearths. The preparation of the site for occupation appears to have involved the terracing of the valley side, and the leading edges of three terraces were indicated by the strips of poorly preserved archaeological levels running east-west across the site.

Phase 2A was represented by a ditch or series of ditches running east to west across the south end of the site. Sections across them (particularly F50) produced the earliest pottery on the site dating from the mid-first to early second century. It is assumed that this ditch was broadly contemporary with the Phase 2B structures to the north, but gradually fell into disuse during this period, becoming completely filled with domestic rubbish well before the end of Phase 2.

Phase 2B comprised one or probably two timber buildings (A and B) in the northern part of the site, represented by sleeper beam trenches (F19-21), with three ditch features immediately to the north-east (F1, 2, and 4), the largest of which (F1) ran northwards and contained a large dump of pottery. Other features included possible hearth structures (F11, 6, and 26).

Pottery in the fills of these features placed the end of Phase 2 in the third quarter of the second century at the earliest. The burnt condition of the pottery particularly from F1, may indicate that the structures were destroyed either accidentally by fire or deliberately during the levelling process in advance of the masonry farmstead (phases 3-5). Roman activity detected 150m to the east on Site 3 was broadly contemporary, and it is possible that a stone trackway connected the two sites at this time.

The Masonry Farmstead (Phases 3-5)

This period witnessed a major reorganisation of the site, and the development of a stone-founded farmstead constructed from locally available Lincolnshire limestone. The lack of later second and early third century samian and contemporary British fine wares on the site, may indicate that the masonry building phase did not begin until at least the early third century, leaving a break in occupation of perhaps fifty years or more.

It would appear from the coinage and pottery evidence that occupation then continued unbroken for at least the next 180 years, and possibly into the early fifth century. During this period a number of alterations and additions were made to the basic layout of the site established in the early third century. These changes have been placed into three phases which are to an extent arbitrary in terms of the duration of individual elements, but based on the most likely sequence.

Phase 3: c.220-270

This was represented by the initial construction phase of Building 1, an aisled barn, at the north end of the site, which overlay Buildings A and B of Phase 2B, and was on the same alignment.

The area to the south consisted of a cobbled yard, which probably incorporated the ironstone bedrock material with locally available limestone cobbling. A division of the yard into an outer (eastern) area, and an inner (western area) through the continuation southwards of the eastern wall line may have occurred at this time, with access given by a gateway defined by an area of worn cobbling. The post settings associated with this gateway were sealed by the dividing wall, and therefore it is proposed that the division could originally have been of timber. The major features in the inner yard at this time comprised a well and a cobbled trackway leading south-westwards. In the outer yard a cobbled area or pathway appeared to lead to a point on the eastern gable end wall of Building 1.

The end of this phase is defined by the dating of the pottery from the well which goes out of use in the last quarter of the third century at the earliest and becomes a dumping place for sheep carcasses and a large amount of masonry rubble. While the abandonment of the well might not on its own be significant, its fill might signal an episode of change on the site.

Phase 4: c.270-350

A masonry boundary wall extending southwards on the line of the east wall of Building 1 was built at this time, if not earlier, to divide the yard and the original gate position was moved southwards, corresponding to an area of worn cobbling flanked by post settings.

The wall at this time extended southwards for a distance of 30m before a return wall ran westwards at right angles to enclose the inner yard on the south side. A keyhole-shaped corn drier was situated in the right angle created. It is likely that the corn drier was actually enclosed within a building, but unfortunately the area immediately north coincided with the leading edge of the third terrace, and had been badly plough-damaged.

Phase 5A and B: c. second half of the fourth century

During this phase the aisled barn was internally partitioned, creating a small room at the southern end, and splitting the remaining area into two portions of 30% and 70%. The partitions are dated by coins of mid-fourth century date which are sealed beneath them. The four extant post bases were retained to support the eastern part of the structure, but the support of the western end is uncertain, and must have been provided by the internal walls to a large extent. Two hearths or furnace structures set into the south wall of Building 1 are likely to have been inserted during this period.

A parallel arrangement of masonry footings, of similar width and length, ran along the eastern gable end of Building 1. The footings sealed pottery of later third or fourth century date at their northern end, and towards the south end covered the pathway leading from the presumed entrance through the gable end wall. The most likely function for these footings is that they supported some form of veranda or porch structure intended to enhance the appearance of this entrance to the building.

A small single-roomed building was constructed against the west face of the yard wall. The masonry was not bonded into the wall, and its foundations lay over an area of worn cobbling, suggesting that it was a later addition. New paving also appeared to seal pottery of later third or fourth century date. Access from the outer yard through the east wall was indicated by a worn threshold. The precise function of the building is unclear.

At some point during this phase the south wall of the yard would appear to have been demolished, save for a metre length, and the corn drier went out of use and was deliberately filled. The east wall of the inner yard was continued southwards, its extension abutting the original section. The truncated south wall was then abutted at right angles by a second section of north-south walling which ran in parallel with the first extension, to form a narrow alleyway, the function of which is unclear. The foundations for the parallel walls were not substantial and indicated that they were not intended to support a heavy superstructure.

In the extreme south-eastern part of the excavated area a complex of post holes was located. Overlapping plans of two buildings, one circular and one rectangular were indicated but their relative sequence was unclear. However, colour-coated ware pottery from two post holes of the rectangular building indicated that it was at least of later Roman date.

Post-Roman Activity

Phase 6

A small amount of Anglo-Saxon pottery was retrieved from the excavations (p.102), but none was securely stratified, and no features of this date were identified. It would appear that the focus of activity shifted 150m to the east to Site 3 at some point in the fifth century, although the precise date for this is uncertain. The occurrence of fourth century Roman pottery within the Early Anglo-Saxon features on Site 3, coupled with the lack of contemporary features of Roman date is interesting but may simply be linked to rubbish disposal from Site 1.

Phase 1

Evidence for prehistoric activity on the site is confined to an unstratified flint scatter, the composition of which is discussed in more detail in the report on lithic material (p.62).

Phase 2 (figs. 4 and 5)

The preparation of the site for occupation appears to have involved the terracing of the valley side, and the leading edges of three terraces are indicated by the strips of poorly preserved archaeology running east-west across the site which are approximately 8m wide and 8m apart. It is assumed that the terracing took place at this time, since if it had occurred later then many of the features belonging to Phase 2 would have been lost. However, the effect of later plough erosion along the leading edge of each terrace is best demonstrated by the differential preservation of the masonry walling of Phases 3-5. The best preserved areas would thus lie at the back of each terrace, protected by hillwash from the collapsed edge of the terrace above.

Evidence from two sections cut to the north of the site in 1971 provided evidence that the ground had been made up along the northern edge. The most southerly of the two showed definite tip lines from the dumping of loam and limestone, whilst the lower one to the north, showed that the clay had been cut away to form a trench into which limestone blocks were inserted, presumably to form a revetment.

Phase 2A: Mid-First Century – Early Second Century

Evidence for occupation during this period is limited, and confined to the extreme south of the excavated area.

Feature 50

A 10m length of east-west ditch, sealed at its eastern end by the phase 5 masonry walling, up to 1.6m wide and 1.0m deep (figs.4 and 5). It was lined on the north side with ironstone, sandy soil on the south side, and clean silt at the bottom. The fill was a brown loam, and this was capped by fine rubble along the northern edge. The pottery comprised only first century material, with no samian or other imported fine wares. Codes: 71 EZ, 71 FA, 71 FD, 71 FE, 71 FG, 71 FH, 71 ZAC, 71 ZAD, 71 ZAE.

Feature 67 and 68 (fig.5)

The westerly continuation of Feature 50 was indicated by Feature 67 detected in a trial trench (A) immediately to the west (71 AV), the primary fill of which contained pottery of the same date. Running parallel to this, 6m to the north west a further ditch or depression (Feature 68) was detected in trial trench B.

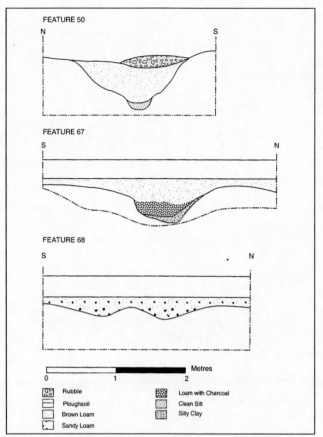

Fig. 5 Site 1 Phase 2A Sections of Ditches

Feature 69 and 70

Two parallel trial trenches running south eastwards across the eastern part of the site detected two portions of the line of a ditch (F70), 15m east of F50 and F69, 28m east of F50, running SW-NE. Feature 69 (70 CY) again contained shell-tempered pottery of first century date.

Features 50, 67, 69, and 70 would appear to belong to a single continuous ditch line.

Phase 2B: Early Second Century to c.160

The earliest excavated features over the rest of the site, indicate occupation during the later first and up to the middle or later second century.

Possible Timber Buildings

The removal of the Phase 3 masonry walling and cobbled flooring in the northern part of the site, exposed an area of sand mixed with patches of clay which, in section, was found to be of 0.75m thickness above the underlying ironstone bedrock. A number of features cut into the top of this sandy surface, and indicated the existence of one, or possibly two, timber-framed buildings side by side, towards the north-western corner of the excavated area.

Building A

Building A, the easterly of the two, was represented by two long narrow features which were probably beam slots (F19 and F21) set at right angles to one another, creating the south west corner of the proposed structure, on the same alignment as the later Phase 3 masonry structure. Feature 19 was a narrow, straight slot running east-west, and was overlain by a Phase 5 partition wall. The slot was 5.8m long, 0.5m wide, had a

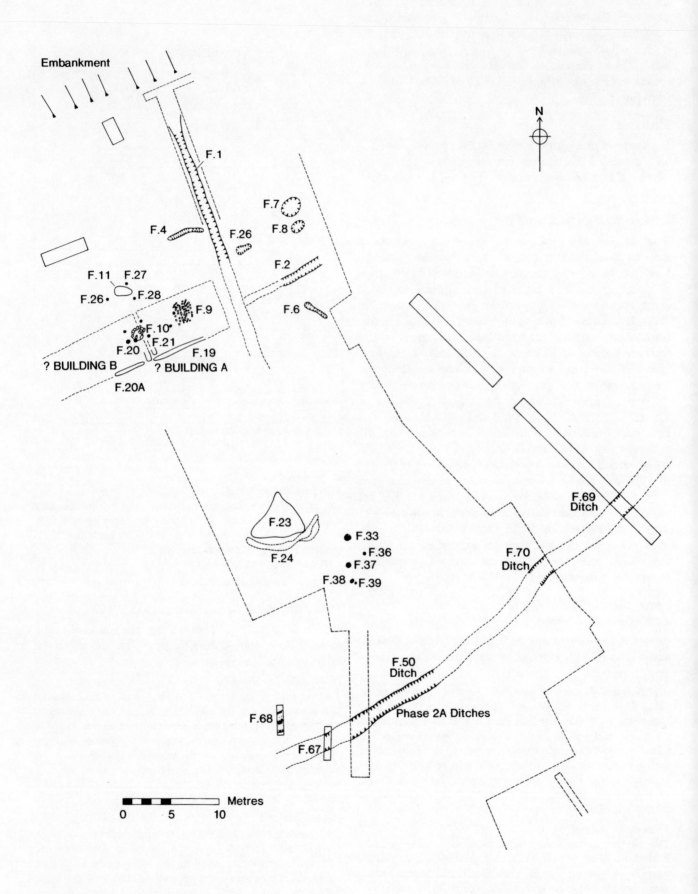

Fig. 4 Site 1 Phases 2a and 2b

rounded western terminal and no detected eastern terminal. F21 abutted on to F19, and was square ended with a width of 0.4m. Only a 1.0m length of it was recorded; it was shown to run under the Phase 5 partition wall, but was not recorded to the north of it.

Building B

Feature 20 ran parallel with F21 only 0.2m to the west of it, and represents the beam trench for the east wall of the proposed Building B. It was of similar dimensions to 21, being square ended and 0.5m wide, with a recorded length of 1.2m. Again it was shown to run under the construction trench of the later partition wall, but not to continue to the north of it. The sleeper beam trench of the south wall was less clearly defined; Feature 20A is similar to 19, and runs at right angles to 20 to form the south east corner of the structure.

Only the fill of F19 produced pottery (69 BO and 69 CK), and it is broadly in character with the other destruction deposits of Phase 2B

Features Associated with the Timber Buildings

A number of features lay immediately north and east of these possible buildings.

Feature 6

This feature is referred to in the excavation records as a deep foundation under the south-east corner of Phase 3, Building 1, but alternatively may represent the deliberate filling of an earlier feature such as a furnace or pit that in consequence provided underpinning for the south-east corner of the building. The feature itself was pear-shaped in plan, with a rounded north-west end which was scooped out to form a bowl-shaped pit 0.55m in width and 0.34m deep with a length of 0.95m. A narrower channel 0.34m wide extended from the south east side of the pit for 1.75m, with a sloping, rounded terminal, giving the feature an overall length of 2.70m. The north west part of the feature was tightly packed with iron-stone, which toward the centre was heavily burnt, giving way to a black soil fill. The filling of the feature was capped with flat slabs and cobbling, over which the Phase 3 walling was constructed. The filling itself (70 GX) contained second century Lower Nene Valley greyware, and the cobbling overlying and surrounding it contained samian of Hadrianic-Antonine date (70 HB), and AD 135-60 (70 GL).

Feature 26 (69 MB)

A second pear-shaped feature lay 8.0m north west of feature 6 and would appear from its position to have been partially cut by the Phase 3 post-base of the aisled barn. The feature was 2.4m long, varied in width from 1.9m and 0.7m, and in depth from 0.5m-0.6m. The nature of the fill is unknown.

Feature 11

This oval shaped feature which is described as a bronze-working hearth in the site records, lay 12m west of F26, and was 2.0m x 1.0m with an east-west long axis. It was surrounded by three post holes F26-28, but it is uncertain whether they relate to it chronologically.

Feature 8

This feature, 1.2m in diameter, was filled by dark soil (70 GU). It was overlain by the Phase 5 footings and was cut by the Phase 3 pit F7.

Feature 10

This pit, 1.75m in diameter, with stones around its north edge, was surrounded by five post holes (F12-16) and the complex as a whole appears to cut the line of the beam trenches of buildings A and B.

Post holes

A further two post holes (F17 and 18) lay 3m east of F10. F17 was shallow, and 0.15m in diameter, while F18 was 0.1m in diameter and surrounded by vertical stones to form a setting. The post holes recorded do not appear to make any coherent sense in terms of possible structures, although F14, 15, 27, and 28 do form an alignment, along the same line as the beam trench F21.

The Drainage System

Three ditches lay to the north-east of the possible timber buildings.

Feature 1

This stone-lined channel or ditch ran north-south across the northern part of the site, and was sealed by the north wall of Phase 3 Building 1. The channel was about 2m wide at the top, along most of its identified length of 15m. Sloping sides gave way to a square-cut central channel 0.5m wide at the base, cut into the ironstone bedrock. The fill (69 AR), contained a large group of pottery, which had been dumped into the bottom of the channel.

Feature 2

This second ditch ran east-west, and was overlain by the east gable end wall of Phase 3 Building 1. It was 4.5m long and 0.7m wide. It had a semicircular profile, was up to 0.5m deep, and the width tapered towards the west end. Fill 70 GY, 70 GW, and 70 HC.

Feature 4

A shallow ditch, partly sealed by north wall of Phase 3 Building 1. It was 4m long, and up to 0.5m wide and 0.5m deep, with rounded terminals. Fill 70 FX and 70 FW.

Features to the South of the Timber Buildings

The area to the south of the buildings contained a cobbled yard surface into which a number of features were cut. It was not always possible to assign these features to a specific phase stratigraphically, but analysis of the artefactual contents has enabled some of the features to be attributed specifically to Phase 2B rather than the later masonry phases.

Feature 23

Some 19m south of the timber buildings a roughly triangular feature or depression (5m by 4m) was located, filled with a dark loam containing much charcoal, and with limestone blocks set into it (contexts 1970 FR, 1971 CD, CE, CK, CM, CN and CP plus CU, CX, and CY). At the northern apex of the feature were small patches of red and yellow. The fill contained Hadrianic-Antonine samian, and colour-coated ware of mid-late second century date.

Feature 24

Along the southern edge of F23 ran a semicircular ditch, although its relationship with the burnt area is uncertain. The feature was 9m in length, with rounded terminals, and lined with cobbles and clay along the eastern half, and sand along the western half. The north-eastern end was overlain by the south-western corner of the Phase 5 Building 2. The fill contained Hadrianic-early Antonine and Antonine samian.

Post holes

Lying immediately south east of F23 was a group of five post holes (F36-40) and a stone-lined pit (F33), but they do not make coherent sense in terms of a possible superstructure.

Discussion of Phase 2

The evidence for this phase is fragmentary, largely because of the damage caused by the later development of the masonry phases. It is likely that not only a series of sub-phases are involved but also, judging by the pottery assemblage, that the major structural evidence for the occupation has not been detected. The Phase 2A ditch (F50) running across the south of the site could fully predate the features attributed to Phase 2B. While it could be late Iron Age in date it was clearly still open in the second half of the first century when wheelthrown pottery was being introduced widely, and it is considered to be broadly contemporary with the earliest part of the occupation, falling rapidly into disuse thereafter.

Phase 2B would appear to comprise a complex of timber buildings and drainage facilities which might have had an industrial function linked to metalworking. The dimensions of the timber buildings can only be conjectured: if drainage channel F1 is assumed to continue further south and to be contemporary, then beam trench F19 cannot have been longer than about nine metres whilst F21 could have extended north for perhaps five metres without encroaching on F11 (assuming that F10 belongs to a later, but undefined, subphase).

The main drainage channel (F1) would have taken waste downslope and over the embankment towards the river to the north of the site. If the line of F1 continued south, it is likely that F2 flowed into it at right angles. The function of F4 is uncertain: while it appears to feed into F1, its small size and orientation might suggest it to be a beam trench.

The interpretation of the features north and south of the proposed buildings is problematic due to a lack of detailed recording. Feature 11 has been termed a 'bronze-working hearth' but there is no evidence of metalworking waste or photographic record to support this interpretation. Likewise the northern apex of F23 exhibited indications of burning but there is nothing to suggest an industrial function rather than a domestic purpose for what might be interpreted as a hearth. Feature 10 is perhaps best regarded as a well or latrine. The post hole arrangements around these features must be assumed to have supported temporary superstructures the exact form of which is uncertain.

The end of Phase 2 is placed in the third quarter of the second century at the earliest, on the basis of the samian from the fill of F.1 which was probably all deposited in the 150s AD, and is supported by the consistently Hadrianic-early Antonine samian from the other features.

The pottery assemblage from Phase 2B is relatively large, rich and varied in origin (see pages 75-85) especially in terms of the proportions of fine and specialist wares such as samian, beakers, flagons and mortaria. This tends to suggest occupation at a scale and status greater than that presently indicated by structural evidence. The suggestion might be that further structural evidence lay in the southern part of the

excavated area where investigation was not so intense and preservation perhaps not as good, or indeed outside it to the east and west. A similar argument has also been made for the apparently 'humble' occupation at the nearby site of Whitwell at this time (Todd 1981, 13).

Phases 3 to 5: The Masonry Farmstead c. 220 – 400 (figs. 6 and 7)

This represented a period of major reorganisation of the site, with the replacement of timber structures by a complex of masonry buildings, constructed from the local Lincolnshire limestone, and developed over the following two centuries (figs.6 and 7).

Phase 3: The Construction of the Masonry Farmstead c. 220 – 270

Building 1 – The Aisled Building.

Construction

The northern part of the site was occupied by a structure originally conceived as an aisled building, without internal partitions, measuring 23.3m east-west by 12m north-south (21.5m x 10.4m internally) The stone wall foundations were 0.65m thick along the north and south sides, and up to 0.9m thick along the line of the gable end walls. The wall structure was of alternating courses of flat slabs and pitched slabs, to give a herringbone effect, in common with the later Building 2 and the yard wall. The flat courses were faced with large limestone blocks infilled with limestone rubble.

It is proposed that the original plan of the building was free of internal partitions, and that north and south aisles were created by two lines of timber posts supporting the roof, either side of a central nave. This proposition is supported by the presence of a line of three substantial post bases, (F41-3) lying 3.5m apart, creating a north aisle 2.5m wide. The internal length of the building would allow for two further post bases to the west and their absence may be due to either plough damage or removal during internal partitioning. There was only evidence for one possible post base (F44) creating a south aisle, which lay half way along the building's length, and was partly cut by the later internal partition wall. While the other posts and post bases of the south aisle could well have been removed to allow for later internal developments, this does not provide a satisfactory explanation for how the roof was subsequently supported.

The dimensions of the post bases were 1.0m to 1.5m wide, and up to 0.75m in depth. Post base F41 was fully excavated, revealing that it had been constructed in a 0.75m deep hollow, with a stepped profile and rounded bottom. Initially two flat slabs were set into the sloping sides of the hollow, which was then filled with irregular ironstone blocks up to the level of the step, acting as the base on which the first layer of flat slabs was laid. At this point the surrounding step was packed with ironstone rubble before the second and final layer of wider, flat slabs was laid.

Hearths F46-F48

Three hearths were located within Building 1, only one of which (F46) was well preserved, the other two (F47 and F48) defined only as areas of burning with scorched ironstone blocks set in. Feature 46 abutted the north face of the south wall, and had a stoking area at the north end. The stone structure appeared to have been built in a natural depression or had been cut into the underlying ironstone bedrock so that the

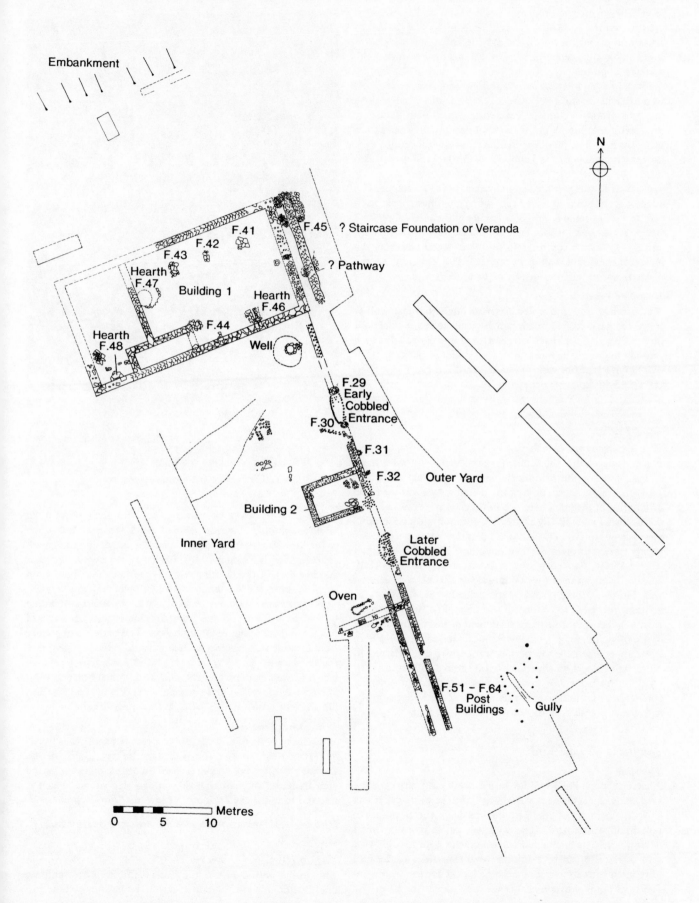

Embankment

N

? Staircase Foundation or Veranda

F.45

F.41

F.42

F.43

Hearth
F.47

Building 1

Hearth
F.46

? Pathway

F.44

Hearth
F.48

Well

F.29
Early
Cobbled
Entrance

F.30

F.31

F.32

Outer Yard

Building 2

Inner Yard

Later
Cobbled
Entrance

Oven

F.51 – F.64
Post
Buildings

Gully

Metres
0   5   10

Fig. 6 Site 1 Phases 3-5 Composite Plan

bed of the stokehole and furnace chamber was lower than floor level. The superstructure was 1.6m by 1.2m and surrounded on three sides by ironstone rubble. The structure was of dressed ironstone blocks infilled by 'fine yellow soil' which was presumably decayed mortar. These blocks surrounded the furnace chamber which was long and narrow (1.2m by 0.25m), and the internal faces and floor were scorched red. At its north end the stoke hole gave way to a roughly circular stoke pit (1.0m-1.4m in diameter), which was filled with dark grey ashy soil, containing a lot of charcoal presumably raked from the stoke hole. The fill of the chamber was a homogenous dark brown with patches of red and yellow mortar, and was 0.20m deep.

Feature 47 was recorded as a circular area of scorching. The edge of it appeared to have been cut by the phase 5 partition wall and so it probably formed a feature of the original phase 3 structure, although it may have continued in use into phase 4 and 5. Feature 48 comprised a setting of stones abutting the inside of the south wall at its western end, scorched on the inside faces, and surrounded by a black area.

Features 3 and 7

An entrance into the aisled barn through the east wall is suggested by a cobbled path which partly sealed a Phase 2B ditch (F2), and was itself overlain by the proposed Phase 5 veranda footings which also sealed a circular shallow pit (F7), 0.2m in depth attributable to Phase 3 or 4. The pit (F7) is filled (70 GO) with limestone cobbling which appeared to provide a hard-standing for the later masonry structure, and contained Lower Nene Valley Colour-coated ware of later third or fourth century date.

Yard Division and Gateway

It is considered that the cobbled area to the south of Building 1, was subdivided into an inner (western) and outer (eastern) yard at an early stage, and that the dividing wall was modified in a series of stages. There are indirect indications that the division was not initially of masonry, and could conceivably have been of timber. This is based upon the fact that a gateway clearly existed through the division, as indicated by a spread of worn cobbles, flanked by two substantial post settings (F29 and F30), 8m south of the building along the line of its eastern wall. However, these settings were sealed by the wall that was subsequently built to divide the two areas. It is not absolutely clear whether a thoroughfare continued at this point, because of the plough damage to the wall, but its function would have been superseded by the new entrance way constructed in Phase 4. A second, smaller pair of post settings (F31 and F32), lay 3.0m further south along the partition line, but only 2m apart. They may indicate the existence of second entrance way and are also sealed by the line of the Phase 4 masonry yard wall.

Features in the Inner Yard

The Well

A circular stone-lined well lay in the north-east corner of the yard, in the angle formed by Building 1 and the yard wall. It was 0.7m in diameter at the top and 5m deep; the bottom 3m remaining waterlogged. The well was set into a clay-lined hollow, forming a lip 3m in diameter which would have allowed spilled water to run back into the well. The sides of the well were lined with courses of limestone blocks for the whole 5m depth, giving way to a layer of blue-grey clay at the base. The surrounding area was paved with cobbles and there was no direct evidence for a well housing, although limestone blocks

Plate 3 Site 1: View down circular stone lined well

found dumped at the bottom may have formed part of it. In addition, amongst the fragments of wood preserved below the water line was a length of 2m, circular in section, and with chamfered ends which may possibly have been a winding rod or another part of the housing. Other fragments may have been vertical staves from a bucket. Unfortunately all the worked wood except the shoe patten (p.110) was discarded at the time of the excavation and the photographic record cannot add further to these tentative identifications. The evidence of pottery from the well indicates that it fell into disuse in the last quarter of the third century (p.85), and was rapidly filled with rubbish which as well as the wood also included animal bone (p.133), plant material (p.139) and associated insect fauna (p.136). Well fills 1970 EG, EM, EN, EO, EQ, ET, EU, EX, EY, FC.

Limestone Trackway

A trackway of angular limestone cobbles led south westwards away from the area of the well. On the south side of the trackway was a small area of pitched limestone blocks, with the appearance of a small wall or platform 1m square which is referred to in the excavation records as the 'storage point'.

Phase 4: Alterations to the Masonry Farmstead c. 270-350

The Yard Wall and Gateway

This initial period of modification to the masonry building complex involved the construction of a wall which ran southwards away from Building 1 following the line of the east wall of the building to replace the conjectured timber boundary and gateway of Phase 3. The wall would appear to have run initially for a distance of 30m before returning at right angles to the west for a distance of at least 6m. It is slightly narrower (0.65m) than the walls of Building 1, with shallower footings suggesting that it was not load-bearing. Its exact relationship to Building 1 is unclear, as the initial 8m of its length coincided with the leading edge of the second terrace, and so was poorly preserved. However, the facing stones at the south east corner of Building 1 were uninterrupted, indicating that the yard wall was not bonded into it, and must therefore have been a later addition. The westerly running return wall was bonded in at right angles to the south end of the yard wall and would therefore appear to be contemporary with it. A second or later gateway was constructed through the Phase 4 yard wall at its southern end, indicated by a spread of worn limestone cobbling 3m wide, flanked by post settings (F34 and F35), 0.4m in diameter.

The Inner Yard:

The Corn Drier (F49)

A keyhole-shaped corn drier was constructed in the south-east corner of the inner yard, lying east-west with the entrance at the east end. The structure was preserved to a height of 0.65m above the internal paving at its west end, and was 2.4m long. The roughly circular chamber was 0.7m in diameter and was paved with large limestone and ironstone slabs, some of which showed signs of burning. The entrance to the chamber was 0.3m wide and lay at the end of a channel 1.6m long, which had an area of paving outside the entrance, forming a stoking area. It was demolished and filled in presumably at the same time as the demolition of the adjacent south wall. Pottery from the fill (70 DL and EL), which includes a late Roman shell-tempered ware jar, suggests at least a mid-fourth century date. However, this could easily also imply that the corn drier

Plate 4 Site 1: Corn drier (F49), looking east

remained in use throughout Phase 5 as well. Plant remains were retrieved from the lower fill at the west end and the evidence is considered below (p.140).

Phases 5A: Late Alterations to the Masonry Farmstead c. 350-400

A number of structural changes are attributable to Phase 5 and arbitrary subphases 5A and 5B, dated c.350, have been defined in order to place these changes in a relative sequence as far as the bonding relationships of walls and other evidence will allow. The changes attributed to Subphase 5A are confined to the south eastern part of the site.

Extension of Yard Wall

The line of the east yard wall was extended southwards for a further 13m at least, its northern end abutting the original rightangled structure.

Timber Buildings

During the 1971 season the extreme south eastern part of the site was stripped by machine and a group of 16 post holes (F51- F66), 6m east of the yard wall, was detected. With the exception of F64, all belonged to either of two structures, one circular and the other rectangular. The post holes of both structures were generally 150-200mm in diameter and at least 100mm deep (the tops of each having certainly been truncated).

Circular

Post holes F59-F63 appeared to form the southern and eastern circumference of a circular structure about 4m in diameter. Post holes F60-63 were spaced 1 metre apart, while the space between F59 and 60 was nearer 2m, possibly indicating an entrance. However, a gully subsequently cut across the floor of the structure, and may have removed evidence for a post at this point. None of the post hole fills contained artefactual material.

Rectangular

F51-55, and F56-58, form the west and north walls of a rectangular structure with the same orientation as the stone buildings. The portholes were placed evenly at one metre intervals, and suggested a rectangular timber building of at least 5m x 3m in size. There appeared to be no internal features over the cobbled floor, except for the aforementioned gully which was cut into the cobbles running north to south across the structure, 5m long and 0.4m wide. Post hole F56 appeared to be cut into its northern end so it may pre-date the building. Only post holes F52 and F54 of the rectangular building yielded pottery, comprising small sherds of Lower Nene Valley colour-coated ware. This would indicate at least a later Roman date for the structure with the lack of any Anglo-Saxon material precluding a date any later.

On tenuous stratigraphical grounds the circular structure is placed earlier than the rectangular one, the former attributed to Phase 5A, and the latter to 5B (Fig.7).

Phases 5B: Late Alterations to Masonry Farmstead c. 350-400

The changes attributed to the second half of the fourth century, Subphase 5B, can be divided between those affecting Building 1, and those affecting the yard area.

Alterations to the Aisled Building

Internal Partitions

The construction of partition walls within the aisled barn occurred at this time, and was dated by the presence of two mid-fourth century coins sealed beneath one of the walls. The coins are one of the House of Constantine, AD335-337 (p.123 no.16), and one of Constans, AD341-347 (p.123 no. 22). Malcolm Dean stated in an interim report on the excavations (DoE 1970) that they were found in a gully running underneath one of the partition walls. This would appear to refer to one of the timber beam slots attributed to Phase 2A, and it is assumed that the coins became incorporated into the top fill of one of them, perhaps during construction of the internal walls.

An internal room 5.7m x 1.6m was created about one third of the way eastwards along the south wall of the building. The internal walls of the room were 0.6m wide, and a wall of the same width projected at right angles to the northern edge of the room towards the north wall of the building, dividing it in two in the ratio of 30% to 70% between the western and eastern halves respectively. The junction between this partition wall and the north wall of the building was not preserved.

Footings for Possible Veranda (F45)

Running parallel to the east gable end wall of the building, about 1m to the east lay a masonry foundation of the the same length and width (12m x 0.85m). The structure sealed pottery of later third or fourth century date.

Alterations to the Inner Yard

Building 2 (Plate 5)

Sixteen metres to the south of Building 1, a small, rectangular, one-roomed building was constructed, abutting the yard wall. Internally it measured 5m east-west by 3m north-south. The walls were preserved for at least two courses above the foundations, and the internal faces of the pitched stone courses were faced with blocks. Excavation of the destruction debris within the building revealed an intermittent floor covering of well-laid cobbles and larger slabs overlying an area of worn cobbling and sealing pottery of fourth century date in between. The larger slabs in the south east corner and pitched slabs in the north east corner may have supported internal structures the nature of which is unclear.

Access to the building from the inner yard may have been through a door in the north wall, indicated by two post holes set into the centre line of the wall, 0.2m in diameter and 1.2m apart. There was a similar post hole set into the west wall. Access from the outer eastern yard through the yard wall is suggested by the presence of worn ironstone slabs which may have formed a threshold. Evidence from the destruction debris inside the building suggested that it was roofed with large limestone slabs of Collyweston slate, 0.35m square.

Alterations to the Yard Wall

The south wall of the yard appears to have been demolished, except for a short 1.5m length at its eastern end. A parallel wall of the same proportions was then constructed 1m to the west of the Phase 4B extension, running along its full length, and therefore forming a narrow alleyway. Fourth century pottery was sealed in a depression (71 FI) beneath the wall. At the south end both parallel walls petered out at the same point without any definite terminals, their removal possibly being due to plough erosion or robbing.

At the north end however, the western parallel wall continued for at least a further 2m, with its east face butting

Plate 5 Site 1: Building 2 looking east

against the truncated south wall of the yard. The exact northern extent of the 'alleyway' is unclear, because of the poor preservation along the northern or leading edge of the proposed third terrace, immediately to the south of Building 2. However if the entrance way through the yard wall was still in use at this time, then the 'alleyway' could not have extended more than a metre further north.

It is impossible to know if the two parallel walls were contemporary, the eastern one could conceivably have been demolished, although there would not appear to be a logical reason to do this. The existence of the 'alleyway' would seem equally illogical, as it would appear to have been too narrow for the passage of most animals, except perhaps for sheep, if indeed its function was to channel animals. Such a function hardly warrants a masonry structure, when a timber arrangement would suffice. The structure could not have acted as an alleyway if the truncated south wall of the yard actually functioned as a cross-wall, and perhaps it only acted as a threshold.

Other Evidence Associated with the Phase 3-5 Masonry Farmstead

Iron Working Complex North of Site 1

A stone-built furnace was situated below the embankment at the north end of the site at SK 94270774 about midway between Building 1 and the river. It was orientated east-west with the stokehole at the east end. The structure was 2.0m long, 1.0m wide at each end, and 0.6m wide in the middle, and appeared to have been bell-shaped. The furnace was unfortunately destroyed by the machines before further investigation could take place. Some unstratified pottery predominantly of fourth century date, and including Lower Nene Valley colour-coated ware was retrieved from the rubble, as well as a coin of Theodosius.

The pottery probably originated from the main part of Site 1, with the embankment forming a convenient dumping ground for rubbish, and this may indicate that the furnace had gone out of use by this time.

It would appear that this structure was associated with an area of industrial activity found immediately below the embankment at SK 9426 0773, covering an area of 9.0m east-west, and 6.0m north-south. Wall footings suggested the presence of a building, and another stone-lined furnace on the west side. There was a considerable spread of slag, clinker, and burnt stone indicating smelting activity. Unstratified pottery was retrieved, but the pace of the development made it impossible to do any further excavation.

Human Burials

During the Autumn of 1971 and Spring of 1972, Bill Thomas recorded five burials in the area around Site 1, which was rapidly being machined during the construction of the dam and the collection drain at the east end of Rutland Water. Most of the records were made under watching brief conditions, and some are simply observations made by the machine drivers themselves.

Burials 1R, 2R, and 3R

These three burials were found south of the river at SK 9432 0765, about 5m south of the most southerly part of the excavated area of Site 1. According to the machine drivers the three burials were lying in line east-west, and approximately 2-3m apart. The bodies themselves were oriented east-west, with feet facing east. There was no sign of any skulls, probably because they had been machined away before discovery. The graves appeared to be ash-filled and possibly stone-lined. Although the drivers collected up the bones, they were accidentally disposed of soon after.

Burial 4R

This burial, at SK 9443 0783, appears to have been an isolated interment 65m north of the Anglo-Saxon cemetery on Site 3, since the surrounding 2500sq m was also stripped by machine, without any further burials being discovered. The body, probably that of an adult male, had been laid east-west, with the head to the west, in what appeared to be a fairly shallow grave, dug into a long mound of quarry waste starting 15m north of Site 3, and ending 10m south of the river. The date of the burial is uncertain as it was not accompanied by any artefactual material. The lack of finds and its orientation may suggest that it was Christian, and while it may be late Roman, it could equally be an outlying grave belonging to a later phase of the Anglo-Saxon cemetery to the south.

Burial 5R

This burial was located at SK 9423 0770, just 15m north west of Building 1 on Site 1, on the very top edge of the south bank overlooking the river. The burial was made in a limestone coffin probably quarried from the nearby Barnack outcrop, and was oriented north-south, with the head to the south. Unfortunately, the coffin had been damaged when the machine uncovered it, as it was only covered by 0.5m of topsoil and it subsequently disintegrated when it was removed. However, full measurements were taken before this. The external dimensions were 2.13m long by 0.64m at the south end (0.65 at north end), with a depth of 0.36m. Internally it was 1.94m long and 0.46m wide at both ends, with a depth of 0.29m. The average thickness was 90mm, though slightly less on the base. The coffin contained a badly preserved skeleton of a probably female adult, accompanied by that of a child, which appeared to have been placed between the lower legs of the adult, and lay in a deep layer of silt that had accumulated at the foot of the coffin. Two ceramic vessels, one inside the other, lay immediately outside the coffin at the north end (see page 90 nos.131-132), both of fourth century date and of Lower Nene Valley origin (fabric C2)

Discussion of Phases 3 – 5 (Fig. 7)

The constructional sequence described above is necessarily based on fragmentary evidence, and there is much about the masonry building phases that simply cannot be ascertained from the excavation records as they stand. Building 1 clearly follows a sequence of development which is common to many examples of aisled buildings (Hingley 1989, 39) and which requires examination regarding its possible function. As in many cases in the East Midlands (Taylor forthcoming a and b), Building 1 is clearly an example where an aisled building is acting as the 'main focus' of an agricultural establishment rather than taking a subsidiary (i.e. specifically agricultural or industrial rather than residential) role next to a winged-corridor villa as at Bancroft, Bucks. (de la Bedoyere 1991, 140). Although Whitwell (1982, 102) has doubted this in the case of Great Casterton further down the valley, the evidence of previous fieldwalking and subsequent machining around Site 1 did not indicate the existence of further buildings. However, the function of Building 1 is ambiguous, being neither clearly industrial nor solely residential, although recent analysis of a number of similar aisled building plans (Taylor forthcoming b) demonstrates that a number of different functions can be performed within the same building. The analysis also shows that not only were these functions consistently carried out in specific areas of the buildings but that also the patterns represent a direct transference from the use of space within Iron Age round houses (Taylor forthcoming b).

It has been convincingly demonstrated that both round houses and aisled buildings (Hingley 1989) were most probably inhabited by extended family groups and that the position of the entrance, usually to the east, and the layout of internal posts, created the framework for activity areas (Taylor forthcoming b). The area inside the circle of posts within roundhouses and within the nave of aisled buildings tends to be the focus for communal activity, often being the location for the hearth, with the entrance providing access to and from the public domain. In contrast, the areas outside the ring of posts and in the aisles respectively, tend to be the location for other activities including both industrial and, typically in the areas furthest away from the entrance, private accommodation for the head of the family. In the developed forms of aisled buildings this division between private and communal areas is expressed through the formal partitioning of the building into upper (western) and lower (eastern) ends respectively, but this must be seen as representing the physical manifestation of a pattern that already existed rather than a change of function.

If this concept of 'public' and 'private' space is related to Building 1, it appears to fit the established pattern very well, and coherent ideas about the layout and function of the complex as a whole can be formulated. In its original unpartitioned form (phase 3) the building would have been entered from the eastern end indicated by the path and the central communal area would be served by the hearth (F47 in Room 1) placed centrally towards the back, a common location for them. The area of the south aisle nearest the entrance appears to have been reserved for metalworking activity as indicated by the hearth (F46), and again this appears to be the most

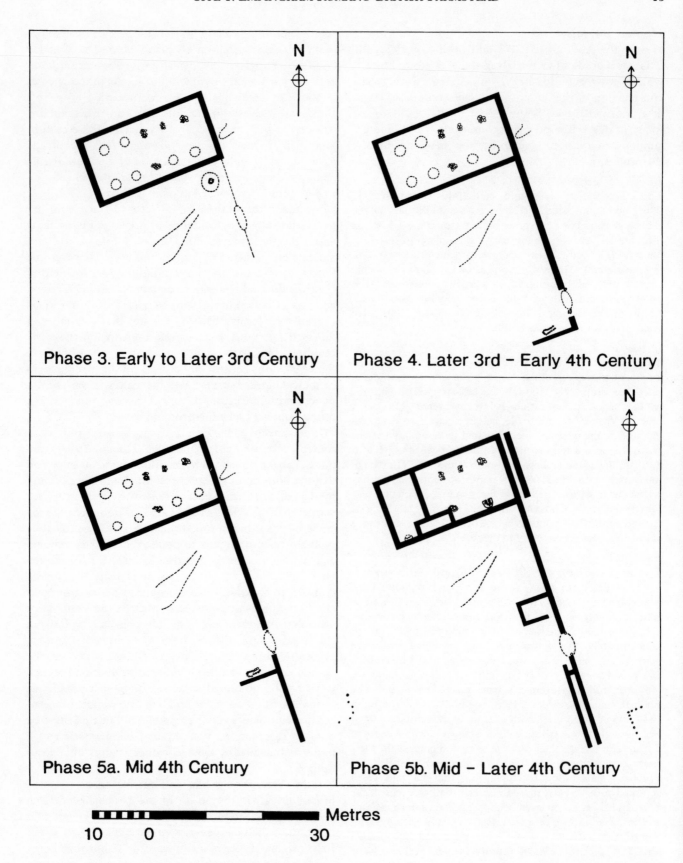

Phase 3. Early to Later 3rd Century

Phase 4. Later 3rd – Early 4th Century

Phase 5a. Mid 4th Century

Phase 5b. Mid – Later 4th Century

10 0 30 Metres

Fig. 7 Site 1 Phase 3-5 The Constructional sequence

common location for industrial hearths (Taylor forthcoming b). It might be assumed that the north aisle and western end of the building were used for private accommodation which has left no archaeological trace, save for the hearth at the far end of the south aisle. However, although this appears to be domestic, it was not necessarily in place at this time.

The developments during Phases 4 and 5 enhance this division between public and private space. The construction of the masonry yard wall as a continuation of the eastern gable wall is effectively restricting access (physical and visual) to household activities in the western or inner yard and presenting a clean facade to the public domain in the eastern or outer yard. The validity of such a division is supported by the evidence of a trackway approaching the site from the east from the direction of Site 3. Public access is therefore limited to the east entrance to Building 1, a gateway through the yard wall and (in Phase 5) possibly an entrance to Building 2.

The subsequent construction of a veranda against the east gable wall, as suggested by the line of footings (F45), embellishes the public perception of the establishment whilst the partitioning of Building 1 makes a clear statement about the desire for privacy amongst certain members of the household. The area of contention concerning this partitioning is the lack of internal upgrading such as the insertion of hypocausts or tessellated pavements as seen in other 'developed' aisled houses of the kind discussed by Hingley (1989, 39 and fig.17), the hearth (F48) representing the only tangible source of creature comfort in Room 2. While the poor preservation of archaeology in the north western part of the building could partly explain this apparent lack, poorly stratified fragments of painted wall plaster hypocaust and flue tiles are the only indirect evidence to support the idea (p.127).

The question of access to the upper end of the building may be answered by considering the function of the small room created by the partitioning of part of the south aisle (Room 3). There is no evidence of thresholds as the walls are only preserved at foundation level, but it would be logical to think of Room 3 as a lobby area entered through the south wall, allowing access to both the upper and lower ends of the building. The daily activities of the household in the inner yard could therefore have been conducted without the need to use the eastern entrance which was reserved for receiving guests into the communal area.

The recognition that a number of both private and communal functions could be performed within Building 1 allows Site 1 to be viewed as a self-contained agricultural establishment. This may have been operated by an extended family (*contra* Cooper 1996, 167) rather than being the productive element of an establishment with a separate residential focus on the sunnier north side of the valley at Site 2. The fact that both sites have associated burial grounds would also support this idea of self-containment. However, the evidence for the opposed stone coffin burials 5R and 7R on either side of the valley does lend support to the idea that Sites 1 and 2 were linked though kinship at some point during the fourth century.

The association of the complex with metalworking both within Building 1 and immediately downslope to the north allows comparisons with a number of East Midlands sites falling into Hadman's industrial category (1978, 192). The best comparable examples come from the Nene Valley, including Lynch Farm near Peterborough (Wild and Dannell 1973) which also contained furnaces and smithing hearths. Two furnaces were also found within Room 4 of the contemporary stone building at Whitwell on the opposite side of the river. Due to potential fire hazard, Todd doubted that they were contemporary with the building (1981,19), although current thinking would tend to support the idea that they possibly were (G Morgan pers.comm). However, the smithing at these sites should probably be seen as serving the requirements of the mixed farming activities of the establishment rather than implying any specialist or intensive metal smelting and working of the kind indicated by the evidence from Wakerley, Northants., where a concentration of smelting furnaces lay outside the southern boundary of the enclosure (Jackson and Ambrose 1978, 151, and fig.25).

The construction of the masonry phase farmstead in the earlier third century coincides with similar episodes of upgrading at the neighbouring three sites along the Gwash valley where aisled buildings also appear, from current evidence, to form the major focus of the establishment. In the case of both Whitwell (Todd 1981) and Great Casterton (Corder 1954, Phase 2), of broadly similar date to Building 1, undivided aisled buildings were both replaced by masonry domestic buildings on the same alignment but not incorporating the original aisle posts. At Site 2 to the north, however, excavation could not demonstrate whether the developed phase of aisled building was preceded by an undivided building incorporating posts, although it would appear likely.

Acknowledgements:
I am grateful to Jeremy Taylor for discussing the function of Romano-British aisled buildings on Sites 1 and 2 and for allowing access to information prior to publication.

SITE 2:
EMPINGHAM NORTH ROMANO-BRITISH VILLA

Nicholas J. Cooper

Introduction

The site (code EPN 71) was located 400m north of Site 1 on the opposite side of the Gwash Valley (SK 942 081), and now lies under the crest of the reservoir dam at its north end. It was first discovered during fieldwalking in 1970 when it showed up as a dense concentration of Romano-British pottery. The area of the scatter was trial trenched in late October 1970 which indicated the need for further work. In July 1971 topsoil was removed by machine and excavation, directed by M.S. Gorin, continued periodically into early autumn. The pace of development meant that there was insufficient time to excavate the site completely.

Two phases of activity were identified. Phase 1 dates to the later Roman period and comprises a masonry building of aisled plan constructed probably during the later third century but possibly as late as the mid-fourth century. Phase 2 sees the area of the aisled building reused as a Christian cemetery in the middle Anglo-Saxon period and may imply that the building was remodelled into a church or chapel.

Note: in common with Site 1, the on-site recording system comprised a series of two letter codes from AA, AB, AC,... to ZZ, assigned to each finds tray and preceded by the year of excavation (i.e. 70 or 71). Several codes may therefore relate to the excavation of one feature or area of the site.

Phase 1: The Aisled House (Fig. 8)

The earliest identified phase of occupation on the site is represented by a large rectangular building measuring at least 21m east-west by 11m north-south, with rooms arranged into an aisled plan. Plough damage removed all evidence of flooring within the building, and the plan revealed is essentially the below-floor masonry foundations (fig. 8). The building was constructed of limestone, with courses of faced blocks infilled with rubble alternating with courses of pitched blocks, to create a herring-bone effect. Wall thicknesses varied from 0.75m along the west gable-end wall, down to 0.6m along the north and south external walls. The internal walls varied between 0.45m and 0.55m in thickness.

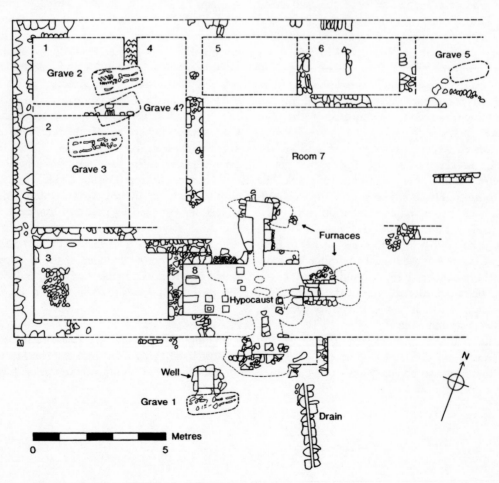

Fig. 8 Site 2 Phases 1 and 2

The plan was divided internally into at least eight identifiable rooms. Unfortunately, much of the eastern half of the building was lost due to plough damage, so the overall plan is not clear. However, the plan appears to have been conceived as a nave and aisle arrangement with ranges of rooms along the north and south aisles of similar width, either side of a central nave which was subdivided to form a central hall (Room 7). Whether this phase represented an upgrading of an undivided aisled building, similar to that on Site 1, was not demonstrated due to the lack of time to undertake stratigraphic excavation. A coin of AD 330-337 (p.124, Site 2 no.13) is described in the site records as having been found in the north wall of the building, while other coinage and pottery dates to the beginning of the third century. However, the majority of the pottery dates to the later third and fourth century.

The North Aisle
The north aisle was subdivided into at least three, or probably four, identifiable rooms of near equal size (Rooms 1, 5, and 6), with a narrow corridor (Room 4) running north to south between Rooms 1 and 5. Room 1 had internal dimensions of 3.4m east-west by 2.4m north-south and did not share exactly the same south wall alignment as the others. Room 5 was 2m by 3.5m, Room 6 was 2m by 3.3m, and the conjectured fourth room was 2m north-south. Room 4, which appears to have acted as a corridor, was 7m by 2m and probably provided access between Rooms 1 and 5 and the nave area.

The South Aisle
The south aisle would appear to have been similarly subdivided into rooms of similar size although only two (Rooms 3 and 8), at the western end, could be identified. Room 3 was 5m east-west and 3m north-south while Room 8 was 2.5m by 4.5m. Room 8, lying towards the centre of the aisle, was a hypocausted room with evidence for a *pilae*-supported floor. The room exhibited a series of modifications, but the exact sequence of construction is unclear from the existing records. It is possible that Rooms 3 and 8 were originally joined, to form a continuous south aisle, as the partition wall and, possibly, a replacement north wall to both rooms would appear to have been inserted at a later date, perhaps when the hypocaust system was built. The south aisle is wider than the north aisle.

The installation of the hypocaust involved the excavation of the underlying ironstone in order to create the under floor space needed. Nine of the original tile *pilae* remained *in situ* in the under floor space, standing in parts on a floor of limestone slabs over a bed of ironstone. The dimensions of the room were 2m north-south and 4.5m east-west. However, there was evidence for a small southern extension to the room which may possibly have been a bath since a stone-lined drainage channel ran southwards away from the building at this point for a distance of 4.0m.

The hypocaust system was supplied with heat from two furnaces situated on the east and north sides of the room. The flue of the eastern furnace was 1.25m long and 0.5m wide. It was lined with tile and faced limestone blocks exhibiting intense scorching, which were backed by irregular limestone blocks. The floor of the flue was formed of limestone slabs. At its east end, the flue gave way to a circular stoke pit 1.5m in diameter, and the scorching of the underlying ironstone which formed the floor of the stoke pit, extended in a 0.5m arc

around the mouth of the flue. The stoke pit had a fill of black ashy soil, presumably derived from the raking out of the flue.

The insertion of the northern furnace, the stokehouse of which extended into Room 7 to the north, necessitated the addition of a double thickness to the north wall of the room, perhaps to support a new floor, and to act as a lining wall for the hypocaust. The flue of the north furnace appeared narrower and longer than that in the east wall, being 1.75m long and only 0.4m in width. It was again lined with tile and faced limestone blocks which were backed by a rubble mixture of tile and limestone bonded with *opus signinum*. The stoke pit at the north end was rectangular and measured 1.0m by 0.6m, the walls surviving to four courses of masonry. This rectangular structure may have represented a modification, possibly to support a hot water tank, as an area of burning of the underlying ironstone extended in an arc to the east underneath the stone structure. To the west, the space behind the west wall was filled with black ashy soil containing broken tile and limestone fragments. The stoke pit itself had a similar black fill containing broken tile.

The Nave
The central portion of the building, at least 18m in length, was subdivided into three portions; a large, central room or hall (Room 7), the continuation of the proposed corridor (Room 4), and Room 2 at the western end. Room 7 was at least 4.5m x 11m and is best interpreted as a central hall. Room 2 was almost square in plan (3.6m x 4.0m), but nothing is known of any internal features.

The Well
A square, stone-lined well was situated just outside the building on the south side and was 3.6m deep. It appeared to have been stone-lined all the way down, with a pitched course surmounted by three flat courses at the bottom. The water level was just 0.5m above the bottom, and the fill at this level contained bone, pottery and burnt stone. Between 3.1m and 2.9m depth, larger stones in a black and yellow sediment had been dumped in, and this was capped by 0.1m of clayey brown fill. From 2.8m-1.4m depth the well was filled with large masonry blocks in a dark grey/black fill. A coin of Claudius II (AD 268-270) was found at a depth of 2.4m. There were no details recorded about the fill above this point. The well head was roughly square with internal dimensions of 0.59m by 0.57m. The aperture was surrounded by flat-edged tiles, the uneven outer edges being infilled with small cobbles, and this gave the structure overall dimensions of 1.2m by 1.4m. In common with the well on Site 1, there is no evidence for any timber superstructure.

Other Phase 1 Roman Period Activity in the Vicinity of Site 2

Agricultural
A key-hole shaped corn drier similar to that found on Site 1 was discovered in April 1972 during the construction of the north collector drain, about 30m east of the building. It was orientated in the opposite direction to that on Site 1, with the stoke-hole at the west end. The flue entrance had been blocked with large limestone slabs, and the interior had also been filled with stones in the same fashion as the example on Site 1. It appeared to have been renovated towards the end of its period of use, as some of the stones used for the walls had been replaced, showing little sign of burning. The lower fill of the corn drier flue comprised a thin layer of charcoal. The discovery of the corn drier would indicate that Site 2 was not

purely residential in function, and that subsidiary buildings may have lain to the east.

Burial

Between the Autumn of 1971 and the Spring of 1972, Bill Thomas recorded two areas of burial associated with Site 2. The stratigraphic details are described below, while discussion of the skeletal evidence is to be found on p.56. The first group lies 50m south-west of the building, and comprises four, or probably five, burials (nos. 7-11), one of which was interred in a limestone coffin. The second group of eight burials lies 80m east of the building (nos. 12-19), but their Roman date cannot be confirmed.

Burial 7R

In common with burial 5R, located directly opposite on the south side of the Valley, burial 7R was interred in a stone coffin, at a shallow depth of 0.5m. It was located about 40m west of Site 2 on the north side of the river, and was one of a group of five contemporary and later intercutting burials. Although this placed it 425m north of burial 5, the two coffins were orientated along exactly the same north-north-west alignment. The coffin was also of Barnack stone, and of very similar dimensions to 5R. Externally it was 2.19m long, and 0.68m wide (0.65 at north end), with a depth estimated at 0.44m. Internally it was 2.01m long and 0.51m wide, with a depth of 0.36m. The lid was too damaged to allow measurement, while the walls were between 70mm and 90mm in thickness. The coffin contained the skeleton of an adult male over 45 years old, with head to the north. This orientation means that the body was literally facing that in burial 5R. Also, in common with burial 5R, two similar ceramic vessels had been placed one inside the other at the foot of the grave (south end), outside the coffin. Again no small finds were present inside the coffin.

Burial 8R

Located 1m west of 7R, and parallel to it, except for the fact that the head was at the south end. There were no coffin remains detected, and the lower left side of the skeleton was missing, having probably been disturbed by the insertion of Burial 9R. A small colour-coated ware vessel lay on the left hand side of the chest (fig.44 no. 136). The individual interred was a probable male adult.

Burial 9R

This burial, probably an adult male, was made in a later cutting of burial 8R, and had an east-west orientation with the head to the east. The skull of 9R lay across the pelvis area of 8R, and the feet, which were missing would probably have overlain the pelvis area of burial 10R which lay parallel to 8R. The burial had suffered plough disturbance, and only parts of the skeleton were present. No pottery was found, but two iron nails were found to the left of the skull, and could be the remains of a coffin, though it is not clear if they belong to burial 8R or 9R.

Burial 10R

This burial, probably an adult male of at least 45 years old, lay 1.5-1.75m west of, and parallel with 8R, though in common with 7R, the head was to the north. The central part of it was disturbed by the later cutting of 9R. A few sherds of colour-coated ware were associated with the burial, as were two iron nails to the right of the skull, suggesting the presence of a wooden coffin.

Burial 11R

This burial lay 2-3m north of burial 7, and was reported by Phil Morris, the driver of the scraper, who saw a skull and two limb bones in his load, but did not recover them.

Burials 12R-19R

This group of burials was located 80m to the east of Site 2 and was discovered by Bill Latimer while supervising the widening of the North Collector Drain. He reported to Bill Thomas that the machines had exposed a ditch containing 8 burials, spaced evenly over a distance of 20m. All the burials were orientated east-west, with their feet to the east, and were only 0.5m deep. Unfortunately the skulls had all been machined away earlier, and the bones were apparently too crushed to be retrieved. However, some Roman pottery was retrieved from around and underneath the burials. Cleaning of the ditch section at the south end showed it to be 2.5m wide and 0.75m deep. The general direction of the ditch was running north-south across the drain, but it appeared to curve away south westwards and north westwards at either end, creating a crescent shape.

Discussion of Phase 1 Roman Period Activity

The aisled masonry structure excavated represents the final phase of building on the site and, although nothing is known of any structures that may have preceded it, it is conceivable that an undivided aisled barn with timber-posted aisles may have been remodelled, as is more apparent on Site 1. In common with the structures on Site 1, the availability of suitable stone makes it likely that the building was constructed entirely of masonry, and the evidence for collapsed walling at Drayton II villa in the Welland Valley (Connor 1993) and Redlands Farm, Stanwick in the Nene Valley (Keevill 1996, 44) also within the 'stone belt', supports this.

The security of the context for the coin of AD 330-337 described as having been found in the north wall of the building must be open to question given the disturbance to the site but would otherwise indicate that the final structure was not built until the middle of the fourth century at the earliest. Evidence for earlier occupation might be indicated by coinage and samian pottery dating to the beginning of the third century, but what little samian there is of this date, is not supported by the presence of similarly dated British finewares such as those from the Lower Nene Valley which would be expected. The pottery is otherwise consistently of later third and fourth century date, and it is therefore most likely that the building was constructed and modified over this period. If earlier structures existed, then evidence for them has been masked and any absence of earlier artefactual material must be attributed to the lack of excavation of such features.

Within the life of the masonry structure visible there is clearly at least one phase of remodelling which concerns the insertion of a bath suite into Room 8. The presence of two furnaces might appear unusual but there is no clear evidence of one succeeding the other that might be suggested by blocking. It is conceivable that one was used specifically for heating water and the other for the hypocaust although this would seem inefficient. Their location on internal walls does not necessarily present a problem. The eastern furnace was probably housed within a specific furnace room accessed directly through the south wall as indicated at Welwyn, Herts. (Rook 1988, 15), whilst the northern furnace could have been accessed through the proposed corridor (Room 4), with smoke exiting through the roof of the central hall as it would have from a domestic hearth. The option to have hypocaust furnaces on internal walls seems to be confined to developed aisled building, as presumably in this architectural form the central hall is still open to the roof. A useful parallel is found at Winterton villa, Lincs., in Phase 2 of aisled Building B (Stead 1976, 28, fig.16).

On the basis of the limited preservation and excavation of the site, the function of the building would appear to have been purely residential, with the discovery of the corn drier to the east indicating the existence of subsidiary timber buildings with an agricultural function. The lack of extant flooring in the building makes it difficult to judge the likely social status of its inhabitants. Although at least one of the rooms possessed a hypocaust, and so presumably a concrete floor, there are no records of tesserae being excavated, however over 12kg of painted wall plaster was retrieved from the rubble layers associated with the bath suite (p.128).

There are many examples of aisled buildings that appear to have a wholly or partly residential or domestic function, and where an originally undivided timber-aisled plan has been modified in order to create suites of rooms acting as 'upper' and 'lower' ends to the building in a fashion comparable to medieval hall houses (see Taylor forthcoming and Site 1 discussion above). Hingley (1989) has reviewed the evidence for this idea, citing the examples of North Warnborough, Hants., and Combley, Isle of Wight (1989, 40 fig.17 a and d), and it is feasible that Site 2 fits into this class of developed aisled house or more broadly into the category of hall-type villas defined by J.T.Smith (1978 a and b). The Site 2 building does not appear to divide nicely into 'upper' and 'lower' ends, but the hypocausted Room 8 may have been part of a private suite of rooms (perhaps along the western part of the south aisle) used specifically by the head of an extended family and the immediate nuclear family (Hingley 1989, 42). The corridor (Room 4) could in effect have separated a working area (or accommodation for other members of the household) in Rooms 1 and 2 from the rest of the house while still allowing access to the central hall (Room 7) for communal activities. A similar through passage was recognised by Todd in the plan of the masonry building at the adjacent site of Whitwell (1981, 14 and fig.8).

Comparable examples of aisled buildings within the Corieltauvian territory have been collected together successively by Todd (1973, 87, fig.20) and Whitwell (1982, 110 and Fig. 19), and the distribution map produced by Hadman (1978, 188, fig.16) illustrates that the area of the Nene and Welland valleys (the Gwash being a tributary of the latter) possesses the densest concentration of this building type within the province. While Hadman points out that the concentration may well reflect an uneven pattern of archaeological discovery, it

could equally be genuine. Aisled buildings are often found in a developed form as subsidiary to the main dwelling house within a villa establishment, as for example at Winterton, Lincs. (Stead 1976), but an increasing feature of the Corieltauvian examples indicates that in many cases they themselves formed the residential part of the farming establishment. This feature was first recognised by J.T. Smith (1964, 75-104) during excavations at Denton 15 miles to the north, and is also a possibility at Great Casterton, just three miles downstream from Empingham, although in both cases there may be reason to believe that the main residence remained undiscovered (Whitwell 1982, 102 ; 111). However, a clearer example comes from the Welland Valley, 12 miles to the south west, where excavations at Drayton II villa, Leics., from 1988-1993 have revealed a large, aisled, masonry building, incorporating two bath suites (with a further external one to the north). The majority of rooms possessed hypocausts, often with tessellated flooring, and from the evidence of excavation and field walking, it appears to stand alone as the major dwelling house, with lesser structures adjoining the north side (Cooper *et al* 1989, Pollard 1991, Connor 1993).

The evidence of human burial from the area surrounding Site 2 suggests the existence of a coherent cemetery related to the household similar to that found close to Site 1. Where dateable objects accompany the burials they are generally of fourth century date and so are broadly contemporary with the Phase 1 building, while the intercutting of burials 8R, 9R, and 10R might also imply that more than one generation is involved.

Phase 2: The Middle Anglo-Saxon Cemetery (fig. 8)

Context of the Burials
The latest phase of activity on the site comes in the form of a group of five burials which lay below Roman floor levels, and by inference must have been cut through the flooring of the Phase 1 Roman building. However, the lack of extant flooring makes this impossible to demonstrate conclusively from the grave cuts. The implications of their location are discussed below.

Note: to avoid confusion with burials from the other sites, those from this site are given the suffix 'MAS' (Middle Anglo-Saxon) in the skeletal report (p.55). This section describes the layout of the cemetery.

The Burials
Though fragmentary, the skeletons in Burials 1-3 were all substantially complete.

Burial 1 (plate 6)
This burial contained a subadult male and was located on the south side of the building, immediately south of the well. The body was supine with its head at the west end.

Burials 2, 3 and ?4 lay in a group in the north-west corner of the building.

Burial 2
This contained an adult female under thirty years of age,

Plate 6 Site 2: Middle Anglo-Saxon Grave 1, looking southwest.

supine with head to the west. The position of the burial crossed the wall line previously separating Rooms 1 and 4. Presumably the wall had been previously removed, although footings for it were preserved to the north of the burial.

Burial 3
Located within Room 2 this contained the skeleton of an adult male which was supine with its head to the east.

Burial 4
By comparison, the remains in Burial 4 were very fragmentary. No detailed plan of the burial was made, and the photographic evidence indicates that it was very badly disturbed. There is considerable doubt therefore whether it represents an actual burial or a scatter of bones derived from another burial, the position of which is unknown. The position of the burial between Burials 2 and 3, would appear logical, but the fact that it overlay extant wall footings between Rooms 1 and 2 (71 NN) is not, given that none of the other burials do. The disturbed nature of the burial is also indicated by the fact that the bones of a large hand which probably belong to it were originally incorporated with those of Burial 2 immediately to the north. The occupant was probably an adult male.

Burial 5
This appears to have been isolated from the other burials located in the north aisle of the building and is the only burial to be accompanied by grave finds. This part of the building was the last to be investigated and under the prevailing rescue conditions no plan or photographic record was made of the burial. However, the written record states that a number of finds were located under and around the head and neck area. These comprised a copper alloy pin with a jewelled head set in

a silver mount, a copper alloy Maltese cross, a glass bead, a jet object, and an object of silver. Unfortunately, all but the copper alloy pin went missing at the time of the excavation. The detailed discussion of this object is to be found elsewhere in this volume (p.107 no.11), but its mid-to-late seventh century date provides the only dating evidence for this burial, and by inference, the rest of the group.

Discussion of Phase 2 Middle Anglo-Saxon Activity

The presence of the mid- to late seventh century pin in Burial 5, implies that these burials are of Middle Anglo-Saxon date and, in addition their east-west orientation and general lack of grave finds, would suggest that they represent Christian interments. If it is accepted that the burials lay below the Roman floor levels, then three possible interpretations exist. Firstly, the burials could have been cut into the floors of a largely intact building, which may have been refurbished or modified (involving the removal of partition walls) for specific reuse as a religious building. Secondly, the burials could have been made through the rubble and into the floors of a partially demolished building which was reused, or held some focal significance, without removing the rubble from the original floors. The third possibility is that the building had been entirely levelled and overgrown by the time the burials were made, and that as a convenient piece of waste ground, the site of the villa building coincidentally became a cemetery.

Accepting the third option would be an easy way of avoiding the possibility that the reuse of the building occurred. However, a number of factors weigh against it. Firstly it is unlikely that the building would not still have featured in the landscape to some extent, since it was clearly occupied until the early fifth century and there was no subsequent reason for its masonry to be robbed during the following two centuries. Secondly, the closer alignment of the burials to the walls of the building rather than precisely east-west must be of considerable significance, and suggests that the walls were to some extent upstanding. Third is the fact that cutting the graves would have involved digging through building rubble and *opus signinum* flooring, which is likely to have deterred all but the most persistent Anglo-Saxon gravedigger, when soft soil lay only metres away.

These factors would support the possibility that the building was still upstanding in the seventh century and was perhaps being reused as a church. No further burials were noted outside the building during topsoil machining after the excavation had been prematurely ended, although it is quite possible that previous ploughing may have destroyed evidence for them. Their presence might have supported the possibility that a cemetery had spread fortuitously over the area of the building or instead, that the building was indeed acting as the focus of a cemetery which made a social differentiation between burials inside and outside the building. Their apparent absence, while supporting the contention that the building was reused, does suggest that the cemetery was rather small and the duration of reuse was perhaps short. The amount of stray human bone excavated does suggest that there were more than five individuals buried in the building, but not many more.

The reuse of villa buildings for burial purposes has been widely recognised on the Continent, not only in France and Belgium where there are hundreds of examples, but also in the Rhine and Danube provinces (Percival 1976, 183, Ripoll and Arce 2000). In his examination of the Continental evidence, Percival acknowledges that in some cases the coincidence of burials and villa buildings is fortuitous, particularly where the cemetery surrounding a nearby church happens to spread over the ruined villa building, but in the vast majority of cases villa buildings have clearly been chosen as a focus for burial either because of previous religious significance or because the building's shape and orientation have made it suitable for conversion into a church. In the absence of any evidence to support the former, the Empingham example would fit the criteria for the latter.

However, the reuse of villa buildings as churches has rarely been demonstrated, and although Percival (1976) cites Continental examples where parts of French villa building plans have been incorporated, for example at Martres-Tolosane (Haute Garonne), there are no definite British examples, despite the fact that the last two decades has seen a gradual rise in the number of recognised examples of burial in villa buildings. In 1972, Applebaum was only able to list six examples, to which Percival added two more (1976, 217), and Rodwell and Rodwell (1985, 106) a further 11, while noting that further examples could be added from recent excavations (Morris and Roxan 1980). There are probably numerous potential examples of the reuse of villa buildings as churches or cemetery sites which have gone unrecognised simply because the burials, which are rarely accompanied by dateable finds, were not considered to be significant at the time of the excavation

and were broadly identified as 'medieval', as (correctly) in the case of those found in the aisled Building D at Winterton, Lincs. (Stead 1976, 49).

Approaching the problem from the other direction, Morris and Roxan (1980) have examined the evidence for extant medieval churches that appear to lie on or near the site of a Roman villa building or other Roman building, or have had Roman building materials incorporated into their structure. While there are numerous examples (Morris and Roxan 1980, Appendix 1), actually demonstrating the direct reuse of an underlying villa building is often precluded by the presence of the church itself or modern burials, as the example of Rivenhall clearly illustrates (Rodwell and Rodwell 1985, 84). Locally the church at Ab Kettleby is thought to lie on the site of a Roman villa (Allsop 1998, 162).

In attempting to explain the relationship between villa buildings and churches it has been observed that the majority of English churches are proprietary in origin, owing their foundation to the initiative of lay lords (Morris and Roxan 1980, 191), and that their location might indicate those villa estates that continued into the Anglo-Saxon period and maintained the same administrative centre. Such an argument could be put forward to explain the evidence from Site 2, despite its apparent 'abandonment' during the later fifth and sixth centuries. The site may then join the growing list of examples where the progression from villa to parish church was arrested at an early stage, when for reasons which are not attestable archaeologically, the focus of activity shifted elsewhere, perhaps to Empingham itself. Parsons has recently suggested that if Site 2 did represent a place of Christian worship, then perhaps it was used by British rather than Anglo-Saxon Christians, the latter choosing to establish a separate system of church organisation, along the lines of the pattern already recognised in the West Midlands by Steven Bassett (Parsons 1996, xx).

SITE 3:
'EMPINGHAM I' EARLY ANGLO-SAXON SETTLEMENT AND CEMETERY

Peter Liddle, Samantha J. Glaswell and Nicholas J. Cooper

Introduction *(NJC)*

This report draws information from an original draft text written by late director Malcolm Dean following his excavations of 1966 and 1967, and incorporates the later findings of the 1969, 1970, and 1971 excavations directed by M.S. Gorin. The site (code EMP/EPS 1966-1971) lay on the south side of the River Gwash at SK 9447 0776 over an ironstone outcrop. In about 1960, a small-long brooch was found on land belonging to Mr Eric Palmer of Church Farm, Empingham who, in 1966, brought it to the attention of Miss Christine Mahany and, on advice from Mr Stanley West, the brooch was given a sixth century date. Subsequently Mr Malcolm Dean, who had excavated Anglo-Saxon cemeteries at Willoughby-on-the-Wolds and Newark, visited Mr Palmer and found that during the intervening period, more material had been recovered by excavation from the same area, including parts of a copper alloy-bound wooden bucket, fragments of a copper alloy bowl, and sherds of an Anglo-Saxon pottery vessel. A small trial

excavation by Malcolm Dean followed in late 1966, and uncovered two pagan Anglo-Saxon inhumation burials with accompanying grave finds (Phase 3 Burials 1 and 2). The threat posed by further ploughing led the Ministry of Public Buildings and Works to fund a three-week excavation over Easter 1967 and further work was carried out in subsequent years. A total area of approximately 800 sq. metres was exposed and evidence for prehistoric, Roman, and Anglo-Saxon activity was recovered.

Note: In common with Sites 1 and 2, the on-site recording system comprised two-letter codes prefixed by the site code and year of excavation (e.g. EPS 70 ZY). In addition, feature numbers were occasionally attributed either during the later part of the excavation or during the post-excavation analysis.

Phasing Summary *(NJC)* **(Fig. 9)**

Phase 1

Prehistoric activity of Mesolithic to Early Bronze Age date was indicated by the presence of worked flint, stratified in two oval

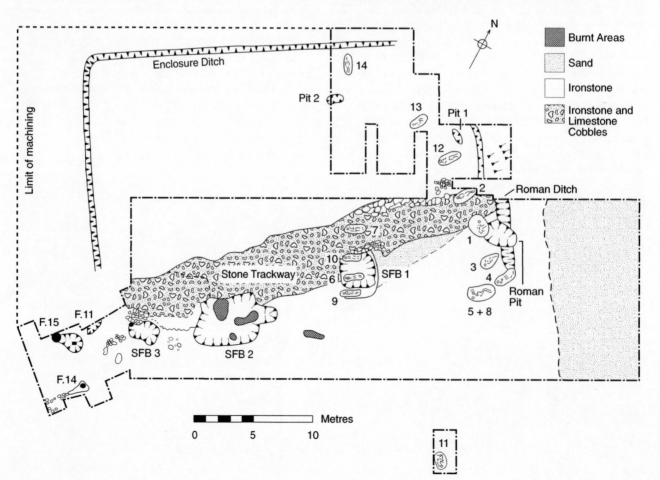

Fig. 9 Site 3 Phases 1-3.

pit features, lying in the northern part of the site, as well as a substantial amount of unstratified material. Material from the area immediately north and east of the excavated area, and also to west, in the area of Site 1, was retrieved during random field walking undertaken at the time.

Phase 2
Romano-British features comprised a cobbled stone trackway and lengths of a possible enclosure ditch and a pit feature of early Roman date. An isolated inhumation burial at the south end of the site also belongs to this phase.

Phase 3
Early Anglo-Saxon settlement evidence comprised three sunken-feature buildings and other associated pit features.

Phase 4
This phase is considered to be broadly contemporary with Phase 3, and comprised an early Anglo-Saxon cemetery of thirteen or fourteen burials immediately to the north and west of the settlement and partly overlies the eastern portion of it.

Phase 1: Prehistoric (NJC)
Two oval-shaped pit features lay towards the northern end of the excavated area. The first of these (Pit 1), excavated in 1969, measured 1.20m by 0.50m and was 0.27m deep. The second, lying 10m to the west, was excavated in 1970 (Pit 2) and measured 0.98m by 0.66m, and was 0.22m deep. The fills of these two features contained no other artefactual material apart from flint. The condition of the material from the 1970 pit was very fresh, suggesting that it had been deposited very soon after being worked, while in contrast, the material from the 1969 pit was heavily corticated, and many of the fragments appeared to come from the same nodule or pebble, with a number conjoined (see p.63). The material from Pit 1 and that from Pit 2 which contained mainly flakes is not closely dated. The unstratified material and that from field walking suggested Neolithic and Early Bronze Age activity. A detailed analysis of the material by Head and Young can be found below (p.63)

Phase 2: Early Roman Settlement (NJC)
The Trackway
A 30m length of stone trackway, cobbled mainly with limestone, ran across the centre of the excavated area in a south-westerly direction, and appears (fig.11) to have been formed by the artificial banking of limestone cobbles over an area of sloping ironstone in order to form a level surface. The trackway was about 5m in width, although the southern boundary was badly disturbed along much of its length by later features. There is possible evidence for a ditch on the northern side which was filled with clay, and was itself cobbled over, perhaps in order to widen the track. The fill contained no artefactual material, and it may in fact be natural in origin.

The attribution of a Roman date to the trackway is based largely on the fact that all other features cut into it and that running south-westwards roughly along the contour line, it appears to head in the direction of Site 1, a further 150m to the west. If the proposed trackway did serve to link Sites 1 and 3 and perhaps other sites along the valley side, then traffic was evidently light, since there was no evidence of wheel ruts or any finds embedded in the surface.

Ditch and Pit Features
At its eastern end, the trackway was cut by a ditch which ran for 6m to the south of it, and tapered to a rounded terminal which was cut by Phase 4, Burial 4. The ditch was 1.5m wide

and 0.5m deep (fig.11), and was cut by a sub-circular pit, 2.5m by 3m in plan, and 0.5m in depth, which was itself cut by Phase 3, Burial 1. Both features were backfilled with a mixture of limestone and ironstone rubble and domestic rubbish comprising animal bone and Roman pottery of later first and second century date (p.89 nos. 115-121). The pottery was rather badly preserved, but dating evidence is also provided by a bow brooch of sawfish type (see p.105 no.3) in immaculate condition, and probably of Flavian date.

Excavation in 1969 indicated that a similar but much narrower ditch continued northwards downslope beyond the trackway for a distance of at least 4.2m, cutting into the ironstone and curving gently westwards. However, it was clearly not a continuation of the same ditch. Excavations in 1970 revealed a further 7m length of ditch (70 ZX), running east to west across the northern part of the site, which would appear to be a continuation of the westerly curving section excavated in 1969, although its eastern end narrowed and appeared to peter out. It varied in width from 0.48m to 0.65m and was 0.25m deep. The fill contained Roman pottery including a sherd of first century samian ware and animal bone. During 1971 (71 ZV), excavation continued during the machining of the area and the ditch was recorded continuing westwards for a further 19m, before turning at right-angles to the south and continuing for a further 16m. The ditch was 0.5m in width and where excavated, was found to contain only Roman pottery.

The single burial (Grave 11) lay 20m south of these features, and appears to have been cut into a masonry hearth structure. There were a number of associated sherds of Roman pottery, but it is uncertain whether they were directly related to the burial itself, or whether the burial is an outlier belonging to the Anglo-Saxon cemetery.

Discussion
The discovery of the ditch continuation during machining in 1971, would appear to suggest the existence of a rectangular enclosure during this period, of which only the northern part has been detected. The portion of ditch lying to the south of the trackway, may represent a recut, and its greater width may be due to a lesser degree of truncation by subsequent ploughing when compared to those sections detected to the north.

An interesting point is that all the Early Anglo-Saxon evidence is actually contained within the perimeter of the enclosure, which may indicate that it continued as an upstanding feature into this period. The main evidence to contradict such a claim is the complete lack of any Anglo-Saxon domestic rubbish within the fill of the enclosure ditch, although this may be explained by the truncation of the upper fills of this ditch.

Phase 3:
The Early Anglo-Saxon Settlement (NJC)
Settlement Evidence (Figs. 10 and 11)
The western half of the excavated area contained substantial evidence for domestic activity of early Anglo-Saxon date, comprising one certain, and two probable, sunken-featured buildings, and a number of associated pits and post holes which may have been structural. All features contained pottery of later fifth and sixth century date (see p.98). Other finds included small finds related

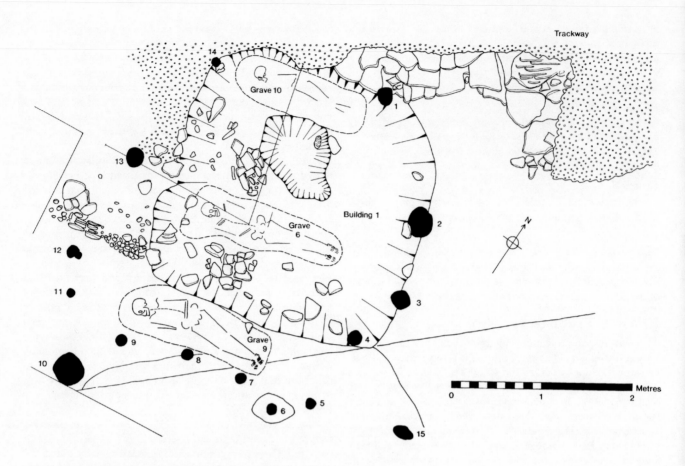

Fig. 10 Site 3 Phase 3, Building 1 and Phase 4 burials 6, 9 and 10 (see pl. 7)

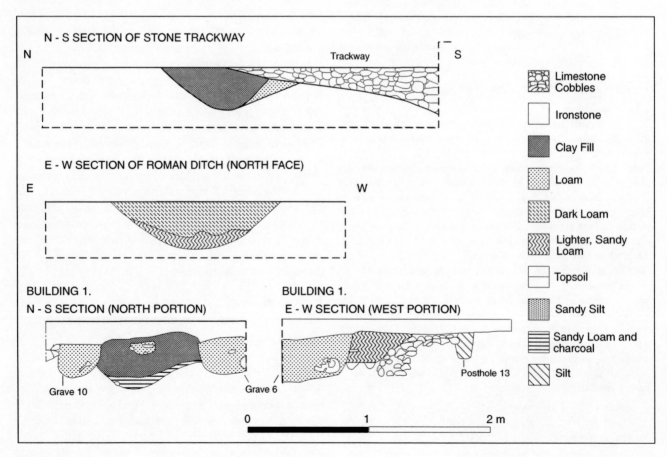

Fig. 11 Site 3 Sections

to weaving (p.113-114 nos. 36, 41 and 42) and metalworking debris (p.130).

Sunken-Featured Buildings

Building 1

This sunken-featured building was cut into the southern edge of the Phase 2 Roman trackway, about halfway along its exposed length, and was itself cut by three early Anglo-Saxon burials (6,9,and 10) belonging to the Phase 4 cemetery. The sunken feature was subrectangular with rounded corners and measured 3.3m north-south by 3.6m east-west. The depth varied from 0.25m to 0.45m (fig.11), with a distinct 'shelf' along the southern and western edges of the sunken feature. The bulk of the occupation material dumped into the structure was concentrated in the 3m by 3m area abutting the north-east corner of the feature.

A total of 14 post holes was associated with the structure. Post holes 1-4 and 14 partially or totally cut the edge of the sunken feature along its northern and eastern edges. Diameters varied from 0.08m (no.14), 0.2m (nos.1,3, and,4), to 0.3m (no.2). Along the southern edge post holes 5,7,8 and 9, which were all of similar size (0.1m in diameter), form a straight line and are evenly spaced at 0.8m intervals. The line ran 0.6m to the south of the edge of the sunken feature, corresponding to the edge of the shelf. Post holes 6 and 10 were larger (0.35m in diameter) and may not necessarily have belonged to the structure. The post holes along the western edge of the structure (11,12, and,13), varied in size, and are more randomly arranged. Post hole 11 was only 0.08m in diameter, 12 may have represent two intercutting post holes of similar size to 11, while 13 is 0.2m in diameter and was set halfway along the western side of the structure, possibly corresponding to post hole 2 midway along the eastern side.

Building 2 (EPS 70 ZY/ZW)

This was represented by a larger (7m by 4m) sunken feature of more irregular plan than Building 1. It lay 6m to the south-west and again cut into the southern side of the trackway. The feature was 0.35m deep, and the floor of the proposed structure showed three areas of intense burning associated with iron-working evidence comprising fragments of furnace bases and tap slag (see p.130). A further area of intense burning also lay just outside the area of the building. There were no associated post holes to indicate any form of superstructure, and so some doubt remains as to whether this was actually a building. It is possible that alterations to the pit

structure related to its later reuse may have removed evidence for post holes, or they may have been truncated by ploughing.

Building 3 (EMP 67 Feature 5).

A third sunken-featured building lay a further 3m to the west. It was sub-rounded in shape and much smaller (3m by 2m) with a single post hole at its western end.

Other Features

Two smaller pit features (F.11 and F.15) and a number of post holes cutting areas of pitched paving (F.14) were excavated immediately south west of Building 3. Feature 15 had a large square post hole located at its centre and a circular area of paving lay at its west end. There were also two linear features with stone lining, interpreted as beam slots or drainage gullies. On the southern edges of the site was a shallow area of occupation debris. In two areas the post holes, at least roughly, form straight lines, and may be the vestiges of post-buildings.

Discussion

It is likely that the excavated evidence for the three sunken-featured buildings and associated pits and post holes represents only a small part of a much larger settlement extending to the west, in the direction of the Roman farmstead on Site 1. The pits and post holes in the south-western part of the excavation are difficult to interpret, but would hint at occupation extending in this direction, perhaps comprising post-built structures. Only the excavation of a much larger area would have revealed such structures and such work was beyond the scope of the project given the financial resources available at the time. The 'rescue' nature of the excavations would also have made the recording of post buildings very difficult and this reason has also been put forward to explain the lack of such buildings on the earliest and southern-most part of the Anglo-Saxon settlement at Mucking (Hamerow 1989, 256).

The relationship between this part of the settlement and the adjacent cemetery, as well as the evidence for metalworking, may indicate that the three buildings represent the eastern limits of the settlement and perhaps the earliest part of it. As will be argued below, the area of Building 1 was subsequently reused to accommodate a proposed later phase of burials, while Building 2 was clearly reused for metalworking perhaps after the removal of its roofed structure. Alterations, poor recording, or simply truncation may explain the lack of post holes around Building 2. Activities such as metalworking produce smoke and sparks, which are not only anti-social, but also present a fire risk in a thatch and timber settlement, and they would thus be confined to its edge. At Medbourne in the Welland Valley, fieldwork has consistently produced a one to one relationship between scatters of Anglo-Saxon pottery and iron slag, suggesting that smelting and smithing were commonly undertaken on domestic sites and it is interesting to see this confirmed by excavation (P. Liddle, pers.comm.)

The above evidence may suggest that the phenomenon of settlement shift, or *Wandersiedlung* as it is known on the Continent, is operating on this site, with a shift westwards. It has been identified at Mucking, Essex by

Plate 7 Site 3: Sunken-featured Building 1 with Graves 9, 6 and 10 inserted (see Fig. 10).

Helena Hamerow, who has argued that it commonly occurs on Early Anglo-Saxon settlements throughout the country (Hamerow 1989). Distinct zoning of settlement has since been recognised at West Heslerton, Yorks (Powlesland 1998), and recent excavations at Eye Kettleby near Melton Mowbray, Leicestershire have revealed evidence for Early Anglo-Saxon settlement over at least four hectares (Finn 1997). The Eye Kettleby site is the largest excavated within Leicestershire and Rutland but study of the pottery and building sequence has so far not demonstrated clear evidence for the sequence of settlement shift (Cooper in prep.).

Phase 4: The Early Anglo-Saxon Cemetery (Fig. 9)

(PL and SLG)

During compilation of the report it was decided that the description and discussion of the finds and the graves themselves should be kept together rather than separating the 'site' and 'finds' elements. However, the human skeletal information has been grouped separately within a report on the Romano-British and Anglo-Saxon population of the Empingham area (see p.55). The graves and their contents have been arranged in order of excavation from 1-14.

Burial 1 (figs. 12 and 13)

Female, 17-25 years (sex only asserted by grave finds).

Badly shattered by ploughing and excavation by Mr Palmer. The excavator, Malcolm Dean, stated that the left clavicle and left hand were *in situ*, but this is difficult to reconcile with the plan. No grave cut was seen, and the orientation uncertain.

Finds

A) Square-headed brooch (1968.158 (13) Sf no.6.)

The square-headed brooch is made of a white metal, presumably silver. The upper surface was originally gilded but this has worn away in some areas. The maximum length of the brooch is 84mm and the maximum width of the headplate is 35mm. The headplate is rectangular, and the frame is defined on both its inner and outer edge by a band decorated with raised triangles. The frame itself comprises zoomorphic feet, hips and eyes. The second panel contains two rectangular sections, each of six connected spirals, above two hips and feet. The upper and lower corners of the frame each contain a single eye. The sections of the bow immediately adjoining the headplate and the footplate are undecorated apart from gilding. The remaining section is divided by a medial ridge, creating two panels bordered by raised triangles, and filled with a jumble of feet and hips characteristic of Salin's Style I beasts. The two panels do not mirror each other but are designed independently. The upper borders of the footplate are decorated with hips, feet, blocks of parallel lines, and two prominent eyes. The lower borders of the foot also carry the hip and blocks of lines motif. The inner panel of the foot has a border bearing the raised triangle motif. The inner panel itself is composed of progressively smaller diamond shapes, one within another. The side lobes follow a similar theme, but in this instance the repeated shape is an angular 'C'. Between the extreme terminal and the main foot is a small rectangular panel defined by a border with the raised triangles motif.

Within the border is a recumbent 'S'. The terminal is in the form of a zoomorphic mask, the eyebrows of which meet and descend, dividing the face into two. The eyes are situated in the curve of the eyebrows and are emphasised beneath with repeating lines. The mask has a long snout decorated with two bands of horizontal lines. The reverse of the headplate has two lugs with corrosion and the remains of a pin between them. The catchplate was made separately, also of white metal, and has subsequently become detached. It is decorated with two uneven zig-zag lines along the plate and gilded mouldings on the catch. The catchplate bears traces of iron from the pin, suggesting that it was fastened when deposited in the ground.

John Hines does not classify this brooch but firmly places it into his Phase 1 for which he suggests dates of AD500-520 (Hines 1984, 169-170; 180; 189). The Style I decoration indicates a date post-AD475.

B) Wrist clasp 1968.158 (5) Sf no.5.

Cast in copper alloy and gilded. The plate is sub-rectangular, with rounded corners. The eye projects from a solid rectangular section along the middle of one edge. The other three sides are decorated with openwork, composed of three outward facing animal heads with scrolled nostrils, which are connected by interlace and zoomorphic features such as eyes and hips, typical of Salin's Style I decoration.

Hines (1984, 98) could find no parallel for this object, but puts it into his Class C. He comments on its similarity to a Scandinavian C1 wrist clasp, suggesting that while it may have been imported there was no clear reason why it should not be of English manufacture.

C) Beads. 1968.15 (12) Sf no.5.

32 beads were scattered around the area of the skull.

i) Rock crystal with central perforation and 22 facets, based on a pentagonal array. The bevelled-edge perforation was drilled between two opposing parallel facets.

From its position, this bead would appear to have formed the centre piece of the string of beads. Meaney has discussed their use. They occur in chatelaines, and the large central perforation and symmetrical facetting also suggest use as a spindle whorl (experimentation with replicas has demonstrated their suitability). They may also have amuletic properties, distracting the evil eye (Meaney 1981, 77-82). Such beads have a widespread distribution, and there are several Leicestershire examples including those from Glen Parva and Beeby. Dated examples tend to be of sixth century date.

ii) seven polychrome beads; four dot and trail, two zig-zag, and one speckled.

iii) 24 monochrome beads; 3 clear blue glass; 7 opaque white glass; 9 red; 3 opaque yellow glass; 1 opaque green glass; 1 opaque blue-green glass.

D) Bucket 1968.158 (16) Sf no.10.

Dimensions: diameter 120 mm. Height 980mm.

An unknown number of wooden staves, possibly of ash or beech, bound by four broad copper alloy straps 16mm wide, and four punch-decorated, copper alloy uprights 91mm long and up to 11mm wide. The rim is formed with copper alloy sheet wrapped round into a split tube, and secured by a minimum of four cleats. Copper alloy rivets were used to secure the structure. The handle mount, of which only one is extant, was formed from copper alloy sheet, decorated with scored lines, and has curling terminals, each secured by a rivet. These seem to be simplified versions of bucket mounts with animal head terminals.

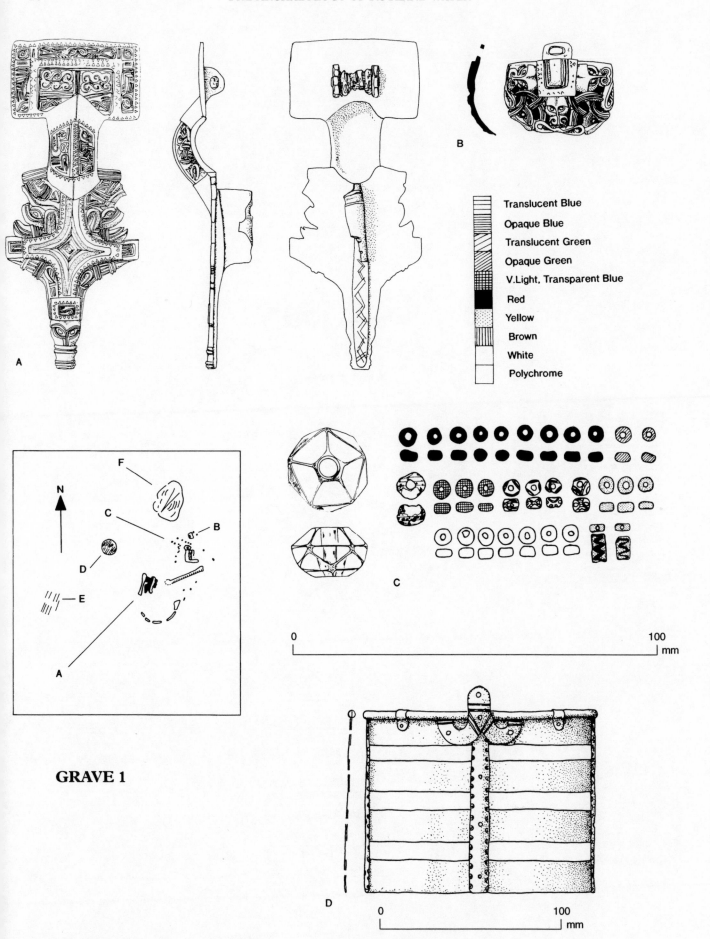

Translucent Blue
Opaque Blue
Translucent Green
Opaque Green
V.Light, Transparent Blue
Red
Yellow
Brown
White
Polychrome

GRAVE 1

Fig. 12 Site 3 Grave 1

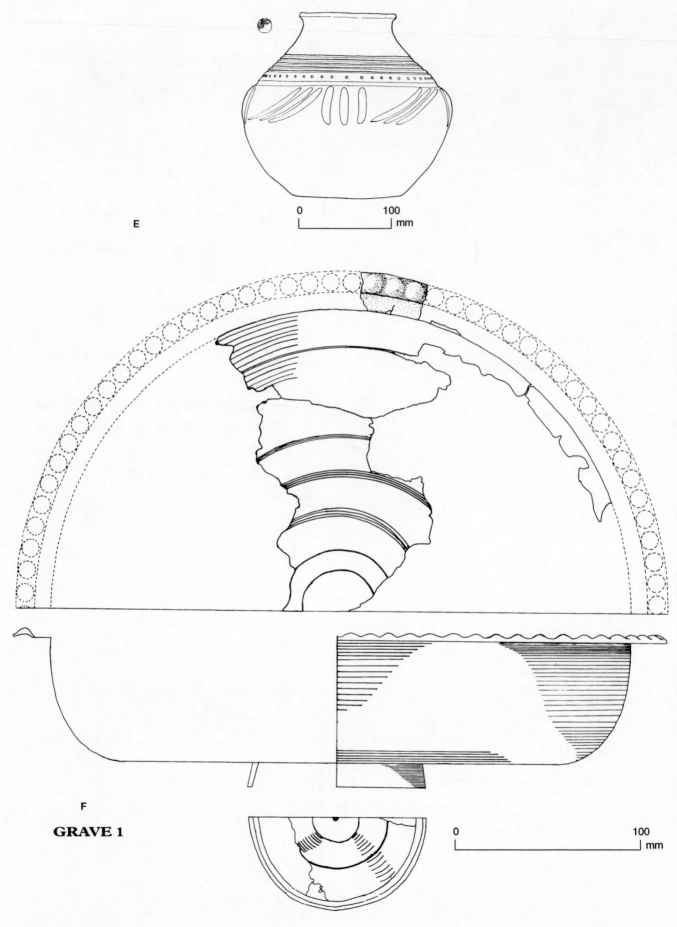

E

0   100
          mm

F

GRAVE 1

0   100
          mm

Fig. 13 Site 3 Grave 1 contd.

E) Pottery vessel 1968.158(8) no Sfno.
Dimensions: Rim diameter 120mm, neck diameter 110mm, maximum girth 260mm, base diameter 135mm, height 220mm.

The vessel was found in several large pieces due to plough damage, but a complete profile was reconstructed. The form is slightly squat with a conical neck and well formed rim, and the decoration comprises five parallel neck grooves below which run a line of circular stamp marks. Below these runs a broad shallow groove. The girth is decorated with alternating triplets of parallel grooves arranged vertically and diagonally. The vertical grooves are on raised panels. The fabric is heavily quartz sand tempered, with reduced black body and burnished black surfaces.

Comment by Paul Blinkhorn
The decoration of bosses, lines, and dots, is similar in style to several vessels from Loveden Hill, Lincs. such as Myres (1977) No.1355, and the general appearance of the vessel and combination of styles, suggests that a date of the late fifth to early sixth century.

F) Copper alloy bowl. 1968.158(14,15) Sf nos.7 and 9.
Plough damaged, with clear plough furrow through base. Only a small proportion of the rim survived.

The bowl is made from beaten copper alloy with a beaded rim and was finished by turning. The heavy footring was soldered separately to the base.

Comment
This is clearly a high status burial. The brooch and wrist clasp are of high quality and it includes both the facetted crystal and a high proportion (7 out of 9) of the polychrome beads from the site. The bowl is also unusual and of high status. In Anglian areas buckets are generally buried with males. The brooches, beads and wrist clasp clearly indicate a female, but the disturbance of the grave means that a double burial of a male and female cannot be ruled out.

Burial 2 (Fig. 14)

Adult male, supine, with legs crossed and hands crossed over pelvis. Aligned SSW-NNE.

Finds
A) Spearhead 1968.158 (69) Sf no.94.
Length 223mm (blade 120mm), width 32mm.

This example has a leaf-shaped blade and a split socket which has wood preserved in it. The rivet is still *in situ*, and is of copper alloy. The blade is stepped in cross-section, and the tip is broken. It falls into Swanton's K2 class, the dating of which is suggested to lie at the end of the fifth and beginning of the sixth century (Swanton 1973, 133). From the remaining impressions, the wooden shaft would appear to be of ash (identification *G. C. Morgan*).

B) Iron knife and other iron objects (probably nails). Sf nos.90-92, located close to the coin at the right hip. The tip of the knife blade is missing and most of the original surface has corroded away. There are traces of a fine-grained hardwood on the tang, but species identification was not possible. Dimensions: Length 103mm; blade width 17mm; back width 4mm.

The back is straight and the cutting edge is curved. This conforms to Evison's Type 2 (1987), which was found in all but the latest phases at Buckland, Dover.

There were at least four other objects. One is a nail (length 47mm) with prominent head; two are nail shanks (40mm and 26mm long), and the fourth appears to be the tang of a knife (43mm long).

C) Pottery vessel 1968.158 (3).
A small crudely made vessel with a pinched out lug or handle. Probably a lamp and not closely datable.
Fabric: Quartz sand tempered.

D) Coin and ?Purse Sf nos.91/93. (Report by *R. A. Rutland*)
A coin of Carausius found by the right hip, and embedded in a mass of a black powdery substance which may possibly have been the remains of a leather purse. Two small pieces of copper alloy sheet may have been fittings for the purse, or part of its contents. The coin is now lost but the drawing of the reverse allows an identification.
Rev. LAETITIA AVG I/ML Laetitia standing left, holding wreath and anchor, javelin or staff.
Probably Mattingly and Sydenham 1933, 467, no.50.
Obv. must be IMPCARAUSIUSPFAVS Radiate, draped [and cuirassed], bust right.
London mint AD 288-9.

Comment
The spear and the knife are common finds, and the small pot is probably a lamp. The Roman coin could well be an amulet (Meaney 1981, 213-6). The nails and broken knife tang are more difficult to explain; they could possibly represent a scrap collection for recycling, and thus reflect the deceased's occupation, although it should be noted that the child in Grave 10 also has a similar collection. They may again be amuletic.

Burial 3 (Fig. 15)

Adult female, 35 years+ (sex only asserted by grave finds). Skeleton was flexed, probably lying on the left side. Aligned SSW-NNE.

Finds
Two copper alloy brooches, both of which were found in the upper chest area of the burial.

A) Cruciform Brooch. 1968.158(17) Sf no.11.
A small, delicate example of Aberg Group II (Aberg 1926. 36). The headplate has three half-round knobs, but no wings. The foot has well defined but not `stalk-like' eyes, and the nostrils are half-round and not joined together. Iron corrosion around the pin lug indicates that the pin was of iron.

Brooches of this type are generally dated to between *c.*500-550 AD.

B) Small long brooch. 1968.158 (10) Sf no.1.
This small long brooch is of a trefoil type. The bow has two medial grooves, and the foot is decorated with transverse grooves terminating in a simple triangular form.

Trefoils are the largest and most varied class of small long brooches identified by Leeds (1945), and he interprets them as a simplified version of the cruciform with the knobs cast flat as an integral part of the headplate. This contrasts with the early cruciform brooches where the knobs were cast separately and attached to the headplate (1945, 8).

This example would fit Leeds' description of the earlier types of trefoil brooch and he suggests a date in the first half of the sixth century (Leeds 1945, 9-11, fig.4a).

C) Iron Knife. 1968.158 (23). Sf no.19.
Dimensions: length 111mm; blade width 21mm; back width 2.5mm

Blade has a curved back and the tip is broken. The cutting edge is also curved, and it can be placed in Evison's (1987) Type 1, which was found in all phases at Buckland, Dover.

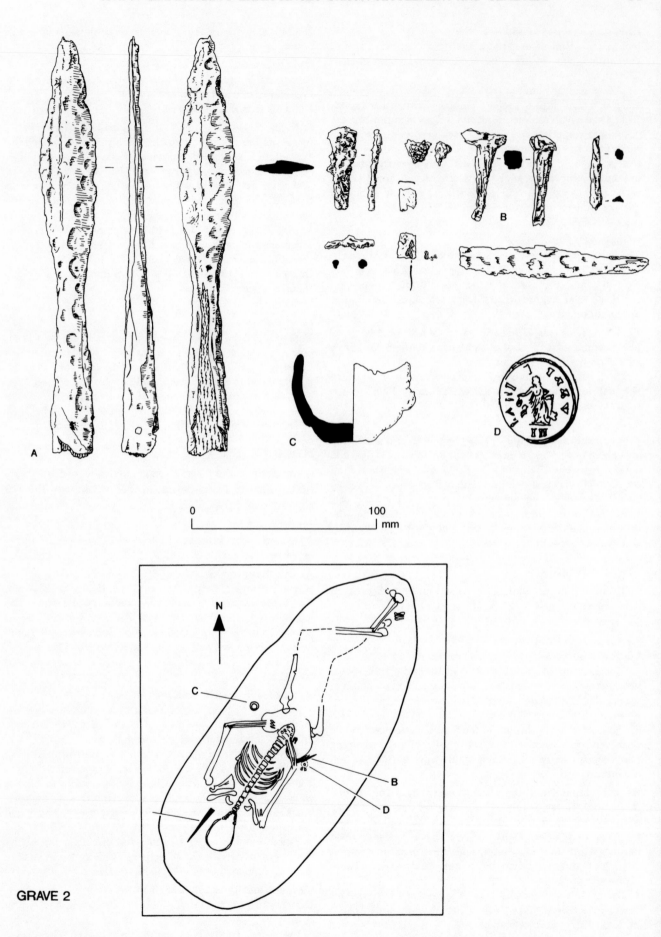

Fig. 14 Site 3 Grave 2

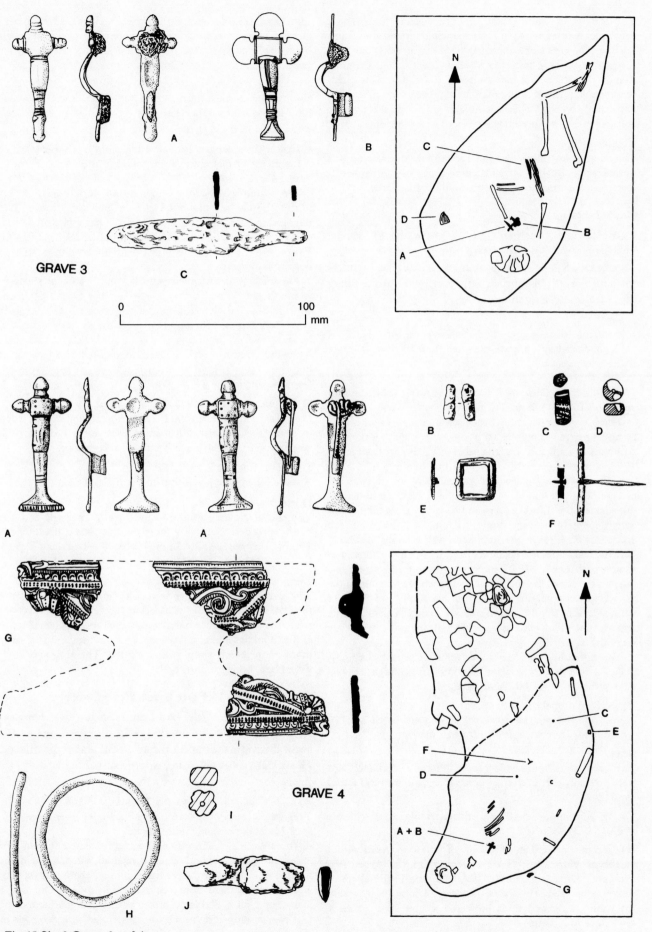

GRAVE 3

0   100
                                 mm

A   A   B   C   D   E   F

GRAVE 4

A   A

B   C   D

E   F

G   H   I   J

Fig. 15 Site 3 Graves 3 and 4

D) Pot base
This object is marked on the grave plan, but is not subsequently mentioned in Dean's original report, and is now missing. The concentric marks indicate that it is wheelthrown (caused by removal from the wheel with wire), and therefore Roman. The deliberate collection and ?reuse of Roman sherds is apparent from a number of domestic Anglo-Saxon features, particularly on Site 7 (Tickencote) (see p.53), and it is possible that this object was intentionally placed in the grave.

Comment
This is a typical female burial. Presumably the woman was buried with odd brooches fastening a peplos-type gown. It seems unusual that no beads were found in the grave.

Burial 4 (Fig. 15)

Adult female (sex asserted by grave finds). Burial posture impossible to assess but edge of grave cut suggests a SSW-NNE alignment, with skull fragments at the south end. This burial partly overlay the stone filling of the Romano-British ditch.

Finds
It is difficult to assign grave finds with any certainty.

Those found in the grave are listed first, followed by those found lying nearby.

A) Small-long brooch 1968.158 (22) Sf no. 8. (Surface find) and 1968.158 (41) Sf no. 44. (Grave 4).

These two copper alloy brooches appear to form a near identical pair, but only one (sf no. 44) was found between the remnants of skull and ribs. The other was found unstratified in 1960, and was probably ploughed out of the grave. Both brooches have a triangular foot and thus probably fall into the category of small long. However, the headplates are somewhat unusual: each is 12mm square and has three projecting knobs which seem to be very crude versions of those found on cruciform types. However, the fact that the knobs are three-dimensional rather than flattened, indicates that they do not fit exactly with Leeds' (1945) interpretation of trefoil types. The lug and the pin of the surface found brooch are missing. In the excavated example, however, the pin lug is offset to the right hand side. Apparently an iron rod was passed through the lug and a copper alloy pin was coiled around the rod, not directly on to the lug itself.

The difficulty in paralleling this pair of brooches closely, makes dating problematic, but the simple form might imply a date in the first half of the sixth century.

B) Iron pin or nail shank Sf no. 45.
Found 50mm from the excavated brooch above (Sf no. 44). 19mm long, 7mm wide. Probably a nail shank.

Beads:
Two beads were found widely spaced due to disturbance, and were probably part of a larger group (see I, a third bead found close by).

C) Polychrome, hexagonal, incorporating four colours 1968.158 (34) Sf no.37.

D) Ceramic bead. 1968.158 (20) Sf no.16. Covered with a pale blue glaze. This is an extremely unusual type. Two examples came from Grave 49A from the Empingham II cemetery on the north side of the valley (Timby 1996), where the other associated finds indicated a later sixth or early seventh century date.

E) Square copper alloy buckle frame. 1968.158 (35). Sf no.38. Pin missing. Decorated with incised nicks or punch marks along the leading edge. Traces of iron pin. No Anglian parallels known, although square buckles are known elsewhere, for example from the Isle of Wight at this time.

F) Copper alloy pin from a buckle. 1968.158(36) Sf no.39.
With a hinge formed from a cross staff with cylindrical collets. No Anglo-Saxon parallels known.

Finds close to Burial 4.

G) Silver (?) equal arm brooch. 1968.158 (37). Sf no.4
3 fragments of this object were found in the topsoil between graves 4 and 5.

Decorated with scrolls and naturalistic animals, and in places the carving has cut right through the brooch. The decoration was finished by gilding. This style of animal decoration shows a provincial Roman influence (Aberg 1926; Evison 1987, 135) which contrasts with the later, more stylistic depiction of beasts.

On the continent similar brooches tend to occur singly in women's graves, and sometimes with other types of brooch, while in England they are almost always accompanied by other types. The equal arm type can occur as a central brooch between two of another type, as at Bury St.Edmunds and Mucking (Evison 1987, 134). This might be the case if it belongs to grave 4, but where dated, the equal arm types are from the fifth century.

H) Copper alloy ring. 1968.158 (11). Sf no.2.
Large cast copper alloy ring. Bent. Diameter 70mm. Described by Dean as a bracelet, but is more likely to be a ring for the suspension of 'chatelaine' objects (i.e. a 'key ring').

I) Glass melon bead. 1968.158. Sf no. 4
A seven lobed blue-green translucent melon bead.

J) Iron knife 1968.158. Sf no. 3
The end of the tang and tip of the blade are missing and it is badly corroded. Surviving length 67mm, max. blade width 19mm, max back width 4mm. Probably a Buckland Type 1 (Evison 1987).

Comment
The damage to this grave is considerable, but most of the material should probably be associated with the grave. All could relate to a single female burial with three brooches (small longs at the shoulders and equal-armed brooch at the centre). Clearly many more beads should have existed. The ring and knife would have hung from the belt.

Burial 5 (Fig. 16 Plate 8 and Rear Cover)

Adult male. The burial had flexed legs and was lying on its left side. One spear was on the grave floor and a second was further up in the grave fill above the bucket. Grave cut across an earlier interment (Grave 8).

Finds

A) Copper alloy-bound wooden bucket 1968.158 (2) Sf no.71. This was located near to the face (facing left), and had one spearhead above it and another below it.

Dimensions: see illustration. It was constructed of 8 wooden staves, 5mm thick, bound by fine copper alloy hoops. The rim is formed of copper alloy sheet rolled into a penannular section, and secured by three cleats, and the handle mount. The handle is of copper alloy, and is decorated with punch marks, and the two copper alloy uprights are each decorated with two pairs of incised lines, one either side of the rivets which secure it.

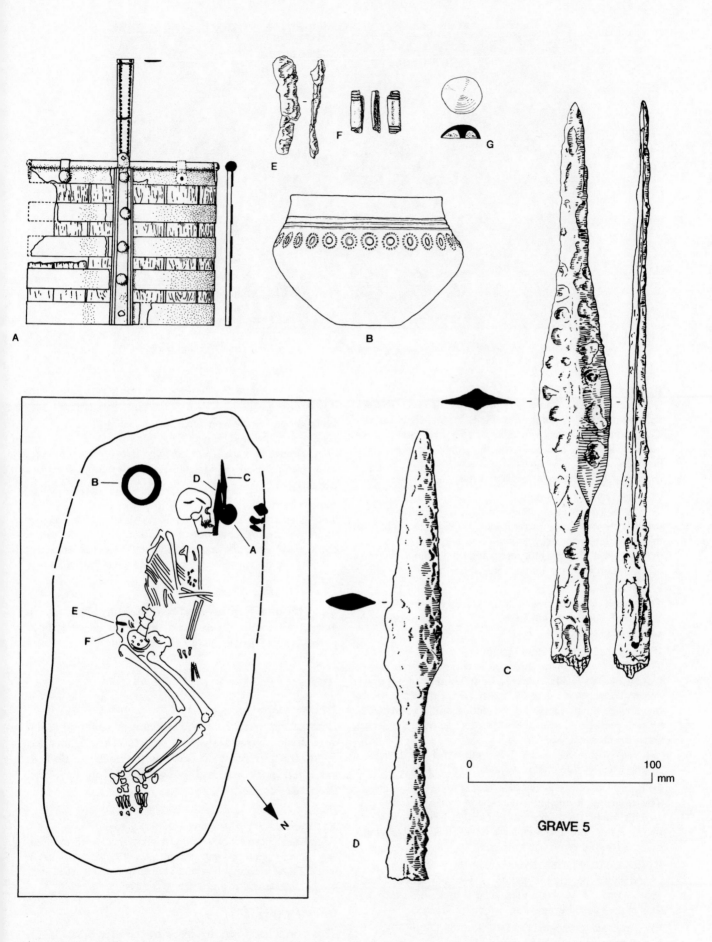

Fig. 16 Site 3 Graves 5 and 8

Plate 8 Site 3: Grave 5 showing detail of wooden bucket (A), ceramic vessel (B) and spearhead (C)

B) Pottery vessel. 1968.158 (1)

Dimensions: rim diameter 150mm, neck diameter 162mm, maximum girth 205mm, base diameter 7mm, height 135mm. The vessel is decorated with three narrow horizontal grooves, below which there is a single row of stamped ornament. The fabric of the vessel is quartz sand tempered, and it has a reduced body with patchy oxidised surface.

Comment by *Paul Blinkhorn*

This stamped vessel is rather unusual, and whilst no exact parallels can be found, the restrained use of the stamping and the lack of linear zone decoration would suggest a date around the early sixth century at the latest, at a time when these forms of decoration were just coming into use.

Iron Spearheads

Two spearheads were present in the grave and both are clearly associated with this individual, rather than the disturbed individual in Grave 8.

C) Spearhead (upper). 1968.158 (56). Sf no. 69.

This is the larger of the two and is without a split socket. Length 298mm (blade 217mm), width 39mm. There is a rivet hole and traces of wood, possibly hazel, in the socket, and an x-ray revealed the presence of a rivet for securing the shaft. The blade is leaf-shaped with the widest section near the socket, and has a pronounced midrib.

It falls within Swanton's B2 group which he dates to a 'relatively early stage of the settlement' (1973, 41).

D) Spearhead (lower). 1968.158 (62). Sf no.77.

This spearhead is missing at the time of writing, but it had an angular blade, the widest part of which lies closest to the socket. It thus falls into Swanton's (1973) E series. Drawing is based upon Malcolm Dean's original.

E) Iron knife. 1968.158 (56). Sf no.70.

Found above the pelvis. Dimensions: surviving length 53mm, width 11mm. A very corroded knife comprising a tang and start of the blade. May possibly belong to Grave 8.

F) Copper alloy strap-end (?). 1968.158 (57). Sf no.72.

Found beneath pelvis. Constructed of copper alloy sheet, bent over and crimped. The decoration consists of three light tooled grooves at both ends. No corresponding buckle was found with it to suggest a belt.

From close to Grave 5 on north side.

G) Copper alloy stud. Sf no.55.

Small copper alloy stud (now missing). Possibly a belt fitting (illustration based on Malcolm Dean's original; scale not certain).

Comment

The occurrence of two spearheads is unusual but not unprecedented. Although often described as a warrior grave, the skeletal evidence suggests that this was not an active warrior, and the spears were presumably status indicators.

Burial 6 (Fig. 17)

Cut through Sunken-featured Building 1. Body in extended position on its back, with arms crossed above pelvis. Adult Female, 35-45 years.

Finds

None.

Burial 7 (Fig. 17)

Located 3m to north of sunken-featured Building 1, and cut into stone trackway. Skull badly crushed against the end of the grave where it cuts into the trackway. Body in extended position, and lying slightly on left side. Probable Female, 17-25 years.

Finds

A) Copper alloy ferrule. 1968.158 (53) Sf no.66.

Found near pelvis. Folded copper alloy sheet with top bent over. Several pin holes, one of which goes through two layers of metal. These presumably secured the ferrule to a wooden stick in a similar fashion to a modern walking stick.

Burial 8 (Fig. 17)

This burial had been disturbed by the later Burial 5.

Finds

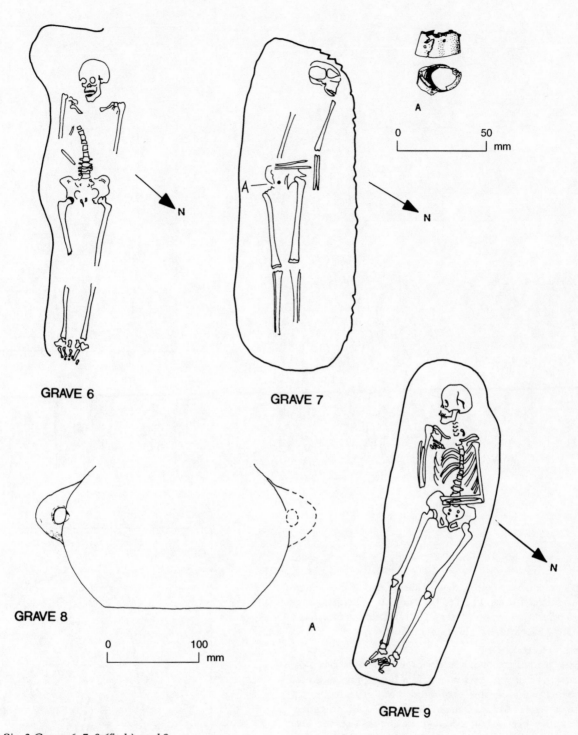

GRAVE 6

GRAVE 7

GRAVE 8

GRAVE 9

Fig. 17 Site 3 Graves 6, 7, 8 (finds), and 9

A) Pottery vessel. 1968.158 (9).
A vessel with a pierced lug handle, in a black, quartz-tempered fabric. Base diameter 150mm, max. girth 250mm.

Comment by *Paul Blinkhorn*.
This handled vessel is very similar in its overall appearance to a vessel from Lackford, Suffolk (Myres 1977, no.858), which is dated to the sixth century by its continental parallels (Myres 1976, 10), although comparisons with vessels such as this must be treated with a little caution, due to their otherwise unremarkable appearance.

B) Iron knife (see detailed description with Grave 5) may have derived from this burial, as may the strap end (?) and the stud.

***Burial 9* (Fig. 17)**

Probable male, 14-15 years.

Finds
None

***Burial 10* (Fig. 18)**

Cut into the floor of sunken-featured Building 1. Body supine in extended position.
    Child of indeterminate sex, 9-10 years.

Finds
A) Iron knife 1968. 158 (56) sf.no 70?

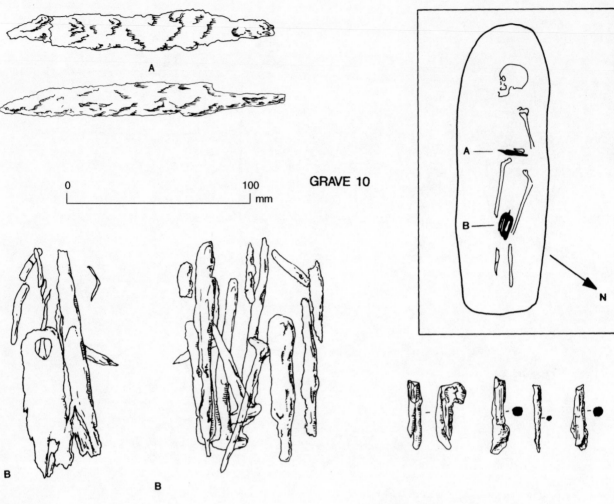

GRAVE 10

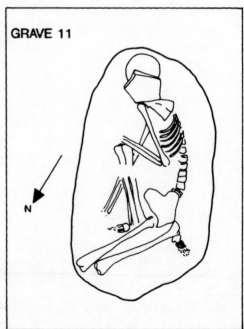

Dimensions: length 147mm, blade width 22mm, back width 4mm.

This knife is very corroded, with almost half of the original surface missing. It has a curved back and curved cutting edge and so belongs to Evison's Type 1 (1987). Drawing from x-ray taken for Malcolm Dean illustrates original shape.

B) Iron objects. Sfno.81.
A closely packed group of iron objects was found between the lower thighs and were presumably in a bag. X-rays taken for Malcolm Dean soon after excavation shows at least a dozen objects, several of which are nails (75mm long) with prominent heads. Others may be iron rods, and one appears to have a hole in it. Dean suggested that this may be a bradawl. This may be the surviving object which has a hooked top, and may in fact be the top of an iron key. A second small find number (95) was assigned to 'iron keys?' from the grave but these cannot be found (unless they have been placed within 81), but this supports the identification of keys as part of this group. Apart from the hooked object, two nails and a rod (key shank?) survive.

Comment
There appear to be keys amongst the group of iron objects and they are probably functional and hung from the belt, although they could also be scrap. The other material is hard to interpret and may be the contents of a bag, as in Grave 2. It could represent a collection of scrap.

Fig. 18 Site 3 Graves 10 and 11

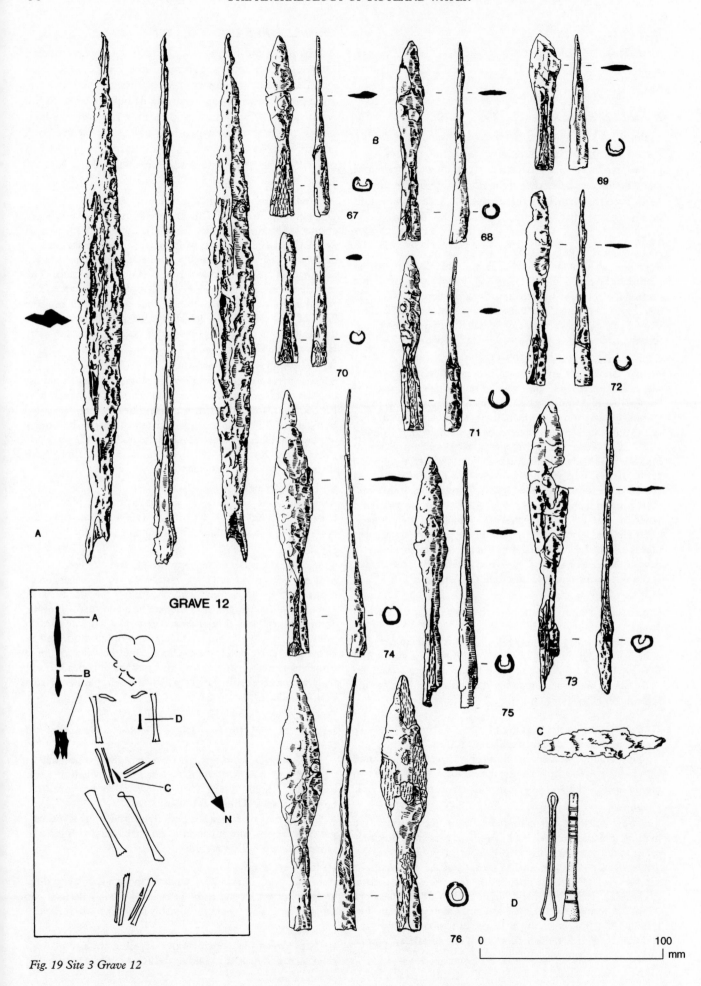

Fig. 19 Site 3 Grave 12

Burial 11 (Fig. 18)

Adult ?male 35-45 years

Finds

None

Burial 12 (EPS 1969). (Fig. 19)

Male, 33-45 years. (Sex asserted by associated finds). Burial supine with legs flexed and arms crossed over pelvis. Knife at belt, tweezers over chest, spear and arrowheads on the body's right side. Nine of the arrows seem to have been contained possibly in a quiver, and one is closer to the spearhead, presumably drawn.

Finds

A) Iron spearhead Sf no. 104.

Surviving length 284mm, width 25mm. This badly preserved example has a leaf-shaped blade with its widest point at the centre. The socket is broken, and the shaft is possibly of ash. The blade is fullered and thus falls into Swanton's I2 class. Few of this type have been closely dated, but a range of later fifth to earlier sixth century is suggested (Swanton 1973, 125).

B) Iron arrowheads Sf nos. 105-114.

All ten arrowheads are made of iron and have split sockets, which are not riveted. They vary in both shape and size, the longest being 156mm, and the shortest complete example 99mm. In common with other Anglo-Saxon arrowheads they are all approximately leaf-shaped rather than angular (Manley 1985, 223). Three of the larger examples (136mm or more) have stepped blade profiles. All examples have traces of wood in the socket, but previous conservation has not permitted accurate identification. 90073 is definitely ash; 90067 and 90070 are probably ash; 70074 is of willow/poplar type, and 90072 is of oak. One example, 90076, which was the last to be excavated, has wood preserved on the exterior which suggests that they may have been held in a quiver or rested next to a bow, or the edge of a coffin. The wood is definitely a hardwood, and is not oak or yew. (identification *G. C. Morgan*)

C) Iron knife Sf no. 116.

Dimensions: length 70mm; blade width 16mm; back width 3mm.

The blade tip is missing and corrosion is extensive. The knife has an angled back and a curved cutting edge, fitting into Evison's Type 3 (1987). This type is the second most common at Buckland, but was not found in the first phase dating to the second half of the fifth century.

D) Copper alloy tweezers Sf no. 115.

Dimensions: length 67mm, max. width 10mm.

Copper alloy tweezers made in one piece and decorated with notches at the top separated by transverse lines, then two border lines, and finally two further groups of transverse lines.

Comment

The bow and arrow is assumed to have been primarily a hunting tool and the variety of arrow size presented here may reflect their use for different forms of prey. However, this weapon was clearly also used in warfare, as illustrated by the discovery of an arrow embedded in the spine of a man at Eccles, Kent (Manchester and Elmhirst 1980, 181). The status of the bow and arrow has always been assumed to be low (Hines 1989, 37), but it might be useful to compare the time and skill expended on the production of one spearhead, against that for ten arrowheads.

Burial 13 (EPS 1969) (Fig. 20)

Adult, probable female (sex asserted by grave finds). Lower half of body apparently lying on left side, with legs flexed. Any brooches have been ploughed away. A large group of beads and a group of objects close to the waist survive. The latter comprises the remains of a bag, a ring probably for suspending objects, a cowrie shell and three wrist clasps, which could have been in the bag or *in situ*. The beads could also have been in the bag.

Finds

A) Wrist Clasps. Sf nos. 127, 128, and 129.

One pair and one hook element were found. The clasps are of copper alloy formed into flat plates, and decorated with applied copper alloy bars, which have subsequently become detached. Each bar has three square elements separated by a rectangular section which has a D cross-section. The rectangular section is decorated with transverse grooves, and would appear to be gilt. There are three perforated lugs at the back of the main plate, allowing the clasp to be sewn to the garment. These wrist clasps fall within class B14a proposed by Hines (1984, 82).

B) Copper alloy ring Sf no. 126.

This ring has a maximum diameter of 45mm, and an almost circular cross-section of uneven thickness. It is decorated with two sets of four short transverse lines, which are now indistinct. While it is possibly an annular brooch, similar artefacts have been found in burials situated near the waist line (Green and Rogerson 1978, 13. Grave 9), and may have suspended objects from belts.

C) Ivory bag ring.

This object was not retrieved during excavation, presumably because it crumbled. Its presence is confirmed from the photograph, and its diameter is estimated at 125mm.

D) Beads

45 glass beads, two red, one polychrome, and 42 blue.

It has been suggested by Hirst (1985, 75) in discussion of the cemetery at Sewerby, Yorks., that blue beads most commonly occur in graves of the late fifth and first half of the sixth century, and that they are generally associated with poorer graves, while amber beads are commonly found in richer graves. However, the evidence from the Empingham II cemetery tends to conflict with this view, as blue beads occur in later sixth century graves which are comparatively rich (Timby 1996).

E) Cowrie shell Sf no.131.

Report by A.J.Rundle, Dept. Geology, University of Nottingham.

Pantherinaria pantherina (Solander 1786). The shell is smaller and narrower than *Cypraea tigris* which it most resembles. Length 59mm. Distribution: Indian province (Red Sea from Suez to Jibute, and Aden).

The opening of the shell is present but the dome is missing, which is the opposite situation to the shell found at Buckland, Dover Grave 6/2 (Evison 1987).

F) Iron keys Sf no. 130.

Four fragments of iron keys survive. One is a shank and three are parts of the looped ends. These are probably parts of two separate keys which were presumably hanging from the belt.

Comment

Barbara Green has convincingly suggested the use of ivory rings as the frames of small bags which would hang from the

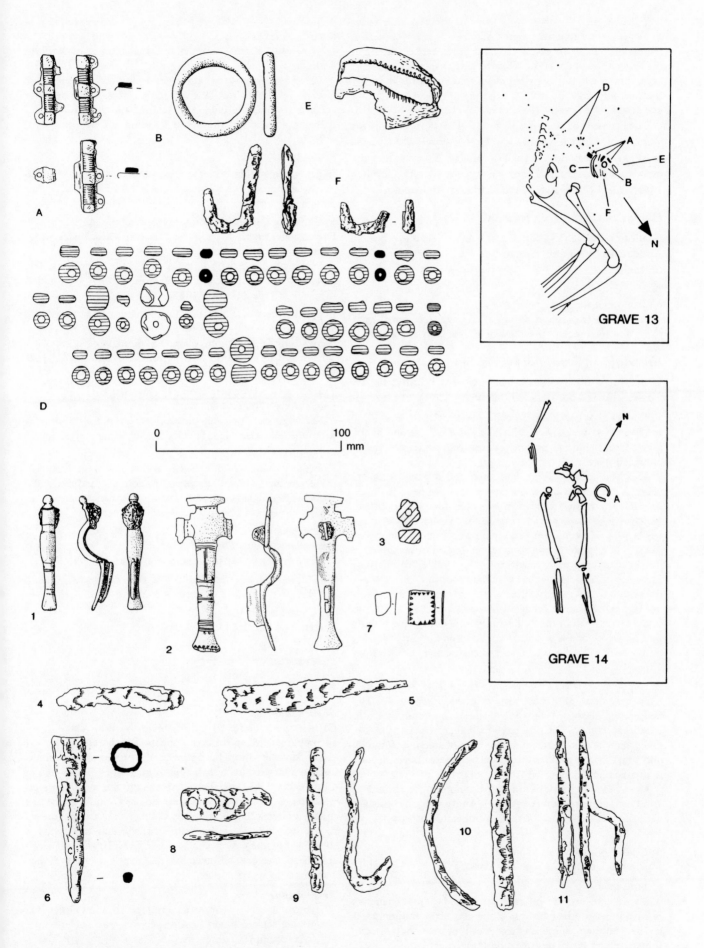

Fig. 20 Site 3 Graves 13, 14 and unstratified grave finds

belt (Myres and Green 1973, 100-103), and this supersedes the earlier view that they were bracelets. It is by no means impossible that all the objects from the grave were contained in the bag, although the ring is likely to have suspended it, or the keys, from the belt. Ivory rings occur mainly in fifth and early sixth century graves, but have been found in seventh century graves at Dover (Evison 1987, 119).

The cowrie shell is clearly an amulet. They are generally (as here) found with adult females, in bags or boxes, and it seems most likely that they were fertility amulets. Although they are mostly dated to the late sixth or seventh century (Meaney 1981, 123-127), this may be too restrictive a date range.

Burial 14 *(EPS 1970)*. **(Fig. 20)**

Adult female, 25-35 years. Lower half of skeleton *in situ*. Appears to be supine with an iron ring on left side at top of thighs.

Finds
A) Iron ring (not illustrated).
A penannular iron ring *c.* 85mm in diameter (estimated from plan). Too fragmentary to be drawn. Presumably a bag ring.

Unstratified Grave Finds **(Fig. 20)**

Other finds unassociated but probably relating to the Phase 3 burials are detailed below.

1) Copper alloy cruciform brooch 1968.158 (24). Sf no. 20. Findspot east of Grave 1. Not likely to be from any of the graves excavated, and possibly comes from an unrecognised, ploughed-out burial.

This brooch has a full round knob and a small headplate which is the same width as the bow. In these respects it closely parallels the earliest cruciform brooches found in England, which Aberg dates to the second half of the fifth century (1926, 26). However, this example has a slightly triangular-shaped foot, rather than a zoomorphic one, and can therefore not be classified as a cruciform. Aberg dates the earliest examples of brooches with a triangular foot to *c.*500 AD, but does not cite any examples that are closely comparable to this one. On this basis, the brooch is probably best assigned a date in the second half of the fifth century. The iron spring is fairly well preserved and is wound around an iron bar through a lug on the back of the brooch, as with the small long brooch from Grave 4.

2) Copper alloy small long brooch. 1968. 158 (38). Sf no. 41. This brooch is of Leeds' (1945) cross potent type. The headplate is decorated with incised lines and a stamp similar to a crescentic moon. The bow has a medial groove. The foot has two groups of transverse lines, two lines of stamp decoration, and a further transverse line near the end of the foot with pairs of incised lines running between it and the edge.

Brooches of this type have a wide but northerly distribution, and Leeds argues that this reflects an Anglian origin consistent with the areas which show their continental ancestry (Leeds 1945, 14).

3) Bead 1968. 158 (33). Sf no. 36.
Melon bead, clear glass, with five lobes.

Comment
The small long brooch and bead were found within two metres of each other south-south-east of the main line of burials and in line with them, suggesting that they represent another early fourth century burial destroyed by ploughing.

4) Iron knife 1968. 158 (29) Sf no. 29. Found *c.* 10m east of the main line of burials.
Dimensions: length 70mm; blade width 8mm; back width 4mm.

Very badly preserved, with tip and tang broken. The knife has an angled back and a curved cutting edge, which becomes concave towards the tang. This feature may be the result of damage, or repeated sharpening. Probably Evison's Type 3 (1987).

Comment
In general, many Early Anglo-Saxon burials are accompanied only by a knife, and so it is possible that this represents another ploughed-out grave.

5) Iron knife ? Sf no. 62. Found to the west of Grave 2.
Dimensions: length 101mm; blade width 15mm; back width 4mm.

Poorly preserved, with tang tip, and blade tip missing. The knife has a straight back, and a curved cutting edge, and is therefore of Type 2 (Evison 1987).

6) Iron butt ferrule. Sf no. 121. Possibly from area of Grave 12 and 13.
Dimensions: length 88mm, diameter 16mm.

Standard form of butt ferrule from an Anglo-Saxon spear shaft.

7) Decorated rectangular 'plate'. Not located
Dimensions: 18mm x 14mm, flat.

Rectangle of copper alloy decorated around all four sides with punched decoration. Reverse has soldering marks.

8) Perforated iron strip. Sf no. 46.
Dimensions: length 50mm, width 16mm.

Rectangular plate with three perforations of equal size, and a probable fourth, larger, perforation which is heavily corroded.

Possibly a buckle, but no close parallels known.

9) Iron hook
Dimensions: length 77mm
Possibly an iron key of Anglo-Saxon date.

10) Curved iron strip. Sf no. ?28 Not located.
Possibly part of an iron bag ring or cauldron handle

11) Forked iron object.
Dimensions: length 83mm, width 25mm

Discussion of Find Types

Weapons

Spearheads
Of the five identified adult male burials, three were accompanied by spearheads, one of which (Grave 5) was accompanied by two. The existence of a further spear burial is indicated by the butt ferrule found unstratified in the area of Grave 12 and 13. Spearheads are usually the most common weapon type, and have been interpreted as symbolic of the free man. Swanton's classification and dating places the spearheads in the late fifth to earlier sixth century, and this range is supported by the dating of associated finds. However, no two spearheads are exactly alike, and this may indicate that they were made to specific order.

Arrowheads
The most notable weapon assemblage is from Grave 12. Arrows are seldom found in Anglo-Saxon graves. Harke lists only six examples, only two of which also contained a spearhead (Harke 1989). From a sample of 205 graves from

Range of Finds

Find Type	Grave													
	1	2	3	4	5	6	7	8	9	10	12	13	14	U/S
Brooches:														
Equal Arm				*?										
Small long			*	*										*
Cruciform			*											*
Square head	*													
Beads:														
Glass	*			*								*		*
Ceramic				*										
Crystal	*													
Cowrie												*		
Wrist Clasp	*											*		
Tag end					*									
Ferrule							*							
Rings:														
Ae				*?								*		
Ivory												*		
Fe													*	
Buckle				*										
Bucket	*				*									
Pottery	*	*			*			*						
Knife		*	*	*?	*					*	*			*
Keys										*?		*		
Spearhead		*			*						*			
Arrowhead											*			
Tweezers											*			
Ae Frags		*		*	*									
Fe Frags		*								*				
Ae bowl	*													
Roman Coin		*												

Table 1: *Matrix of finds types from Site 3 Graves.*

Anglian areas only 1.5% contained arrows. The dating of such graves, where possible, lies between the mid-fifth and mid-sixth century (Harke 1989). Of the classes of weapons absent from the cemetery, shield bosses might have been expected, but as they normally occur in every third grave accompanied by a spearhead, the small sample may be the explanation.

Personal Adornment

Brooches

Of the eight brooches recovered from the cemetery, four can definitely be assigned to specific graves (1, 3, and 4), and two more probably belong to Grave 4. Of these, the equal-arm brooch, probably belonging to Grave 4, is the most unusual and, like the unstratified small long with full round knobs, is datable to the fifth century. The equal-armed brooch was probably worn as the central of three brooches and, as it was flanked by a pair of small longs of late fifth or early sixth date, may already have been old at the time of burial.

The two unmatched brooches from Grave 3 and the unassociated cross-potent small long are also of later fifth to early sixth century date, and the square headed brooch should not be dated much after AD500-520. There are no examples of later sixth century types, and also no examples of annular brooches which are normally very common (many examples came from Saxby and the Empingham II cemetery, for example).

The wearing of brooches at each shoulder is consistent with the wearing of a peplos-type gown which is made from a single piece of material, sewn together along one edge to form a tube, and fastened at each shoulder with a brooch, which sometimes form a matching pair. The gown could also be fastened at the waist with a belt, for which there is evidence in the form of a buckle from Grave 4. Occasionally a third brooch, placed centrally on the chest is found as in the case of the equal arm from Grave 4, and this probably fastened a cloak.

Wrist Clasps

Two of the graves were accompanied by wrist clasps. The single plate from Grave 1 is an unusual example, decorated in Style I, and perhaps imported or following an imported example. The three elements from Grave 13 are of a more common type. Wrist clasps are typical of 'Anglian' areas (Yorkshire, the Midlands and East Anglia) and are not commonly found in the 'Saxon' south, which suggests that they reflect a regional dress style. They indicate the wearing of a long-sleeved under-garment with tight sleeves slit at the wrists and fastened with the clasps.

Beads

A total of 81 beads were derived from female burials 1, 4, and 13 and one was unstratified. The majority of the beads are glass, but there is also a crystal bead, and a glazed ceramic bead.

Monochrome glass beads

Seventy of the beads were of this type, of which twenty-four came from grave 1, forty-four from grave 13 and one from grave 4, and one unstratified. They fall into six colour classes, although it should be noted that there are several shades within each hue, particularly in translucent examples.

Dark blue translucent	42
Red	11
White	7
Pale blue translucent	3
Yellow	3
Green	2
Blue/green translucent	2

The range of colours represented is comparable with beads found from other Leicestershire cemeteries such as Saxby (Leicestershire Museums unpublished archive).

The form classification follows Evison (1987), although the method of bead production means that boundaries between forms are to an extent arbitrary. Most of these beads were probably made by trailing molten glass on to a revolving rod, until the required thickness and shape was attained (Coles 1987).

Five form classes are identified:

Disc: the central perforation is narrower than the thickness of the bead; the bead is much broader than it is long.

Annular: the diameter of the perforation is wider than the thickness of the bead, and the bead is broader than it is long.

Globular: more elongated than the disc or annular forms, and tending towards a spherical shape.

Barrel: an elongated disc or annular form with slightly tapering ends.

Melon: the Anglo-Saxon form of lobed bead, rather than the Roman type.

Annular	38
Disc	22
Globular	7
Barrel	1
Melon	2 (five-lobed and seven-lobed)

Polychrome glass beads

There are nine examples from the cemetery; seven from grave 1, and one each from graves 4 and 13. Four beads incorporate the 'dot and crossing trail' motif against a white ground, three of which have blue dots and trails, and one a red dot and blue trail. There were two examples of rectangular yellow beads with red zig-zags on opposite faces. There were single examples of a bead with a blue body and red and white speckles; an elongated hexagonal blue bead with red, green and white spirals, and white trails parallel to the axis, and a red bead with a yellow spot overlain by an irregular, green curvilinear design.

Most of the beads are of types paralleled at numerous other sites. The rectangular yellow beads with red zig-zags, are however, less common and can only be closely paralleled with similar examples from the Empingham II Anglo-Saxon Cemetery (Timby 1996). The most unusual aspect of the assemblage is the glazed ceramic bead, and again the only obvious parallel comes from the Empingham II Cemetery (Timby 1996, Grave 49A).

The most striking absence amongst the bead types also comes from comparison with Empingham II, and concerns the use of amber. 81% of the 1565 beads from Empingham II were of amber and were present in all but three of the graves that contained beads (Timby 1996). In sharp contrast, no amber beads were found from the Empingham I graves, and the most likely reason for this is that they did not reach their peak of popularity until the second half of the sixth century, by which point the cemetery had probably gone out of use.

There is some slight evidence for glass working from the site, including a fragment from the wall of a glass furnace and a fragment of fused glass (p.130), but whether this relates in any way to the manufacture of beads is uncertain. However, the occurrence of small-scale bead production, leaving little trace, might explain the localised nature of some of the more unusual beads from the grave.

Belts and Fittings

There are remarkably few belt fittings from the cemetery. The buckle and pin from Grave 4 are highly unusual and may be intrusive. Beyond this, there is a possible strap end and a stud from Graves 5 or 8 which suggest a leather belt. However, the evidence of several rings, knives, a possible purse, and bags that appear to have hung from the waist indicate that belts were present, and were possibly of cloth, perhaps tablet woven.

Containers: Pottery, Buckets, Bowl

Of the 14 burials excavated, four were accompanied by containers of various types. Grave 1 had a pot, a bucket, and a bronze bowl, Grave 2 had a small ceramic vessel, Grave 5 had a pot and a bucket, and Grave 8 had a handled pot.

The function of containers in Anglo-Saxon graves is not fully understood. They are generally found close to the head (as in Graves 1 and 5), and may have contained food or drink, or have been considered proper equipment for an after-life in the feasting halls of the gods. The small vessel in Grave 2 was, however, found close to the waist and may be a cup or lamp.

The buckets were stave-built with copper alloy fittings. They are widely found but appear in only a few graves in each cemetery, and are common to both Anglian and Saxon areas. In the former, they are mostly found with males. Vera Evison has pointed out that, unlike those with iron hoops which could be shrunk on, the bronze-bound buckets would not be water tight (Evison 1987, 105), unless the staves were very closely fitted, or the gaps between them sealed.

The bronze bowl from Grave 1 is one of a series made on the Continent and imported into England. They are found most commonly in the Rhine and Meuse valleys but outliers occur in Thuringia, France and England. Other local examples occur from burials at North Luffenham, Wigston and Queniborough, Leics. They are (where a context is recorded) found with high status burials. An example from the Buckland cemetery, Dover, was found with brooches dated to the first quarter of the sixth century (Evison 1987, 104).

Personal Equipment

Knives

Six graves, both male and female, produced knives and two more were unassociated. They are, in general, poorly preserved but three of Evison's Type 1 (1987, 113) (Graves 3, ?4, and 10), two of Type 2 (Grave 2 and unassoc.) and two of Type 3 (Grave 12 and unassoc.) were identified. One other from Grave 5 or 8 was unclassified.

Keys

Iron keys are common finds from Anglo-Saxon female graves, and two of the burials in the cemetery have them. Grave 12 has surviving fragments associated with other material which hung from a belt, while Grave 10 is more problematic. What appear to be key fragments are associated with nails (while other fragments now appear to be lost). The keys may have hung from a belt with a bag of nails or been contained in the same bag as scrap.

Ferrule

The copper alloy ferrule from Grave 7 is unusual, but is paralleled with Grave 93 Buckland, Dover (Evison 1987, 313).

Tweezers

Only one pair of bronze tweezers was recovered, from Grave 12, and was associated, as so often, with a male accompanied by weapons.

Rings (Bronze, Iron, and Ivory), Bags and Amulets.

Rings are generally found at the waist of female burials. Those of smaller diameter appear to have been used to suspend objects from a belt, and larger ones formed the framework for the mouths of small cloth or leather bags. The bronze rings from Grave ?4 and 13 are probably suspension rings, while the ivory and iron rings from 13 and 14 respectively are probably bag rings.

Ivory rings, cut from the upper part of elephant tusks, are widely distributed across the country (Evison 1987, 387) and are clearly imported from India or Africa. They are also found on the Continent in Frankish and Allemannic graves, where they are generally associated with open-work discs. They are found in graves ranging in date from the 5th to the 7th centuries (Myres and Green 1973, 100-103).

The putative bag in Grave 2 was noted as a mass of a black powdery substance, thought possibly to be the remains of leather. Associated with it were two pieces of copper alloy sheet which may have been fittings, and a Roman coin of Carausius. Coins are commonly found in Anglo-Saxon graves, and are sometimes pierced for use as pendants or kept for curiosity of amuletic value (Meaney 1981, 213-222). The cowrie shell from Grave 13, which may also have been in a bag, is most likely to have been a fertility amulet because of its shape, and are almost always found in a container. They are widely distributed throughout the country, and may have been obtained through the same contacts producing the ivory bag rings (Evison 1987, 388).

Two graves (2 and 10) produced closely grouped iron objects, mostly nails, that appear to have been in bags hanging from the belt. This is difficult to explain, and has not been traced on other sites. They may be scrap collections or have some kind of amuletic property.

Discussion

The evidence for the 'Empingham I' Early Anglo-Saxon cemetery on Site 3 is fragmentary and not easy to interpret. Although only 14 burials were excavated, it seems almost certain that there were originally more. A consideration of Graves 1 and 4 shows how extensive plough damage has been in parts of the site, as they are close to the point of being unrecognisable. The close proximity of small finds 36 and 41 (a bead and a brooch) might well suggest an additional but totally disturbed grave, and other unassociated finds may indicate further graves. The recorded plan and orientation of the cemetery would also tend to support the idea that further graves were unrecognised.

Plan and Burial Orientation

The burials can be divided plausibly into two major groups and two outliers.

Group 1 comprises a row of six burials (13, 12, 2, 1, 3, and 4). Four of these (13, 12, 2, and 3) and one other (burial 5/8) are on the same alignment, roughly SW to NE (with heads to SW), while Burials 1 and 4 were severely damaged by ploughing. Nothing can be said about the alignment of Burial 1 beyond the head being broadly to the South. Burial 4 can probably be assigned a common alignment with the other four based on the southern edge of the grave cut. Burial 5 is also best assigned to Group 1, lying close by, as though starting a second row. The alignment, however, is more WSW-ENE than the others. Burial 8 is problematic since it was completely destroyed by Burial 5, and although it might be assigned to Group 1, the later cutting would indicate that its position was unrecognised by the time Grave 5 was dug.

Group 2 comprises a row of four burials (6, 7, 9, and 10) aligned WSW-ENE, three of which are cut into Sunken-featured Building 1.

Burial 14 lies some distance to the north of the two groups, aligned NNW-SSE, and may represent a genuine outlier. However, it does not lie far from the projected line of the Group 1 row of burials. Its alignment is noticeably at right angles to the Roman enclosure ditch (although dating suggests that the ditch was at least partly filled by the early Roman period), and this may account for the change in alignment.

Burial 11, a the south end of the site is crouched, and cut into a Roman hearth structure, and the complete lack of Anglo-Saxon material might suggest that it is of Roman date.

Dating

At the outset it should be said that the dating of Early Anglo-Saxon material is imprecise and that for many classes of object dating is based on very old typological schemes that may well need considerable revision. However, eight graves produced material that can be dated (albeit tentatively). The dates are broadly consistent, falling into a period from the late fifth to early sixth century. Only the cowrie shell from Burial 13 would normally be considered later than AD 550, as examples from other sites seem to be associated with late sixth or seventh century objects. Audrey Meaney has argued that such shells only reached England due to trade with the Continent instigated by Aethelberht of Kent in the latter half of the sixth century (Meaney 1981). However, other exotic items do appear to be available at an earlier date such as ivory bag rings, which have been found in late fifth / early sixth century burials such as that at Glen Parva, Leics. (Liddle forthcoming). The shell in Burial 13 was found associated with such a bag ring, and it seems not unlikely that they were both acquired from the same source.

The datable burials are not randomly distributed within the cemetery. In fact, all the Group 1 burials are dated, while those of Group 2 and the outliers are not. The excavator, Malcolm Dean was firmly of the opinion that Group 2 represented Christian burials and suggested that there was a gap of between 70 and 200 years between the two. His argument was based on the 'shortage of grave goods, greater depth... and extended burials' (unpublished excavation report). He also mentioned that the graves were 'neat and rectangular' and aligned differently to those of Group 1. It is not impossible that these burials are Christian, but there is nothing to positively substantiate such a claim. The burials are a genuine group with a consistent alignment and character: one male and one female (6 and 9) had no grave finds, whilst another possible female (7) had a ferrule or ring, and the unsexed child (10) had a knife, keys, and a bagged collection of iron objects. A certain number of burials with few grave finds will be present in any cemetery of the Pagan period. Clearly, as the group cuts across a disused building it is unlikely to be the earliest phase of the cemetery. It seems reasonable to associate Group 1 with the early buildings in the late fifth or early sixth centuries, and Group 2 with later buildings further to the west. However, the distinctive late sixth and seventh century material such as the florid cruciform brooches, great square-headed brooches, and amber beads which are so prominent a feature of the Empingham II cemetery across the valley (Timby 1996) are all absent from Empingham I, and would tend to indicate that it did not continue in use for long after the mid-sixth century.

SITE 4: 'EMPINGHAM WEST' IRON AGE AND ANGLO-SAXON SETTLEMENT

Nicholas J. Cooper

Introduction (Fig. 21)

During the Autumn of 1971, the activity of mechanical scrapers on the north side of the valley at SK 9372 0795, immediately south of Sykes Lane (76m contour) exposed a complex of archaeological features, appearing as cuts into the underlying ironstone, which were excavated periodically until Autumn 1972 under the direction of M.S. Gorin. The site (code EPW 1971/72) was located on slightly sloping ground, of about 5% dip to the south, and both ploughing and the machine damage may have caused considerable truncation of some features.

The excavated features fall into two clearly defined areas, both spatially and chronologically (fig.21), which can be summarised as follows:

Phase 1

Iron Age occupation consisted of three house structures indicated by penannular eaves-drip gullies, and a number of associated pits and post holes. Two subphases were identified, 1a and 1b.

Phase 2

Early Anglo-Saxon occupation comprised two sunken-featured buildings and associated pits and ditches, lying (with the exception of Pit C) upslope and to the west of the Phase 1 settlement.

Phase 1: The Iron Age Settlement

Phase 1a

The evidence for this subphase comprised a single pit (Pit D, fill AF), and possibly the adjacent Pit E, which lay to the north of the later Building 2 (fig. 22). Pit D was cut by Pit A of Phase 1b, and its contents suggest that it predates the rest of the occupation evidence. It had a maximum diameter of 1.0m and following the deposition of a single, large and complete jar, the pit was rapidly backfilled entirely with ironstone, with no loam accumulation in the fill. The single vessel (p.67, No.1), which probably broke as a result of the backfilling process, did not contain any bone or charcoal and so does not appear to have been a cremation deposit. The form and the band of thumbnail impressions suggests an earlier Iron Age date. The adjacent Pit E is of uncertain date, as it is cut by

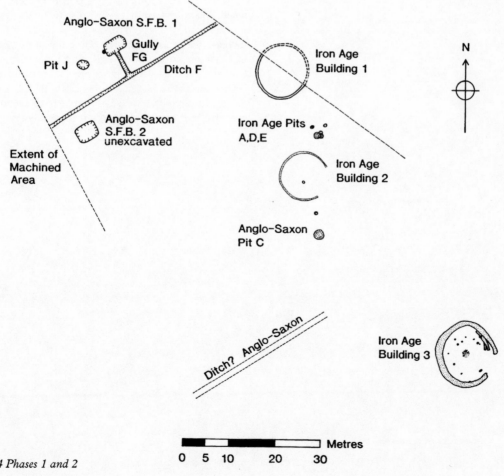

Fig. 21 Site 4 Phases 1 and 2

neither Pit A nor D. It has a maximum width of 0.7m, and the fill contained only flint and bone.

Phase 1b

This subphase comprises the remaining features of Iron Age date.

Building 1

Only about 50% of the ground plan of this building was exposed, the north-western half lying beneath the ungraded area (fig. 21). The internal diameter of the eaves-drip gully circuit is estimated at 10m, but the dimensions of the gully itself were not recorded. A central hearth was recorded as a circular setting of burnt stones 0.5m wide.

Building 2

This structure lay to the south of House 1, and a full ground plan was exposed (fig. 22). It was defined by a narrow circular eaves-drip gully, 0.25m wide, and 0.25m deep, which had a fill of dark soil. The south eastern part of the circuit was interrupted by an entrance. The gully terminal on the south side of the entrance was clearly defined and at this point it had been filled with burnt limestone which may have acted as a hard-standing for a door frame. A one metre length of the gully fill was excavated at this end and a small amount of scratch-decorated pottery was retrieved. However, the gully terminal on the north side was indistinct due to the disturbance caused by the grading machinery. The eaves-drip gully circuit had an internal diameter of ranging from 9.8m north-south to 10.4m east-west.

No evidence of internal post settings was recorded, but a probable hearth was indicated by a 0.5m wide circular setting of burnt soil and stones towards the centre of the area enclosed by the gully.

Features in the Area of Building 2
Pit A (Fill AA) (Fig. 22)

This was the largest of the group of three pits lying immediately north of House 2, and the only one that would appear to have been contemporary with it. It cut Pit D, and was sub-round in plan, ranging in diameter from 1.4m to 1.6m, with a depth of 0.35m.

Post holes

A pair of circular pits or post holes was recorded lying 3m apart, 1 metre to the north of pits A, D, and E. The easterly of the two was 0.65m in diameter and was filled with burnt limestone fragments up to 0.25m in size, which were pitched on edge. The west pit was 0.5m in diameter, and was also filled with burnt limestone fragments of the same size. These may have acted as stone foundation settings for timber uprights, but no further evidence for an associated structure was recorded. A single post hole of similar size lay 2m south of Building 2, but the lack of any artefactual evidence in the fill made it impossible to ascertain if it was contemporary with the building.

Building 3 (Fig. 23)

This building was isolated on the south edge of the site and evidence comprised an eaves-drip gully and 13 associated post holes. The gully appeared to have been recut completely or at least modified on two separate occasions. The entrance opening to the south-east was maintained throughout, and the recutting would appear mainly to have been in order to widen the gully, judging by the narrowness of the original cuts.

The existence of the recuts was only apparent at the points where the gully terminates either side of the entrance, where the later cuts diverged from the original line in order to increase the overall diameter of the dwelling. The original cut was clearest on the north side of the entrance, with a 1.5 m length of a 0.3m wide gully visible. The first recutting of it was 0.5m wide, and a 5m length of it was visible, along the western part of its circumference. The southern terminal of this recut was also indicated. The final cutting of the gully, widened it

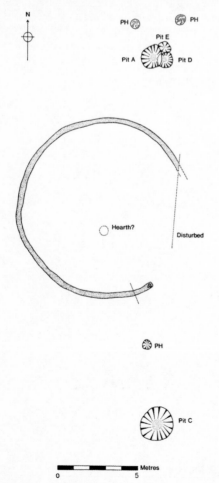

Fig. 22 Site 4 Phase 1 Building 2

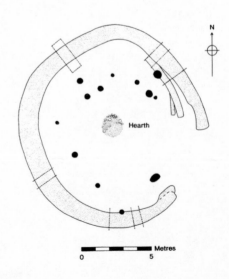

Fig. 23 Site 4 Phase 1 Building 3

considerably, giving it a maximum width of 1.5m, tapering to 0.9m at the terminals either side of a 4.25m wide entrance.

Internal Features

A hearth was indicated by a 1.5m wide circular spread of burnt soil and stones, lying at the centre of the structure. Additionally (but not recorded on the excavation plan) a pear-shaped feature was recorded 2.1m west of the hearth. It was 0.8m wide, and was 0.6m deep at the tapered end and 0.47m at the rounded (south) end.

The thirteen internal post holes varied in diameter from 0.25-0.6m, but it was difficult to identify a truly coherent pattern. Post holes 7, 9, 10, 13 (and possibly 5) may have formed a coherent circular pattern, and 12 clearly belonged to the final phase of rebuilding, as it cut the earlier gully fills. However, the remaining post holes did not appear necessarily to relate to the circular structure. Post holes 2-5 ran in a straight line across the western half of the building, and the fact that no.2 cut the final recut of the gully indicates that they may have formed the west wall of a later rectangular building superimposed over the circular structure. In support of this, post holes 6 and 8 may have belonged to the north wall of such a building.

Discussion of Phase 1

Poor conditions of excavation did not allow for a full appreciation of the extent of Iron Age occupation on the site, but the three identified round houses represent the only such structures to be excavated in the valley. There is no evidence that the buildings were enclosed in any way, although the length of east-west ditch to the south of the site could feasibly be of Iron Age date rather than Anglo-Saxon as postulated below. If it is part of an enclosure, then Building 3 would appear to have lain outside it.

Analysis of the pottery, which came predominantly from Pits A and D, and Building 3, indicates that the site was occupied initially in the Early Iron Age, giving rise to Pit D (c. fifth-sixth century BC), and most intensively in the Middle to Late Iron Age, the period to which the other pits and three round houses belong. These later features consistently contained handmade, shell-tempered, Scored Ware which dates from the beginning of the third century BC to the end of the first century BC (Elsdon, 1992). The forms represented within the assemblage suggest that they belong to the latter part of the production period, indicating that Phase 1b probably lies in the first century BC. Comparison with other assemblages from Leicester-shire sites, namely the adjacent site at Whitwell (Todd 1981), Enderby (Elsdon 1992) and Tixover in the Welland Valley (Elsdon forthcoming) would tend to bear this out.

Further Late Iron Age settlement evidence was detected during the excavation of Empingham II Early Anglo-Saxon cemetery 250m north-west of Site 4 (fig.2). It comprised a trackway, better described as a hollow-way, which later formed the southern boundary of the Early Anglo-Saxon cemetery. Significantly, the sections excavated across it are the only reminder of Rutland Water's archaeology still visible today to those visiting the Anglian Water leisure area at Sykes Lane.

Additionally, a number of other associated features were detected, including ditches, pits and a hearth. In common with the trackway, the fills of these features contained pottery of Later Iron Age and Early Roman date (Timby 1996, 14)

In addition to this site, there is evidence for two others in the valley. Firstly at Whitwell, where the corner of a possible enclosure was encountered together with a number of shallow pits which were not considered to be structural (Todd 1981, 7 and fig.3). Secondly, the existence of an Iron Age enclosed farmstead is indicated by cropmark evidence from the Hambleton Peninsula (SK 919 069), which appears to contain at least two circular buildings (Fig 64 no.16). Fieldwalking of the site in April 1992 yielded only two sherds of Scored Ware, alongside a large assemblage of late Roman pottery, which tends to indicate that firstly, the lower fills of the enclosure ditches have not yet been disturbed by ploughing, and secondly that settlement continued on the site right through the Roman period, which is in contrast to the evidence from Site 4. The excavation of the enclosure at Enderby, four miles south of Leicester, remains the only detailed analysis of a farmstead of this type (Clay 1992).

Phase 2: The Early Anglo-Saxon Settlement (Fig. 21)

A series of occupation features of Early Anglo-Saxon date were recorded in the area immediately north west of the Phase 1 Iron Age settlement, and slightly upslope of it, closer to Sykes Lane. They comprised one certain sunken-featured building (SFB 1) on the northern edge of the site, and one less certain sunken-featured building (SFB 2) 15m to the south. The two were separated by a 40m long straight ditch (Feature F), which ran east-west across the site, continuing to the north of the Iron Age Building 1. A 4m length of gully (Feature FG) ran southwards away from the south side of SFB 1, to meet Ditch F at right angles. A large pit (Pit J) lay 5m to the west of SFB 1.

Sunken-Featured Building 1

This sunken-featured structure was rectangular in shape, with rounded angles, 4m east-west x 3m north-south. Grading had probably truncated the top of the feature, but the structure had only been cut very shallowly into the underlying ironstone, the depth up to a maximum of 0.2m. The depth of topsoil removed from over the ironstone in this area was up to 0.2m, giving a maximum possible feature depth of 0.4m (not allowing for hillwash or plough erosion).

The superstructure was supported at the west end by a single large timber post placed centrally, and set into a substantial post hole approximately 0.3m in diameter, cut into the ironstone to a depth of 0.2m, immediately outside the line of the sunken feature itself, and appearing to cut it slightly. The support at the eastern end of the structure was less clear with a possible corresponding post hole located centrally at the east end of the hut.

Gully FG, cut the rectangular feature of SFB 1, and continued to cut deeper into the ironstone to a depth of 0.2m. The gully varied in width from 0.5m-0.75m, and ran for a length of 4m, entering the east-west ditch F. The function of the gully would appear to have been for drainage, as it ran downslope, and cut deepest where it left the sunken feature, in order perhaps to collect water accumulating in the sunken area of the structure.

Sunken-Featured Building 2

This would appear to have been of similar dimensions to SFB 1, being rectangular, with the long axis east-west, and parallel with it, perhaps suggesting that they are contemporary. The feature remained unexcavated.

Ditch F

A 40m length of this ditch was recorded, running east-west, and it appears to have been the continuation of a 17m length of ditch recorded in 1971 to the north of Iron Age Building 1. The ditch was 1.0m in width, and excavation of a small section of the ditch in 1971 yielded only two small sherds, one of Iron Age and one of Early Anglo-Saxon date. However, more extensive excavation of the ditch in the area of the sunken feature buildings in 1972 yielded only Early Anglo-Saxon material, which supported an Early Anglo-Saxon attribution. A second length of ditch was also recorded in 1971, running east-west for an unrecorded (but similar) distance, 30m to the south of House 2. The width varied from 1-1.5m. It would appear to run in parallel with Ditch F, some 65m to the north. No excavation was undertaken so its relationship to the other features remains uncertain.

Pit J

This feature lay approximately 5m to the west of SFB1, and was 1m in diameter. Its initial function is uncertain, but its secondary use was clearly for rubbish disposal, as its fill (BM) contained the largest group of Anglo-Saxon pottery from the site, as well as animal bone.

Pit C

This pit was located 50m south-east of the main focus of the observed settlement, about 10m south of Iron Age Building 2. It was 2m in diameter, and of shallow depth. Its fill (AD, AG, and AH) indicated that it had been used for rubbish disposal, as Early Anglo-Saxon pottery, animal bone, a bone comb and a clay spindlewhorl were retrieved from it (see p113 nos. 31 and 37).

Discussion of Phase 2

Analysis of the pottery from the Early Anglo-Saxon features indicates that the area of settlement excavated was probably of later fifth and early sixth century date, making it broadly contemporary with the settlement evidence from Site 3, but earlier than that from Site 7 at Tickencote. In common with those sites, it is considered likely that the recorded evidence represents only a fraction of what was probably a much larger settlement, and that over time the area of occupation gradually shifted, with disused house structures and pits becoming dumping grounds for domestic rubbish. While this situation can only be conjectured for Sites 3 and 7, there is evidence to support the idea on Site 4. Observations were made by a local amateur archaeologist Bill Thomas in 1973, at the time that the area immediately north of Sykes Lane was being graded by machinery, which indicated that the excavated area of Site 4 may have formed the southern part of a much larger settlement. In the area between Sykes Lane and Empingham II Anglo-Saxon cemetery (not discovered until 1974) approximately 20 possible sunken-featured buildings, as well as hearths were observed. Unfortunately, no excavation was undertaken and no written or photographic record made, since the evidence was completely destroyed the following day. However, while such information must be treated with caution, it cannot be dismissed out of hand.

It is logical to assume that this settlement generated the individuals occupying the 135 burials recorded at Empingham II Anglo-Saxon cemetery in 1974 and 1975 (Timby 1996), the dating of which spans the early fifth to the early seventh century. The portion of the settlement represented on Site 4 would thus be one of the earliest parts occupied.

SITE 5: 'EMPINGHAM 1968'
ROMANO-BRITISH MASONRY BUILDING
AND CORN DRIER

Anthea Diver and Nicholas J. Cooper

Introduction

This report on the 1968 excavations has been edited from an original unpublished report written by the director Anthea Diver. The corn drier was excavated in 1971 and planned by Bill Thomas. Between Easter and Midsummer 1968, a small excavation was carried out at SK 9425 0800, about 200m north of the river Gwash, just above the 60m contour. The site (code EMP 68 Site 3) had originally shown up as a dark soilmark after ploughing. An area of approximately 100 sq. m was stripped and a number of features were identified below about 0.25m of ploughsoil. Further excavation on the site was not possible because the field was needed for cropping. Further evidence of the site was detected in 1971, 10m to the south of the 1968 excavation at SK 9423 0798, when a stone-built structure was exposed by the mechanical scrapers.

Features Excavated in 1968

In the south-west corner of the excavated area, a 5m length of limestone walling faced on both sides, 0.75m thick and with a rubble core, ran in an easterly direction. The wall had been constructed within a foundation trench, the edges of which were filled with yellow sand. The wall then narrowed to 0.6m and began to curve north-eastward for a distance of 2.0m before being cut by a field drain running north-south across the site. The drain was of semicircular profile and covered with irregular limestone slabs along its entire length. East of the drain, a roughly aligned scatter of limestone rubble wall footings about 1.0m wide continued to curve northwards to form a shallow crescent but it is not clear whether they form a continuance of the same wall, as the alignment is slightly off set. The northern part of the stripped area was excavated more fully, and the walling was found to be mortared. At the northern end of this section of walling were traces of burning, though this was not intense enough or large enough to suggest a hearth. On excavation, the field drain was found to cut an oval-shaped pit feature with a dark fill, but containing no finds.

Features Excavated in 1971

Clearance of the overlying rubble left by the machines revealed a structure resembling a corn drier. Unfortunately, the south and west sides of the structure had been completely destroyed, but the remaining part comprised a flue running west to east for 1.75m, which turned at right angles to run south for 2.75m. The internal wall of the flue was created by a rectangle of well-jointed, smooth and very flat limestone slabs that showed signs of gentle heating and might have formed a drying floor. The external wall surrounding the flue was constructed of flat, faced limestone slabs of which three courses survived. The fill of the flue comprised a 50-70mm depth of dark, sooty material, indicating the lengthy use of the structure before its abandonment. However, the internal faces of the slabs forming the external flue wall showed no evidence of the burning apparent on the internal wall. Eight fragments of thin Collyweston limestone slabs (20-30mm thickness), were found in the flue on the north side, and these may have been used as roof covering. At the north-west corner of the structure was an area of intense burning to the limestone, mixed with dark charcoal-filled soil, indicating the stokehole.

Discussion

The features excavated in 1968 were associated with Roman pottery of later third and fourth century date (p.89). The sections of walling would thus appear to relate to one or more phases of buildings of later Roman date, but no overall plan is clear. Disturbance and robbing of the masonry probably occurred during construction of the field drain (undated, but probably medieval or post-medieval), as well as subsequent ploughing. No pottery was associated with the corn drier excavated immediately downslope to the south, so it is not possible to confirm the contemporaneity of the two structures. However, it is likely that the corn drier is also late Roman, and that together the structures formed part of a complex of outbuildings or a separate farmstead, contemporary and perhaps associated with, the villa on Site 2, lying 100m to the north.

SITE 6:
RENNER'S PARK ROMANO-BRITISH FARMSTEAD

Nicholas J. Cooper

Introduction

During 1973 and 1974, construction work continued to be monitored along the south-east bank of the proposed reservoir. The site (code EMP 73) was initially discovered in June 1973, in an area known as Renner's Park about 100m north east of the north end of Normanton Hall gardens at SK 9362 0670, and excavations were directed by M.S. Gorin. The site comprises a series of loosely associated features excavated separately which seem to centre on a group of masonry buildings, and include a well, an H-shaped corn drier, and an ironworking furnace. Unfortunately, only the corn drier was planned in detail (fig. 24), and no overall plan of the features was made. This report is based on the photographic evidence and site records.

Description of the Excavated Features

The Buildings

The buildings and well were discovered during the construction of a large pipe trench on the south shore of the reservoir. The pipe trench cut directly through the complex of buildings which could not be recorded before they were destroyed. A portion of the complex was temporarily preserved under a roadway for construction traffic, but by the time this area was available for examination, the traffic had caused so much damage that the surviving evidence was impossible to record. The buildings were clearly constructed with foundations of limestone masonry blocks and spread over an area of 60m east-west by 30m north-south.

The Well

The well lay in the western part of the building complex. During the excavation of the pipe trench, a machine operator noticed that a well had been cut through and that half of it was preserved in the south section. The well had been cut to a depth of 2.85m, but fortunately the remaining depth of 1.75m below this was undamaged. The well was circular and constructed almost entirely of ironstone blocks, with occasional limestone blocks as well. The lowest two courses were of larger blocks, giving an irregular squared off impression. The internal diameter of the structure at the bottom was 0.68m east-west, and 0.57m north-south.

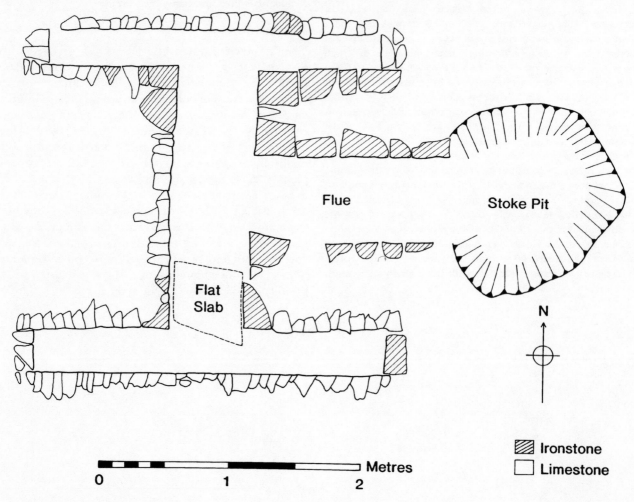

Flue

Stoke Pit

Flat Slab

N

0   1   2   Metres

Ironstone
Limestone

Fig. 24 Site 6 H-shaped Corn Drier

The total depth of 4.6m was backfilled with a mix of domestic rubbish and masonry rubble. The lowest 0.75m was taken up by a large square masonry block, with a mortice slot cut into its upper surface, probably the pivot for a door or gate post. In addition there was a discrete group of substantially complete pottery vessels of Lower Nene Valley colour-coated ware and grey ware (p.89 nos. 122-129), and a fragment of leather which may have been from a sandal, but which is now lost. The fill immediately above this for a metre comprised mainly animal bone, and a small amount of pottery. The bulk of the fill in the top 2.85m had fallen out of the open section, but it was clear from what remained that the top part of the well had been filled with domestic rubbish including animal bone and limestone and ironstone rubble, but no pottery.

The Corn Drier

About 30m north of the complex of buildings, lay a corn drier (fig. 24), built on a north-south axis with the firing chamber at the south end. Machinery had already removed the 0.25m of topsoil overlying the structure and ploughing may well have caused some damage. However, the lack of surrounding rubble suggested that the structure had survived more or less intact. The flue leading from the firing chamber was constructed of ironstone and limestone blocks. The rest of the structure was constructed of pitched limestone slabs, in places formed in herring-bone fashion, set into the surrounding ironstone. The flues would appear to have been covered by large limestone slabs, one of which was found in the main flue. The slabs varied from between 50-90mm in thickness. The fill of the flue contained a small colour coated ware beaker of later third or fourth century date (p.89 no.130), and more pottery was recovered from the fill of the main firing area.

The Ironworking Furnace

In June 1974, a hearth was discovered 40m to the east of the corn drier. Only the lower 0.25m of the structure remained undamaged; it was orientated in a west-east direction, with the flue to the west. The structure had been dug into the natural ironstone and was 0.95 – 1.0m long. The flue was 0.35m long, and 0.15m wide. The floor of the flue and the chamber was covered by a 20-30mm thick layer of fine (?fire) deposit. Lying partially in this layer within the large chamber, was a large slab of stone (0.5m x 0.35m x 0.07m) which was heavily burnt. A larger slab of the same thickness overlay this (0.5m x 0.6m), and was partially burnt on its lower surface. It became apparent once the chamber had been fully excavated that it was rectangular in shape rather than circular, and its dimensions were identical to that of the large slab, suggesting that the slab may have acted as a covering to the chamber. The rubble filling of the structure above these slabs, contained two crushed pots, one in greyware, the other buff. Unfortunately this feature was neither planned nor photographed.

Discussion

The evidence for this settlement is very fragmentary but appears to reflect the pattern more clearly defined on Site 1, with a collection of features of agricultural and industrial function centred around a masonry farmstead. The dating derived from the fills of the features indicates a fourth century date for their abandonment, but the previous development of the site is unknown.

During periods of low rainfall in the summers of 1990 and 1991 the level of the reservoir was low enough to expose the area of the site, and it was observed that the building complex destroyed by the pipe trench extended further to the east. The topsoil that had previously masked it had been washed away to reveal sections of masonry walling (B. Thomas pers. comm.). However, no records of these observations were made.

SITE 7:
TICKENCOTE
EARLY ANGLO-SAXON SETTLEMENT

Josephine Buckley

Introduction

A watching brief undertaken by the Trust for Wessex Archaeology during the laying of a pipeline by Fina plc in April 1990, located a previously unknown site to the south-west of Tickencote (SK 985 093), 26 miles east of Leicester and 3 miles north-west of Stamford (fig. 1a). The site (Acc.Code A44.1990) lies 3 miles east of Empingham in the lower part of the Gwash valley, close to its confluence with the Welland near Stamford. Excavation directed by the writer, was subsequently undertaken by the Leicestershire Archaeological Unit and revealed two Early Anglo-Saxon sunken-featured buildings with associated pits and hearths, on a natural subsoil of Jurassic clay and ferruginous limestone.

Contractors for Fina plc had topsoil-stripped a trench 14-15m wide to a depth of 0.2m for most of the pipeline's length, but at the south end of the site, this opened out to 70m to enable a bore to be driven under the River Gwash. The area under investigation covered 270 sq.m on the gently sloping north side of the Gwash valley, about 150m north of the river (fig.25).

The archaeological features clustered into two groups, about 100m apart (fig. 26). Prehistoric activity was indicated by a scatter of flint over the site, but no corresponding features were detected. Time constraints precluded the cleaning of the whole area, but random 5m grid squares were troweled between the two groups of features. Soil samples for sieving were retrieved from each feature to enable the recovery of environmental information, but their full analysis has not been possible for the purposes of this report.

Description of the Excavated Features

The southernmost group of features, included a sunken-featured building (F1), within which there were 50 stake holes,

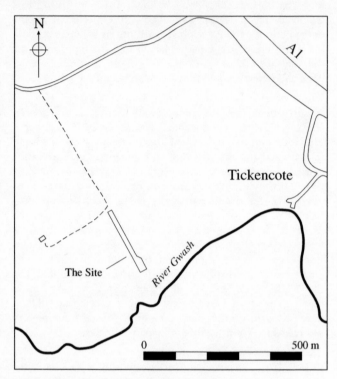

Fig. 25 Site 7 (Tickencote) Location of Site

three post holes, and a hearth (F2) with a flue. The features were filled with dark yellowish-brown clay loam containing five sherds of Roman pottery, 100 sherds of Early Anglo-Saxon pottery and much charcoal (fig. 27). Five metres north-west of F1, there was a small sub-rectangular hearth (F6), with a fill of dark yellowish brown clay loam, which contained many small charcoal fragments, some slag, and one sherd of Roman pottery. A ditch (F7) crossed the site on a south-west to north-east alignment 5m to the south of F1. It was v-shaped in section, 1m in width, and 0.5m deep, with a fill of dark yellowish-brown clay loam. Some animal bone, one small

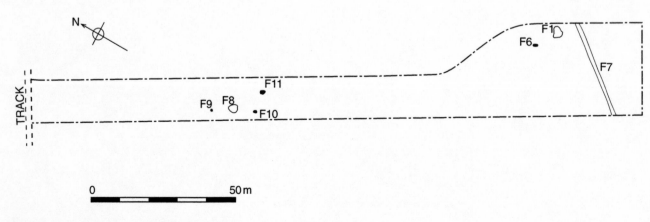

Fig. 26 Site 7 (Tickencote) The Excavated Area

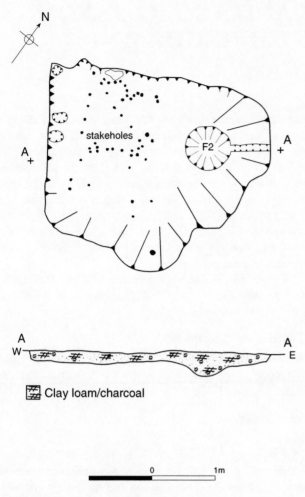

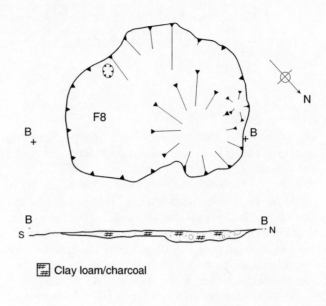

Fig. 28 Site 7 (Tickencote) Building 2

Fig. 27 Site 7 (Tickencote) Building 1

sherd of Saxo-Norman Stamford ware and one small sherd of Early Anglo-Saxon pottery were recovered from this feature.

The second group of four features lay 100m to the north, and was initially visible as a small scatter of pottery and bone fragments. Excavation revealed a second sunken-featured building, F8, with a fill of dark yellowish brown clay loam which contained much charcoal and ironstone fragments, as well as more than 200 sherds of Early Anglo-Saxon pottery and three iron nails. Removal of the fill revealed one possible post hole close to the southern edge (fig.27). Five metres north-west of F8, lay a small circular hearth, F9, with a fill of dark brown clay loam which again contained fragments of burnt ironstone and much charcoal, but no associated dating evidence. Seven metres to the south of F8, an area cleaned at random exposed two sub-rounded pits (F10 and F11), the dark brown clay loam of which contained animal bone and charcoal. F10 was the smaller of the two at 1.0m across and contained 50 Early Anglo-Saxon pottery sherds while F11 measured 1.2m and yielded 23 sherds.

Discussion

The sunken-featured buildings on Site 7 are, in general, smaller than those on Sites 3 and 4, and the evidence for timber superstructures is problematic. The shallowness of the features suggests that their tops had been severely truncated and this could well have removed evidence for post holes surrounding the sunken area. The aridity of

the site and the rescue nature of the excavation also made recognition of post holes difficult. The large number of stake holes found cutting into the compacted floor of F1, would not appear to be structural, and may, as in the case of similar structures at West Stow (West 1985), represent the shifting position of an internal structure such as a loom or drying rack. The single large post hole towards the southern edge of F1 could, however, be structural as could the three larger depressions along the western edge. The circular hearth and flue, F2, would tend to suggest an industrial function for this building, such as iron smelting.

Despite the lack of dating evidence, the two external hearths would appear to be contemporary with the sunken features and pits which became filled with pre-dominantly domestic rubbish, the charcoal possibly deriving instead from industrial activity. The second sunken structure was far less well defined, as well as being somewhat more irregular in plan, and there are no obvious internal features to suggest a function. It is likely that the structures represent workshop activity within, or to the edge of, a scattered settlement. In common with Sites 3 and 4, no evidence for timber-framed structures was detected. While, in contrast to those sites, the area under examination was certainly large enough to encompass the plans of such buildings, the excavation conditions could well have hampered their detection. Analysis of the pottery suggests that this activity dates to the sixth century (see p.103). The ditch F7 running across the south of the site would appear, from the lack of domestic rubbish in its fill, to be a later feature, perhaps of medieval date.

THE ROMANO-BRITISH AND ANGLO-SAXON POPULATION OF EMPINGHAM

J. Wakely and R. Bellamy

Introduction

The purpose of this section is to bring together the disparate and fragmentary skeletal evidence from the five cemeteries recognized during the excavations; three of Roman date associated with Sites 1 and 2, one Early Anglo-Saxon on Site 3, and one of Middle Anglo-Saxon date on Site 2. The stratigraphic details of the cemeteries have been incorporated into the relevant site reports.

The generally poor condition of the skeletal material placed limitations on its analysis and consequently on any interpretation relating to the population from which it derived. Although evidence for at least 38 individual burials was identified, the remains of only 26 individuals were retrieved for analysis. Of these, eight were of certain or probable Roman date, thirteen were of Early Anglo-Saxon date and five of Middle Anglo-Saxon date. For a more comprehensive picture of the Early Anglo-Saxon population this report should be read in conjunction with that from the Empingham II cemetery (Mays 1996, 21)

Methodology used for Age, Sex and Stature Estimates

Juvenile age was estimated primarily by dentition using the chronological chart of dental development compiled by Ubelaker (1978). The technique was developed from work on Native Americans, and so its applicability to British material should be questioned. However, where possible (Grave 10 AS) agreement with the degree of epiphyseal union and synostosis of the pelvis was confirmed. The ageing of adult skeletal material using dentition is less reliable, but where dentition was present, rate of tooth wear was the method used, by employing the system devised by Brothwell (1981). The lack of the pubic symphysis in any of the individuals, meant that the only other information that could be taken into account was the state of degeneration of the spine, or the sutural fusion of the skull, which can be used to assign skeletons to a broad age range (Stewart 1958, Brothwell 1981, Meindl and Lovejoy 1985).

The sexing of some of the adult skeletons also proved problematic because of poor preservation, particularly of the skull and pelves. Both morphological and metrical methods of assessment were used, in order to minimize error (Brothwell 1981). However, it was found that in all cases where 'biological' sexing was dubious, and the skeleton was classified as a 'probable male' or 'probable female', the associated grave finds did support the tentative diagnosis. The method developed by Hunt and Gleser (1955) was used to provisionally sex the sub-adults in the group, and involves the comparison of skeletal and dental maturation. It is dependent upon the fact that, in general, while dental maturation occurs at a consistent rate between sexes, skeletal maturation generally occurs earlier in females than males. The technique is now considered to be rather unreliable. Since these skeletons were examined, Duncan (1998) has developed a method for ageing juvenile skeletons from individuals aged eight years or more, using dental measurements and discriminant function analysis, similar to that applied to adults by Mays (1996), which appears to have general validity.

Stature was estimated using the system devised by Trotter and Gleser (Bass 1987), the equations for which are only applicable to adults.

Results of Analysis

Information relating to age, sex, stature, and palaeopathology was obtained for 26 individuals, and is summarised in Table 2 below.

Discussion

Age

The number of individuals is too small to allow meaningful statistical analysis of age, but comparison with data from the Anglo-Saxon and medieval cemetery at Raunds, Northants. (Boddington 1996), indicates a distinct lack of juvenile and early infant burials in the Empingham group. In contrast, the highest mortality rates at Raunds, as in pre-industrial populations generally (Roberts and Manchester 1995), are within the 2-6 year age group. In the Anglo-Saxon cemetery at Great Chesterford, Essex, 40% of the burials were of individuals less than five years old (Waldron 1994). The most likely reason, considering the plough damage to the site and the generally poor preservation of the bone, is that destruction of the fragile bones of infants, and the smaller, less-calcified bones of females and the elderly could produce a biased sample (Brothwell 1972, Weiss 1972, Walker *et al.* 1988).

Stature

The heights measured are found to fall within the range represented by the Anglo-Saxon burials from Polhill, near Sevenoaks, Kent (Miles 1969), Portway (Cook and dacre 1985, Great Chesterford (Waldron 1994), and raunds (Boddington 1996), as well as those from the Empingham II cemetery (Mays 1996). They also resemble the statures estimated for Romano-British skeletons from Trentholme Drive, York (Wenham 1968), and Newarke St, Leicester (Wakely 1996).

Palaeopathology

Osteoarthrosis

Osteoarthrosis or osteoarthritis is the term used for

Grave	Age	Sex	Stature	Palaeopathology Detected
Roman				
4 R	Adult	?M	-	
5a R	17-25	?F	-	
5b R	6-8	-	-	
7 R	45+	M	1.76	healed ?weapon injury
8 R	Adult	?M	-	
9 R	Adult	M		
10 R	45+	?M	-	osteoarthritis, benign tumour, dental abscess
11 AS	35-45	?M	-	degen.spondylosis, osteoporosis, anaemia, caries
Early A/S				
1 AS	17-25	?F	-	caries
2 AS	Adult	M	1.78	degen.spondylosis, Schmorl's nodes
3 AS	Adult	F	-	
4 AS	Adult	?F	-	
5 AS	Adult	M	1.83	respiratory disease
6 AS	Adult	F	1.64*	osteoarthritis, healed injury enamel hypoplasia,dental abscess
7 AS	17-25	?F	1.64*	caries
8 AS	-	?F	-	
9 AS	14-15	?M	1.69	anaemia, enamel hypoplasia, caries, dental abscess
10AS	9-10	-	-	enamel hypoplasia, caries
12AS	35-45	M	-	Caribelli's cusp 2nd molar.
13AS	Adult	F	-	
14AS	Adult	F	-	
Middle A/S				
1 MAS	Subadult	M	1.66	?tuberculosis, enamel hypoplasia
2 MAS	20-30	F	1.58	?tuberculosis, enamel hypoplasia
3 MAS	25-35	M	1.69	Schmorl's nodes
4 MAS	?Adult	?M	-	
5 MAS	45+	F	-	

* Height estimated at time of excavation only.

Table 2: *Age, Sex, and Stature of the Romano-British and Anglo-Saxon Population.*

degenerative changes which occur in the synovial joints. They may form part of the natural ageing process, but are also associated with repetitive stress on the joints, possibly of occupational origin (Martin *et al.* 1979; Merbs 1983; Rogers *et al.* 1981), though Waldron (1989, 1993) doubts any clear link with any particular type of work.

One 35-45 year old female (Grave 6) from the Early Anglo-Saxon cemetery, shows evidence of osteoarthrosis on the 2nd-4th cervical vertebrae. There is considerable and asymmetrical development of osteoarthrosis in their facet joints. All three show the same pattern of features, but cervical 3 is the most affected with the right facet joint showing clear signs of eburnation and the beginnings of excoriation of the bony surface in the central area. The joint has been partially eroded (post-mortem) immediately around and below the joint surface, but it is still possible to see substantial osteophytic growth around the margins of the joint surface. The corresponding left facet joint shows a completely different pattern of degeneration. The joint

surface is distorted by osteophytic growth, extended beyond the margins of the joint, thereby considerably enlarging it. The different appearence of the two sides suggests asymmetrical stresses on the neck, which could conceivably be of occupational origin, or alternatively due to injury. This female also has evidence of two healed right arm fractures (see bony injuries), but it is not possible to say if they are linked to the neck condition.

One Roman skeleton (Burial 10), that of an elderly man, showed osteoarthritis of the cervical spine and in the shoulder region, suggesting that this individual's lifestyle involved prolonged neck and shoulder stresses, perhaps caused by carrying or pulling heavy loads. The sternoclavicular joint is particularly involved in wide arm swinging in which the whole limb, including the scapula, is moved (Moore 1985).

Degenerative Spondylosis / Spinal Osteophytosis
Degenerative Spondylosis is the term used for degenerative joint disease of the articular surfaces of the vertebral bodies. Together with osteoarthrosis, it is the

most common condition found in skeletal material (Roberts and Manchester 1995), and there are seven instances, three from Anglo-Saxon burials on Site 3, two Middle Anglo-Saxon, and two Roman, none of them severe. It is probable that there were more cases in the group, but the lack of vertebrae in some cases, makes this impossible to assess.

Osteophytic growth was evident in the lower thoracic and lumbar region of all affected skeletons. Roberts and Manchester (1995) have noted that of all the vertebrae, the lumbar region is the most commonly affected by degenerative spondylosis in modern humans. Similarly in other Anglo-Saxon cemeteries such as Great Chesterford (Waldron 1994), and Romano-British cemeteries such as Poundbury (Farwell and Molleson 1993), the lower lumbar region is the most affected. In particular, lipping around the fifth lumbar vertebra, as in the 35-45 year old female (Site 3, Grave 6 AS) would be expected in an individual of advanced age.

Degenerative spondylosis was identified throughout the spines of both Burial 2 AS and in the possible male Roman burial on Site 3 from Grave 11AS, who also suffered from osteoporosis of the spine. The combination of conditions would tend to suggest that the individual in Grave 11AS was of mature to senile age. Osteophytosis is a response to stress on the ligaments of the vertebral column, and can be almost regarded as 'normal' in the skeletons of aged individuals who had lived physically strenuous lives (Miles 1989).

Schmorl's (cartilaginous) Nodes

Schmorl's Nodes are depressions within the central area of the surface of the vertebral plates. They can vary from irregular, complex openings, to smoother, regular depressions, and it is now thought that the different types may be caused by different processes (Miles 1989, 116). Within the Empingham group, only the smooth, regular depressions occur, and these may be caused either by disturbance of the disc-vertebral plate relationship induced by stresses such as lifting heavy loads during development in adolescence, or weaknesses in the bony end-plates (Miles 1989).

Schmorl's nodes were found in the adult male in grave 2AS, where they occured on the underside of the twelfth thoracic, both surfaces of the first and second lumbar vertebrae, and the upper surface of the third and in the lumbar spine of the male skeleton 3MAS. This area of the spine is one of the regions where stress is at maximum concentration (Roberts and Manchester 1995), and this would explain the absence of nodes elsewhere in the spine. The nodes in skeleton 2AS are accompanied by slight development of osteophytosis, but it cannot be ascertained whether they developed coincidentally or from totally separate incidences of spinal stress.

Muscular Development as Evidence of Strenuous Activity

The points of attachment of muscles and ligaments to bone are visible as ridges or tuberosities on the bone surface, and muscle enlargement through strenuous activity is reflected by increased roughness or enlargement around these areas of attachment (Dutour 1986). Such enlargements, known as enthesopalthies, may be observed in individuals, both modern and archaeological, who have lived a physically strenuous life, but, as with joint disease, one must be wary of relating them too closely to specific occupations (Stirland 1991)

Possible activity-induced muscle hypertrophy is indicated in the right forearm of the adult male in Grave 2, which features enlarged muscle attachments not present in the left arm. This would indicate that the individual was right handed, and had used his right arm for strenuous physical activities such as scything or felling trees for example.

A second example of hypertrophy is evident in the foot bones of the possible male adult from Roman Grave 11AS. In particular, the metatarsals in both feet have very accentuated ligamentous attachments at the tarso-metatarsal joints. Roberts and Manchester (1995) have suggested that this is indicative of movement over rough, uneven ground, where gripping and movement of the muscles is necessary for balance, and this would be consistent with activities in rural areas, which might, for example, involve walking over ploughed fields.

Bone Injuries

There are only two examples of healed fractures, and they both occur in the 35-45 year old female from Grave 6AS. These comprise a slight healed fracture midway along the shaft of the right humerus, and another healed fracture in the right radius. In the humerus, the area of break is covered by reactive bone tissue; it only affected a small area of the bone and healing was complete. The adult male from Grave 7R showed a well-healed penetrating injury of his right temporal bone, near to the ear. Its round shape suggested that it could have been made by a pointed weapon or implement.

Infectious Disease

Sometimes infection can be recognised by the presence of periostitis, with deposition of new bone on surfaces. Two skeletons, 1R and 2R, showed this change on ribs, indicating a chronic chest infection, probably tuberculosis (Wakely *et al.* 1991). Chronic respiratory disease is also implicated in the widespread periostitis in Burial 5AS (Ortner and Putschar 1985).

Neoplastic Disease

No evidence of malignant tumours was found, but one Roman skeleton (10R) showed a benign tumour (ivory osteoma) of the surface of the frontal bone.

Deficiency Disease

Porotic-hyperostosis and cribra orbitalia are now recognized to be part of the same pathological process caused by a reaction in the bone to anaemia (Martin *et al.* 1985; Stuart-Macadam 1987). They can be caused by various types of anaemia, but in Europe and North America have been linked most specifically to iron-deficiency anaemia.

They occur in one individual from the Early Anglo-Saxon cemetery, the 14-15 year old, possible male from Grave 9AS. Cribra orbitalia is present in the left eye socket only, as the right socket is missing. Porotic hyperostosis is only visible in one small area of the parietal bone, probably because of the extensive post-mortem erosion of the skull surface. The adult male of Roman date (11AS) also showed slight, healed cribra in both orbits. Iron deficiency could have been linked to deficiency within the diet or intestinal parasites, chronic infection, or even lead poisoning (Stuart-Macadam 1991), but would be unlikely to be fatal in itself.

Unfortunately the poor preservation of skull bones does not allow us to confirm whether these were isolated cases or reflected a more generalised iron deficiency in the diets of both Roman and Saxon communities. No evidence of other dietary deficiencies such as rickets were recorded, but the existence of enamel hypoplasias may indicate poor nutrition in childhood. The osteoporosis in the adult male from Grave 2AS, is possibly also of dietary origin.

Dentition

Eighteen of the individuals had surviving teeth, of which ten had over 50% survival of the dentition, but only five of these have over 50% of the teeth *in situ* in the maxilla and mandible. The large number of missing teeth precludes the statistical analysis of the distribution and prevalence of dental caries, periodontal disease, or other conditions.

Tooth Eruption and Positioning

It has not been possible to make any general assessment of the regularity of tooth eruption and positioning across the group, but some examples merit discussion.

The dentition of burial 9AS, a 14-15 year old, exhibits several irregularities. The upper left adult canine has been unable to erupt because of the retention of the deciduous left canine, and this has caused the adult canine to grow horizontally towards the front of the mouth. Similarly the upper left second deciduous molar is unshed, and the upper left second permanent molar has therefore started to erupt between it and the erupted first premolar, on the lingual side. In the mandible, the left second deciduous molar is still present, and x-rays show that there is no unerupted lower left second premolar, despite the fact that the roots of the former have begun to be reabsorbed. The abnormalities on the left, are in contrast to the right where eruption has proceeded normally, and it is probable that they are congenital in origin.

Tooth Rotation

The lower right second premolar of burial 9 is slightly rotated, as are the lower left canine and first premolar of the female in Grave 6, and this feature is probably caused by overcrowding, which most commonly affects second premolars (Bass 1987).

Extra Cusps

The phenomenon of Caribelli's cusp, occurs only once, on the upper left second molar of the adult in grave 12AS. This tubercle or extra cusp is located on the anterior portion of the lingual surface of the tooth, and is a feature that occurs in varying frequencies in ancient and modern populations.

Enamel Hypoplasia

This is a condition caused by the faulty structural development of the tooth enamel, and is visible macroscopically as continuous or discontinuous transverse grooves. It occurs during development of the tooth and may be caused by malnutrition (Rose *et al.* 1985), by systemic disturbances such as disease, particularly infectious diseases inducing fever, or by both acting synergistically (Dobney and Goodman 1991).

The condition is evident in the upper and lower incisors of the female in grave 6AS, in the surviving incisors and canines of burial 9AS, and in the left adult incisor of the pre-adolescent in grave 10AS. Nutritional deficiency or disease would appear to have occurred in early childhood, with weaning being a possible influence on health (Molleson 1989). This condition was not observed among the Romano-British burials, but does occur in two of the middle Anglo-Saxon burials from Site 2 (1MAS and 2MAS). The number of skeletons is too small for any general conclusions about differences in health and nutriton between the Romano-British and Anglo-Saxon communities to be made. In the Empingham II Anglo-Saxon cemetery Mays (1996) notes a low frequency of hypoplasis compared with urban Anglo-Saxon cemeteries, perhaps indicating low levels of childhood ill health in the local area.

Dental Attrition

Wear of the occlusal surfaces of teeth is not a pathological state, but a natural consequence of chewing hard abrasive foodstuffs. The extent of wear on the teeth of all individuals was as great as that found in Anglo-Saxons from Breedon-on-the-Hill, Leicestershire, and Polhill, near Sevenoaks in Kent (Miles 1969), as well as the Romano-British populations represented at Poundbury (Farwell and Molleson 1993) and Newarke St, Leicester (Wakely 1996). The levels of wear generally in Anglo-Saxon and Roman dentitions are high, reflecting in both cases a diet probably composed largely of fibrous foods and foods contaminated with hard substances from processing such as stone-grinding.

Dental Calculus

Dental Calculus is a mineralised form of plaque, the sticky substance composed of layers of saliva and food debris which accumulates on the surfaces of uncleaned teeth. Calculus may form both supragingivally (above the gum margin) or subgingivally (below the gum margin), but in the Empingham group only the former is evident.

Four early Anglo-Saxons, all middle Anglo-Saxons, and three Romano-British individuals showed varying amounts of dental calculus, from slight in the case of burials 1AS and 9AS which had small accumulations on the labial surface of the molars, to severe as in burial 6AS with large deposits on the lingual and labial surfaces of the lower premolars and molars (the upper premolars and molars are not present due to post-mortem loss). In Burial 10R, calculus deposition is severe and widespread throughout the dentition.

The presence of supragingival calculus, conflicts with the evidence for substantial toothwear, since the fibrous diet which the latter indicates is not conducive to the formation of calculus. However, Miles (1969) found the same phenomenon to be widespread amongst the 180 late Anglo-Saxon burials at Breedon-on-the-Hill, Leicestershire, and suggested that it resulted from the period of illness before death, during which the individual might have been largely immobile and on a diet of very soft foods. Mouth breathing may also have been a cause, as it would tend to dry the food debris on the tooth surface, and could explain its occurrence on incisors and the lingual surface of the posterior teeth. The evidence from Grave 6 would certainly support this, although slow accumulation over a long period may also be possible, particularly in older individuals. It was present in half of the jaws examined from Raunds (Powell 1996) and the majority of individuals at Great Chesterford (Waldron 1994), sometimes to a severe degree. Similarly it is a common feature of Romano-British populations such as that represented at Poundbury (Farwell and Molleson 1993).

Dental Caries
The presence of caries in both Romano-British and Anglo-Saxon skeletons indicates a high-carbohydrate diet. There are two examples of enamel caries from the early Anglo-Saxon cemetery. Burial 1AS has a small cavity on the labial surface of the lower left third molar, and burial 7AS has small cavities on the labial surface of the right lower first and second molars. Caries of the occlusal surface, occurring secondarily to tooth-wear, is a common form of caries within Anglo-Saxon popula-tions (Miles 1969). The upper right second molar of burial 9AS is, however, the only example from the group.

The 9-10 year old Burial 10AS exhibits an interesting example of caries in an unerupted permanent second premolar. The unshed deciduous second molar which overlies it has no evidence of caries. The teeth were not *in situ*, but it is possible that the caries developed after the formation of a dental abscess at the root tip of the overlying tooth.

Three of the Romano-British skeletons showed carious teeth. In one instance, the possibly Roman burial (Burial 11AS), decay was widespread.

Chronic Inflammatory Periodontal Disease and Abcesses
Recession of alveolar bone and infection of the tooth sockets is encouraged by the presence of plaque or tartar around the teeth. It is to be expected, therefore, in populations where dental hygiene is poor or non-existent. The only evidence of the disease is the presence of dental abscess pockets at the base of the root socket in the lower right third molars of burial 6AS, and the deciduous lower left canine of burials 9AS and 10R. It may have been more prevalent, but the post-mortem erosion of the thin alveolar bone, and the relatively small number of teeth left *in situ*, prevent a fuller assessment. In a preliminary survey of 130 skulls of Neolithic to Saxon date, Brothwell (1959), found it to be present in 74% of the sample. Comparison with other recent reports of Anglo-Saxon and Romano-British cemeteries reveals a variable picture suggesting a complex aetiology and relationship to diet, hygiene and general health. For example at Newarke St, Leicester severe degrees of alveolar bone loss are rare (Carter 1996). However, at both great Chesterford (Waldron 1994) and Raunds (Powell 1996) moderate or severe levels were noted in approximately half the samples.

THE LITHIC MATERIAL

Ruth Head and Rob Young

Introduction

This report considers the assemblages of flint retrieved from excavations on Sites 1, 2, 3, 4, and 5, and that collected during the fieldwalking survey which accompanied the excavations of Sites 1 and 3 from 1967 to 1971.

A total of 769 pieces of lithic material was collected during excavation and fieldwalking. Unfortunately, the circumstances of recovery dictate that precise information on the spatial distribution of the material is lacking. Material deriving from primary contexts is limited to two oval-shaped pits (Pits 1 and 2) excavated in the northern part of Site 3 in 1969 and 1970. The bulk of excavated material occurs in residual contexts of Iron Age, Roman and Anglo-Saxon date, and much of this is poorly stratified. The fieldwalked material was predominantly collected during random survey of the fields surrounding the areas of Sites 1 and 3 during 1967 (the work which initially identified the location of Site 1), and can only be grouped by field rather than by a grid within any one field. This clearly limits the definition of specific activity areas, but it was considered that the intrinsic quality of much of the material collected still made it worthy of analysis. Initially the assemblage was treated as one in order to assess the overall range of raw materials used and artefact types present. The individual site and fieldwalked assemblages were then analysed in order to look at the composition by artefact type.

Raw Materials and Condition

766 of the recorded pieces are of pebble flint of various shades of grey all of which has probably been obtained from local gravel and boulder clay deposits. Two pieces of chert and one piece of haematite were also recorded. 45 pieces of flint (5.85% of the total assemblage) show varying degrees of patination while a further 273 pieces (35.5%) show evidence of either total or partial cortication. 293 pieces (38.1%) retain cortex. 352 pieces (45.4%) show evidence of damage either by ploughing (321) or thermal fracture through frost or burning (31).

Typological Analysis (Fig. 29)

The assemblage was classified into types with reference to Tixier (1974), Young (1987) and Wickham-Jones (1991).

Table 3 and Figure 29 show the breakdown of the assemblage into artefact types. Throughout the following analysis, the catalogue numbers used refer to the archive catalogue from which objects have been chosen for illustration.

TYPE	NUMBER	%
Hammerstone	1	0.13
Microlith	1	0.13
Bladelet	1	0.13
Chunk	147	19.12
Chip	7	0.91
Core	38	4.94
Scraper	26	3.38
Arrowhead	8	1.04
Blade	49	6.37
Blade-like flake	59	7.67
Total Flakes	429	55.79
Retouched flakes	60	7.80

Table 3: *Typological Analysis of Excavated and Fieldwalked Flint from the Gwash Valley 1967-72*

Cores

The assemblage included a total of 38 cores which were classified according to Clark *et al.*'s 1960 scheme (1960, 216) and this information is tabulated below (Table 4). Two of the cores (132; class B2, and 767; class E), have evidence for retouch along the edges.

CLASSIFICATION		NUMBER	%
A	One platform		
1	Flakes removed all round	4	10.53
2	Flakes removed part way round	4	10.53
B	Two platforms		
1	Parallel platforms	4	10.53
2	One platform at oblique angle	8	21.05
3	Platforms at right angles	1	2.63
C	Three or more platforms	8	21.05
D	Keeled: flakes in two directions	2	5.26
E	Keeled: one or more platforms	6	15.79

Table 4: *Classification of Cores from the Gwash Valley*

18) Discoidal core of grey flint. Clark Class C. Some wear and abrasion evident on edges. Smooth, buff pebble cortex retained. 45mm x 39mm x 15mm.

Scrapers

26 scrapers were recorded and classified with reference to Clark *et al.*'s scheme (1960, 217). The data are tabulated below (Table 5), and eight examples are illustrated.

CLASSIFICATION		NUMBER	%
A	End Scraper	1 Long	0	0
		2 Short	22	84.62
B	Double ended	1 Long	0	0
		2 Short	0	0
C	Disc	0	0
D	Side	1 Long	1	3.57
		2 Short	1	3.57
E	On broken flakes	2	7.14

Table 5: *Classification of Scrapers from the Gwash Valley*

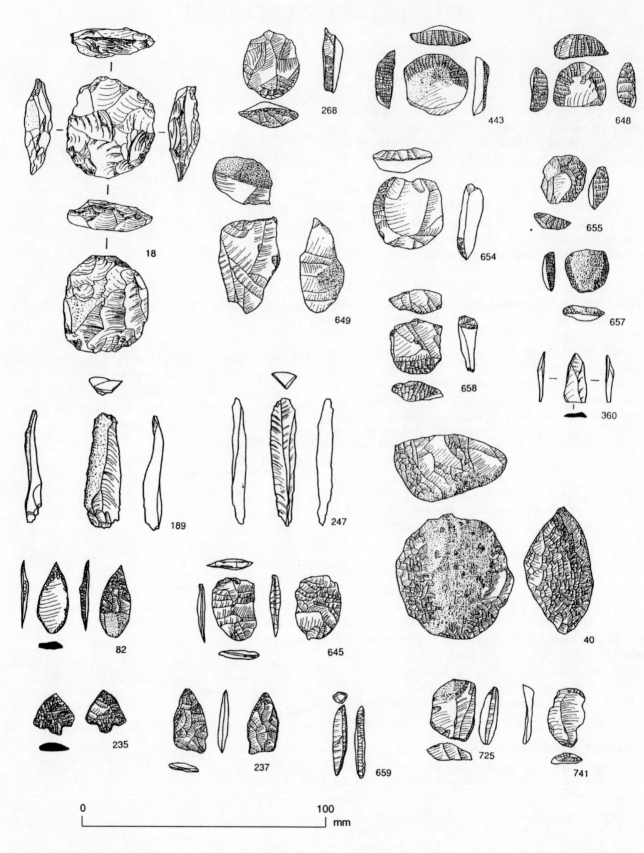

Fig. 29 Objects of flint scale 2:3

268) Scraper on distal end of grey, slightly corticating secondary flake. Clark Class A2. Retains buff pebble cortex on left edge. Cortical striking platform and diffuse bulb.
30mm x 30mm x 13mm.

443) Dark grey flint scraper. Clark Class A2. Smooth buff pebble cortex on retouched face in centre. Plough damaged at bulbar end. 26mm x 29mm x 9mm.

648) Scraper of grey flint. Clark Class A2. Retouched on sides and distal end. Plough damaged. 19mm x 24mm x 9mm.

649) Scraper of dark grey flint. Clark Class A2. Retouched along sides and distal end. Diffuse bulb and plain striking platform. Retains patch of smooth buff cortex on distal face. 29mm x 26mm x 11mm.

654) Scraper of grey flint. Clark Class A2. Pronounced bulb. Plough damaged. Retouched at distal end and both edges. 33mm x 33mm x 13mm.

655) End scraper of dark grey flint. Clark Class A2. Incipient cortication. Diffuse bulb, plain striking platform. Retains small patch of smooth buff pebble cortex. Retouched at distal end and both edges. 19mm x 20mm x 7mm.

657) Scraper of dark grey flint. Clark Class D2. Plain striking platform, diffuse bulb. Hinge termination. Smooth buff pebble cortex retained. Retouched along both sides. 17mm x 19mm x 6mm.

658) Scraper of grey flint. Clark Class A2. Faceted striking platform, diffuse bulb. Retouched at distal end. Plough damaged. 24mm x 25mm x 9mm

An analysis of the breadth:length ratios of 16 complete scrapers confirms that the majority conform to the metrical criteria set out for 'short' end scrapers (Clark *et al.* 1960, 217)

Blades
Note: Flakes were placed into this category if they were twice as long or more than they were broad and had regular, almost parallel edges.

49 blades and one bladelet were recorded. Of these, 19 were on secondary removals and 30 were tertiary or inner removals. 45 are in varying shades of grey flint, one of brown, and two of white flint. Only five blades are complete, and of the incomplete ones, 18 are plough damaged. Two examples show evidence of patination and 12 show signs of recortication. Three examples are illustrated (fig.29).

189) Blade of dark grey flint. Diffuse bulb, plain striking platform. Smooth brown cortex on right side. Fairly fresh edges. Slight retouch at distal end. Slight plough damage. 50mm x 16mm x 8mm.

247) Light grey flint blade. Irregular fracture at bulbar end. Broken transversely at tip. Edges very fresh. 57mm x 10mm x 6mm.

659) Blade of grey corticated flint. Diffuse bulb. Faceted striking platform. Retouched along right edge. 31mm x 6mm x 4mm.

Arrowheads
Eight arrowheads were recorded and classified according to Green's typology (1985, 21). Six were leaf-shaped, and two were barbed and tanged. Of the six leaf-shaped examples, two are of Green's Class 3A, one of 4A, one of 4B and one of 4C. The sixth example is highly fragmentary and was only identified as a leaf-shaped arrowhead because of the presence of shallow, invasive retouch on both faces of the fragment. The fragmentary nature of the barbed and tanged examples meant that they could not be classified using Green's scheme. Four examples are illustrated (fig.29).

82) Leaf-shaped arrowhead of grey flint. Green Class 4C. Bulbar face exhibits retouch around all edges. Smooth grey cortex on dorsal face. 32mm x 13mm x 4mm.

235) Barbed and tanged arrowhead of grey flint. Barbs broken. Both faces exhibit shallow invasive retouch. 18mm x 18mm x 4mm.

237) Leaf-shaped arrowhead of dark grey flint. Green Class 4B. Broken transversely at base. Invasive shallow retouch on both faces. Plough damaged on both edges and tip. Incipient cortication on both faces. Traces of copper oxide patination. 27mm x 15mm x 3mm.

645) Leaf-shaped arrowhead of grey flint. Green Class 3A. Distal end only. Snapped transversely. Invasive retouch on both surfaces. 27mm x 20mm x 4mm.

Hammerstone
One hammerstone was recorded from the assemblage.

40) Hammerstone of grey flint. Shows some evidence for frost spalling. Retains rough buff cortex on the dorsal face. The hammer surface is crushed and smooth from wear. 54mm x 58mm x 30mm.

Microlith
One microlith was recorded from the assemblage.

360) Microlith of dark grey flint. Broken transversely at the bulbar end. Retouched along right edge. Edges are fresh. 21mm x 9mm x 3mm.

Flakes
429 flakes were recorded, which represents 55.8% of the assemblage as a whole. Of these, 59 were recorded as blade-like flakes, and 60 were retouched or utilised. The flakes were analysed by class, colour, bulb-type, and platform type, and the results are summarised in Table (9-15) held in archive. Two examples of the retouched/utilised flakes are illustrated (fig.29).

725) Grey secondary flake. Faceted striking platform, diffuse bulb. Retains hard, pitted cortex. Left edge retouched. 26mm x 20mm x 8mm.

741) Grey tertiary flake. Plain striking platform, diffuse bulb. Retouched at distal end. Plough damaged. 26mm x 18mm x 4mm.

Site 1

A total of 60 lithic artefacts was retrieved from Site 1 during the excavations of 1969-71, and is supplemented by a further 249 pieces that were randomly fieldwalked from the field in which the site lay during 1967.

The breakdown of the excavation and field-walked assemblages by type is tabulated below (Table 6 and 7).

TYPE	NUMBER	%
Blade	4	5
Flake	37	50
Blade-like flake	2	2.5
Core	5	7
Chunk	13	17.5
Scraper	8	11
Chip	1	1.5
Arrowhead	4	5
Total	74	100

Table 6: *Analysis of Excavated Flint from Site 1*

TYPE	NUMBER	%
Core	19	7.63
Chunk	23	9.24
Flake	140	56.22
Blade	26	10.44
Blade-like flake	25	10.04
Scraper	10	4.01
Arrowhead	2	0.80
Bladelet	1	0.40
Chip	3	1.20
Total	249	99.98

Table 7: *Analysis of Fieldwalked Flint from Site 1*

Site 2

A total of 52 lithic artefacts were recorded from Site 2 during the trial excavations of 1970, and the full excavation of 1971. The breakdown of the assemblage by type is tabulated below Table 23 and fig 17.

TYPE	NUMBER	%
Scraper	2	4
Blade	7	13
Flake	19	37
Blade-like flake	6	11
Chunk	16	31
Core	2	4
Total	52	100

Table 8: *Analysis of Excavated Flint from Site 2*

Site 3

A total of 256 lithic artefacts were recorded from these excavations, a proportion of which came from two oval-shaped pit features in the northern part of the site which were filled with sand, and contained only flint. A selection of material from Pit 1 has been illustrated (fig.30), which contained a total of 43 flint flakes, flake tools, and

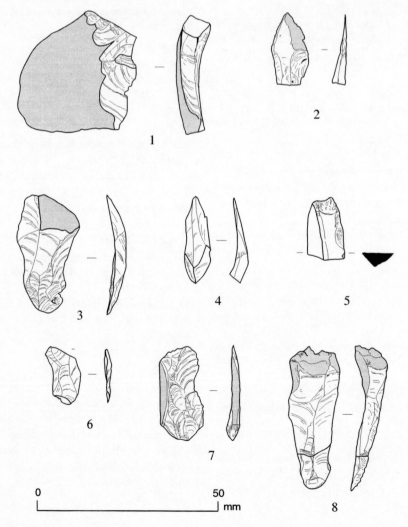

Fig. 30 Objects of flint from Site 3, Pit 1 Scale 1:1

cores. The flakes would appear to have been struck from at least two but probably not more than four separate pebbles. All of the material was heavily recorticated, and flake no.8, broken during excavation illustrated that the recortication penetrated 0.5mm into the surface. 8 of the 43 flakes show clear signs of secondary working, and of the remaining 35, three were found to be conjoining. Pit 2 contained 71 pieces of flint, predominantly flakes, of which 12 were complete.

Random fieldwalking survey of the two fields across which the site lay turned up a further 78 pieces and the proportions of types are tabulated below (Table 9).

TYPE	NUMBER	%
Blade-like flake	18	7.03
Chunk	76	29.69
Hammerstone	1	0.39
Flake	147	57.42
Blade	2	0.78
Core	6	2.34
Scraper	3	1.17
Arrowhead	1	0.39
Chip	2	0.78
Total	256	100

Table 9: *Analysis of Excavated Flint from Site 3*

TYPE	NUMBER	%
Flake	50	64
Microlith	1	1
Blade	4	5
Blade-like flake	8	10
Scraper	3	4
Chunk	6	8
Core	6	8
Total	78	100

Table 10: *Analysis of Fieldwalked Flint from Site 3*

Site 4

39 pieces of lithic material were retrieved during the excavation of Iron Age Building 3 on this site, and the proportions of types are tabulated below.

TYPE	NUMBER	%
Chunk	10	26
Flake	24	61.5
Chert flake	2	5
Blade-like flake	1	2.5
Blade	2	5
Total	39	100

Table 11: *Analysis of Excavated Flint from Site 4*

Discussion

The assemblage as a whole provides evidence for both the manufacture and use of stone tools in the area of the Gwash Valley. It is difficult to be conclusive about a date for this material beyond the level of broad generalisation. There is certainly a Mesolithic element present, as indicated by the proportion of blades and blade-like flakes recovered (just under 15% of the total material),

by the material from the two pits on Site 3, and the single microlith. The barbed and tanged and leaf-shaped arrowheads would indicate later activity and the scraper data is also of some interest in this respect.

The overall ratio of cores to waste flakes is approximately 1:12.5. Bradley (1970) has suggested that for the Neolithic period in the South of England this sort of ratio becomes very wide indeed, so taken at face value it may be that the core:waste ratio suggests an early date. However 16 of the cores (just over 42% of all cores recorded) show evidence for multi-platform/multi-directional working. Saville (1973) has argued that multi-platform flaking is rare on early sites in the Midlands. For example, at the Mesolithic site of Honey Hill, Northants. only 7.8% of the cores (18 examples of 231) are multi-platform cores (Saville 1981, 11). Similarly in northern England, multi-platform flaking is rare in the Mesolithic and becomes more common in the Neolithic and Bronze Age Periods. In the Wear Valley, Co. Durham, for example, multi-platform cores account for just over 18% of all cores from Mesolithic sites, whereas they represent over 38% of the Neolithic and Bronze Age sample (Young 1987, 45-49). Other northern British Mesolithic sites exploiting pebble flint also show a similarly low representation of multi-platform cores (Young 1987, 51).

Of the 26 scrapers recorded, 16 are complete and the majority are of the 'short, end of flake' type. In terms of length, the complete examples range from 37mm-17mm, with an average length of 27.3mm. In terms of breadth, they range from 37mm-19mm with an average breadth of 27.1mm.

It must be borne in mind that the localised nature of the raw material may predicate the size of tools manufactured and used (see Moore and Williams 1975, Young and Kay 1989), but in the absence of published comparanda from the East Midlands, a comparison with other pebble flint exploiting areas of the North East and North West of England suggests that the Empingham scrapers fit best into a broad Neolithic/Bronze Age context (Young 1987, 53-58 and figs. iv.14-iv.19).

The predicatory nature of the raw material may be further supported with reference to the arrowheads recovered from the valley. As mentioned previously, all the classified leaf-shaped examples fall into Green's categories 3 and 4. The formal variation in these categories, Green suggests, is related primarily to the quality of raw material available. 'Typological variation among arrowheads of Size Group 4 is probably normally meaningless in view of the constraints imposed upon the knapper by small size and low quality raw material' (Green 1980, 68). He goes on to say that, 'in the case of leaf-shaped arrowheads of Types 3A-C and 4A-C we have considered that their dimensional and formal variability are related primarily to raw material factors and that this part of the typology may have no significance beyond that of description of geographical variations in typology' (Green 1980, 68).

A consideration of the metrical data for complete

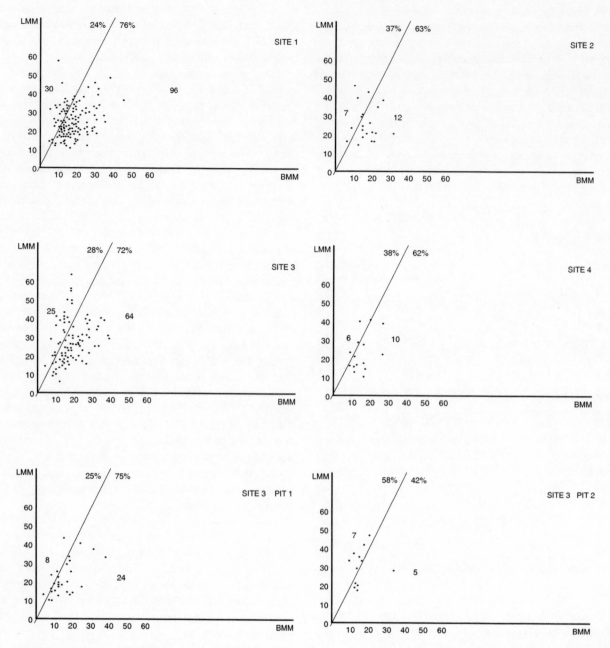

Fig. 31 Metrical Analysis of Flint Flakes

flake/blade-like flakes is hampered by the lack of published comparanda from the Midlands region. Fig.31 shows that the majority of flakes from Sites 1-4 are predominantly short and squat. In all of these figures complete flakes and blade-like flakes, including miscellaneous retouching were included. Site 5 was excluded because of the small number of complete pieces.

Only 24% of the material from Site 1 reaches blade-like proportions while the figures from Sites 2 and 4 are 37% and 38% respectively. If the two pits on Site 3 are excluded from the calculations, then the figure for blade-like proportioned flakes is 28%. If the pit data are included then the figure rises to 30%. On all sites there appears to be no selection of blade-like flakes for retouching or utilisation.

Pitts has shown that in the south of England the changes in dimensions of waste flakes can be a useful chronological indicator (1978). However, we should be wary, in the absence of detailed metrical work for the Midlands, of assuming that his observations also apply to this region. As Pitts himself pointed out, 'Any generalisations made relate to southern England. The situation further north may, interestingly, be significantly different' (Pitts 1978, 25). Indeed, one of us (RY) has shown that for north-eastern England, again due to the nature of the available raw material, Pitts' observations carry no chronological importance. The same may be true of the East Midlands.

The published regional data are not very useful in this discussion. The later Neolithic sites of Ecton, Northants. and Mount Pleasant, Derbys, have similarly low proportions of blade-like flakes (Moore and Williams

1975, 22 fig. 7.23; Garton and Beswick 1983, 30). However, at the henge site of the Bull Ring, Dove Holes, Derbys., almost 29% of the waste flakes are of blade-like proportions (Barnatt and Myres 1988, 18, fig. 6). The dimensions of the waste flakes from Beedles quarry, Leics., and Honey Hill, Northants., were not analysed.On Mesolithic sites in Northern England, flakes of blade-like proportions account for less than 30% of the material from each site. The percentage figure for Neolithic and Bronze Age sites, falls well within the range of variation exhibited on the Mesolithic scatters (Young 1987, 83).

For a more comprehensive view of lithic use in the valley this report should be read in conjunction with the study of the fieldwalked assemblages from the vicinity of Empingham (Herepath 1993) and the fieldwalked and excavated assemblages from the head of the valley at Oakham (Hale 1993; Clay 1998). Clay has also recently made a broader consideration of lithic distribution within Leicestershire and Rutland (1999) and particularly within the context of the East Midlands claylands (1996 and forthcoming). In addition, a number of detailed analyses of lithic assemblages from Leicestershire and Rutland sites have recently been published or are currently underway. Material of Neolithic to Iron Age date has been considered from Wanlip (Cooper and Humphrey 1998, 63); Launde has produced an assemblage of late Upper Palaeolithic date (Cooper L. forthcoming a) and the assemblage from Eye Kettleby near Melton includes stratified Late Neolithic groups (Cooper, L. forthcoming b). Most recently, a substantial assemblage has been excavated at Uppingham (Cooper L. pers. comm.).

THE IRON AGE POTTERY

Nicholas J. Cooper

Introduction

A total of 717 sherds of Iron Age pottery, weighing 11.081kg was recovered, giving an estimated vessel equivalent (EVEs) measure of 3.77 (not including complete vessel 8 and part of vessel 1, not available for study). Judging by the number of identifiably separate rims, it would appear that at least 44 vessels are represented. The pottery was entirely derived from Site 4 during the excavation of the Iron Age house structures, and their associated pits and post holes, and no other pottery of identifiably Iron Age date was retrieved from any of the other sites.

Of the above total, 232 sherds (32%), weighing 5.038 kg (45%), 1.29 EVEs (34%), was retrieved from the two pit fills (A and D) lying between Building 1 and 2, excavated in 1971. Of the remaining material some was retrieved from the partial excavation of the eaves-drip gully of Building 3, while the rest was uncertainly located within and around that building, probably having been disturbed from its original sealed contexts by the machinery. This assertion is supported by the observation that, in general, the pottery was in good condition, often with little weathering of the shell-tempered fabric in which, with few exceptions, it is made. Occasionally the outer surface of the sherd is weathered, giving the characteristic vesicular or corky appearance, and the differential weathering of sherds from the same vessel attests different burial conditions.

Form, Fabric and Decoration

With the exception three vessels (7, 21, and a burnished base in a grog-tempered fabric) all the material fits into the Ancaster-Breedon tradition, now usually termed Scored Ware in the East Midlands, recently defined by Elsdon (1992a) equating to Knight's Group 2 (1984, 40). Scored Ware is characterised by randomly incised decoration, which is predominantly vertical but also occurs as intersecting arcs, or occasionally as horizontal strokes, executed using twigs. Generally speaking, the material matches Elsdon's Style no.6 (1992a, fig.1.6).

The fabric of the material is almost without exception shell-tempered (Marsden 1998, Fabric S1), and any variation in the coarseness of the crushed shell inclusions (fragments usually up to a maximum of 5mm) can be attributed simply to the clay preparation activities of different potters. The occurrence of quartz sand inclusions which may be natural or added, is also detectable. Most of the material has no sand, and the shell-tempered fabric therefore feels quite soapy, but in a small number of cases, it is moderately sandy and micaceous.

The vessels are coil built as demonstrated by the occurrence of bodysherds with false rims, and the bonfire firing gives rise to the expected pattern of variation in surface, core and margin colour from orange (oxidised) to black (reduced). The use of light burnishing or smoothing on one or both surfaces is common, with the incising of the scratch decoration on to an already lightly burnished surface apparent (no.3). Smoothing is usually internal, and would have aided cleaning, although carbonised food residues do occur indicating breakage during use.

The range of forms is similar to that from the Iron Age occupation at Whitwell, which lies only 1km to the west, on the next spur of land on the north side of the Gwash Valley. As at Empingham, tall, shouldered vessels with flattened upright rims appear common at Whitwell, with occasional fingertipping (Todd 1981, fig.12.7), but in contrast to Empingham there do not appear to be any flat rims with diagonal fingernail incisions.

Vessels with less pronounced shoulders, and plainer upright rims are also common from both sites, and there are also examples of thick-bodied, barrel-shaped vessels with incurving flat or slightly beaded rims (e.g. no.14 and Todd 1981 fig.12.15). Fig. 32.12 represents an unusual occurrence of a vessel with an open flaring rim with internal corrugations.

Three of the vessels excavated (7, 21 and an unillustrated base) do not fit into the Scored Ware tradition, occurring in distinctly finer fabrics with a burnished finish. They probably represent vessels imported from outside the region. Only the highly burnished vessel (7) from Pit A, is securely stratified with Scored Ware vessels.

Pottery from Phase 1a (fig. 33)

Pit D (fill AF)

The remains of a single vessel derived from this pit, comprising 153 sherds weighing 3790g.

1) Shouldered jar with upright or slightly flaring rim, which has diagonal fingernail impressions on its upper surface. The point of maximum girth is decorated externally with a single row of finger or thumb impressions, that have been executed by supporting the inside of the body with the fingers of the other hand, just above the point of impression, and then pressing the finger and nail into the external surface at 90 degrees, leaving a vertical nail impression. Immediately above this band is a corresponding band of faint finger pad impressions. Remainder of external surface is smoothed with straw or grass impressions. Diam. 280mm; EVEs 0.57.

The form and decoration of the vessel fits broadly into Knight's Group 1 (1984, 39) of Late Bronze Age or Early Iron Age date or Cunliffe's Ivinghoe-Sandy group dated from the sixth century BC (1974, 320, fig. A:5.11). Closer parallels come from the Reading Business Park excavations in the Thames Valley (Hall 1992, fig.45.67 and 69) and from the Welland Valley at

Gretton, Northants., (Jackson and Knight 1985, fig.6.12).

Pottery from Phase 1b (figs. 32 & 33)

Pit A (fill AA)

A total of 79 sherds, with an EVEs value of 0.72, and weighing 1248g, was retrieved from this feature. Six separate vessels are represented, as well as an additional 21 bodysherds weighing 90g which are not attributable to specific vessels.

2) Jar with incipient shoulder, and upright, flattened rim with diagonal finger nail impressions. Evidence of coil building from 'false rims' on some body sherds. Irregular scratch decoration extends up to shoulder only. Internal surface smoothed or lightly burnished. Diam. 340mm; EVEs 0.21.

3) Jar with flaring rim, the upper surface of which is decorated

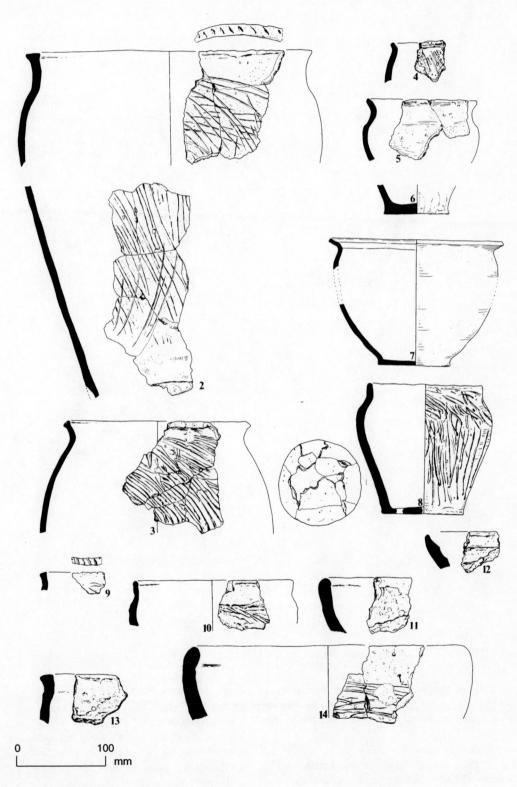

Fig. 32 Iron Age Pottery Scale 1:4

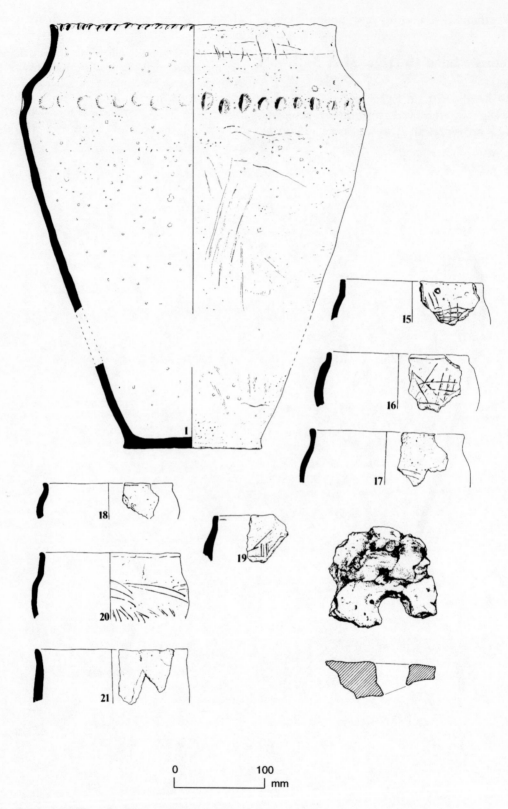

Fig. 33 Iron Age Pottery and Clay oven fragment Scale 1:4

with circular dimples, spaced evenly. The rim and external surface are burnished, with irregular scratch decoration executed over this, and extending to just below the rim. Diam. 230mm, EVEs 0.16.

4) High shouldered or neckless jar with pinched out everted rim, and irregular scratch decoration extending to immediately below the rim. Similar fabric and surface finish to no.3. Diam. 220mm, EVEs 0.06.

5) Squat jar with S-shaped profile. Vessel is well formed, with a burnished internal surface, on which carbonised residue adheres. Shell-tempered fabric is reduced, and weathered, with no external decoration. Diam.130mm, EVEs 0.2.

6) Base from small jar, with finger-formed chamfer. Shell-tempered fabric is slightly micaceous.

7) Rim and base of wide-mouthed jar in fine, hand made, shell-tempered fabric. Core and margins oxidised, with surfaces reduced black, and burnished externally. The vessel is thin-bodied, and well formed, with a bevelled or lid-seated rim. Diam.150mm, EVEs 0.09.

This represents a vessel of distinctly higher quality which may represent a regional import. Similarly burnished hand made pottery from a site of Middle Iron Age date is known from a small enclosure site at Weelsby Avenue, Grimsby excavated by J.Sills and G.Kinsley (forthcoming).

Building 3

The following 14 vessels were excavated in the area of Building 3 in 1972, but unfortunately from existing records it is not possible to determine the stratified location of many of the vessels by reference to their two-letter codes. Where possible this information is provided.

8) Complete shouldered jar with upright rim. Irregular scratch decoration over entire external surface. The base of the vessel has been perforated with 2 or 3 holes after firing, which have been drilled from both sides, creating an hour glass profile. Possibly used in cheese making. 1972 BE
A similarly perforated base was excavated at Enderby, Leics. (Elsdon 1992b Phase 2.2B fig.24.42).

9) Upright rim with incised grooves on the upper flattened surface. Fabric oxidised, and tempered with predominantly coarse shell fragments. 1972 AP.Diam.160mm, EVEs 0.08.

10) Shouldered jar with upright rounded rim. Hard reduced black fabric, with coarse shell temper. Scratch decoration is deeply incised, and extends up to the shoulder. 1972 AP. Diam. 180mm, EVEs 0.06.

11) Jar with upright rim in friable shell-tempered fabric. 1972 AR. Diam.220mm, EVEs 0.09.

12) Flared rim jar with internal corrugations. Part of a perforation shows on one edge of the sherd. 1972 AS. Diam.120mm, EVEs 0.08.

Jars of this type have been excavated at Fiskerton, Lincs., where they are associated with La Tène I swords. They were found *in situ* crushed beneath a wooden jetty, the timbers of which have felling dates of 457 and 339 BC (Hillam 1985, 96, 21-27). A similar jar came from Gretton, Northants., with radio-carbon dates centring on 290-260 BC (S. Elsdon pers.comm; Jackson and Knight 1985, fig.79.65). At least six other examples are known with similar dating and so a Middle Iron Age or earlier date would appear most likely.

13) Upright flattened rim from shouldered jar. Thick bodied, hard, with profuse shell temper. 1972 AT. Diam.uncertain, EVEs 0.03.

14) Barrel-shaped vessel, with in-turned bead rim. Scratch decoration below rim. 1972 AT. Rimsherds from the same (or similar) vessel come from AP, AW, and AZ. Diam.420mm, EVEs 0.05.

15) Shouldered jar with plain upright rim. Scratch decoration. 1972BC. Diam.160mm, EVEs 0.21.

16) High shouldered vessel with short upright rim, in sandy shell-tempered fabric. 1972 BH. Diam.160mm, EVEs 0.08.

17) Upright, flattened bead rim. 1972 BK. Diam.130mm, EVEs 0.08.

18) Upright rim. Sandy and micaceous, shell-tempered fabric. 1972 BP. From bottom fill of first cut of eaves-drip gully. Diam.120mm, EVEs 0.08.

19) Upright rim. Sandy shell-tempered fabric. 1972 BQ. From second recut of eaves-drip gully. Diam.160mm, EVEs 0.05.

20) Long upright rim with slight bead. 1972 BT. From second recut of eaves-drip gully.
Diam.140mm, EVEs 0.5.

21) A funnel necked vessel, in a fine shell tempered fabric (similar to 7). Oxidised dark red body, and reduced black burnished surfaces. Sole occurrence of this form. Diam.140mm, EVEs 0.15.

Objects of Clay

Perforated baked clay oven (fig. 33)

Forty-four fragments of baked clay, weighing 2.3kg were retrieved from the eaves-drip gully of Building 3. All the fragments are in the same clay fabric, tempered with grass, and grog, fired to a uniform orange colour, and clearly come from one object. Most of the fragments show signs of finger smoothing, and about 15 incorporate the edges of circular perforations which are on average 30mm in diameter. The remains of at least six perforations are represented, though no complete examples could be reconstructed. The perforations are 40-45mm deep, and appear to be made by inserting a finger through the top surface of the structure and smoothing the sides.

The remains of such ovens are not unusual, but they are rarely preserved to any degree of completeness, and so it is difficult to assess their overall shape and function. The examples from Little Woodbury, Wilts., (Brailsford 1949, 161), would tend to indicate that they are beehive-shaped, with large central openings in the base and top, and with a ring of small vents ringing the top one. Examples also come from Willington, Derbys, (Elsdon 1979, 209), and most recently from Tixover, Leics., in the Welland Valley, 6 miles to the south of the Empingham site.

Discussion

With the exception of the Early Iron Age vessel from Pit D, the homogeneity of the material in terms of both form and fabric, as well as poor stratigraphical information, has not enabled any internal site chronology to be determined on the basis of the pottery alone. Vessel profiles 18, 19, 20, which derive from the first cut and second recut of the eaves-drip gully of Building 3 are similar enough to indicate that no such chronology could be constructed in this case, although comparison of the profiles from Pit A and Building 3 indicates that plain upright rims are confined to the latter.

Parallels with the Whitwell assemblage have already been alluded to, and comparison with other Iron Age pottery assemblages then known, led Todd (1981) to date the pottery from Whitwell, to between the 400 BC and 100 BC, based necessarily on its loose association with dateable metalwork from Ancaster. Based upon the lack of associated early Roman pottery with the Iron Age material from Whitwell, Todd (1981) proposed a break of occupation of uncertain duration (but probably at least a century) between the two phases of occupation. The occurrence of Early and Middle Iron Age vessels (1, 7 and 12), might tend to suggest an earlier date for the assemblage than at Whitwell.

Comparisons between the Empingham material and the much larger assemblage from the enclosure site at Enderby, Leics. (Elsdon 1992b), indicates that it compares well with that from Phase 2.2A (fig. 23.17-26) where both plain upright rims and those with finger-tipping occur. Phase 2 at Enderby, when comparison with the material from Weekley, Northants, (Jackson and Dix 1987) is made, is thought to fall between 175BC and AD20, with Phase 2.2A presumably falling towards the centre of this band, somewhere in the first century BC. The rounded forms (15-20) compare well with those from Weekley Phase 1 (Jackson and Dix 1987).

The distribution and dating of East Midlands Scored Ware has been reviewed by Elsdon (1992a), illustrating a tradition (formerly Ancaster-Breedon) stretching from the Trent and Soar Valleys to the north and west, to the Ouse, Nene, and Welland Valleys to the south and east. Evidence suggests that scoring begins in the fourth century BC, which may be pushed back to the fifth on evidence from Wanlip (Marsden 1998, 49), but is not common until the middle of the third century BC, and that in the Nene valley it stops before the introduction of wheelmade pottery (Elsdon 1992a). The evidence from both Whitwell and Empingham would tend to support this end date, but further excavation and research in the southern part of the distribution area may alter this view. As the evidence stands, there is no stratified Roman pottery from Site 4, and no sign of Roman occupation nearby with Site 2 being some 300m to the east. A number of large assemblages have been studied since the publication of Whitwell, and Elsdon argues that in the Trent and Soar Valleys at least, Scored ware does continue into the first half of the first century AD (Elsdon 1992a). The most recent study from Humberstone, Leics., would tend to confirm this idea (Marsden 2000)

Acknowledgements
I am grateful to Sheila Elsdon for commenting on the material, to Patrick Marsden for suggesting changes to the final report, and to Patrick Clay for access to unpublished reports on material from the sites of Enderby (now published as Elsdon 1992b) and Tixover. The catalogue illustrations were by Martha de Bethune.

THE ROMAN POTTERY

*Nicholas J. Cooper**

Introduction

A report on the Roman pottery from Sites 1 and 2 was undertaken by Martha de Bethune in 1977, at the same time as the pottery from the Whitwell excavations (Todd 1981). A preliminary catalogue and brief discussion of the important groups as well as the illustrations were completed by de Bethune, but there was no attempt to create a fabric series, or undertake any kind of quantification or detailed discussion of the material. Since that time, a fabric series has been developed by Leicestershire Archaeological Unit (Pollard 1994, Clark 1999 and summary below) now held by Leicester City Museums, and so further work has been undertaken to tie the material in with this existing series and advance the understanding of the chronology, production and distribution of wares found in Leicestershire and Rutland.

Rutland has seen few Roman pottery assemblages published from it. Among the nearest and most important have been those from the excavations at Great Casterton (Corder 1951, 1954 and 1961), as well as the nearby site of Whitwell (Todd 1981), but no quantification work was undertaken during either study. The fact that none of the pottery was discarded at the time of the Empingham excavations, thus presented an opportunity to undertake quantitative work on the more important groups. Work on another large assemblage from Greenfield's excavations at Thistleton Roman villa has been completed (Symonds, forthcoming) but remains unpublished

A total weight of 270kg of pottery was retrieved from all the excavations, the greater proportion (83%) deriving from Site 1. The extent of plough damage to all sites dictated that much of the pottery was unstratified, and while this material has been examined for dating implications, and to select material of intrinsic interest, attention has focused on the important stratified groups. The report has been laid out in order to emphasise these stratified groups which are arranged in site and phase order. The two major stratified groups from Site 1 (the Phase 2 Ditch F.1, and the Phase 3 Well), have been quantified by number of sherds, EVEs (Estimated Vessel Equivalents), and weight.

The smaller site assemblages (Sites 2, 3, 5, and 6) have been quantified by weight only, since the small number of rims would give a misleading EVEs quantification. Additionally, as three of the groups are fourth century in date, the division between 'fine' and 'coarse' wares is less marked and so the biasing effect of 'heavier' fabrics is lessened. The intention is to provide an

*Incorporating information from an original report by Martha de Bethune and with samian ware by Brenda Dickinson.

impression of the composition of these smaller groups, rather than data for rigorous statistical comparison.

Where no important phase groups occur from a site, then a short discussion of the material is included, and any pottery of intrinsic value is included in a section at the end of the report which brings together unusual forms, or forms present but not represented in any of the stratified groups. The policy has been to avoid illustration of common or well-known types which have been published elsewhere such as Lower Nene Valley colour-coated ware forms (Howe, Perrin and Mackreth 1980).

A Summary of the Leicestershire Roman Pottery Fabric Type Series

To allow this report to be used independently, a summary of the fabric codes used, their common names, and concordance with the National Roman Fabric Reference Collection (Tomber and Dore 1998; Pollard 1999) when appropriate, is provided below.

C   Colour-coated Wares

C2   Fine white fabrics usually Lower Nene Valley origin (LNV CC) but also from the Lower Rhineland (Cologne KOL CC)

C3   Pale oxidised fabrics. Number of sources but here denotes a probable Lower Nene Valley origin

C7   Variant of C11 probably from Lower Nene Valley

C11   Dark oxidised fabrics. Here probably from Lower Nene Valley

C13   Oxfordshire red or brown colour-coated ware (OXF RS).

C17   Fabrics similar to C2,3 and 11.

MO   Mortarium Fabrics

MO4   Mancetter-Hartshill as WW2 (MAH WH)

MO6   Lower Nene valley (LNV WH)

WW   White Wares

WW2   Fine as M04. Mancetter-Hartshill or Lower Nene Valley origin (MAH PA)

WW3   Fine sandy. Here probably denotes Upper or Lower Nene Valley origin

WW4   Medium sandy. Verulamium region or Mancetter Hartshill (VER WH?)

OW   Oxidised Wares

OW2   Fine or fine sandy of uncertain Midlands sources.

OW3   Coarse sandy as OW2

OW9   Much Hadham burnished ware (HAD OX; Going 1987, Fabric 4).

GW   Grey Wares

GW3, 5, 6, 9 A gradation from fine to very coarse for fabrics of unknown source.

GW4 Lower Nene Valley grey ware. Fine light grey fabric (LNV RE).

GW12 Used here to denote grey ware of 'London ware' type (Perrin 1980).

BB Black-Burnished Wares
BB1 of South-East Dorset origin.

CG Calcite Gritted Wares
CG1A Fossil shell tempered fabrics (low sand content) of Late Iron Age to second century date.

CG1B Fabric as A but becoming widespread in the later Roman period from Harrold, Beds. (Brown 1994) (HAR SH).

CG3B of mid-Roman date. Production locally at Bourne and Greetham (BOG SH)

GT Grog Tempered Wares
GT3 coarse fabric not in 'Belgic' forms. Also used here to denote Soft Pink Grogged ware (GT3A; PNK GT; Booth and Green 1989).

MG Mixed Gritted Wares
MG3 Fine to medium sandy grey ware with calcite. Local and early in date.

SW Sandy Wares
SW2 fine sandy fabric usually in 'Belgic' style.

The Samian Ware

In an attempt to move away from the more traditional layout of Roman pottery reports, where the samian ware is reported on separately, it is instead placed within the relevant phase groups, and the discussion is placed within that for the pottery as whole. Only the stratified material is catalogued, and the occurrence of forms across all assemblages is tabulated below.

Summary
A total of 164 sherds of samian ware weighing 1.883 kg was retrieved almost exclusively from Empingham Sites 1 and 2, with only two sherds coming from Site 3. None of the other Roman sites yielded any samian, which is due almost certainly to their later Roman date. A total of 149 sherds (91%) weighing 1783g (95%) was retrieved from Site 1, while 13 sherds (8%) weighing 90g (5%) came from Site 2, and two sherds (1%) weighing 10g (<1%) derived from Site 3.

The occurrence of identifiable forms from Sites 1, 2, and 3 is summarised in Table 12. All forms are Dragendorf unless otherwise stated.

Form	Site 1	Site 2	Site 3	Total
Decorated				
30 or 37	2	-	-	2
37	7	-	-	7
Plain				
27	1	-	-	1
33	13	-	-	13
33?	1	1	-	2
15/17	-	-	1	1
18	-	-	1	1
18/31	2	-	-	2
18/31R	10	-	-	10
18/31 or 31	7	-	-	7
31	15	2	-	17
35	1	-	-	1
36	2	-	-	2
42	1	-	-	1
Curle 15 or 23	1	-	-	1
Curle 23	1	-	-	1
Walters 79	-	2	-	2
38	1	3	-	4
Curle 11	2	-	-	2
Total	**67**	**8**	**2**	**77**

Table 12: The Occurrence of Samian Forms at Empingham

Abbreviations used in the catalogue entries of samian ware.

D. = figure-type in	J.Dechelette (1904).
Hermet 1934	F.Hermet (1934).
O. = figure-type in	F.Oswald (1936-7).
O.& P.1920	F.Oswald and T.Davies Pryce (1920).
Rogers = motif in	G.B.Rogers (1974).
S.& S. 1958	J.A.Stanfield & Grace Simpson (1958).

Stratified Groups from Site 1 (EPR 1969-71)

A total weight of 223 kg of Romano-British pottery was retrieved from the site, of which 102.610 kg (46%) belonged to stratified groups. This is by far the largest assemblage from the sites under consideration, and the generally good condition of the stratified groups yielded much useful information.

Phase 2A (figs.34 and 36)
Feature 50 East-West Ditch partly sealed by phase 5 walling.
Codes 71 FA, 71 FD, 71 FE, 71 FF, 71 FG, 71 FH, 71 ZAC, 71 ZAD, 71 ZAE.

A total of 664 sherds of pottery with an EVEs value of 5.45 and weighing 9.163 Kg was retrieved from the fill of this feature. The quantification of this group by fabric is summarised in Table 13 below.

Fabric	No.Sherds	%	EVES	%	Weight(g)	%
CG1A	439	66.1	3.61	66.2	5859	64.0
MG3	211	31.8	1.35	24.8	3124	34.1
GW5/6	14	2.1	0.49	9.0	180	1.9
TOTAL	**664**	**100**	**5.45**	**100**	**9163**	**100**

Table 13: Quantification of Roman Pottery from Feature 50

This group probably represents a relatively gradual accumulation of refuse during the Phase 2 occupation of the site, and is broadly datable to the second half of the first century AD, and probably into the early second. All drawable rims are illustrated, and this covers examples of all forms present. The very small number of clearly intrusive sherds found in the top fill of the feature have not been quantified, but are discussed briefly below.

The primary silting at the bottom of the ditch contained the rim and bodysherds of a handmade vessel

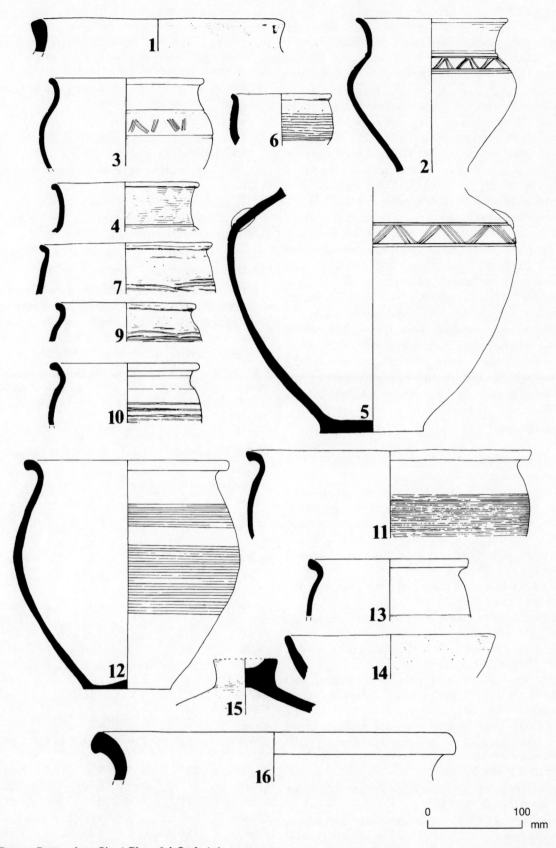

Fig. 34 Roman Pottery from Site 1 Phase 2A Scale 1:4

of later Iron Age date (no.1). It is the only occurrence of the form on Site 1, and it is closer in character to the Iron Age scored ware material from Site 4, than anything else in the ditch group.

The main filling contained a number of jars with outcurving rims in fabric CG1A with horizontal combing below the shoulder (nos.6-12). There are also three examples of carinated bowl/jar forms each with a band of diagonally incised decoration around the shoulder in grey ware or mixed-gritted fabrics (nos.2-5). The mixed gritted fabrics display some variation, but are mainly a mix of quartz and a variable amount of shell inclusions, representing the transition to the later grey ware fabrics.

A number of large storage jars in oxidized shell-tempered fabric CG1A, with irregular horizontal combing, are also present, including one (no.16) with an incised diagonal shoulder band identical to that in the Flavian group from the fill of Pit II at Great Casterton (Corder 1961 fig. 14 no.19). There are general similarities with Great Casterton groups of this date.

The ditch appears to have been substantially filled well before the end of the Phase 2 occupation, as there is little overlap with those fabrics and forms represented in the Phase 2b 'destruction' deposits. However, a slight depression must have remained open for some time, as the upper fill (71FA) contained two sherds of Hadrianic or Antonine samian (71 FA) and abraded sherds of Nene Valley colour-coated ware. The main fill, in contrast, contained no samian or other early fine wares.

The pottery from Feature 67 which appears to be a continuation of Feature 50, supports the suggestion that the ditch was filled in the later first century AD (nos.17 and 18).

Primary Silting
1) CG1A. Hand-made jar with upright rim and fingertip impressions below rim.

Main Filling
2) GW 5/6/7 or MG3. Shouldered or carinated jar with horizontal band of herring-bone burnished decoration around shoulder, separated from flaring neck by a cordon. 71 FG.
3) MG3. Jar with beaded rim and shoulder band of burnished herringbone decoration.
4) MG3. Neck of carinated jar as no.2, but with burnished external surfaces. 71 ZAC.
5) GW 5/6/7 or MG3. Coarse grey ware fabric with fine shell inclusions. Shouldered jar with horizontal band of herring-bone incised decoration around girth. 71 ZAE. Same fabric as no.70 from 69 ET.
6) CG1A. Small jar with regular horizontal combing. Mid first century. Similar to a vessel from Great Casterton (Corder 1961 fig.14 no.12).
7) CG1A . Handmade neckless jar in hard, dark grey fabric, with fine shell inclusions. Decorated with irregular horizontal incised lines. Mid first century. (Corder 1961 fig.15, nos.25 and 26).
8) CG1A. Handmade jar as no.7, but larger, with similar decoration. Not illustrated.
9) CG1A. Necked jar, with beaded rim. Decoration as no.7. burnished surfaces.71 ZAC. Mid first century (Corder 1961 fig.14 nos 13-15 and fig.15, no.41).
10) CG1A. Necked jar with bead rim. Decoration as no.7 .
11) CG1A. Jar with slightly hooked bead rim, and regular combed decoration.
12) CG1A. Complete jar with beaded rim. Regular combing.
13) CG1A. Jar as nos.11 and 12. Regular combing.

14) CG1A. Dish or possibly a lid, with plain rim. Burnished surfaces.
15) MG3. Lid in hard light grey fabric, with dark grey surfaces. Mixed inclusions of sand, grog and shell. Sole occurrence of this version of the fabric.
16) CG1A. Large storage jar. Non-joining bodysherds with incised decoration on shoulder.

Feature 67 71AV and 71BY

17) CG1A. Jar with everted, and slightly lid-seated rim, fabric and appearance as no.12.
18) OW3. Rim of carinated jar with corrugated neck similar to no.76 from Phase 2, Feature 4.

Phase 2B: 'Destruction' Groups Sealed by Phase 3-5 Masonry Structures (figs. 35-39)

Feature 1, the north-south ditch sealed by Building 1. 69 AR.

This is the largest well stratified group from the site, comprising more than 44 vessels in a limited range of fabrics, many of which are substantially complete, and all of which are illustrated. A total of 1495 sherds weighing 35.4kg, and with an EVEs value of 22.42 was retrieved from what formed the primary fill in the base of the ditch. The quantification by fabric is illustrated in Table 14 and by EVEs only in pie-chart (fig.46 Ceramic Phase 2).

Fabric	Sherds	%	EVES	%	Weight(g)	%
C.G Samian	47	3.0	2.22	10.0	903	2.6
C2 L.Rhine	24	2.0	0.27	1.0	95	0.4
Comb. Imps.	**71**	**5.0**	**2.49**	**11.0**	**998**	**3.0**
WW2	98	6.5	1.85	8.3	700	1.9
WW3	38	2.5	1.62	7.2	585	1.5
WW4	19	1.25	1.00	4.5	178	0.5
OW2	2	0.25	0.28	1.0	20	0.1
Comb. WW/OW	**157**	**11.0**	**4.75**	**21.0**	**1483**	**4.0**
GW3	54	3.5	4.46	20.0	1648	4.8
GW4	61	4.0	3.20	14.4	831	2.5
GW3/4	465	31.0	0.19	0.9	8411	23.9
GW5/6	99	6.4	2.09	9.4	1814	5.1
GW12	15	1.0	-	-	119	0.3
SW2	1	0.1	-	-	5	0.01
SW misc.	16	1.0	-	-	125	0.4
Comb. GW/SW	**711**	**47.0**	**10.00**	**45.0**	**12953**	**37.0**
CG3B (Bourne)	446	29.4	3.91	17.0	10481	29.0
CG1A	9	0.6	0.66	3.0	986	3.0
GT3	111	7.0	0.61	3.0	8495	24.0
Comb CG/GT	**556**	**37.0**	**5.18**	**23.0**	**19962**	**56.0**
TOTAL	**1495**	**100**	**22.42**	**100**	**35396**	**100**

Table 14: *Quantification of Roman Pottery from Feature 1*

The group appears to be in its primary context, as there is little contamination from earlier or later material, and there are very few sherds that cannot be attributed to a specific vessel. This would indicate that its deposition was a single event, and the fact that much of the material, including the samian ware, shows signs of burning would support the possibility that it derives from the levelling of the site by fire. The burning could have been either accidental, and thus perhaps caused an abandonment, or deliberate in order to level the site before rebuilding.

The imported fabrics (samian and Cologne ware C2) provide the closest dating evidence. They form 11% of the assemblage by EVEs, but only 3% by weight.

The Samian Ware by Brenda Dickinson

Forty seven sherds of samian weighing 903g came from this context. This represents over half (52%) by weight but only 32% by sherd count of the samian from the site, and represents the most complete and securely stratified group.

The samian from Site 1, F.1 (Ditch 69 AR), is heavily burnt and a few burnt sherds in other contexts belong, or could belong, to it. Some of the vessels are substantially complete; footrings, where present, showed varied signs of wear. The group includes a bowl of Curle 11 (particularly heavily worn) which would have reached the site before c.AD150, or so. The decorated bowls, in the styles of Cinnamus ii (with scarcely-worn footring) and Criciro v, could in theory be as late as AD 170, but it is more likely that the material was deposited in the 150s, presumably after some domestic accident.

The Other Pottery

The cornice-rimmed (not developed), bag-shaped beaker with roughcast decoration in Lower Rhineland Fabric 1, was probably produced between AD 100-150 (Anderson 1980 fig. 7 nos.1-3).

The white wares include a 'segmental' or hemispherical flanged bowl with red-brown paint decoration which, if of Lower Nene Valley origin, would have to be one of the earliest products of the range produced in the second half of the second-early or middle third century as found at Water Newton (Perrin 1999, 111, fig.67 nos.348-352).

The grey wares are very consistent in form comprising necked jars with beaded rims and a distinctive band of burnished wavy line decoration below the neck cordon. They are produced in a range of fine grey fabrics including GW4, Lower Nene Valley grey ware. There is kiln evidence from the Lower Nene Valley to support the production of this general jar form there during the mid- to late second century, for example from Normangate Field (Perrin and Webster 1990, fig.4 no.36) and Water Newton (Chesterton) (Perrin 1999, 80, fig.56 nos.19-20) and possibly later at Stanground (Dannell, Hartley, Wild and Perrin 1993, fig.24 nos.193-196). The production sites for the other grey ware fabric represented here is unknown although the type is well known further up the Nene at Brixworth (Woods 1970, fig.21 nos.134-136, with 3rd century types generally being undecorated

(Perrin 1999, 80). Jar (37) with grooved bead is paralleled from the kiln group at Sulehay, dated to the second quarter of the second century (Wild 1975, fig.7 no.2)

The domestic pottery was augmented by the shell-tempered products which match closely those identified from kilns of the Bourne-Greetham industry to the north of the Gwash Valley.

A date in, or soon after, the 150s appears most likely for the group, and is supported by the lack of the later second and early third century colour-coated ware products of the Lower Nene Valley, such as bag-shaped beakers with *en barbotine* decoration with either plain or cornice rims, the presence of which might have been expected if the deposit had been later. The Cologne beaker is the only colour-coated vessel from the group which is perhaps surprising, and while this may simply be a peculiarity of the group, the date is supported by the colour-coated wares in the possible destruction group from Feature 23, which contains roughcast beakers of both Cologne and Nene valley origin, and also hunt cups and scale-decorated bag-shaped beakers. The ditch group is also interesting in that not a single mortarium sherd is represented.

The Samian (Fig. 35)

i) Forms 18/31 or 31, 31, 36 (burnt) and Curle 11 (burnt), Central Gaulish. The last is largely complete and has a joining sherd in 69 EA. The footring is heavily worn. Hadrianic or early-Antonine.

ii) Two fragments of form 31, heavily burnt, Central Gaulish. Early- to mid-Antonine.

iii) Forms 31, 33 (2) and Curle 15 or 23, Central Gaulish. Antonine.

iv) Form 37, burnt, Central Gaulish. Eleven Fragments, many joining (possibly including no.168). A panelled bowl in the style of Criciro v, with a single-bordered ovolo (Rogers B12) and his beaded junction-masks (Rogers C132). Each alternate panel contains a caryatid (O.1207A). The top part of a split panel contains a single festoon with a sea-cow (D.29 = 0.42) amid partly-impressed acanthi (Rogers K22?). A full panel has an Apollo (D.52 = O.83, on a stand), in a medallion with beaded outer border (Rogers E2). Two signed Criciro bowls from Corbridge have a similar arrangement of panels (S.& S.1958, pl.117, 4, 11). c.AD140-170. (Illustrated fig.35)

v) Form 37, heavily burnt, in the style of Cinnamus ii. A substantially complete small bowl, with scarcely-worn footring. The four panels, presumably repeated four times, comprise: 1) a vertical series of lozenges (Rogers U33). 2A) A goat (D.889 = O.1836), in a double festoon; 2B) a hare to left (D.950A =O.2116). 3) A mask to right, on an ornamental column made up of a motif approximating to Rogers Q95. 4) A double medallion with a kneeling stag (D.847 = O.1704), over an acanthus (Rogers K12). This is a standard Cinnamus bowl, with his ovolo 3 (Rogers B143) and his characteristic small rings in panel 4. All the other details are attested for him, too. c.AD150-180. (Illustrated fig.35)

Other Fine Wares and Coarse Wares

19) C2. Lower Rhineland Fabric 1 (Anderson 1980). A very fine Cologne product with fine clay roughcasting. Fabric

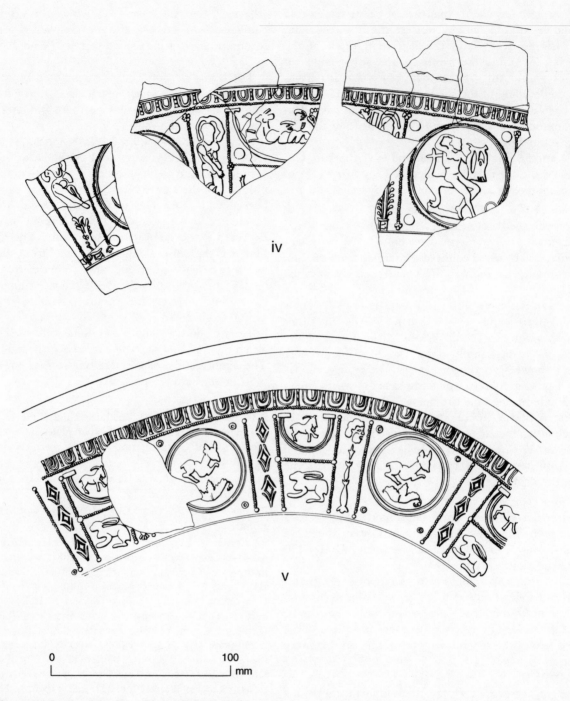

iv

v

Fig. 35 Decorated Samian from Site 1 Phase 2B F1 Scale 1:2

white, with light grey core; coating matt olive brown. Sherds rather abraded. AD 80-150. The fabric is very fine, with no trace of ironstone inclusions, making a Lower Rhineland attribution likely. However, two examples of Lower Nene Valley origin come from F23 below (nos.82 and 83).

20) WW3. Dish with down-curving flange. Similar fabric to flagon 22 . Powdery with abraded surfaces and traces of grey-brown slip.

21) WW2. Segmental bowl, similar to Nene Valley self-coloured ware (Howe *et. al.* 1980 No.99), but with a down-turned flange tip.

22) WW2. Small jar with bead rim. Traces of brown paint under rim and on shoulder.

23) WW2 or 3. Devolved ring-neck flagon, with top ring enlarged into a bead. Gillam 5. AD 110-150.

24) WW3. Devolved ring-neck flagon Gillam 7. AD130-220. Surface has traces of pink slip or wash.

25) WW 4. Devolved ring-neck as above. Sandy fabric.

26) OW2 or GW3. Globular beaker with everted rim.

27) WW2. Small beaker with everted rim.

28) OW2 or GW3. A misfired grey ware vessel. A near complete vessel abraded through burial. Band of burnished lattice below shoulder cordon.

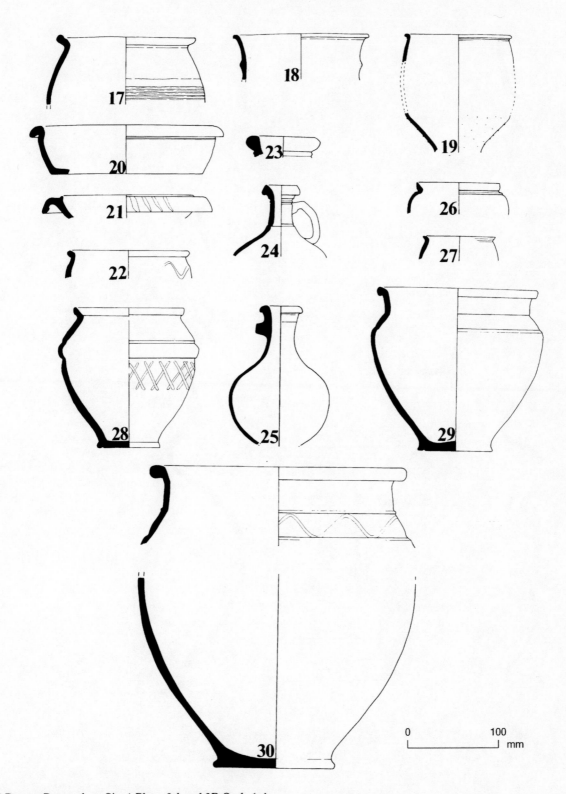

Fig. 36 Roman Pottery from Site 1 Phase 2A and 2B Scale 1:4

29) OW2 or GW3. Necked jar, with beaded rim. A near-
complete vessel.

Vessels 30-36, represent a range of necked jars, with 30-
32 in particular being substantially complete, and in the
same fabric.

30) GW5/6. Necked jar with burnished wavy line below neck
cordon.

31) GW5/6. Similar to 28. Rim distorted during firing.

32) GW 5/6. As 28, but with slightly hooked bead rim.

33) GW3 Sharp neck to shoulder angle. Double burnished
wavy line.

34) GW4. Mottled grey surfaces. Similar in appearance to
products of Lower Nene Valley kiln at Sulehay (see
Hadman and Upex 1975). Burnished slashes. Sharp neck
and shoulder angle.

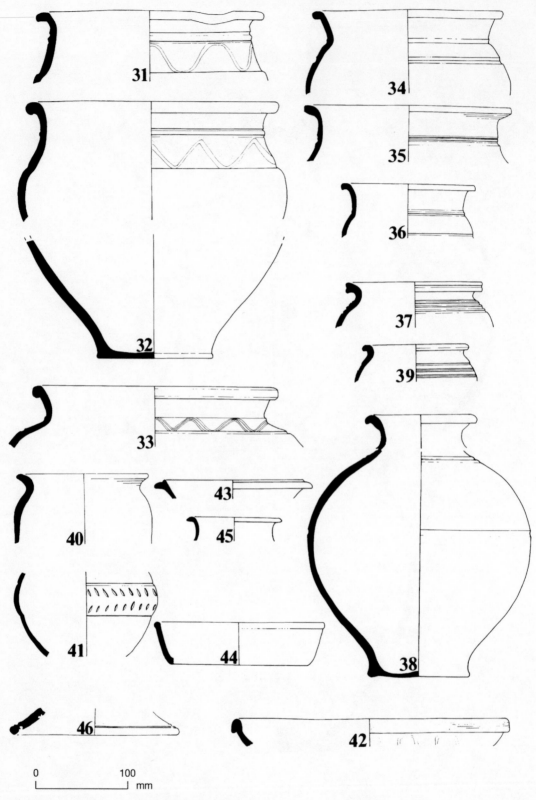

Fig. 37 Roman Pottery from Sites 1 Phase 2B F1 Scale 1:4

35) GW5/6. Neck groove as 29, but with no burnished wavy line decoration below.

36) GW4. Small jar. Rim slightly hooked.

37) GW4. Hard, with mottled grey surface, possibly caused by burial (Wild 1975, fig.7 no.2).

38) GW3. Near complete narrow mouthed, necked jar. Light grey with pink-buff surfaces.

39) GW3. Small jar with horizontally grooved shoulder. Slightly micaceous fabric.

40) GW5/6 or 1. Jar in very coarse, sandy fabric, with

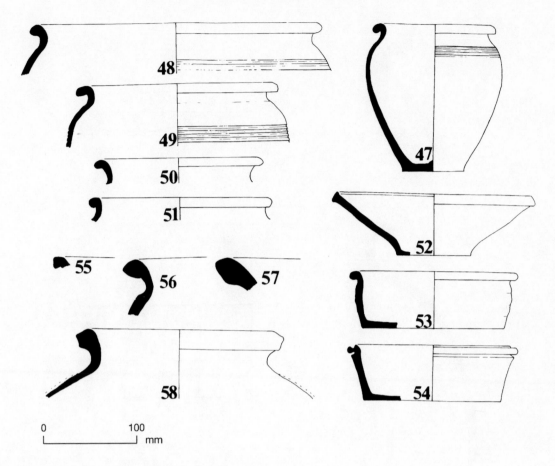

Fig. 38 Roman Pottery from Site 1 Phase 2B F1 Scale 1:4

distorted rim. Sole occurrence of this fabric variant.

41) GW4. Mottled surface. Form and fabric are similar to products of the mid-second century lower Nene valley kiln at Sulehay (Wild 1975, fig.7 no.9).

42) GW4. Curved-sided bowl or dish with turned-down flange.

43) GW4. Nene Valley grey ware No.21. Flanged bowl with incipient bead.

44) GW4. Straight-sided dish with slightly beaded rim. Nene valley grey ware No.19.

45) GW3. Small necked jar with out-curving rim.

46) GW4. Lid with grooved rim.

Vessels 47-54 are in shell-tempered fabric CG3B and conform to the products of kilns identified to the north of the valley at Bourne and Greetham. The products of these kilns usually have a fully reduced, black fabric and surfaces, and for the bulk of the material from the site this holds true. However the vessels from this context, have a proportion of their surfaces re-oxidised to orange. Much of the material from the ditch as a whole, but particularly the samian ware, shows signs of burning, and it is likely that the shell-tempered products have been affected in the same way.

47) CG3B. Jar with rolled bead rim, which is down-curving, and a band of horizontal combing.

48) CG3B. Jar as 47, but with more pronounced step below the neck.

49) CG3B. Jar as 47, but with more pronounced neck.

50) CG3B. Jar as 48.

51) CG3B. Jar with rim tightly rolled into a bead.

52) CG3B. Probably a lid, but possibly a dish. No lids have been recognised from the available kiln material.

53) CG3B. Bowl with slightly curving sides, and rolled over bead rim.

54) CG3B. Straight-sided bowl with bead and flange rim which has been undercut.

Vessels 55-60 are large storage jars in shell-tempered fabric CG1A.

55) CG1A. Jar with grooved bead rim.

56) CG1A. Necked storage jar.

57) CG1A. Storage jar.

58) CG1A. Storage jar.

59) CG1A. Storage jar, with band of incised decoration on shoulder.

60) CG1A or GT3. Combing on lower body, and incised panel decoration on shoulder. Midlands pink grog-tempered ware (Booth and Green 1989)

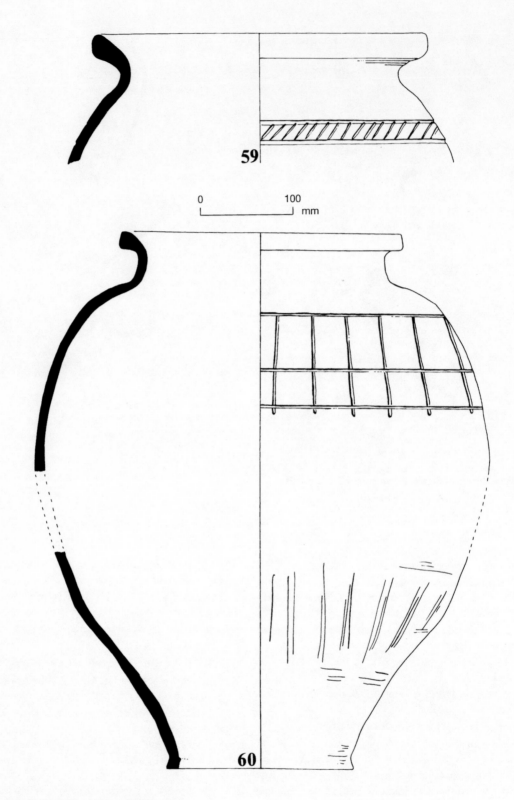

Fig. 39 Roman Pottery from Site 1 Phase 2B F1 Scale 1:4

Other Phase 2B Groups (figs. 40-42)

Feature 19 sleeper beam trench 69BO/CK. 69 AO/AJ (fig. 40 Nos. 61-65)

61) CG3B. Cooking pot with down-curving rim. Horizontal parallel grooves on shoulder. Surfaces orange to black with soapy feel.

62) GW5/6 or MG3. Narrow-mouthed jar with sparse fine shell tempering. Burnished wavy line decoration around neck.

63) GW3. Colander formed from a shallow flanged dish with perforated base, with surfaces lightly burnished.

64) GW12. Imitation samian form Dr.30/37 with impressed decoration typical of so-called London Ware (Perrin 1980)

65) MO6. Mortarium with down-curving flange and upright 'wall' rim which is beaded. Pink buff fabric grey core, black grits. An unusual form.

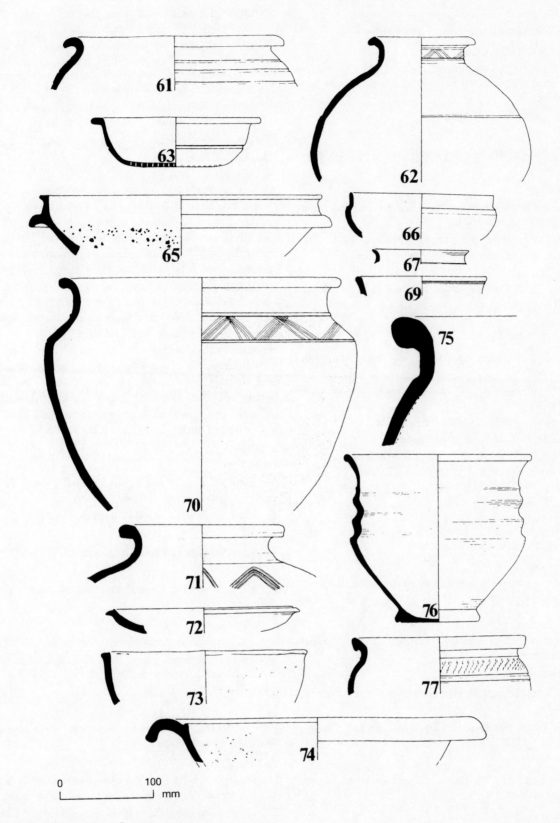

Fig. 40 Roman Pottery from Site 1 Phase 2B Scale 1:4

Feature 26 Pit fill 69 MB

66) C2. Howe *et al.* 1980 no. 89 'Castor Box', without normal rouletted or chattered decoration. Burnt. Small size and suggested narrow base indicate an early date of mid-late second century.

67) C11. Out-curving beaker rim probably from a folded beaker of late second-early third century (earlier than AD 225.)(Howe *et al.* 1980 no.40). Probably Lower Nene Valley. Burnt.

68) WW2. Beaker with out-curving rim and faint internal brown slip up to junction of neck. Mid-second century.

Feature 11 Hearth 69CC

69) WW3. Straight-sided bowl with groove below rim.

Feature 70 Pit 69ET

70) GW5/6 or MG3, with fine shell. Necked jar with bead rim, and band of burnished herringbone decoration around shoulder.

Feature 2 Ditch 70GY, 70GW

Samian

Form 18/31R, slightly burnt, Central Gaulish. Hadrianic or early-Antonine.

Other Pottery

71) GW5/6. Narrow-necked jar with beaded rim, and incised arc decoration on shoulder.

72) OW2. Shallow flanged dish or most probably a lid.

73) CG3B. Curved-sided bowl with incipient flange.

70 GL and GM Pottery sealed beneath footings of east wall of Building 1.

Samian

70GL

i)   Dish or bowl, from Les Martres-de-Veyre. Hadrianic-Antonine.

ii) Form 18/31R, Central Gaulish. Hadrianic or early-Antonine.

iii) -, Central Gaulish. Hadrianic or Antonine.

iv) Form 31, Central Gaulish. Antonine.

v)   Form 37, in the style of Cettus of Les Martres-de-Veyre, with ovolo Rogers B263 and a lion (O.1516). Cf. S.& S. 1958, pl.141, 16. *c.*AD135-160.

70GM

Two joining fragments of form 18/31 or 31, burnt, Central Gaulish. Hadrianic or early-Antonine.

Other Pottery

74) MO4. Mortarium with bead and down-curved flange.

Feature 6 70HB

Samian

Four fragments, two joining, form 31, Central Gaulish. Hadrianic-Antonine.

Other Pottery

75) GT3. Large storage jar. First century. cf Great Casterton I fig. 5.16.

Feature 4 Gully partly sealed by north wall of Phase 3 Building 1. 70 FW, FX, HA.

Samian

Forms 38 and 31, both burnt. Central Gaulish, Lezoux. Antonine.

Other Pottery

76) OW3 Carinated jar with corrugated upper body and flaring rim. *c.*AD 70 cf Great Casterton fort (Todd 1968b fig. 17, 34).

77) GW4. Jar with hooked bead, and band of chattered decoration on shoulder above parallel grooves. Very similar to Howe *et al.* 1980 no.9 and products of kilns at Park Farm, Stanground, Peterborough (Cooper 1989 nos.3 and 9)

78) CG3B. Straight-sided bowl with internal lid-seating.

79) MO6 Mortarium with bead and down-curved flange. Over-fired. Mid-second (-early third?).

80) CG1A Cooking pot in handmade fabric. Barrel-shaped with bead rim. Horizontal groove on upper body, and suspension holes above this drilled after firing. First century Iron Age /Transitional.

81) CG1A Handmade cooking pot. Food residues on internal surface. First century Iron Age /Transitional.

Feature 23 Triangular depression in yard 71 CE, CK, CM, CO, CX, CY, FR.

This group included the fragmentary remains of at least twelve bag-shaped beakers, six of which were cornice-rimmed, three had outcurving rims, and the remaining three had no surviving rims. Two of the beakers had applied scale decoration, one of which was cornice-rimmed (no. 82), while at least three had fine clay roughcast decoration, and again one of these had a cornice rim (no. 83). One of the roughcast beakers was clearly folded, and had roughcasting on the base. Two beakers had *en barbotine* decoration, one of which represented a hunting scene. All sherds were quite heavily abraded, which hampered vessel reconstruction, and so only two vessels are illustrated. The abraded nature of the material made fabric identification difficult, but it would appear to be all of Lower Nene Valley origin, rather than Lower Rhineland.

Samian

70 FR

i)   Eight fragments from a dish, Central Gaulish. Hadrianic or early-Antonine.

ii) Form Curle 23, Central Gaulish. Antonine.

71 CE

-, Central Gaulish. Hadrianic or Antonine.

71 CK

Form 18/31 or 31, Central Gaulish. Hadrianic or early-Antonine.

71 CM

i)   -, Central Gaulish. Hadrianic or Antonine.

ii) Two joining fragments of form 18/31R, Central Gaulish. Early- to mid-Antonine. Riveted.

iii) Form 33, Central Gaulish. Antonine.

71 CO

Form 18/31R, grooved for riveting, Central Gaulish. Hadrianic or early-Antonine.

71 CX

i)   Joining a sherd in CY. Form 30 or 37 rim, from Les Martres-de-Veyre. First half of the second century.

ii) -, burnt. Probably Central Gaulish and second century.

iii) Form 33, Central Gaulish. Antonine.

71 CY

i)   Four fragments of form 37 rim, one joining a sherd in CX.

ii) Form 18/31R, Central Gaulish. Hadrianic or early-Antonine.

Other Pottery

82) C2. Lower Nene Valley. Bag-shaped beaker with cornice

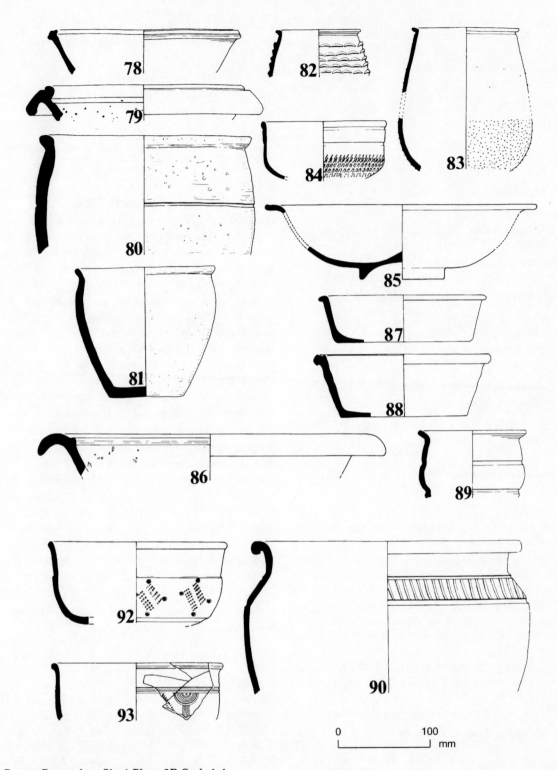

Fig. 41 Roman Pottery from Site 1 Phase 2B Scale 1:4

rim, and applied scale decoration. Late second to early third century. Rather abraded. 71 CX.

83) C2 Lower Nene Valley? Bag-shaped beaker with fine clay roughcast decoration. Mid-second century. Rather abraded. 71 CY.

There is no direct evidence for the production of roughcast beakers amongst the earliest products of the Lower Nene valley, the only kiln evidence coming from Great Casterton (Corder 1961, 50, fig.18 no.2),

although a growing number of excavated examples from Northamptonshire sites are clearly in the Lower Nene Valley fabric (for example from Ashton and Bannaventa, E. MacRobert pers. comm.).

84) C3 Copy of samian form Drag.37 (Howe *et al.* 1980 no.82), with rouletted decoration. This vessel has a much thinner body than the normal fourth century imitations, and is more likely to be part of the late second century repertoire. 71 CY.

85) GW12. Copy of samian form Drag.36 with kicked base.

The fabric is identical to that used for the so-called 'London Ware' copies of form Drag.37, also represented in Phase 2b.

86) MO4. Mortarium with bead and downcurving flange.

Feature 24 Semi-circular clay-lined depression around south side of F23.

Samian

71 DC

i) Form 18/31 or 31, Central Gaulish. Hadrianic or early-Antonine.

ii) Form 33, Central Gaulish. Antonine.

Other Pottery

87) GW3/4. Straight sided flanged bowl.71 DC. Woods 1970 fig.10 26-39.

88) CG3B. Straight-sided bowl with incipient bead and flange which is rolled down into a hook. second cent. 71 DC.

Feature 80 Depression North of Building 2, 71 CI.

Samian

i) Dish or bowl, Central Gaulish. Antonine.

ii) Form 31, Central Gaulish. Mid- to late-Antonine.

Other Pottery (Fig. 42)

89) GW4. Hard light grey fabric, mid-grey surfaces. sooting on exterior. 71 CI.

71 CS and BZ below rubble of Phase 3 stone structures beside trackway in the Inner Yard.

Samian

i) Dish, from Les Martres-de-Veyre. Trajanic or Hadrianic.

ii) Form 31, Central Gaulish. Antonine.

Other Pottery

90) GW5/6 with some shell inclusions. Necked jar with band of shoulder decoration of near vertical slashes. 71 CS.

91) GW4. Mottled grey fabric. Wide mouthed jar with beaded rim. 71 BZ. see Woods 1970 figs 14-16 esp 80-85. See MK Group 3 no.17; late first early second century.

92) GW12. Imitation Samian form Drag.37 with impressed decoration. 71 CS. London-Type ware (Perrin 1980; Howe *et al.* 1980 no.23). second quarter of the second century.

93) GW12. Imitation samian form Drag.37 with compass drawn concentric circles. 71 CS and BZ. London-Type ware as 92 above.

94) CG1A with sand. Jar with hooked bead rim. 71 CS

Samian from other Phase 2 Contexts

70 GB

Form 18/31R, Central Gaulish. Hadrianic or early-Antonine.

70 GO Feature 7 (top fill)

Form 42 (Oswald & Price 1920, pl.LIV, 7), slightly burnt, Central Gaulish. Hadrianic or early-Antonine.

70 HQ

Form 33, Central Gaulish. Three fragments, two joining, one stamped IO[. Antonine.

71 CA

i) Dish, Central Gaulish. Antonine.

ii) -, burnt, Central Gaulish. Hadrianic or Antonine.

iii) Form 31, Central Gaulish. Mid- to late-Antonine.

71 CB

-, Central Gaulish. Hadrianic or Antonine.

71 CC

i) -, Central Gaulish. Hadrianic or Antonine.

ii) Two joining fragments of form 33, Central Gaulish. Antonine.

71 CF

Form 18/31, Central Gaulish. Mid- or late-Antonine.

71 CG

-, Central Gaulish. Hadrianic or Antonine.

Phases 3-5 Pottery from Building 1 and Associated Structures (Fig. 42 and 43)

While ceramic refuse resulting from the third and fourth century masonry phases of occupation on the site makes up the bulk of the material excavated, very little of it is securely stratified due to both the lack of subsequent activity that might seal it, and the extent of plough damage. Most was completely unstratified in the ploughsoil or lay either directly on the cobbled yard surface or within the masonry building rubble. Occasionally sherds are clearly stratified beneath masonry structures attributable to Phases 4 and 5, and these help to define the chronology of the subsequent developments of the Phase 3 Building 1.

The Well (EPR 1970 EY, FO) (fig.42)

This represents the only securely stratified large group from the masonry phases of the site. The majority of the pottery formed the primary filling of the well (70 EY), at a depth of below 2.05m, which was also the water level at the time of the excavation. The pottery was not unduly affected by the water. A total of 279 sherds weighing 9.771 Kg, and with an EVEs value of 7.97 was excavated and found to belong to 21 substantially complete vessels. The quantification of the group by fabric is illustrated in Table 15.

Fabric	No.Sherds	%	EVES	%	Weight(g)	%
C2	67	24.0	1.75	22.0	1323	13.7
C3	7	2.5	-	-	41	0.5
C2/11	46	16.5	0.74	9.5	450	4.7
C17	8	3.0	0.58	7.5	200	2.1
Comb. NVCC	**128**	**46.0**	**3.07**	**39.0**	**2014**	**21.0**
WW3	3	0.8	0.39	5.0	10	0.2
MO6	1	0.2	0.65	8.0	43	0.8
Comb. WW/MO	**4**	**1.0**	**1.04**	**13.0**	**53**	**1.0**
GW4 (LNVGW)	120	43.0	2.9	36.0	4869	49.8
GW1	2	1.0	-	-	7	0.2
Comb.GW	**122**	**44.0**	**2.9**	**36.0**	**4876**	**50.0**
CG1	20	7.5	0.03	0.3	1573	15.0
CG1B (S.Mid)	5	1.5	0.93	11.7	1255	13.0
Comb.CG	**25**	**9.0**	**0.96**	**12.0**	**2828**	**28.0**
TOTAL	**279**	**100%**	**7.97**	**100%**	**9771**	**100%**

Table 15: *Quantification of Roman Pottery from Primary Fill of Phase 3 The Well*

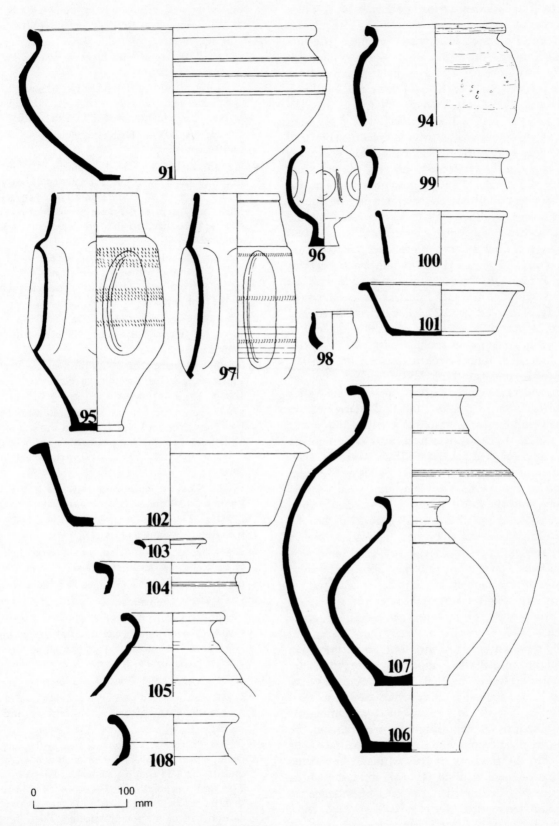

Fig. 42 Roman Pottery from Site 1 Phase 2B and Phase 3 Well Scale 1:4

The group is dominated by burnished grey wares (44% by sherd count, 50% by weight and 36% by Eves) and Lower Nene Valley colour-coated wares (46% by sherd count, 21% by weight, and 39% by EVEs), the remaining pottery comprising the rim of a parchment ware (self-coloured ware) bottle and three shell-tempered vessels.

The dating of the group would appear to lie in the last quarter of the third century at the earliest and may possibly extend into the early fourth. It falls at a point before the establishment of the late Lower Nene Valley colour-coated ware repertoire in the late third and fourth century, which otherwise dominates the late material from the site with colour-coated versions of formerly grey ware types such as plain rimmed, bead and flange bowls, and necked jars (Howe *et al.*1980 nos. 87, 79, and 75-77 respectively). Of those only the necked jar is represented. Interestingly there are both grey ware and colour-coated versions of flanged bowls of Lower Nene valley origin. While the flanged bowl is quite a common Lower Nene Valley grey ware product (Howe *et al.* 1980 nos. 17/18) it does not emerge as one of the staple colour-coated products in the fourth century range, and appears to be replaced by the ubiquitous bead and flange bowl (Howe *et al.* 1980 no.79), which itself was rarely produced in grey ware (Howe *et al.* 1980 no.21). How chronologically strict this progression is, is uncertain, but it would tie in with the similar progression in black-burnished ware bowls of Gillam Types 220, 227, and 228. The lack of Howe *et al.* 1980 no.79 may thus support a later third rather than fourth century date for the group.

The indented, funnel-necked beakers, 95 and 97, belong to the mid-late third century range of colour-coated beakers produced in the Lower Nene Valley (Howe *et al.* 1980, 18, nos.38-9 and 42-3), deriving from the East Gaulish form produced at Trier, and imported during the third century, to which no.97 is particularly closely paralleled. There is no evidence so far for their production at the Lower Nene valley kilns at Stibbington, and so it is perhaps unlikely that such beakers continued into the fourth century. However, no.96 is problematic and may be fourth century in date. It derives ultimately from the other main East Gaulish import, the globular or 'motto' beaker, which were closely imitated in the Lower Nene Valley in the third century, with the addition of alternate circular and slit folds possibly being a feature of the later forms.

The group of narrow-mouthed jars nos.104-107, are in fabric GW4, Lower Nene Valley grey ware, and probably represent some of the latest products of that strand of the industry which appears to cease in the later third century (Howe *et al.* 1980). All four examples have a highly lustrous metallic finish, which would, in part, appear to be due to burnishing, but is predominantly due to a slightly higher firing temperature, and the probable application of a thin slip over the surface. The jars fit into the tradition of East Midland burnished wares first outlined by Todd (1968a), and although he states correctly that there is no direct kiln evidence for their production in the Lower Nene Valley (1968a, 198), the fabric indicates that they clearly originate from there.

95) C2. Indented beaker with bands of chattered decoration around the body, which has been executed after the colourcoating had been applied, causing it to smear and wear away. Howe *et al.* 1890 no.43, mid- to late third century.

96) C2. Small funnel-necked or bulbous indented beaker similar to Howe *et al.* 1980 nos.52/53, with circular folds framed by narrow slit folds or grooves. Rather crudely executed vessel. Later third or fourth century?

97) C2. Indented beaker with funnel neck, and single chattered bands across the body. Howe *et al.* 1980 no.43. Mid-late third century.

98) C3. Lower Nene Valley. Small cup with upright rim, in a coarse orange fabric with white calcareous `splashes'. An unusual type with no parallels. Fourth century? 70 FO .

99) C2. Necked jar with bead rim. Howe *et al.* 1980 no.75, fourth century.

100) C2. Straight-sided bowl with bead rim. An unusual form in this fabric, possibly based loosely on a copy of samian form Drag.30 or 37? Vessel is thin-bodied suggesting that it does not belong to the main run of thick-bodied bowls and jars produced in the fourth century. Later third century? 70 EU

101) C2. Straight-sided flanged bowl without bead. Colour-coated version of Howe *et al.* 1980 no.18. The slope of the sides creates a lid-seating ledge internally. Late third-early fourth century.

102) C2. Colour-coated version of Howe *et al.* no.18. Similar to no.101 above, but larger and lacking internal lid-seating.

103) WW2. Out-curving rim, with red painted band around upper edge. Probably from a narrow necked jar or bottle (Howe *et al.* 1980 no.94/95).

104) GW4. Rim of necked jar in East Midlands burnished grey ware (Todd 1968a), produced in the Lower Nene Valley and identical in appearance to 105-7 below. High firing temperature give almost metallic grey finish to surface.

105) GW4. Narrow-mouthed jar with neck and shoulder grooves. Surface has very lustrous metallic appearance.

106) GW4. Large narrow-mouthed jar in burnished grey ware, with neck and shoulder grooves.

107) GW4. identical to 106, but smaller and slightly more globular. Highly burnished surface.

108) GW4. Necked, narrow-mouthed jar with bead rim.

109) GW4. Necked jar with bead rim. Howe *et al.* 1980 no.8 . Highly fired, giving lustrous appearance to surface.

110) GW4. Flanged bowl with internal lid-seating ledge. Howe *et al.* 1980 no.17. Darker grey surface produced by a thin slip coating which gives a lustrous appearance.

111) GW4. Flanged bowl. Howe *et al.* 1980 no.18.

112) GW4. Plain-rimmed dish or dog dish. Howe *et al.* 1980 no.19, with unusually thick base. second or third century. 70 EQ .

113) CG1B. Necked jar or cooking pot, in the soapy fabric characteristic of the late Roman shell-tempered products of the south Midlands e.g. Harrold, Beds. (Brown 1994). This form has an elongated squared-off bead rim rather than the typical hooked bead of the jars common in the second half of the fourth century. There is a groove immediately under the neck, and two more at the shoulder. This vessel may indicate a date in the first half of the fourth century.

114) CG1B. Similar in form and appearance to 113, with a more pronounced neck and elongated or everted bead rim. First half of the fourth century? Form is very similar to Lower Nene Valley grey ware (Howe *et al.* 1980 no.7) usually given a third century date.

Pottery from Site 2

A total weight of 32.5kg of pottery was retrieved from the site of which 5.962kg were stratified. This relatively small assemblage was in generally poor condition, with a high level of abrasion and plough-bashing evident, and there were few joins between sherds and few reconstructable vessel profiles. The plough damage to the site disturbed much of the pottery, and consequently a lot of that described as stratified, save that from the well, is not securely sealed. The quantification of the stratified material by weight is illustrated in Table 16.

Fabric	Wt(g)	%
C12 (Lezoux)	2	0.04
C2/3 (LNVCC)	2426	41
C7?	12	0.2
C13 (Oxford RCC)	10	0.2
OW9 (Hadham)	15	0.3
OW2	2	0.04
MO6 (LNVM)	448	8
BB1	63	1
GW4 (LNVGW)	226	4
GW3/5/6/9	719	12
CG1B (S.Mids)	826	14
Other CG	1213	20
TOTAL	**5962**	**100**

Table 16: *Quantification by Fabric of Stratified Pottery from Site 2*

The stratified material comes mainly from the rubble filling around the hypocaust in room 8, and from rubble layers within each room. The condition of this pottery does not suggest that it is a primary deposit, and may have been integrated from ploughsoil or levelling up after the building fell into disuse. The presence of Roman pottery and other domestic rubbish in the building at all, needs explaining if the postulated period of re-use as a church and/or cemetery in the Middle Anglo-Saxon period is to be supported. Such re-use would presumably have entailed the clearing out of any rubbish that had accumulated during the immediate post-Roman abandonment.

There is no material from contexts pre-dating the final phase masonry building since there was insufficient time to excavate the building fully, and so it is assumed that the pottery belongs predominantly to the period of use and abandonment of the final phase building. Despite its condition, the assemblage is very homogeneous in character, and dates almost exclusively to the fourth century, with an emphasis on the second half of the fourth century since hooked-bead rim jars in South Midlands shell-tempered ware (CG1B) are common, and do not gain wider distribution from their known production centre at Harrold, Beds., until this time (Brown 1994).

However, both pottery and coins indicate that there was activity on the site in the third century, although the samian ware present may well be residual (13 small sherds weighing only 90g less than 0.3% of the assemblage by weight). It all belongs to later forms, of Antonine or later date, which are not well represented on Site 1. There is however very little pottery of a comparatively early date, and this is particularly noticeable among the products of the nearby Lower Nene Valley industry.

Not surprisingly, the Nene Valley colour-coated ware forms belonging to the later third and fourth century repertoire produced in the Stibbington area, dominate the assemblage. Of the stratified material, 2.426 kg (41%) comprised these forms, of which Types 79 (bead and flange-rimmed bowl) and 87 (plain-rimmed dish) were the most common, along with necked, wide-mouthed jars of Types 75-77. In comparison, the range of imitation samian forms 31, 36, 37, 38 and, 45 (Types 80-84 respectively) are conspicuous by their absence, with only a few examples of Type 80 present. This may support the dating of much of the assemblage to the second half of the fourth century, as Types 81 and 82 are not thought to have been produced after c.AD 350 (Perrin 1981).

In contrast Lower Nene Valley colour-coated forms belonging to the later second and third centuries are rare on Site 2. Cornice or plain rims are absent, as is any form of *en barbotine* decoration. Where decorated beaker sherds occur, the decoration is of white painted scroll over the colour-coat, which is unusual before the middle third century, although the technique probably overlapped rather than superseded *en barbotine* (Howe *et al.* 1980). Beaker rims when present, derive from funnel neck with bead rim forms of Howe *et al.* 1980 no. 50 which are copies of the globular beakers from Trier (Niederbiebe Type 33) dating c.AD 250 onwards. The earliest beaker form present is a plain folded beaker with a short funnel with beaded rim probably a variant of Howe *et al.* no. 42 dating to the middle third century. The illustration of Lower Nene valley types is restricted to forms not represented in Howe, Perrin and Mackreth (1980), and not widely recognised elsewhere.

Other Fine wares

Besides samian ware, the only evidence of continental imports was provided by a sherd of a Central Gaulish folded beaker from Lezoux probably dating to the early third century.

Three sherds of Hadham ware (OW9, burnished) belonging to a bossed form (Going 1987) were present as were seven sherds of Oxford red colour-coated ware (C13) including a copy of Drag.37 with stamped rosette decoration.

Compared with its contribution to the Phase 2 and 3 groups from Site 1, Lower Nene Valley grey ware (GW4) makes up only a small part of the Site 2 assemblage (4%), and grey wares overall make up only 16%. This would tend to support the predominantly fourth century nature of the assemblage as the Lower Nene Valley switches to colour-coating its more robust grey ware forms during the later third and early fourth century, to produce a flexible 'oven-to-table' ware. At the other end of the spectrum the cooking pot function of the grey wares is squeezed by the increasing contribution of the shell-tempered products of the south midlands which contribute 14% to the overall share of 34% taken by shell-tempered wares.

The 1% share taken by Dorset black burnished ware (BB1), is also worth noting (one G.329 dish is represented), as while it demonstrates the easterly penetration of the ware, a comparison with its role in Leicester (up to 10-15% R. Pollard pers.comm.), shows that it did not reach far into the countryside.

Pottery from Site 3

A total weight of 4.45kg of pottery was retrieved from the excavations in 1967, 69, and 70. 2.88kg (65%) was derived from stratified Roman features excavated in 1967, comprising a ditch, pit, and the fill of Grave 11, and the fill of the Anglo-Saxon sunken-featured building 1, and the ditch excavated in 1969 and 70. The remainder of the pottery is unstratified and comprises predominantly small and abraded sherds.

Stratified Material

The stratified material suggests occupation during the first and second centuries AD. However the unstratified material includes sherds belonging to Lower Nene Valley colour-coated forms of later third and fourth century date, as does the fill of sunken-feature Buildings 1 and 2, and this presumably derived from the late Roman occupation phases on Site 1, 150m to the west.

The Ditch (fig. 43)

115) MG3. Wheel-thrown jar, with horizontal combing.

116) MG3. Squat jar with horizontal combing.

Other fabrics present include GW4 (Lower Nene Valley grey ware) suggesting that, unless intrusive, the group extends into the middle of the second century.

The Pit

117) GW3 carinated bowl/jar with band of lattice decoration defined by neck cordons.

118) GW3 Jar with everted rim and shoulder cordon.

119) MG3 Jar with lid-seated rim.

120) CG1A or B. Necked jar with beaded rim. Very similar to the form typical of the Late Roman shell-tempered ware CG1B, which is widespread in the Midlands and South of England during the fourth century. However, the hooked bead is not so fully developed, the fabric is not characteristically soapy, and there is no fine rilling on the external surface. If the vessel is indeed of late date then it is intrusive.

Fill of Grave 11

121) CG 1A. Large storage jar with oxidised orange fabric, and incised decoration.

Pottery from Site 5

A total weight of only 2.92kg of pottery was excavated from the site in 1968. The material is largely unabraded and of broadly fourth century date, but none is securely stratified, as far as the excavation records indicate. The quantified breakdown of the fabrics present measured by weight is illustrated in Table 17.

Fabric	Wt(g)	%
C2 (LNVCC)	2175	74.4
C13 (Oxford RCC)	40	1.4
MO6 (LNVM)	10	0.2
GW4 (LNVGW)	177	6
GW3/5/6/9	267	9
CG1B	253	9
Total	**2922**	**100**

Table 17: *Quantification of Roman Pottery from Site 5*

The assemblage is dominated by Lower Nene Valley colour-coated ware (fabric C2) which accounts for 74% of the pottery and consists solely of later third and fourth century forms including jars and bowls (Howe *et al.* 1980 nos.75/6, 79, 83, and 87), and beakers (Howe *et al.* 1980 nos.49 and 55/56). In contrast, Oxford Red colour-coated ware (fabric C13), accounts for only 1% of the assemblage. The presence of fabric GW4 of Lower Nene valley origin (6%) amongst the grey wares (15% overall) suggests third century occupation, but the shell-tempered wares (9%) are all of the fabric CG1B, reinforcing the overall fourth century date.

Pottery from Site 6 (fig. 44)

A total weight of 7.6kg of pottery was retrieved from Site 6 (this figure does not include four vessels that were unavailable for study), nearly all of which was derived from the lower filling of the well, with an additional vessel coming from the H-shaped corn drier.

Stratified Material

The well

A small group of eight substantially complete vessels was retrieved from the lower fill (bottom to 0.75m) of the stone-lined well. The group probably dates to the earlier part of the fourth century.

122) C2. Girth and base of bottle, with wavy white paint decoration running vertically.

123) C2/3. Lower half of bottle or narrow mouthed jar.

124) C2/3 Base of bottle or narrow-mouthed jar in an orange fabric. The external surface coating is highly lustrous varying from purple to metallic green. Probably a waster or 'second' as shape is distorted.

125) GW5 Narrow-mouthed jar with collared rim and neck cordon. Scars on neck and rim indicate the presence of two or possibly 3 handles. Decoration comprises burnished bands and wavy lines.

126) GW5 Narrow-mouthed jar with ribbed rim, and lustrous surfaces.

127) GW6/9 cooking pot with outcurving rim.

128) CG1 Jar with beaded rim.

129) GW4 Plain rimmed dish. Howe *et al.* 1980 no.19 .

The Corn drier

130) C11. ?Lower Nene Valley. Undecorated funnel-necked bulbous beaker with matt orange colourcoat.

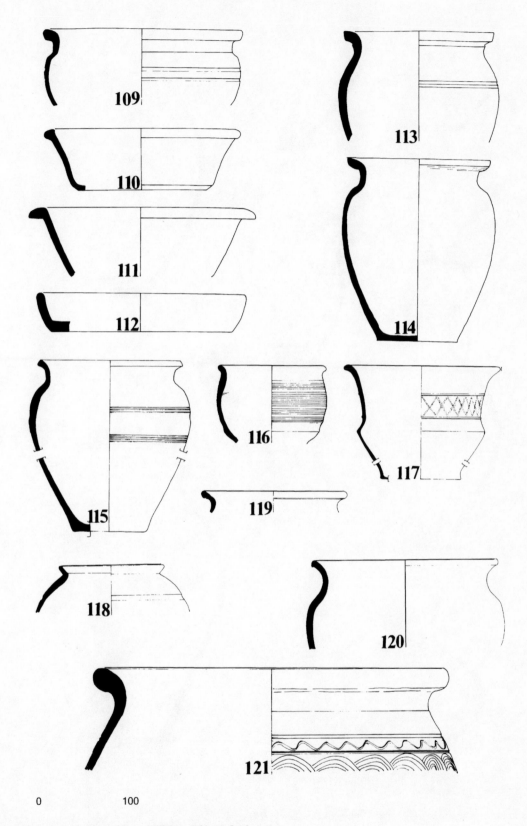

Fig. 43 Roman Pottery from Site 1 Phase 3 Well and Site 3 Scale 1:4

Pottery from Burial associated with Site 1 (fig.44)

Grave 5R (stone coffin burial)

Four vessels were associated with this burial, and had been placed outside the foot of the coffin. All the vessels suggest a fourth-century date.

131) C2. Large narrow-mouthed jar with beaded rim, and shoulder grooves. Similar to Howe *et al.* 1980 no.70.

132) C2. Upper part of funnel-necked beaker with traces of white paint decoration on shoulder. Howe *et al.* 1980 no.54.

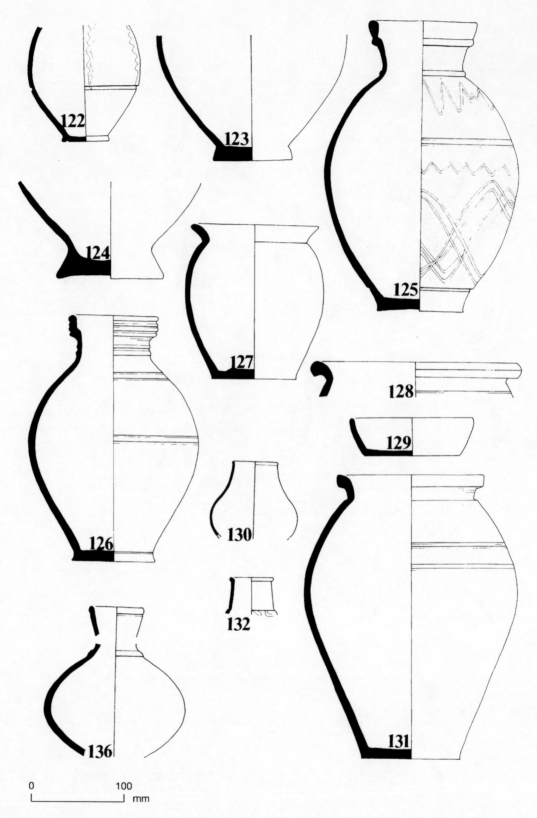

Fig. 44 Roman Pottery from Site 6 Well and Roman Burials Scale 1:4

133) C2. Three large joining sherds from a large funnel necked beaker of 'pentice-moulded' type with rouletted decoration around the body (Howe *et al*. 1980 nos 56/57). Not illustrated. The freshness of the breaks suggest that these sherds derived from a complete vessel that was damaged by the reservoir grading machinery, and that therefore not all of the vessel was retrieved.

134) C2. Complete base and rim sherds of a large bead and flanged bowl (Howe *et al*. 1980 no.79). Not illustrated. As 133, probably a complete vessel, not all of which was retrieved.

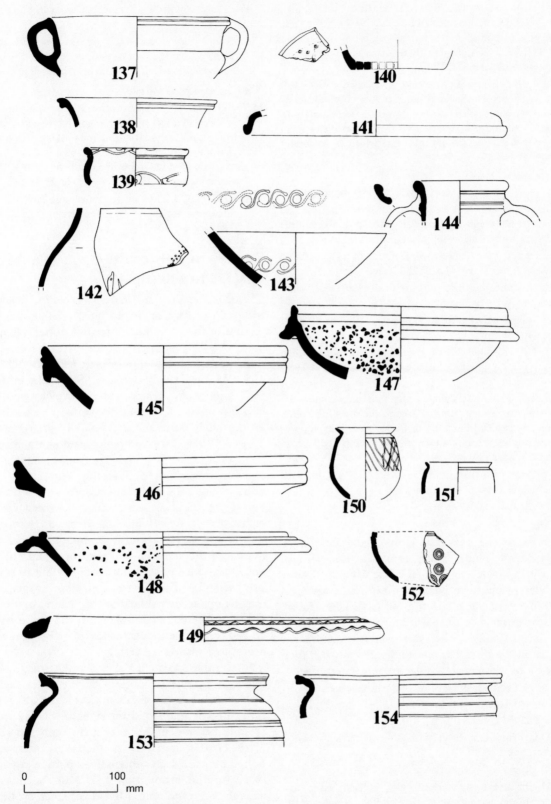

Fig. 45 Roman Pottery of Intrinsic Interest Scale 1:4

Pottery from Burials associated with Site 2

Grave 7R: Stone coffin burial

135) C2 Abraded sherds forming the complete base of large jar. Not illustrated.

Grave 8R

136) C2. Globular bottle with flaring rim. Similar to Howe *et al.* 1980 no.69. Abraded.

Pottery of Intrinsic Interest (fig.45)

Pottery from unstratified contexts or unillustrated groups of intrinsic interest from all sites. This has been arranged by ware type.

Samian Ware

Two samian stamps were recovered from unstratified contexts on Site 1.

i) Site 1 1969 Sf. no. 167. Form 31, heavily burnt, stamped ALBVC[I.OF]: Albucius ii of Lezoux, Die 3a. There is no site dating for the stamp, but its use on forms such as 18/31R, 27, 31R, 79 etc. R and occasionally, 18/31 suggests a range c.AD150-180.

ii) Site 1 1969 Sf. no. 169. Form 33, stamped BVRDOM: Burdo of Lezoux, Die 8a. A stamp used on both forms 27 and 80, suggesting that the potter worked both before and after AD160. Stamps from other dies appear in early-Antonine groups from Castleford and Alcester c.AD140-170.

Colour-Coated Ware

137) C2. Three-handled bowl (Howe et al. 1980 no.78) of later fourth-early fifth century date. One of the range of late products of the Lower Nene Valley industry; this example lacks the more usual white paint decoration. 69AC.

138) C2. Handled jar (Howe et al. 1980 no.74). Handle scar present. Later fourth to early fifth century

139) C2. Small bowl (Howe et al. 1980 nos.85/6) with white painted scroll decoration.

140) C2. Colander derived from Howe et al. 1980 no.79 bead and flanged bowl.

141) C2. Lid with hooked rim. An unparalleled form which was probably suitable for use with Howe et al. 1980 no.79.

142) C2. Bossed sherd with white paint decoration comprising vertical strokes, and stipples around the top of the boss. Probably comes from a jug or flagon form. The stipples could possibly represent hair around the top of a face on the boss, which is now lost.

143) C2. Body of a dish of Howe et al. 1980 no.88, with internal white paint decoration.

144) C2. Handled jug or flagon.

Mortaria

Amongst the mortaria excavated from all the sites, only a relatively narrow range of rim forms was represented, and nearly all the vessels were in fabric MO6, of Lower Nene Valley origin, with black iron tap slag trituration grits. Products of the Mancetter-Hartshill kilns (fabric MO4) are confined to the earlier forms with bead and down-curved flange. The vast majority represent variations on the bead and reeded flange type, of which only the more complete examples are illustrated here.

145) MO6. Wall-sided with grooves. No trituration grits.

146) MO6. ?Devolved wall sided form with grooved surface. Site 1 69 BU.

147) MO6. Prominent bead with almost vertical reeded flange. Site 1 69 BC.

148) MO6. Bead and reeded flange. Site 1 71 AH.

149) MO6. Flanged mortarium with incised wavy line decoration. Hard orange fabric with lighter orange core; could be mis-fired Lower Nene valley product, or a Lincoln Swanpool product? Gillam 277? Late third-early fourth century. Site 1 Unstratified 70 AC.

Grey Wares

150) GW4. Bag-shaped beaker in hard off-white fabric and grey surfaces, with crude incised lattice decoration. Site 1 69 CL. Mid-second century (cf. Frere 1972,fig.117,616) and at Water Newton (Perrin 1999, 79, fig.56 nos.11-15).

151) GW12. Small bag-shaped beaker with simple cornice-type rim.

152) GW12. Fine micaceous orange-brown fabric with black, slightly burnished surfaces. Incised circle decoration. 70 AL unstratified, and 70 DT from tumble in Building 2.

Shell-Tempered Wares

153) CG1. Large jar with grooved bead rim, and shoulder grooves, in a soft shell-tempered fabric with red margins, grey core, and dark brown to black surfaces. Inside building, above ditch (AR). 69CZ. Late third-early fourth century. One other example from EPR 69 BK. Great Casterton II, 1954, fig.6,9 and 10.

154) CG1/ GW3. Similar to above but fabric is fine and micaceous with sparse fine shell tempering. Red core and dark grey surfaces.

Pottery Supply to the Gwash Valley c.AD50 to 400 (fig.46)

The quantification and analysis of selected groups across the phases of a site or group of related sites allows a picture of the changing pattern of pottery supply to be charted, and this approach has proved successful in a number of recent studies (Going 1987; Going and Ford 1988; Marney 1989; Cooper 1998b). The pottery from the Empingham sites presented a similar opportunity to create a series of ceramic phases and so data from the groups analysed in the main part of the report (Tables 13 to 17) have been simplified and summarised in the form of a series of pie-charts (fig.46) in which fabric types are quantified by EVEs for Ceramic Phases 1 to 3, and by weight for Phases 4a and 4b

It is important to bear in mind the small size of some of the groups from which the data has been drawn, as well as special behavioural (taphonomic) factors which may have dictated the make up of a particular group, and determined its variation from the 'life assemblage' in use every day. Fine wares and other specialist vessels may be under represented in the 'death assemblage' due to the care taken in curating them and the relatively high cost of renewal, and what is therefore being measured is access to replacement vessels.

Sites in the Gwash Valley would presumably have obtained supplies of pottery from markets held in the nearby small town of Great Casterton which lies four miles downstream of Empingham, having developed around the first century fort at the point where Ermine Street crosses the river. Additionally, potters may have visited individual sites themselves, particularly if they lay closer to the production site than the market. The assemblages represented by sites higher up the Gwash Valley will therefore tend to be a reflection of those excavated at Great Casterton. Although no comparable quantification data exists for the assemblages excavated by Corder, the catalogues reveal the range of material available to the lower part of the valley, and so qualitative comparisons can be made. The assemblage excavated from the Roman settlement at Whitwell (de Bethune 1981) immediately upstream of the Empingham sites also allows comparison with a site of similar status.

Fabric	CP1 c.50-100 F50 Ditch 5.5 EVEs % EVEs	CP2 c.100-200 F1 Ditch 22.4 EVEs % EVEs	CP3 c.200-300 Ph.3 Well 8.0 EVEs % EVEs	CP4a c.300-400 Site 5 3kg %Wt.	CP4b c.350-400 Site 2 6kg %Wt.
Samian		10			
C		1	39	76	41
WW/OW		21	5		<1
MO			8		8
GW	9	45	36	15	16
BB1					1
MG	25				
CG	66	23	12	9	34
Totals	100	100	100	100	100

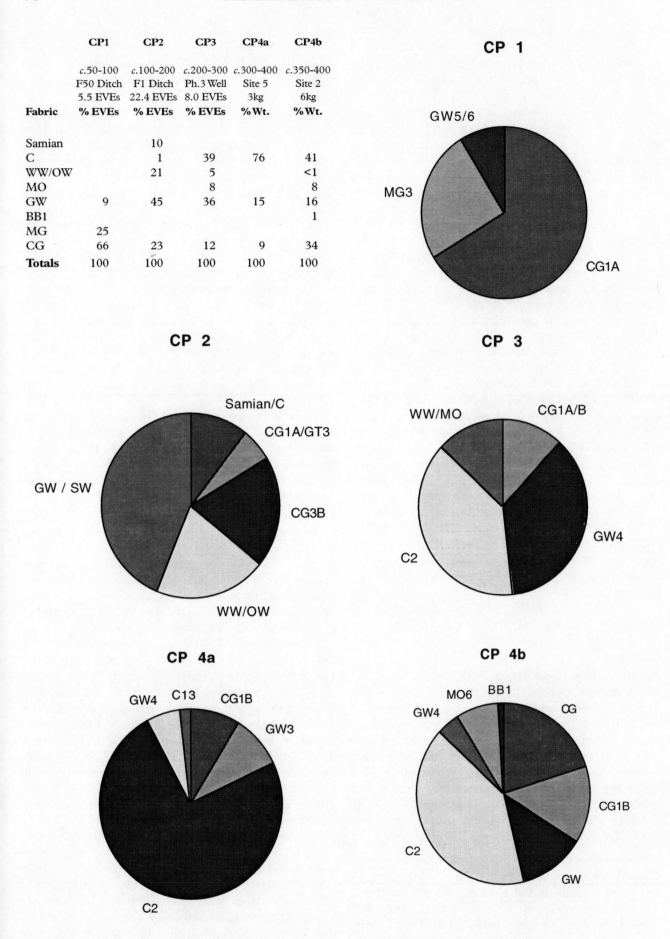

Fig. 46 Roman Pottery Supply to the Gwash Valley c.AD 50-400

Ceramic Phase 1 c.AD50 to 100

The Phase 2A group from Site 1, (fig.46) would tend to indicate that pottery supply to the Gwash Valley during this period was confined to a narrow range of coarse/transitional grey wares (MG3, 25%; GW6, 9%) and a mix of handmade and wheel-thrown shell-tempered wares (CG1A 66%) supplied almost exclusively as jars, and for which the production sites are unknown but presumably local. However, the other published assemblages of this date from the valley indicate that this is a rather conservative impression. Notable differences can be discerned in comparison with the neighbouring site at Whitwell, for example. Although the amount of samian from Whitwell is less than that from the Empingham sites, six out of the eight decorated vessels and nine out of 14 plain vessels are South Gaulish and of first-century date, the earliest decorated piece being Claudio-Neronian (figures calculated from catalogue by Joanna Bird in Todd 1981, 25-26). This contrasts markedly with the complete absence of first-century samian from Empingham Sites 1 and 2. In addition the Whitwell assemblage from Enclosure Ditch 43 (de Bethune 1981, 26 and fig.14) comprised a large group of first-century vessels including a range of Belgic-type forms matching those from the fort at Great Casterton (de Bethune 1981, 26), but absent from Phase 2A on Site 1.

Whatever the reasons behind the observed differences, it is clear from the evidence from Whitwell that sites in the valley were benefiting from their proximity to the fort which was occupied from the AD 40s to late AD 70s (Burnham and Wacher 1990, 130), and more significantly in the long term, the north-south route way of Ermine Street, that brought an exotic range of wares intended for the military market, within easy reach of the civilian population. It is not certain to what extent the River Gwash itself was navigable, but presumably trackways, of the kind excavated on Site 3 ran along the valley sides and gave easy access to Great Casterton.

Ceramic Phase 2 c.AD100 to 200

The quantified picture of supply illustrated (fig.46), is derived from the material in Ditch F1 (Site 1, Phase 2B) and reflects the situation in the middle decades of the period, by which time the pattern has changed considerably, and a number of key producers are identifiable. Since this period is the only one during which imports (dominated by Central Gaulish samian) make any kind of impression on the pattern of supply to the Empingham sites (11%), the discussion of the samian has been placed in this section of the report.

Samian Ware discussion by Brenda Dickinson.

With the exception of the two first century sherds from Site 3, it is possible that all the samian from Sites 1 and 2 is second century in date. The bulk of it comes from Lezoux, but there are a few sherds (all from site 1) from Les Martres-de-Veyre, including one from a bowl by the Hadrianic-Antonine potter, Cettus. The two South Gaulish pieces certainly belong to the later exporting period of La Graufesenque and will be Trajanic. The three sherds of East Gaulish ware (two of which come from Site 2) probably all from Rheinzabern, need not in theory be much later than AD160.

Much of the plain ware can only be loosely dated to the Hadrianic or early-Antonine period, but Antonine form 31s feature prominently and this suggests that the rouletted dishes of form 18/31R, also fairly numerous, may be contemporary with them, rather than Hadrianic. They should not be later than c.AD160, however. The absence of forms 31R and 45, both first made in the later second century, could be significant, though there are two examples of form 79 (both of which come from Site 2), which should fall within this range. On this evidence it seems likely that the East Gaulish ware is also second century, rather than later. It must be noted, however, that the quantity of samian recovered from the sites is really too small for reliable statistical analysis.

On the evidence of the plain ware the samian should go beyond AD160, but the scarcity of anything demonstrably later suggests the possibility of a change in the nature of Site 1 in the last few decades of the second century.

The material from Site 2 is all of Antonine or mid- to late-Antonine date, and taking into consideration the lack of other contemporary pottery on the site, it is possible that the samian (which is all unstratified), represents survival material, and the site was not necessarily occupied at this time.

Other Pottery

In addition to the imported table wares, which also included roughcast beakers in Lower Rhineland Fabric 1 from Cologne (19), British fine wares become apparent in the Empingham assemblage at this time. Although there are no examples of Lower Nene Valley colour-coated ware products from the F1 ditch group, some of the earliest beaker forms with roughcast, *en barbotine*, and scale decoration occur elsewhere in Phase 2B contexts (notably F23). While the early core of the Lower Nene Valley industry centred on *Durobrivae* lay only 12 miles away, south along Ermine Street, it is important to note the possibility of supply to the Gwash Valley from the kilns situated at Great Casterton itself. Two kilns have been identified, firstly in 1958 (Corder 1961, 50 and fig.18) and secondly in 1966 (Whitwell and Dean 1966, 46), which were producing a range of colour-coated vessels including beakers and 'castor box' casseroles during the later second century and into the early third.

Another distinctive, locally-produced, fineware apparent during this period is 'London-type' ware which consistently occurs in a fine, black, micaceous fabric (GW12) and includes imitations of samian form 37 (64, 92, and 93) with incised and impressed decoration similar to the range identified by Perrin (1980), and in one instance, form 36 with a kicked base (85). On evidence from the Nene Valley, such vessels appear to have been produced in the second quarter of the second century, probably as a response to declining samian supply (Howe *et al.* 1980, 10), and although production in the Nene Valley appears likely, it was not in the same fabric as the Empingham examples, for which the source remains uncertain. Other fine wares including flagons, beakers and small jars in white and oxidised fabrics contribute 21% (20-29), their production sites are unknown, although red-painted examples probably derive from the Nene Valley.

In the supply of utilitarian grey ware vessels, the Lower Nene Valley also begins to figure largely as fabric GW4 (14%) and fine and coarser light grey fabrics resembling it (GW3, 3/4, 5/6) together contribute over 45% of the overall supply. With production starting in the second quarter of the second century (Howe *et al.* 1980, 7), this signals the increasing domination of supply by products of this industry over the succeeding centuries.

However, nearly a quarter (23%) of the pottery supply still comprises shell-tempered pottery, 17% of which is in fabric CG3B (Bourne-Greetham ware) manufactured in a narrow range of jars and dishes (47-54) for which two kiln-sites have been recognised, firstly at Bourne Grammar School and secondly at Greetham excavated in 1962 (*TLAHS* **43** (1967-8), 14), the latter lying four miles to the north of the valley, while the former is situated 10 miles to the north east, on the fen edge. A preliminary typology of the products of the Bourne kiln has been constructed but is unpublished (R. Pollard unpub. Leics. Archaeol. Unit internal document), while three examples of jar forms from the Greetham kiln were published for comparative purposes in the report on the pottery from Whitwell (de Bethune 1981, fig.16.81-83). The range represented at Empingham and also recognised at Whitwell (de Bethune 1981, fig. 16.80) compare well with the excavated kiln material.

Ceramic Phase 3 c.AD200 to 300

This period of supply is represented by the Phase 3 well group from Site 1 (fig. 46) which dates to the last quarter of the third century at the earliest. While this does not provide a true reflection of the entire supply period, none of the sites produced groups dating to the first half of the third century and there does appear to be a genuine lack of any pottery that might be securely dated to the first half of the third century even amongst unstratified material. Defining earlier third-century groups is a common problem within Romano-British assemblages, and the existence of economic longwaves incorporating lag phases of low production and slow typological change has been put forward to explain it (Going 1992). The existing dating criteria used have a tendency to either pull ceramic dates back into the second century or push them into the later third and fourth centuries.

While Site 1 is, in any case, the only settlement that on excavated evidence, could have been occupied during this period, none of the pottery from Phase 2B contexts, sealed by the Phase 3 masonry structures need extend into the third century. Notably, the assemblage lacks

Lower Nene Valley colour-coated ware beakers of the later second and first half of the third century and, given the occurrence of roughcast beakers from Phase 2B, is somewhat surprising perhaps indicating a genuine break in occupation before the Phase 3 structures are built.

An examination of the pottery from the later part of the supply period represented by the well, highlights a number of differences from the mid-second century situation. The first of these concerns the complete lack of imported fine wares. While there is no evidence for samian supply extending into the third century on the Empingham sites, sherds of 'Rhenish' wares from both Trier and Lezoux are present in the Site 2 assemblage (the former being unstratified, the latter contributing just 0.04% to the assemblage by weight).

The second change concerns the supply of shell-tempered wares. While large storage jars were still produced locally, the production of Bourne-Greetham ware had ceased, to be replaced by jars which appear to be in fabric CG1B (12%, 113 and 114), and thus belonging to the South Midlands shelly ware industry for which a major production centre has been identified at Harrold, Beds., (Brown 1994). The products of this industry, which operates throughout the Roman period, become widespread across the south of Britain during the fourth century, being common at Cirencester in the west and Billingford, Norfolk to the east, being characterised by jars with hooked bead rims and flanged bowls, all with a distinctive 'soapy' fabric. The two jars lack the hooked bead of the fourth century form, being closer in form to the jars produced by the industry during the later third century (Brown 1994 Phase 4).

The remainder of the supply (88%) could all come exclusively from the Lower Nene Valley comprising colour coated ware (39%), white ware and mortaria (13%), and grey ware (36%). As has been argued above, the well group appears to fall at a transitional phase of the Lower Nene Valley industry, before the establishment of fourth century repertoire of colour-coated vessels, and possibly during the latest phases of grey ware production in the second half of the third century. By this time also, mortaria are supplied exclusively by the Lower Nene Valley (145-149), with isolated examples of Mancetter-Hartshill mortaria confined to the earlier form with bead and downcurving flange coming from Phase 2B(74).

Ceramic Phase 4 c.AD300 to 400

This period of supply is represented by the assemblages from Sites 5 (CP4a) and 2 (CP4b), (fig.46). The variation between the two, particularly with regard to the contribution of the Lower Nene Valley colour-coated ware industry (Fabric C2) ranging from 41% on Site 2 to 74% on Site 5, highlights the dangers of basing judgements on such small samples. However, the pattern of continuing domination of supply by the Lower Nene Valley is clear. While the contribution from the grey ware strand of the industry declines, it is replaced by the ubiquitous range of fourth century colour-coated wares comprising, in particular, jars, bead and flanged bowls and plain-rimmed dishes (Howe *et al.* 1980, nos. 75, 79 and 87 respectively).

While the contribution of colour-coated ware on Site 5 (74.4%) is probably exaggerated by the small sample (and perhaps by biased collection), it is clear from the huge sample of material excavated from the destruction deposit of the villa at Great Casterton that colour-coated ware could make up over 50% of an assemblage (Perrin 1981, 449). The fourth century repertoire of colour-coats functioned as both kitchen and table wares, thus negating the need for a wide range of grey wares and shell-tempered wares, which make a correspondingly smaller contribution to both groups. The destruction deposit groups from the Great Casterton villa remain, after 40 years, the most closely datable late fourth century groups from the area. The pottery was initially examined by John Gillam (Corder 1951 and 1961), and was reappraised by Perrin in order to try and establish a chronology for the fourth century products of the industry (Perrin 1981). Some of the latest products of the industry can also be identified at Empingham Site 1 including a handled bowl and jar (137 and 138) thought to date to the later fourth or early fifth century (Howe *et al.* 1980 nos.74 and 78). Proximity to the industry also led to the availability of more unusual or uncommon forms including a colander (140), a lid (141), and a closed form incorporating a large boss (142).

Colourcoated or finer wares were not exclusively supplied by the Lower Nene Valley, as Oxford red colour-coated ware (C13), and Hadham oxidised ware (OW9) are both present on Site 2 at levels of less than 1%, and on Site 5, C13 contributes 1.4%. However, such products (particularly C13) normally make a greater impression at sites more distant from their source than Empingham.

The continued presence of Lower Nene Valley grey ware (GW4) at levels of 4% and 6% perhaps indicates that the two groups are not exclusively fourth century in date, although it is not clear from present evidence how clear-cut the end of the grey ware industry was in the Lower Nene Valley towards the end of the third century (Howe *et al.* 1980, 9).

Of the remaining wares that can be provenanced at this period the mortaria from the Lower Nene maintain a contribution of between 2% and 8%, while the South Midlands shelly ware (CG1B), in the more typical fourth-century forms contribute between 9% and 14% by weight. The low contribution made by Black Burnished Ware 1 (1% on Site 2) is perhaps surprising, amounting to only two vessels from Site 2, and a single sherd from Site 1, but might be explained by the easterly location of the sites, their isolation from a major urban centre and possibly the similarity of the flanged bowl and plain rimmed dish 'casserole' combination to those produced by the Lower Nene Valley (see Allen and Fulford 1996).

The Empingham sites do not add significantly to the picture of pottery supply at the very end of the Romano-British period already painted by the destruction deposits at Great Casterton lower down the Gwash Valley, except to confirm or infer from the evidence of pottery and coins that Sites 1 and 2 were also occupied right up to the end of the fourth and quite probably an undefinable number of years into the fifth century. Without coins it is impossible to estimate how far into the fifth century normal production continued in the Lower Nene Valley, although it is clear that no new forms were introduced. What is clear from the gradual centralisation of pottery supply by the large scale industries such as Oxford and the Lower Nene Valley during the fourth century in particular is that the skills needed to produce pottery were being held in fewer and fewer hands and that economic breakdown for whatever reason would throw production back into the hands of households who had never learned how to make pots themselves. In the East Midlands at least, there seems to be little evidence for the late flowering of localised handmade industries of the kind apparent in the south (Cooper 1996a).

THE EARLY ANGLO-SAXON POTTERY

Paul Blinkhorn

Introduction

This report considers a total of 988 sherds of Early Anglo-Saxon pottery weighing 9.077kg retrieved from Sites 1, 3, 4, and 7. A total of 542 sherds of Early Anglo-Saxon pottery, weighing 5.811kg, was retrieved from stratified contexts on Sites 3 and 4. Of this total, 263 sherds weighing 3.017 kg came from the excavation of Site 3, during 1967-70, and 279 sherds weighing 2.794 kg were retrieved from Site 4 on the north side of the valley, excavated during 1971 and 1972. A further nine unstratified sherds weighing 120g were retrieved during the excavation of the Romano-British Site 1 from 1969-71, with only one sherd weighing 35g being retrieved from trial excavations on Site 2 during 1970. A further 436 sherds weighing 3.111kg were retrieved from stratified contexts on excavations at Tickencote (Site 7) in 1990.

This report deals only with the pottery considered to be from domestic contexts and therefore of domestic use; the four substantially complete vessels belonging to the grave find assemblages on Site 3 are described separately within their appropriate grave groups.

Most of the material derives from unreconstructable vessels and there is a fairly small average sherd-size (<10g). For this reason fabric analysis is particularly important in helping to form an overview of the material.

The definition of fabric groups has been kept fairly broad in an effort to accommodate the inevitable variations which occur in Early Anglo-Saxon domestic pottery. In general however, the material was quite easily classified, which is probably due to the small size of the excavated areas and the apparently short lifespan of the structures therein. Twelve fabrics have been identified within the Empingham material. The material from Tickencote (Site 7) has been placed in a separate fabric series of eight.

The Fabrics from Sites 1, 3, and 4

Fabric Descriptions

EM1: Moderate temper of sub-angular, clear, crushed metaquartzite up to 1mm, with sparse shelly limestone up to 5mm, and rare, rounded reddish brown ironstone up to 3mm.

EM2: Moderate to heavy temper of white oolitic limestone, with rounded ooliths up to 2mm. Rare Bryozoa platelets up to 2mm.

EM3: Moderate temper of angular crushed granite up to 2mm, with occasional sub-rounded reddish brown ironstone up to 3mm.

EM4: Moderate temper of angular crushed granite up to 2mm.

EM5: As EM4, with sparse to moderate chaff voids.

EM6: As EM4, with white limestone up to 0.5mm. Sparse to moderate chaff voids.

EM7: As EM1, without the shell.

EM8: Moderately heavy temper of finely crushed white metaquartzite up to 0.5mm.

EM9: Sparse to moderate temper of subangular red ironstone up to 2mm.

EM10: Moderate to heavy temper of angular, crushed white limestone upto 2mm.

EM11: Moderate temper of subrounded, white, orange and grey quartzite up to 1mm.

EM12: Soft, chaff-tempered fabric with few other visible inclusions except for very fine subangular quartz.

Pottery from Site 3 (Fig. 47 and 48)

The pottery from this site derives from the fill of three sunken-featured buildings, and a number of other associated pit features. The fabric proportions of the pottery from these contexts, quantified by weight (g) and numbers of sherds are summarised in Table 12.

Sunken-Featured Building 1

As well as Anglo-Saxon material, the fill of this feature also contained a small amount of Romano-British material, of fourth century date in Lower Nene Valley colour-coated ware fabric.

1) EM3. Upright rim from narrow-mouthed vessel.
2) EM2. Plain rim from straight sided bowl.
3) EM11. Plain rim from closed form.
4) EM8. Bowl with pinched-out, flaring rim.
5) EM8. Bowl with upright flattened rim.
6) EM7. Narrow-mouthed vessel with plain, upright rim.
7) EM4. Straight-sided bowl.
8) EM8. Upright rim from closed form.
9) EM7. Bodysherd from carinated vessel, decorated with two parallel horizontal incised grooves above the girth.
10) EM8. Bodysherd decorated with 3 horizontal, parallel incised grooves.

Sunken-Featured Building 2 (70 ZW/ZY)

11) EM8. Globular vessel form with upright rim.
12) EM3. Similar to 11.

Sunken-Featured Building 3 (1967 F.5)

13) EM4. Shouldered or globular vessel with everted, slightly lid-seated rim.
14) EM8. Globular vessel with upright, slightly outcurving rim.
15) EM7. With joining sherds from F.13. Globular vessel with upright thickened, and flattened rim. Circular perforation in neck, presumably for suspension, made after firing.
16) EM4. Bowl with flared rim.
17) EM7. Small sherd with two vertical striations and the beginnings of two vertical bosses. Possibly a carination.

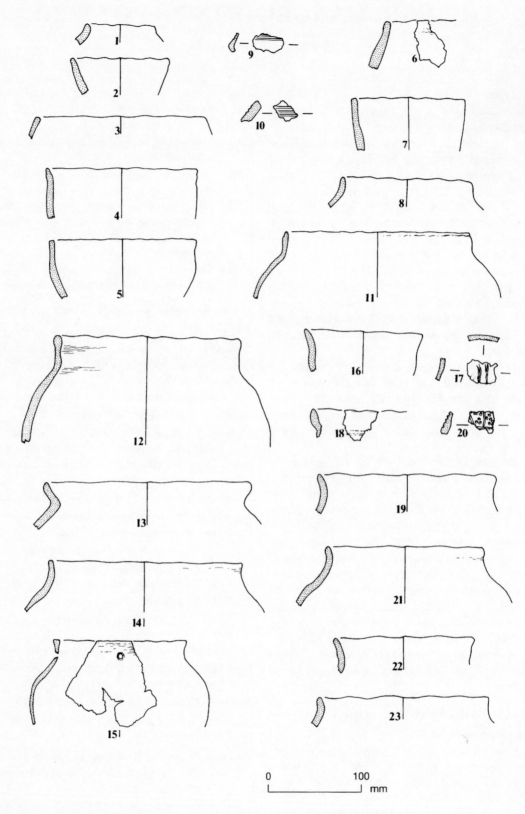

Fig. 47 Anglo-Saxon Pottery nos. 1-23 Scale 1:4

Feature 14

18) EM8. Everted rim, with rounded external surface, from narrow-mouthed vessel.

19) EM4. Flaring rim.

20) EM8. Decorated bodysherd probably from shoulder of vessel. Incised lattice and trefoil stamps; overall scheme uncertain.

Feature 15

21) EM4. Globular form with slightly flaring rim.

22) EM4. Outcurving rim.

23) EM4. Upright rim.

24) EM4. Upright rim, slightly beaded.

25) EM4. Upright rim, rolled over.

	EM1	EM2	EM3	EM4	EM5	EM6	EM7	EM8	EM9	EM10	EM11	EM12
	2	0	6	12	0	0	59	3	13	0	2	0
	20	0	55	150	0	0	625	50	105	0	15	0
	1	0	28	2	0	0	0	14	0	0	0	0
	3	0	590	10	0	0	0	245	0	0	0	0
	2	0	2	9	1	0	1	31	3	1	1	1
	10	0	15	60	10	0	10	135	15	15	5	20
	3	0	4	0	0	0	15	1	0	2	1	0
	15	0	35	0	0	0	70	5	0	10	5	0
	0	0	3	4	0	0	7	5	9	0	0	2
	0	0	90	40	0	0	100	35	270	0	0	60
	0	1	0	6	0	0	1	4	1	0	0	0
	0	50	0	47	0	0	5	16	1	0	0	0
	8	1	43	33	1	0	83	58	26	3	4	3
	48	50	785	307	10	0	810	486	391	25	25	80
	2	2	26	10	<1	0	27	16	13	<1	<1	3

*roportions of Early Anglo-Saxon pottery fabrics represented on Site 3, quantified by
nd numbers of sherds.*

w in number, the decorated and other
erds from the Site 3 assemblage are useful
rposes.

ce of a carinated bowl fragment in SFB1
fifth century date (Myres 1977), and
y do occur in small numbers in sixth and
ury contexts at Mucking, Essex (Hamerow
date is supported by the presence of a
rd, another typically fifth century decorative
The lack of stamped sherds would also
idea, although caution should be exercised
relatively small group. The decorated sherd
which would appear to be from a vessel in
panel style, suggests a date in the late fifth or
ntury.

small amount of decorated material from
unken-featured buildings and associated
s impossible to confirm their contemporaneity, but the fact that fabrics containing crushed
granite (EM3 and EM4) and quartzite (EM7 and EM8)
are common in all contexts, would tend to support the
idea. Overall, granite-tempered fabrics (EM3-6) make
up 36% of the assemblage by weight, while the major
quartzite-tempered fabrics (EM1, 7 and 8) make up
nearly 45% by weight.

While it is difficult to make a strong case for the dating
of Site 3 on the basis of the decorated sherds discussed
above, three of the substantially complete vessels from
the adjacent cemetery do add further support to the idea

that the settlement was occupied during the later fifth
and early sixth century.

The complete vessel from Grave 1, which is decorated
with bosses, lines, and dots, is similar in style to several
vessels from Loveden Hill, Lincs., (Myres 1977 No.
1355), and the general appearance of the vessel and
combination of styles, suggests that a date of the late
fifth to early sixth century would be in keeping.

The stamped vessel from Grave 5 is rather unusual,
and whilst no exact parallels can be found, the restrained
use of the stamping and the lack of linear zone decoration would suggest a date around the early sixth century
at the latest, at a time when these forms of decoration
were just coming into use.

The handled vessel is very similar in its overall
appearance to a vessel from Lackford, Suffolk (Myres
1977, no.858), which is dated to the sixth century by its
continental parallels (Myres 1977, 10), although such
comparison with vessels such as this must be treated
with a little caution, due to their otherwise unremarkable
appearance.

Pottery from Site 4 (Fig. 48)

The material from was retrieved from the fill of Sunken-
Feature Building 1 and a number of pits and gullies
associated with it. The conjectured Sunken-Feature
Building 2 was not excavated. The fabric proportions of
pottery from this site, quantified by weight (g) and
numbers of sherds is summarised in Table 19.

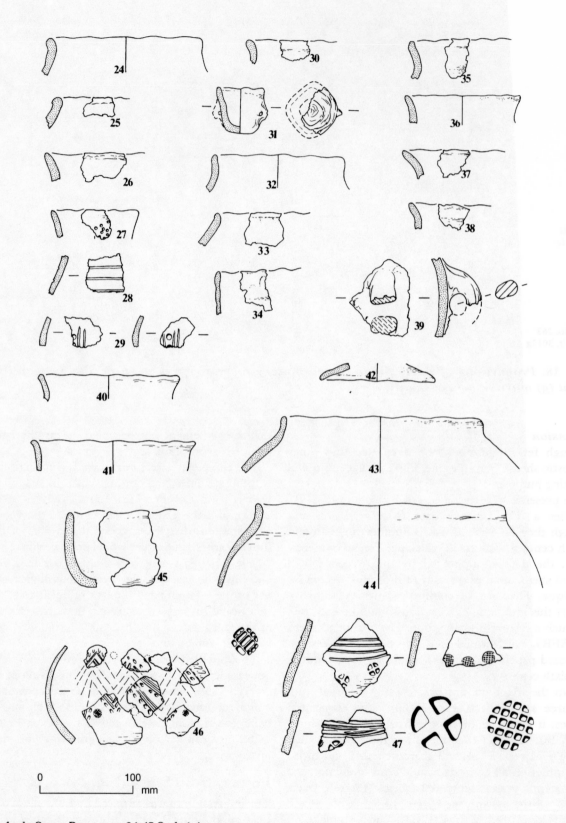

Fig. 48 Anglo-Saxon Pottery nos. 24–47 Scale 1:4

Fabric	EM1	EM2	EM3	EM4	EM5	EM6	EM7	EM8	EM9	EM10	EM11	EM12
SFB1												
(Pit G)												
No.	3	2	2	3	0	0	10	1	14	2	0	0
Wt.	10	25	25	15	0	0	55	10	45	10	0	0
Pit C												
No.	13	2	3	28	2	3	4	1	0	0	0	0
Wt.	205	40	60	465	60	50	15	5	0	0	0	0
Pit J												
No.	0	1	1	55	0	0	50	1	0	5	4	0
Wt.	0	5	5	675	0	0	475	5	0	35	10	0
Ditch FG												
No.	0	0	0	11	0	0	2	0	2	3	0	0
Wt.	0	0	0	55	0	0	15	0	10	25	0	0
72AX												
No.	0	1	2	10	1	0	3	1	0	0	2	0
Wt.	0	5	5	50	10	0	15	10	0	0	5	0
Other												
Contexts												
No.	2	0	0	21	3	0	3	1	0	1	0	0
Wt.	12	0	0	240	15	0	10	5	0	2	0	0
Total												
No.	18	6	8	128	6	3	72	5	16	11	6	0
Wt.	227	75	95	1500	85	50	585	35	55	72	15	0
%Wt	8	3	3	54	3	2	2	1	1	2	3 <1	0

Total No. 279
Total Wt. 2794g

Table 19: *The proportions of early Anglo-Saxon pottery fabrics represented on Site 4, quantified by weight in grams, and by numbers of sherds.*

Sunken-Feature Building 1 (Pit G) (72 AK, AM) (fig. 48)

26) EM11. Flaring rim.
27) EM8. Rim with punched decoration. Overall scheme uncertain.

Pit C (72AD, AG, AH)

28) EM4 but inclusions more finely crushed. Three sherds from same vessel, not joining. Incised with a maximum of three horizontal lines. Surfaces very lightly but evenly burnished.
29) EM6. Two sherds from the same vessel, not joining. Vertical incised lines with rounded, punched decoration between (plain stamps).

Pit J (Code BM)

30) EM11. Outcurving rim.
31) EM4. Lamp with pinched-out lug handles.
32) EM4. Globular vessel with upright rim.
33) EM8.
34) EM7. Straight-sided bowl.
35) EM7. Outcurving rim with tip pinched upright, possibly to form lid-seating.
36) EM4. Outcurving rim.
37) EM3. Outcurving rim.
38) EM10. Outcurving rim.

Context AL

39) Handled vessel with very sparse temper. Possibly Iron Age?

Discussion

While the small amount of decorated material from Site 4, makes precise dating of the site difficult, there are broad similarities with the range of fabrics from Site 3 which would suggest that the two sites are broadly contemporary and span the later fifth and earlier sixth century. However, the relative proportions of the two major fabric groups, may be of significance. The granite tempered fabrics make up 62% of the assemblage by weight, while the major quartzite tempered fabrics make up 30% by weight.

Pottery from Site 1 (Fig. 48)

A number of sherds were found unstratified over the area of the Roman buildings on the site.

40) EM4. Rim (71BE)
41) EM6. Rim from bowl (71BM).
42) EM4. Lid.
43) EM9. Closed form with upright rim 70ED.

The small size of the assemblage, and the lack of contemporary associated features would indicate that this material is the result of rubbish disposal from the adjacent Site 3, and the range of fabrics represented would tend to support this contention.

Pottery from Tickencote (Site 7)
(Fig. 48 & 49)

The difference in character of the pottery from this assemblage dictated that a separate fabric series was constructed, comprising eight fabrics described below.

The Fabrics

TK1: Moderate temper of subangular clear quartzite up to

0.5mm and white oolitic limestone up to 2mm. The latter is often leached out of the sherd surface.

TK2: Moderate to heavy temper of sub-angular lumps of granite up to 2mm.

TK3: As TK1, without the oolitic limestone.

TK4: As TK1, with sparse to moderate fragments of angular limestone up to 1mm.

TK5: Chaff-tempered, with sparse to moderate sub-rounded red ironstone up to 3mm.

TK6: Moderate temper of sub-angular red ironstone up to 2mm.

TK7: Chaff-tempered, with sparse to moderate subrounded quartzite up to 1mm.

TK8: Few visible inclusions.

The fabric proportions of pottery from stratified contexts was quantified by weight (g), and numbers of sherds, and is summarised in Table 20.

Fabric	TK1	TK2	TK3	TK4	TK5	TK6	TK7	TK8	Total
SFB1 (F.1)									
No.	1	3	3	0	0	0	0	0	7
Wt.	10	25	30	0	0	0	0	0	65
Feature 2.									
No.	4	1	103	7	3	1	6	1	126
Wt.	50	10	980	55	85	60	35	5	1280
FB2 (F.8)									
No.	0	3	67	0	0	169	1	0	240
Wt.	0	10	490	0	0	695	5	0	1200
Feature 10.									
No.	1	8	15	0	0	18	0	0	42
Wt.	10	65	70	0	0	220	0	0	365
Feature 11.									
No.	1	5	9	0	0	6	0	0	21
Wt.	1	40	85	0	0	75	0	0	201
Total									
No.	7	20	197	7	3	194	7	1	436
Wt.	71	150	1655	55	85	1050	40	5	3111
%Wt.	2	5	53	2	3	34	1	<1	100

Table 20: *Proportions of early Anglo-Saxon fabrics from stratified contexts on Site 7, quantified by weight (g), and numbers of sherds.*

Pottery from Sunken Feature Building 1

Pottery came from both Features 1 and 2 within the building, but predominantly from the latter.

Feature 1

This small group of seven Early Anglo-Saxon sherds, was also accompanied by six Romano-British sherds in a buff fabric. Since all of them were rimsherds it is likely that they had been specifically collected and curated for an unknown function rather than being residual.

Feature 2

44) TK3. Large rim and shoulder sherd.

45) TK4. Profile of shallow bowl.

46) TK3, with inclusions more finely crushed. Seven sherds from same vessel. Decorative scheme is uncertain, but appears to consist of pendant triangles with lines surrounded with shallow punch marks and a single grid stamp in the space between each of the triangles. Exact parallels are not known,

but the use of triangles, stamps, and dots would suggest a date in the sixth century.

47) TK3. Eight sherds from the same vessel. Overall scheme is unclear, but combed lines, and two different stamps, one a cross and the other a round grid, are used. Highly scorched surface, possibly a waster? Sixth century.

48) TK3. Single sherd decorated with three annular stamps and a horizontal combed line. Sixth century?

49) TK2. Single sherd. Pendant triangle with a single triangular grid stamp. Sixth century ?

Pottery from Sunken Feature Building 2 (Feature 8)

50) TK6. Two non-joining sherds possibly belonging to the reconstructable vessel making up the bulk of this group.

51) TK6. Single rimsherd from a cooking pot.

52) TK6. 78 sherds providing full profile of almost complete cooking pot.

53) TK3, but with very finely crushed inclusions as in no.44. 54 sherds from a stamped vessel, the form of which is uncertain, but appears to be bag-shaped with a flaring rim, rather than carinated with an upright rim. Thus, the form is closer to that of a cooking pot rather than an urn. Parallels for the form come from Fonaby, Lincs., (Myres 1969 no.1482), and Loveden Hill, Lincs., (Myres 1977 no.580). Overall decorative scheme is uncertain, but appears to be two rows of incised chevrons, with alternate chevrons filled with 'hot cross bun' stamps. No exact parallels are known, but there are similarities to Myres nos.145 and 776 (1977 figs.147 & 148). Almost certainly sixth century.

Discussion

There seems little doubt that the features from this site containing decorated pottery all date to around the middle of the sixth century, with the predominance of stamped decoration being the delineating factor. The range of fabric types would also tend to support a different dating to Sites 3 and 4. Granite tempering is almost entirely absent, while fabrics containing ironstone (TK5 and 6) form 37% of the assemblage by weight.

Overall Discussion

Taken as a whole, the ceramic material from all the sites in question is very typical of the south-east Midlands at this time. The evidence of fabric and decoration indicate that the areas of Empingham Sites 3 and 4 excavated, are not contemporary with the site at Tickencote, the former spanning the later fifth and early sixth century, and the latter dating around the middle of the sixth century.

On the sites, the most common temper consisted wholly or partially of granite, with other minerals such as ironstone and limestone present. The granite appears to be the Charnwood Forest type, which is found in pottery on many sites in the area, such as Orton Hall Farm, near Peterborough, Cambs., (Mackreth 1996). The source of the clay containing these minerals actually lies in the area to the south and west of Charnwood Forest, with sand deposits in the Soar Valley area not containing the mineral (Vince and Young 1992). The occurrence of pottery from the Gwash valley tempered with this

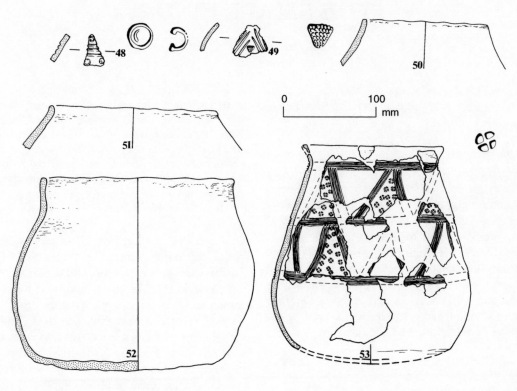

Fig. 49 Anglo-Saxon Pottery nos. 48-53 Scale 1:4

material therefore makes a useful addition to the corpus of data currently being analysed in order to resolve the question of its source.

The proposed early date for the settlement on Site 3 and 4, combined with a high proportion of granite-tempered pottery paints a picture not too dissimilar to that found by Mackreth at Orton Hall Farm (1996), and it may well be the case that pottery of this type is characteristically early on sites in this part of the Midlands.

In contrast the Tickencote assemblage contains a high proportion of ironstone tempered pottery. Fabrics containing this mineral only (EM9) represent 2-13 % of the pottery from the Empingham sites by weight, and while it does occur in other fabrics it is only as a minor constituent of the mix alongside granite or quartzite.

The presence of the two hearths on Site 7, containing slag and ironstone, suggest that iron was being smelted and so it represented a readily available raw material that may have eclipsed the more usually favoured temper.

However, the Empingham sites also lie over ironstone, and produced evidence for both the smelting and working of iron.

The most likely explanation for the observed difference may be chronological, with a gradual transition from using predominantly granite-tempered pottery in the fifth and early sixth century, towards greater use of ironstone during the sixth century. This is supported by the very low proportion of granite-tempered pottery from Site 7 (5% by weight). The range of granite-tempered fabrics also becomes smaller over time as there were four represented at Empingham and only one at Tickencote (Site 7). Most recently a large assemblage of Early Anglo-Saxon pottery has been excavated from the settlement site at Eye Kettleby, near Melton, Leics. and contains a small proportion of the ironstone tempered fabrics with the vast majority being tempered with Charnwood Forest granite (Cooper in prep.).

THE SMALL FINDS

*Shannon M. Fraser**

*with additional catalogue entries by *Nicholas J. Cooper* (nos. 29, 37, 41, 42, 44-47, 50, and 51) and *Sian Davies* (nos. 57 and 58).

Introduction

With the exception of the grave finds from the Anglo-Saxon cemetery on Site 3, all the small finds from Sites 1 to 7 have been grouped together in one report for ease of access. Therefore, while the majority of the material is of Roman date, some objects of Iron Age, Anglo-Saxon, and medieval date are included. The artefacts are arranged within functional categories, a method which is perhaps more informative than categorisation by material, and which has been refined by Nina Crummy (1983). Metals which had not been conserved at the time of writing were identified by chemical spot-testing.

Objects of Personal Adornment or Dress
(Figs. 50-52)

Brooches

1) Site 1, 1969.147.
Fragment of a copper alloy bow brooch, Hod Hill type. Lateral lugs at base of bow, which is decorated with three lines of longitudinal moulding. Both lugs are damaged. Strong cross-mouldings at junction of bow and foot. Only upper tip of catchplate remains. Length 26mm, maximum width 11mm.
The Hod Hill type is found in Britain from the Conquest to *c.*AD 65; exact parallels are not common (Mackreth 1973, 26).

2) Site 1, 1970.322 Unstratified.
Complete cast copper alloy 'head-stud' bow brooch, Lamberton Moor type (Hull 1968, 82). Extremely well preserved. Hinged pin with solid catchplate. Bow of flat, sub-rectangular section, with circular stud at head cast solid with the bow, and foot decorated with transverse moulding. Fixed head-loop for the attachment of a chain; ribbed arms. Possible traces of black enamel remain in head-stud. Bow decorated with lozenges of yellow enamel bounded on either side by triangles of red enamel; the iron in the latter has concealed most of the colour in green corrosion products. Transverse grooves above foot. Length 47.5mm, width at arms 17mm.

This is a British type, fashionable from the AD 70's through the second century. Such brooches were often worn in pairs high up on the shoulders, linked by a chain. A very similar brooch, both in colour and decoration, was found at Balkerne Lane, Colchester, in a context dated *c.* AD 80/85 to 100 (Crummy 1983, 13). Crummy notes that the head-stud cast solid with the bow is not an early feature of these brooches (1983, 13).

3) Site 3, 1967.84 Roman Ditch.
Complete copper alloy bow brooch, Sawfish type (Hull 1968, 82-3). Probably tinned. Hinged pin with solid catchplate. Bow of convex section, with crouching dog crest at head attached by a rivet. Dog's tail forms a loop, probably for the attachment of a chain. Circular stud at foot faces forward. Arms decorated with a single longitudinal groove at each end; lead or tin solder visible at each end, holding axis bar in place. Bow decorated with lozenges of copper alloy, bounded on either side by triangles of enamel (probably originally red, but now covered in green corrosion products) and by a longitudinal groove. Each side of the bow is edged with projecting 'teeth'. Length 39mm, width at arms 24mm.

Although the Sawfish brooch is geographically widespread, it is not a common find (Hattatt 1985, 96). This is a fine example of the type, and comes early in a series beginning in the Flavian period, and most likely continuing well into the second century. In later examples the dog devolves into a thin, flat crest (Hull 1968, 83, and pl. 29). The riveting of the dog crest to the head would seem to be a fairly unusual feature, as Hattatt notes in his discussion of an example of cruder design from Northamptonshire (1985, 96;99).

4) Site 3, 1967
Copper alloy bow brooch, Dolphin type. Metal stripped, with only the core remaining. Zinc and tin present in alloy. Hinged pin missing; seemingly solid catchplate damaged. Strongly arched bow of convex triangular section tapers towards plain foot. Pronounced central rib and very faint bulge on either side of the head. A single piece of wood, now fragmented, was recovered from within the arms. Length 41mm, width at arms 24mm.

The bulges at the head are a form of decoration most often seen on brooches of the Polden Hill group (Hull 1968, 79). A good parallel was recovered during excavations at the Romano-British settlement at Rotherly (Pitt Rivers 1888, pl. 98.10). An example with rather more extreme features comes from Wylye (Mackreth 1973, 20). The type dates from the late first to the mid-second century. The discovery of wood within the arms is interesting. It would not appear to be modern as both ends were sealed with mud; it may be the case that small wooden plugs were inserted into the arms of the brooch to keep the axis bar firmly in place.

5) Site 1, 1970.328. NW corner of Building II. Depth 0.1m below top of pitching. 2865 6559.
Complete copper alloy penannular brooch, with pin and ring apparently of different alloys (G.Morgan, pers. comm.). Extremely well preserved. Fowler type Aa (1960, 150). Strongly humped pin with well-defined, moulded tongue, moving freely on ring; top flattened and wrapped around ring. Flattened terminals slightly distended. Internal diameter 23mm, pin length 31mm.

6) Site 1, 1969.148.
Fragment of a copper alloy penannular brooch. Probably Fowler type D2, or possibly type E – her small, zoomorphic brooch (1969, 152-3). End of ring turned back on itself to

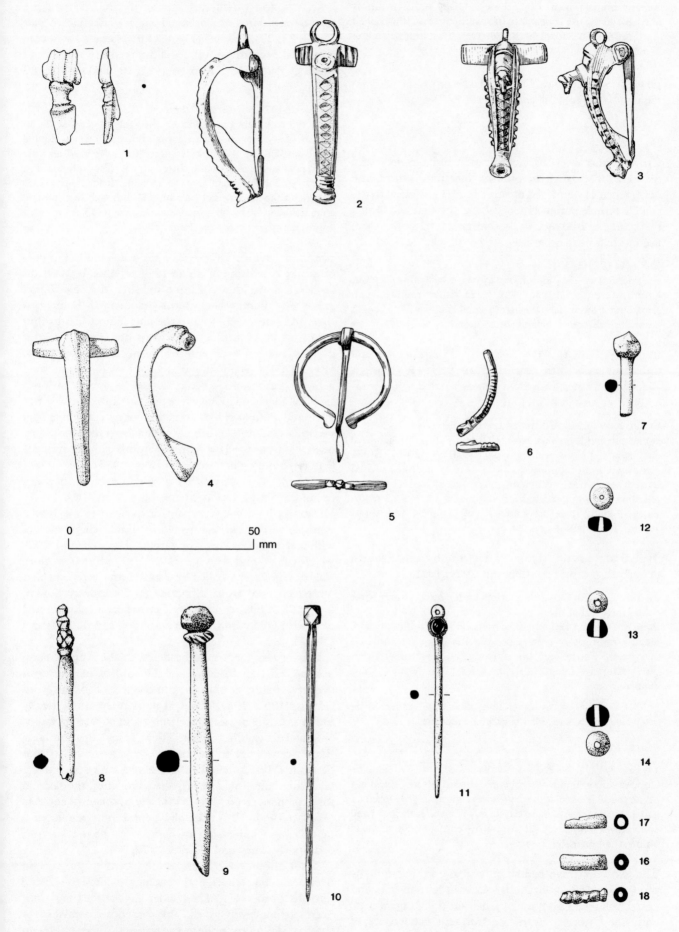

0   50
                         mm

Fig. 50 Objects of Personal Adornment and Dress 1–18 Scale 1:1

create terminal which is both longitudinally and transversely notched, giving the appearance of an animal head. Ring ribbed along upper face for 14mm. Postulated internal diameter 27mm.

Fowler considers type D2 to have been produced from the first to the fourth centuries (1969, 52-53).

Bone Pins

Crummy discusses the identification of large bone and metal Romano-British pins as hairpins, noting the occurrence of pins fixed in surviving hair or close to the skull in female burials (1983, 19). As she states, although the available evidence suggests that the majority were used as hair pins, other uses are not precluded.

7) Site 2, 1971.513.
Fragment of a bone pin, with tip and most of shaft broken off. Crummy type 3b (1983, 21-2). Head rather irregular, with semicircular lower half and slightly conical upper half. Length 22mm (head 7mm), shaft diameter 3mm.

Crummy dates this type from c. AD 200 to the late fourth or early fifth centuries (1979, 161), although MacGregor notes finds from contexts dated to the mid-second century (1985, 117).

8) Site 1, 1970.315. Unstratified.
Bone pin with broken tip. Extremely high polish. An elaboration of Crummy's type 6 (1983, 24-5). Head comprises, from top, bead/reel/long bead with deeply incised lattice decoration, producing pineapple effect/reel. Cross-hatching of long bead has left cut marks on reel above it. Faceted shaft tapers just under head. Length 47mm (head 14mm), max. shaft diameter 4mm.

Type 6 pins are dated from c. AD 200 to the late fourth or early fifth centuries (Crummy 1979, 162).

9) Site 1, 1970.436 E/W section under large stones, over cobbling, S end of site.
Bone pin with broken tip. An elaboration of Crummy's type 6. Head comprises from top, bead/reel with oblique incised decoration. Cancellous bone apparent on bead. Shaft swells quite strongly. Length 73mm (head 10mm), max. shaft diameter 6mm.

Shaft fragments of two other bone pins were recovered on Site 1, and are included in the archive catalogue.

Metal Pins

10) Site 2, 1971.585 ?NE corner of site.
Copper alloy pin with faceted cuboid head. Excellent preservation. Head has thirteen facets comprising five lozenges and eight triangles. Shaft swells slightly just under the head and comes to a very fine, sharp point. Length 81.5mm (head 5mm), shaft diameter 2mm.

The extremely high patination visible on this pin is the product of long contact with leather or human skin, and could well result from use as a hairpin (G.Morgan, pers. comm.). Crummy notes the frequent occurrence of faceted cuboid motifs on third to fourth century

jewellery, and postulates a date of c.AD 250 to the fourth century for similar metal pins found at Colchester (1983, 23; 29). Two silver pins of the same design were recovered from mid-fourth and fifth century contexts at Barnsley Park, Glos. (Webster 1982, 107 and fig. 22; 109 and fig. 30).

11) Site 2 1971.561 Grave 5. Phase 2.
Brass pin with dark red cabochon, probably of glass, set in an oval, beaded silver mount which is soldered to a flat, double disc head. The jewel is now separated from the head and the setting damaged. Shaft quite corroded. Circular perforation in upper disc for the attachment of a chain. Head tinned. Lead present in the solder, and possibly tin, although this may be contamination from the tinned surface. Length 52.5mm (head 9mm), max. shaft diameter 2mm.

This is an example of a type of pin usually found as part of a suite consisting of a pair of pins linked by a chain; such suites are known from a number of Anglo-Saxon graves. At Chamberlains Barns Cemetery II, Beds., two silver pin suites were found, the pins almost identical in form to our example, apart from being set with flat garnets, one on each side of the head (Hyslop 1964, 181-2; 185). It is possible that this pin was originally set with two cabachons, as traces of solder appear on both sides of the head. However, pins of this type are not invariably double-sided, as is demonstrated by a single, very plain example in bronze with a jewel socket on only one face, from the late sixth to seventh century sunken-featured building at West Stow (West 1985).

Linked pins were also worked in gold; with a secondary inhumation in the barrow at Cow Lowe, Derbys., a gold pair very similar in form to the Site 2 example was found, connected by a gold chain and set with dark red glass jewels or garnets (Bateman 1848, 93-94; Meaney and Hawkes 1970, 37). Slightly more elaborate gold pins linked by a substantial jewelled chain were recovered from a barrow on Roundway Down, Wilts.; these pins were set with garnet cabachons framed in beaded gold wire (Akerman 1855, 1 and pl. I; Youngs 1989, 53).

Pins of this form may be dated to the Anglo-Saxon pagan/Christian interface of the mid-to late seventh century, being found in cemeteries of both types (Hyslop 1964, 194). When in pairs, they are generally found near the necks of skeletons, and so were presumably worn near the throat. Those from Chamberlains Barns were used to fasten an outer garment to that beneath (Hyslop 1964, 198). Linked pins may have taken over the function of paired brooches, the fashion for which petered out in the early seventh century (Hyslop 1964, 198). Certainly, these pins represent a new fashion appearing in cemeteries of the seventh century (Meaney and Hawkes 1970, 36).

Associations have been termed 'female' (e.g. bead necklaces, chatelaines, and pendants), although skeletal remains from most of the older excavations have not been independently sexed. This evidence is available for some of the more modern excavations; for example, an adult female (30-35 years) was buried with a silver pin suite at Winnal, Winchester, while the burial of a female of about 30 years included a single bronze example of the type (Meaney and Hawkes 1970, 11). The skull and mandible is all that now remains of the skeleton from Site 2; examination of the teeth indicates an individual of at least 45 years, of indeterminate sex.

The pin from Site 2 was found associated with a number of other items under the skull and neck of the skeleton (sf no. 582), comprising a copper alloy 'Maltese cross' (possibly a pendant cross, another seventh century type, worn alone or as part of a necklace, Hawkes and Grove 1963, 30), a glass bead, and an object possibly of silver. Unfortunately, these objects were lost at the time of the excavation or subsequently.

The pin represents the only such discovery in Leicestershire, and may demonstrate an Anglo-Saxon presence at a date later than previously recognised in the county (P.Liddle pers. comm.). It is interesting to note that one of the pin suites from Chamberlains Barns was found in association with a silver disc pendant of the type recovered from Site 1 (No.25).

Beads

12) Site 4, 1972.901 AH Pit C. Found associated with bone comb (29).
Plain annular bead of bright yellow vitreous material. The surface is extensively abraded, probably deliberately (G.C. Morgan pers. comm.). Circular section. Height 3mm, diameter 7mm.

13) Site 1, 1969.118.
Plain globular bead (i.e. height more than half the diameter [Guido 1978, 69]), of opaque blue glass with white specks. Circular section. Height 10mm, max. diameter 11mm.

This is a common form of bead, produced over a long period. The type is probably Roman, but may extend into the post-Roman period (Guido 1978, 70).

14) Site 1, 1971.413. Over cobbling E of parallel walls.
Plain spherical bead of opaque blue glass. Circular section. Height 6mm, diameter 6mm.

15) Site 1, 1970.317.
Fragment of a plain cylinder bead of opaque green glass. Slightly curved. Circular section. Length 9mm, diameter 3mm.
Not illustrated.

The earliest British examples of this type date to the first centuries BC/AD, carrying on into the post-Roman period. Their height of popularity was reached after the third century AD (Guido 1978, 95).

16) Site 2, 1971.535.
Plain cylinder bead of translucent blue glass. Circular section. Length 13mm, diameter 4mm.

Guido notes that this type is common throughout the Roman period, becoming more popular after the second century and continuing in production in the post-Roman period (1978, 94).

17) Site 2, 1971.581 RZ.
Fragment of a plain cylinder bead of translucent green glass. Tapered at one end. Circular section. Length 11mm, max. diameter 4mm.

18) Site 2, 1971.583
Small segmented bead of translucent blue glass. Five segments taper slightly towards one end, probably a result of the production method of wrapping a molten glass rod around a wire (Guido 1978, 91-2). Circular section. Length 13mm, max. diameter 3.5mm.

This form is a Roman one, found on sites in Britain from the second century and produced well into the post-Roman period. It seems to have been very fashionable in the third and fourth centuries (Guido 1978, 92-3).

Bracelets and Armlets

19) Site 1, 1970.323 Dark sandy loam and limestone/charcoal scatter over Phase 3 well.
Fragment from a plain shale bracelet or armlet, with convex D-shaped section. Height 6mm, thickness 6mm, postulated internal diameter 48mm.

20) Site 1, 1970.304. Unstratified.
Fragment of a copper alloy cable bracelet or armlet. Good preservation. Three strands of wire of oval section twisted together. At one end, two strands wrap less obliquely around the third strand and terminate, leaving final strand free-perhaps the hook of a clasp. Thickness 2mm, postulated internal diameter 60mm.

Similar clasp ends appear on a three-strand cable armlet from Butt Road, Colchester; Crummy dates the cable form at Colchester from c. AD 320 to c. AD 450 (1983, 38-9).

21) Site 3, 1967.97 Near F9. Unstratified.
Plain copper alloy bracelet or armlet with damaged hook and eye clasp. One rounded terminal incorporates a tear-shaped eye which is quite roughly cut, while the other terminal is sheared off. Rectangular section; bent. Width 7mm, thickness 0.5mm, postulated internal diameter 60mm.

22) Site 1, 1970.300.
Plain copper alloy bracelet or armlet. Good preservation. One terminal is bent slightly outwards, the other is broken off; possibly a hook and eye clasp. D-shaped section. Thickness 2mm, swelling to 2.75mm at hooked end and tapering to 1.5mm at the other. Internal diameter 64mm.

23) Site 1, 1971.433. Phase 5?
Penannular iron bracelet or armlet. Very badly corroded. One terminal possibly spherical, the other broken off. Max. thickness 6mm, internal diameter 64mm.

Finger Ring

24) Site 1, 1971.434. Large stones over cobbling at south end of site.
Fragment of a jet (or jet-like material such as cannel coal) finger ring. Bezel in the form of a slightly raised circle, incised with a deep central dot surrounded by a ring and bounded on either side by a vertical groove. On the more complete side, two smaller, fainter vertical lines lie parallel to the first. Oval

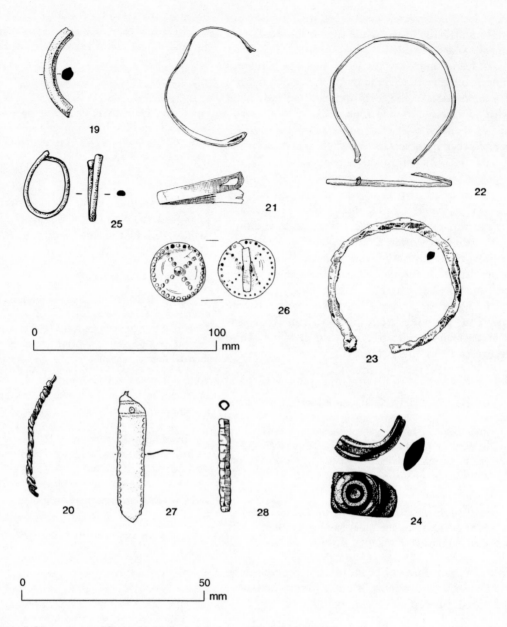

Fig. 51 Objects of Personal Adornment and Dress 19-28 Scale 1:2 (except 20, 24, 27, 28 1:1)

section. Height at centre of bezel 11mm, thickness at centre of bezel 3.5mm, postulated internal diameter 18mm.

This ring has been biconically worked, produced by drilling a jet disc from either side. The central internal band has an extremely high patina, due to extended contact with and friction against human skin (G.C. Morgan, pers. comm.) The outer surface of the ring is quite highly patinated, probably also the result of wear in use.

?Suspension Ring

25) Site 3, Fill of F.15 Sf. no. 98
Copper alloy bracelet with flattened terminal (?Roman 'snake' bracelet) which has been broken and bent to form a smaller ring. Similar bent copper alloy rings are used for suspending smaller objects from a belt in Anglo-Saxon burials. Probably represents opportunist re-use of a Roman object. Internal diameter 28mm.

Pendant

26) Site 1, 1969.164.
Copper alloy disc pendant. Traces of tinning on obverse. Flat disc with central repousse boss. Lines of smaller repousse dots radiate from this to form a cross within a circle of similar dots around the circumference. The suspension bar, now detached, is formed from a rectangular copper alloy sheet with a central kink, originally soldered to the reverse. Traces of tin solder remain on both pendant and suspension bar. Both zinc and tin are present in the copper alloy, although the latter may be contamination from the tin solder. Thickness 0.5mm, diameter 30.5mm.

A silver pendant of almost identical pattern, although smaller in diameter, was recovered from a late sixth to seventh century sunken-featured building at West Stow (West 1985, 145 and fig. 33). At the Christian Anglo-Saxon barrow cemetery on Sibertswold Down, Kent, two identical 'brass gilded ornaments' were found near the neck of a skeleton; the edge of one of the pendants retained a suspension loop with the remains of string in it (Faussett 1856, 117 and pl. II). The design is again very similar to that on the Empingham pendant, except that the cross is formed from three parallel lines of dots rather than one. Silver pendants of similar form also come from Sibertswold and Chamberlains Barns Cemetery II, Beds., the latter in association with pins of the type found on Site 2 (11) (Hyslop 1964, 181 and fig. 13). A gold version was recovered from an Anglo-Saxon cemetery on Kingston Down, Kent (Faussett 1856, 78 and pl. I). The Anglo-Saxon cemetery at Burwell, Cambs. produced a disc pendant 'of embossed silver on a bronze base'; no suspension loop is apparent (Fox 1923, 262 and pl. 34).

The disc pendant would seem to have been fashionable in England from the late sixth/early seventh century, continuing in popularity through to the end of the seventh century. The type is generally confined to Christian contexts, although pagan associations are known (Hyslop 1964, 200).

Several authors have discussed the Christian significance of the cross motifs commonly found on disc pendants (e.g. Hawkes and Grove 1963; Meaney 1981; Evison 1987), and opinions range from considering all cruciform designs as symbolic of Christianity, to restricting 'semi-Christian' significance to the later examples. In any case, it would seem that these pendants may well have been regarded as protective amulets, by analogy with European parallels found in association with model weapons (Meaney 1981, 162). In this light, their resemblance to shields with central bosses and arrangements of studs (hence their occasional classification as 'scutiform' pendants) is not entirely fortuitous. An extraordinary amulet necklace from Szilagy-Samylo, Romania, includes a disc pendant with a miniature handgrip on the reverse, very similar to the suspension bar on the pendant from Site 1. It should be noted that the Romanian pendant is also provided with a functional suspension loop (Evison 1987, 56; see Meaney 1981 for a detailed discussion of model weapons, including the Szilagy-Samylo shield pendant).

It has been suggested that the protective function of the shield amulet took on a new significance with the transition to Christianity, the pendants thereby acquiring cruciform motifs (Evison 1987, 56); Meaney notes that the concept of God as a shield is a reasonably common metaphor (1981, 162). I think it is fair to note here that the pendant from Site 1 would have displayed an 'X' motif when worn, rather than a cross, as did three parallel examples from Buckland cemetery, Kent (Evison 1987, 55 and fig. 37). However, the 'X' as Greek letter *chi* is also a component of Christian symbolism.

Disc pendants are considered to form part of female attire, often worn as part of a necklace or festoon (Meaney 1981, 162). Again, many older excavations have relied on finds associations for sex determination, but some pendants have been found with skeletons independently sexed as female (e.g. Buckland cemetery,

Evison 1987, 123-4). Detailed descriptions and/or illustrations of disc pendants without visible suspension loops are generally lacking, but the provision of a suspension bar as opposed to a loop may be an unusual feature. In common with the dress pin from Site 2 (Phase 2, Grave 5) this object is a unique find in Leicestershire, and may represent Anglo-Saxon presence here later than previously thought.

Belt Fitting

27) Site 1, 1969 Unstratified, but found with copper alloy vessel rim (43).
Copper alloy strap-end. Long parallel-sided form with rounded terminal end. The rivet, which is apparently of different material remains in place at the other end, with a possible second rivet hole immediately above it. Decorated with a border of punched crescents; rivet(s) separated by incised transverse grooves. On the reverse, possible traces of solder remain at the terminal end for attachment to a backplate (for method of attachment see West 1985, fig. 37). A fine, well-made piece. Length 34mm, width 7.5mm, thickness 0.3mm.

A strap-end of similar form, but with more elaborate punched decoration comes from an Anglo-Saxon cemetery at Reading, associated with a late Roman belt buckle; Hawkes and Dunning note only that it is of 'early type' (1962, 45 and fig. 14).

Two parallels – one with incised line decoration, the other undecorated – formed part of a complete belt set buried with a male inhumation in the Anglo-Saxon cemetery at Kempston, Beds. Kennet dates this burial to the early fifth century, while noting that the ornamental style of the strap-ends is reminiscent of late Roman work (1983, 90; White 1988, 49).

Ferrule

28) Site 1, 1969.135.
Copper alloy cylinder, with grooved decoration creating the appearance of segmentation. Made from a thin sheet rolled into shape. Plant material, possibly wood, recovered from the interior. Length 24mm, diameter 2.5mm.

Probable ferrule. Undecorated examples have been identified from Gadebridge Park villa (Neal and Butcher 1974, 37 and fig. 59).

Footwear (Fig. 52 and pl. 9 and 10)

29) Site 1, 1970 Fill of well. Phase 3.
Left shoe patten or sandal made from a single piece of wood, the base of which has a large proportion cut away to leave blocks supporting the heel and ball of the foot, the vertical edges of which, appear to have been sawn. The upper surface is smooth and has been lightly polished through wear. It is contoured slightly to accommodate the ball of the foot more comfortably. No upper parts have survived, but the attachment of a band or strap across the centre is indicated by the presence of pinholes along the vertical sides of the central part of the sole. Additionally, there is a square hole of 4mm towards the rear of the sole on the right hand vertical side, which may also be for attachment.
Max. length 270mm, max. width 94mm, max. height 47mm, max. thickness of sole 19mm.

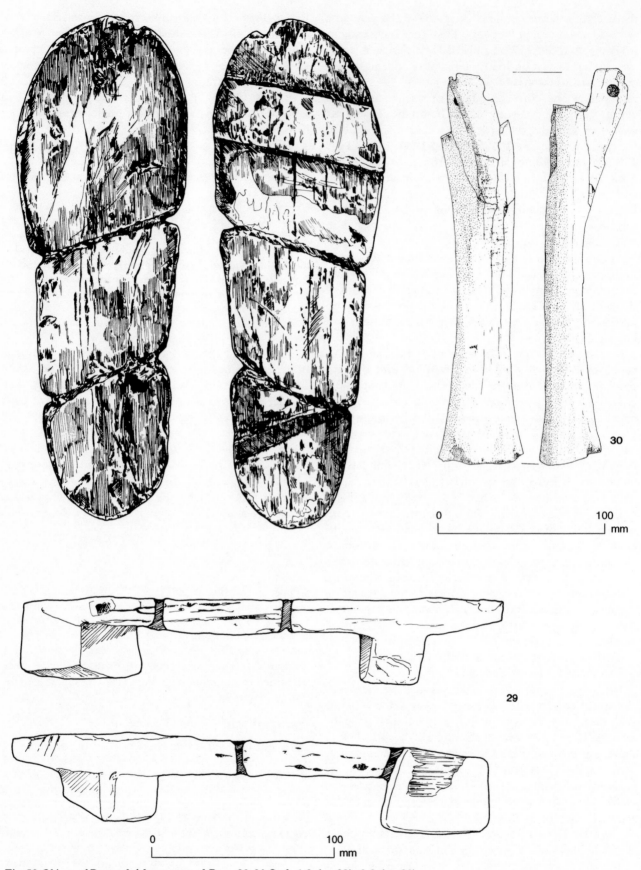

Fig. 52 Objects of Personal Adornment and Dress 29-30 Scale 1:2 (no. 29), 3:8 (no. 30)

Examples of wooden shoes or sandals of this type are unusual in Roman contexts. A group of four examples of wooden sandals described as 'bath-house slippers' were excavated from a period II pre-Hadrianic floor of one of the stone forts at Vindolanda (Birley 1977, 125 and fig. 38). They are ostensibly identical to the Empingham

Plate 9 Footwear: wooden pattern on sandal top view

Plate 10 Footwear: wooden pattern on sandal lower view

example, and have an angular piece of leather across the centre, pinned at either side to form the uppers. The slippers apparently acted as protection from hot concrete floors while bathing, and similar examples were recovered from excavations at Carlisle by Dorothy Charlesworth (Birley 1977, 126 and note 116). It is debatable whether the Empingham example performed the same function. Whilst there was a broadly contemporary bath suite across the valley at Site 2, pattens could also act as temporary footwear for walking across muddy ground, lifting the feet up on a high platform in order to protect more delicate footwear. Wooden pattens of very similar form were commonly worn in the medieval period while pattens with metal soles were used into the 19th century to perform a similar function (T.McK. Clough pers. comm.)

30) Site 1, 1969 CM and CS.
Cow right tibia, with distal end sawn or chopped away. The greater part of the proximal end has been removed by sawing or chopping transversely from the posterior side, about 20mm into the bone, then splitting off the end. Lower part of cnemial crest has been removed to reduce ridge on shaft; upper part drilled with two horizontal holes. Transverse tooth marks or scratches visible on shaft. Posterior side patinated. Length 242mm, max. width 59mm, max. thickness 46mm.

This is most likely a bone skate drilled with strapholes, with part of the proximal end removed to create an upswept, pointed toe. All three elements are common features on bone skates (MacGregor 1985, 142). Thus, the distal end may have been removed to create a flat surface upon which to skate, while the removal of the cnemial crest would have provided a flat surface for the

foot. The gloss on the posterior side may be the result of friction on ice, although it is possible that post-depositional processes may have been responsible (A. Gouldwell pers. comm). MacGregor (1985, 142) notes that no tibia skates have been found, although elsewhere (1977, 72) he lists a horse tibia skate from Thetford.

Toilet Instruments (Fig. 53)

Combs

31) Site 4, 1972.900 AH Pit C. Found with vitreous bead (12) and Anglo-Saxon pottery.
Triangular-backed, single-sided, composite bone/antler comb (no bone structures were visible to aid positive identification). Elongated form with outswept endplates, upon which teeth cut gradually shorter towards either end. Two endplates, five tooth-plates. Identical, symmetrical ring and dot decoration on each sideplate, with border of three incised lines. Groove marks from sawing of teeth visible along lower edges of sideplates. Originally held together by twelve iron rivets, of which six remain. Postulated height 65mm, length 192mm, thickness 6mm.

This comb form appears in the late third or early fourth century and continues in production until the eighth (MacGregor 1985, 83).

32) Site 4, 1972.905 Fill of Sunken-Feature Building 1.
Fragmentary double-sided, composite bone comb. Plain, rectangular endplate with rounded corners and teeth which are all shorter than those on the toothplates, rather than being graduated in length. One endplate, two toothplates, and fragments of one sideplate remain. The only visible decoration comprises six vertical incised lines at the end of the sideplate. Sideplate, of flat cross-section, swells towards the centre of the comb; groove marks from sawing of teeth evident along part of one surviving edge. Tooth spacing identical on both sides. The comb is held together by a single line of iron rivets along the centre of the sideplate, four of which survive (two *in situ*). Height 48.5mm, length 103mm, postulated thickness 10mm.

The lack of teeth of graduated height on the endplate(s) may be an unusual feature.

Nail-Cleaner

33) Site 1, 1970.333 Feature 4. Phase 2.
Copper alloy nail-cleaner in two fragments. Probably brass. Flat shaft swells gently towards suspension loop which is in the same plane as the shaft. Slightly bent; suspension loop broken. Length 53.5mm, max. width 7.5mm, thickness 1mm.

The form falls between Crummy types 1a and 1b, which she has dated mid-to late first century at Colchester (1983, 57-8). Broken suspension loops are a common form of damage on nail-cleaners.

Toilet Spoon

34) Site 1, 1969.178.
Copper alloy toilet spoon with small, round scoop. Extremely good preservation with high degree of patination. Top of shaft and bottom of scoop broken off. Shaft of circular cross-section. Length 52mm, diameter 2mm.

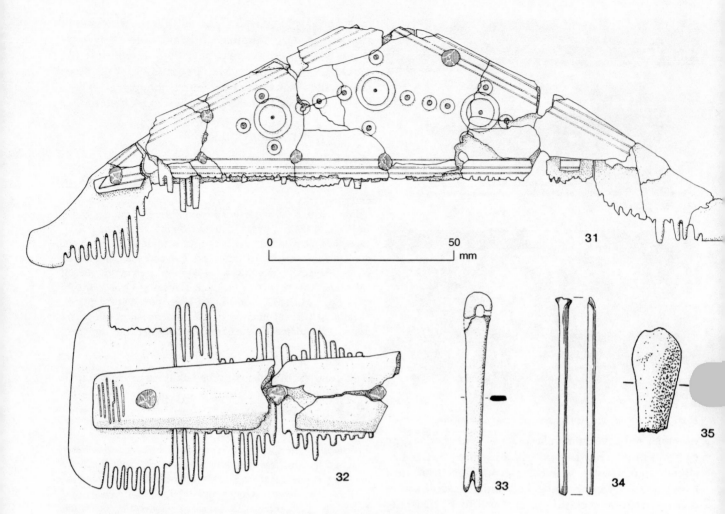

Fig. 53 Toilet Instruments and Objects used in the Manufacture of Textiles 31-37 Scale 1:1

Toilet spoons were most likely used to remove cosmetics and unguents from their containers. A close parallel was recovered from Balkerne Lane, Colchester (Crummy 1983, 60, no. 1907). Several examples from the Roman villa at Gadebridge Park are also very similar (Neal and Butcher 1974, 143 and fig. 63). Crummy notes that such spoons were used throughout the Roman period (1983, 59).

Wig Curler

35) Site 1, 1971.431 Unstratified.
Fragment of a pipeclay wig curler of hourglass shape. Handmade, solid. Length 27mm, max. diameter 13mm.

Wig curlers or *bigoudis*, originated in France in the late sixteenth century. The wearing of wigs was popularised by the court of Louis XIV and continued to be fashionable until the early nineteenth century. Locks of hair were wrapped around the curlers with moist paper strips, after which the wig was baked in a bread oven to set. This example probably dates to between 1690 and 1730, according to Le Cheminant's typology (1978, 188).

Objects Used in the Manufacture of Textiles (Fig. 54 and 54)

Spindle Whorls

36) Site 3 1968.158 (64) Sf. no. 80
Fired clay spindle whorl. Almost identical form to 37 below. Diameter 37mm, diameter of perforation 9mm.

37) Site 4, 1972.902 AH Pit C.
Fired clay spindle whorl with biconical profile. Cylindrical perforation, flared at each end. Quartz tempered fabric, slightly oxidised, with reduced grey core. Plant impressions on surface. Height 21.5mm, diameter 40mm, diameter of perforation 10mm.

Spindle whorls of a similar shape have been recovered from sunken-featured buildings at West Stow. (West 1985, 27 and fig. 91.14 from the early to mid-fifth century; 37 and fig.150.10 from the late sixth century; 15 and fig. 30.9, from the late sixth to seventh century).

Pin Beaters

38) Site 5, 1968.
Double-pointed bone pin beater, with one point thicker than the other. Extensive but faint transverse grooving extends from each point along lateral edges, 26-31mm down the shaft. Oval

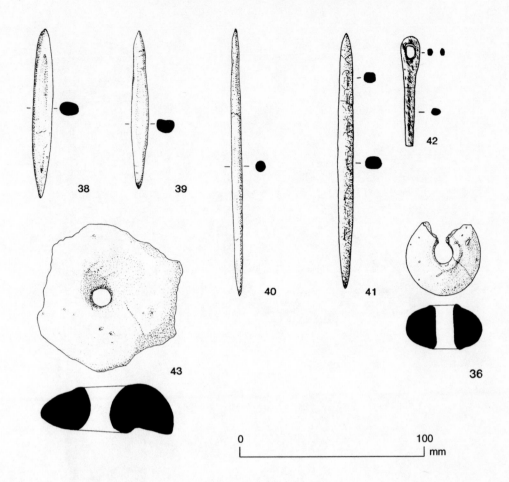

Fig. 54 Objects used in the Manufacture of Textiles 38-43 Scale 1:2

section. Length 92mm, max. width 10mm, max. thickness 7.5mm.

Pin beaters were used during the weaving process, being inserted between the warp threads to beat down the weft, ensuring a firm and even weave. The transverse grooving results from the friction against the warp (MacGregor 1985,188). Pin beaters were produced from the Roman period into early medieval times (MacGregor 1985, 188). From its context this would appear to be a late Roman example.

39) Site 1 1970.320 Unstratified.
Double-pointed bone pin beater. Extremely high polish, especially at the points. Waisted appearance at both points, with faint grooving 13-14mm down the shaft. Ovoid section. Length 84mm, max. width 10mm, max. thickness 6.5mm. The patina is probably due to friction in use.

40) Site 4 1972.906 AQ Fill of Sunken-feature Building 1. Found associated with hook (272) in archive catalogue.
Double-pointed bone pin beater. Extremely high polish. Slightly waisted appearance at one point. Circular section. Length 146mm, max. diameter 6mm.

A very similar example in terms of size, shape, and polish has been recovered from the Anglo-Saxon village at West Stow, in a fifth century context (West 1985, 50 and fig 210).

41) Site 3 1967.158 (67) Sf. no. 54.
Double-pointed bone pin beater. Highly polished on both ends consistent with use in pushing loose threads back into place during weaving. Slightly flattened section. Length 132mm, max. width 9mm.

Bone Needle

42) Site 3 1967 Feature 5 (Sunken-feature Building 3)
Eye and shaft of bone needle with shaft tip broken off. Flattened section, eye slightly elongated. Length 57mm, width of shaft 6mm, width of eye 5mm.

MacGregor states that 'Bone needles were developed to a high degree of uniformity of style and standard of production in the Roman period' but that they 'are much scarcer in the succeeding centuries' and are completely displaced by metal needles by the start of the medieval period (1985, 193). The width of the eye would indicate use with coarse thread. The ovoid head is unusual for needles of Anglo-Saxon date, which often have triangular heads as at West Stow (West 1985).

Loom Weights

i) *Circular*

43) Site 1, 1969.136
Oolitic limestone loom weight. Roughly circular with central hourglass perforation. Max. thickness 40mm, approx. diameter 77mm, min. diameter of perforation 12mm, weight 174.2g.

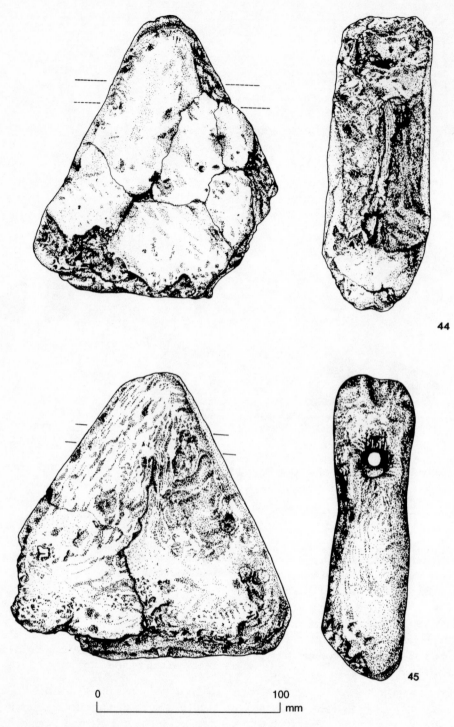

0   100
⊢————————————⊣ mm

Fig. 55 Objects used in the Manufacture of Textiles 44–45 Scale 1:2

ii) *Triangular*

Four fragments belonging to four different triangular, baked clay loomweights were excavated from Site 1. Two are nearly complete and of similar size, the third is an edge fragment, again from a weight of similar size, and the fourth is from a similar but smaller object of slightly different design.

All are made from the same (presumably local) grey, slightly micaceous clay, with red grog inclusions. The bodies are uniformly reduced grey with black surfaces,

except (44) where later exposure to fire has resulted in orange surfaces.

All the loomweights are in the form of isosceles triangles, with the narrow side forming the base. A circular perforation, presumably for suspension, is set horizontally through the sides of the triangle towards its top (46) has two perforated angles. All the angles have 'pulley-wheel' grooves set centrally, which are probably caused by wear rather than being pre-formed and are particularly pronounced on (44) and (47).

The type is pre-Roman with examples coming from Maiden Castle (Wheeler 1943, 294-7 fig. 100.1), and Willington, Derbys. (Elsdon 1979, 208 fig. 87). They have been found in early Roman contexts at Old Winteringham villa (Stead 1976, 226, fig. 123.211), Gorhambury (Wardle 1990, 162 fig. 145), and Verulamium (Wheeler and Wheeler 1936, 178, fig. 26.1).

44) Site 1, 1969CT
Height 150mm, length of side 170mm, thickness 58mm, width of perforation 9mm, weight 1175g.

45) Site 1, 1969EA
Height 150mm, length of side 180mm, thickness 48mm, width of perforation 11mm, weight 1173g.

46) Site 1, 1969EA
Edge fragment of similar length to (39) and (40). Weight 240g.

47) Site 1, 1969.151A.
This example has one deeply-grooved angle, with evidence for straight perforations across the other two angles, suggesting it is of smaller dimensions than the other weights. Postulated length of side 110mm, thickness 30mm, weight 158g.

Household Utensils (Fig. 56)

Metal Vessels

48) Site 1, 1969 Unstratified. Found with strap-end (27).
Rim fragment from a copper alloy vessel, decorated with a row of repousse bosses, three of which are visible. Rough, parallel, incised lines run around the interior of the rim.
Height 14mm, width 39mm, max. thickness 1mm.

The association of this vessel with strap-end (27 above) may indicate that the two objects belonged to a pagan Anglo-Saxon grave group that had been disturbed by ploughing. Similar objects were found within such burials on Site 3.

49) Site 2, 1971.580 Fill of Room Six
Fragments of heavily mineralised copper alloy sheet, with

Fig. 56 Household Utensils 48-59. Objects used for Recreation 60-62 Scale 1:1 (except 54-59 and 61, 1:2)

much fossilised plant material adhering. Both zinc and tin are present in the alloy. Largest fragment: length 58mm, width 34mm, thickness 0.5mm. Not illustrated.

Probable dish or bowl.

50) Site 3. Close to Feature 15. Sf. no. 102
Twisted rim fragment of a copper alloy vessel of indeterminate diameter.

51) Site 3 1968.158 (60) Sf. no. 75. Fill of Sunken-feature Building 1.
Rim fragment of a copper alloy bowl similar to that from Grave 1 of the Anglo-Saxon cemetery.

Glass Vessels

A total of 32 fragments of vessel glass of Roman date was retrieved from sites 1, 2, and 7, and a further vessel of possible Anglo-Saxon date came from Site 4 (49). A full list of the material is held in archive, and only the best preserved examples of diagnostic vessel fragments are published here.

52) Site 1, 1969 unstratified.
Body and handle fragment from a prismatic bottle in dark blue-green glass. Simple lower attachment of reeded handle, with part of shoulder and straight side of vessel remaining. Heat affected. Vessel thickness 6mm, original handle width 43+mm.

The prismatic bottle fragments from Sites 1 (three fragments) and 2 (one fragment) are of late first to second century date, possibly extending into the third century (H. Cool, pers. comm.).

53) Site 2, 1971.552.
Reeded handle fragment from a blue-green glass bottle. Only one edge remains. Original handle width 26+mm, thickness 3mm.

This handle fragment may be of slightly later date than the blue-green colour suggests (first to third centuries), possibly forming part of a mould-blown barrel jug, or 'Frontinus bottle', (Isings 1957, Forms 89 and 128) rather than of a cylindrical or prismatic bottle (H. Cool, pers. comm.). Frontinus bottles were popular in Britain during the later third to fourth centuries, though on the Continent they have been found in first century contexts (Price and Cool 1983, 117; Cool and Price unpublished). Such vessels are generally made from greenish colourless glass, although blue-green examples are known. For example, a blue-green fragment from Greyhound Yard, Dorset has been tentatively dated to the third century (Cool and Price forthcoming).

54) Site 1, 1970 FC. Industrial Area North of Building 1
Rim fragment from a conical beaker in light green colourless glass with many small bubbles. Out-turned rim with fire-thickened edge. Straight side of body slopes inwards. Height 28mm, thickness 1mm, postulated rim diameter 65mm.

Greenish colourless glass takes over from blue-green in popularity, and is on the whole a fourth century phenomenon. Hemispherical cups and conical beakers with fire-thickened rims would seem to have been in use in Britain from at least the mid-fourth century (Price 1982, 117). Several examples of this date come from excavations at Towcester (Price 1982, 122 and fig. 47), while Charlesworth identified similar vessels from Gadebridge Park villa, dating them to the last quarter of the fourth century (1974, 206-7 and fig. 205).

55) Site 1, 1969.171.
Rim fragment, possibly from a cup, in light green colourless glass with many small bubbles. Out-turned rim with fire-thickened edge. Height 14mm, thickness 1mm, postulated rim diameter 75mm.

56) Site 2, 1971
Body fragment from a mould-blown, hexagonal bottle, in light green colourless glass with many small bubbles and streaky iridescent surfaces. Lower body and edge of base remain. Parts of three straight sides survive, with very faint diagonal ribbing on the exterior. Height 26mm, approx. bottle width 55mm (point to point), thickness 1mm.

This is a fragment from a variant of Isings Form 100 (1957), which is a cylindrical bottle with cracked-off rim, cylindrical neck and two dolphin-shaped handles. In this case, the bottle has a ribbed hexagonal body rather than a cylindrical one. The bases of such bottles are sometimes decorated with a raised design. The type occurs in the Lower Rhineland and in southern Gaul, but it is extremely rare in Britain (Price 1982, 184). The only parallels would seem to have been found at Colchester (Cool and Price forthcoming), Greyhound Yard (Cool and Price unpublished), Barnsley Park (Price 1982), Caistor by Yarmouth (unpublished, and Claydon Pike (unpublished). The example from Empingham is smaller and less prominently ribbed than is usual (H. Cool, pers. comm.). It is interesting to note that an example of Isings Form 100 has been found to contain wine (S. Davies pers. comm.).

57) Site 7 A44 1990 (1)
Handle fragment of square bottle. Lower attachment of a multi-ribbed ribbon handle retaining part of curved shoulder and flat vertical side. Many small bubbles. Present height 31mm, max. handle width 39mm, thickness 6mm. Not illustrated.

Square bottles are very common container forms on first and second century sites.

58) Site 7 A44 1990 (11)
Rim and shoulder fragment of small globular jar. Outbent rim with edges rolled inward. Remains of a flat shoulder. Many small bubbles. Wear mark on rim edge. Present height 12mm, rim diameter 70mm, rim thickness 5mm, wall thickness 1.5mm

The 'rolled in' rim of this vessel is more usually found on jug or flask forms rather than jars. A similar example, however, is known from Fishbourne (Harden and Price 1971, fig. 141.71) and is dated typologically to the early second century AD.

59) Site 4, 1972.910 AH Pit C.
Rim fragment from a beaker or cup, in dark yellow-brown glass with small bubbles. Slightly out-turned rim with edge rolled in. Fine horizontal trail on upper body. Height 17mm, thickness 1mm, postulated rim diameter 55-60mm.

This is not typically Roman and may be of Anglo-Saxon date (H. Cool pers. comm.).

Objects Used for Recreational Purposes
(Fig. 56)

Gaming Counters

60) Site 2, 1971.569 Unstratified.
Bone disc gaming counter with central perforation and single incised ring on obverse. Max. thickness 2.5mm, diameter 15mm.

Most bone counters are lathe turned, but this example has been excised from the bone using the principle of a centre bit, scribing a circle from both sides (G.C. Morgan pers. comm.). Both plain and grooved bone disc counters with central perforations were found at Jewry Wall, Leicester (Kenyon 1948, 266-7), South Shields Roman fort (Allason-Jones and Miket 1984, 56-61), and Gorhambury (Wardle 1990, 158). As this find is unstratified, it is as well to note that it does resemble bone buttons of the medieval period, although it does not share their straight-sided profile (MacGregor 1985, 99-102).

61) Site 2 1971 Unstratified.
Hard chalk or limestone gaming piece, carved into a perfect sphere. Diameter 17mm.

62) Site 4 1972.907 AW.
Flat, rectangular, antler gaming counter. Highly polished, with bevelled corners and slightly convex long edges. Six ring and dot motifs on obverse, placed in two parallel lines. Possibly burnt. Length 19mm, width 11mm, max. thickness 3.5mm.

Building Materials

Window Glass

Twenty-two fragments of window glass were recovered from Site 2, while one fragment came from Site 5. The majority of these are light green colourless, blown glass with many small bubbles, and ranging in thickness from 1-2.5mm. Fragments of dark green colourless and dark blue-green verging on peacock are also represented among the blown window glass. This type of glass is not closely dateable, but its use in Britain begins in the late third to early fourth century (S. Davies, pers. comm.). Five fragments of matt/glossy, cast panes, of 3-4mm thickness, came from Site 2, all except one being of blue-green glass; these can be dated to the first to third centuries. A full catalogue of the window glass is held in archive.

Tools (Figs. 57 and 58)

Implement Handle

63) Site 2 1971.517 Unstratified.
Fragment of a one-piece antler handle. Cylindrical, with central cavity along entire length. Decorated at one end with three parallel grooves. Traces of polished surface visible, especially around decoration. Fragment of an iron tang remains in the central cavity at decorated end. Length 80mm, diameter 29mm.

Blades

64) Site 1, 1971 EX over cobbling of eastern (outer) yard.
Iron knife. Manning type 11a (1985, 114 and fig. 28). Convex edge with rounded tip. Broken tang continues straight line of blade back. Length 104mm.

65) Site 2 1971 PK Fill of Room 2.
Iron knife. Manning type 17. Straight edge; tip and tang broken off. Back slightly arched. Length 94mm. Not illustrated.

66) Site 2 1971 RO.
Fragment of an iron knife. Manning type 13 or 18a. Convex edge stepped down from tang. Arch of back begins at base of tang. Blade broken as is end of tang. Length 55mm.

67) Site 1, 1971.404 Unstratified. Over cobbling of eastern (outer) yard.
Iron blade from a pair of small shears. Manning type 3 (1985, 34) type 3 with straight edge and slightly arched back. Tip broken off. Small fragment of omega-shaped spring remains. Length 129mm.

Shears of this size would have been suitable for domestic and personal use. The omega spring provided greater strength than the simple U-shaped form which is also found on shears of this type (Manning 1985, 34). Small shears of similar form come from a late fourth/early fifth century context at Verulamium (Manning 1972, 176 and fig. 65), and an almost complete pair was recovered from Richborough (Bushe-Fox 1928, 51 and pl. 24).

Hone

68) Site 1, 1971 CO Feature 23, Phase 2B
Fragment of a hone of fine-grained, calcareous, micaceous sandstone. Rectangular to ovoid section. Faint transverse grooving visible on broad faces. One end broken off. Length 54.5mm, max. width 20mm, max. thickness 12mm.

A hone of similar form was found at Balkerne Lane, Colchester, in a context dated to the second half of the third century (Crummy 1983, 113 and fig. 114).

Miscellaneous Iron Tools

69) Site 1 1970.318 Unstratified over cobbling in Building 1
Iron file with tapering blade of rectangular section. Teeth on all four faces; ten teeth per cm. Length 215mm, max. width 9mm, max. thickness 5mm. Iron collar which bound the end of the handle also remains; width 11mm, thickness 1mm, diameter 17mm.

This is a metalworking tool. The collar would have prevented the wooden handle from splitting during use.

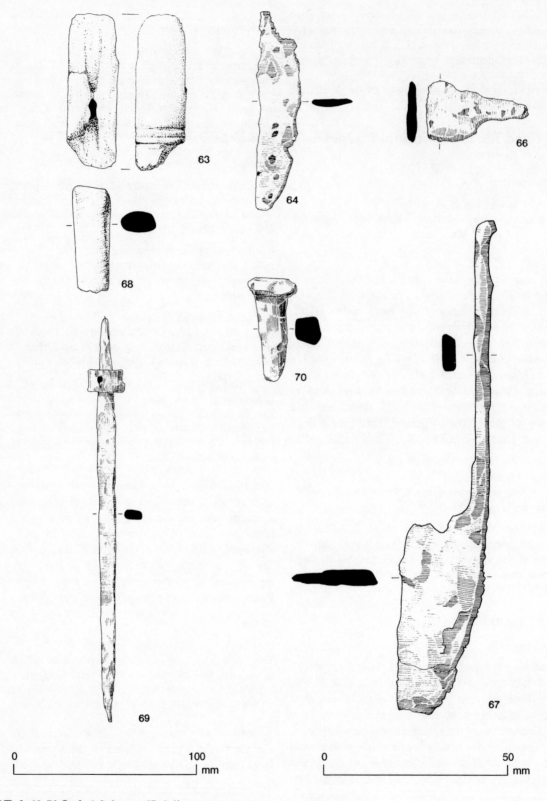

Fig. 57 Tools 63-70 Scale 1:2 (except 67, 1:1)

70) Site 1, 1971.412 Over cobbling of eastern yard.
Iron smith's punch. Square section, coming to a blunt point. Large head with evidence of hammering. Length 53mm, width of head 36mm.

This type of punch would have been used to make holes in hot metal (Manning 1985, 9).

71) Site 1, 1970.301
Iron chisel with fragmentary tang of square section, broad blade with gently sloping shoulders and slightly splayed, unifacially bevelled cutting edge. Length 128mm, max. width 30mm, max. thickness 8mm.

The form of the cutting edge suggests that this was a

carpenter's mortise chisel, intended for fairly heavy work. This example does not bear much resemblance to the Romano-British forms outlined by Manning (1985, 23). However, a close parallel from Shakenoak Farm site A has been dated to the fourth century (Brodribb, Hands and Walker 1968, 102 and fig. 34), while a shouldered chisel with a tang of square section has been recovered from first century levels at Balkerne Lane, Colchester (Crummy 1983, 113 and fig.115).

72) Site 1, 1970.327 Unstratified.
Miniature iron hammer head. Two identical, flared striking heads of square section are separated by a centrally placed circular shaft hole. Length 42mm, diameter of shaft hole 6mm.

This is probably a metalworking tool. A miniature bronze axe-hammer of similar dimensions came from the inner stone fort ditch at Richborough, Kent (Henderson 1949, 146).

73) Site 1, 1969.186.
Iron ring with bar attached. Ring of circular section; end of bar curved. Length of bar 59mm, thickness of ring 7mm, internal diameter of ring 40mm.

Either a loop-headed spike or a fragmentary snaffle bit.

74) Site 1, 1971 BB.
Iron fragment of square section, swelling to flat cross-section and curving in hook-like fashion. Both ends broken. Length 49mm, max. width 16mm, max. thickness 3.5mm.

Probably part of a shaft and U-shaped spring from a pair of shears.

75) Site 1, 1971.429
Long iron bar of square section, twisted in the middle, and flattened at one end. Both ends broken off. Length 440mm, max. width 18mm, max. thickness 10mm.

This is most likely the handle of a fire-shovel. Handles with a twisted element are characteristic of Romano-British hearth tools, especially of the shovel (Manning 1985, 13). A very good close parallel comes from a mid-second century context at Verulamium (Manning 1972, 64 and fig. 60; Frere 1972, 97-98). Another example was recovered from a third century context in Carrawburgh Mithraeum (Manning 1976, 39 and fig. 23). In the latter case the shovel would have been used to feed fuel on to the altar fires (Richmond and Gillam 1951, 20; 28), but it should be noted that in most cases fire shovels are considered to be smith's tools (Manning 1985, 13).

Military Equipment (Fig. 58)

Catapult Bolt

76) Site 2, 1971.579 Fill of Room 6.
Iron catapult bolt head. Manning type IIb (1985, 176). Flat, leaf-shaped blade with flanged socket. Length 60mm (blade 29mm, socket 31mm), max. width 19mm, external diameter of socket 11mm.

Manning notes that flanged forms were probably rapidly made either due to lack of supplies on campaign or to a shortage of arms reaching military units (1985, 176). This example is at the lowest end of the size range, but the socket diameter is comparable to those of larger bolt heads.

Fasteners and Fittings (Figs. 58 and 59)

Iron Studs

Four iron studs were excavated from Sites 1 and 2; only the largest example is described here.

77) Site 1 Unstratified.
Convex iron stud with shaft of square section. Length of shaft 51mm, diameter of head 97mm, thickness of head 3mm.

Iron Nails

A total of 363 complete iron nails was retrieved during the excavation of Sites 1, 2 and 5; these were classified in accordance with Manning's British Museum catalogue (1985, 134-5 and fig. 32). The complete catalogue is held in archive, and the following includes representative examples of Types 1, 2 and 4.

There were 258 complete examples of Type 1, six of Type 2, two of Type 3, one of Type 4, five of Type 5, one of Type 10, and 90 of indeterminate type.

78) Site 1. 1971 CF
Manning Type 1 with square section. Length 79mm.

79) Site 2, 1971 QY.
Manning Type 2 with rectangular section. Length 70mm.

80) Site 1, 1971 DE.
Manning Type 4 (or a variant), with square section and L-shaped head, flattened and splayed. Length 43mm.

Rivet

81) Site 2, 576.
A lozenge-shaped piece of brass sheet, with the two ends folded towards the centre and back on themselves. Length 20mm, width 9mm.

Probably an improvised rivet or split pin for leatherworking, a function attributed to similar objects from Gadebridge Park villa (Neal and Butcher 1974, 137).

Joiner's Dogs

Five examples were identified in all from Sites 1,2, and 5.

82) Site 1, 1971.430 Feature 23 Phase 2.
Iron joiner's dog with pointed arms. Arm length 34mm, width 8mm, max. thickness 5mm.

Joiner's dogs acted as staples for holding timbers together.

T-Clamps

83) Site 5. Unstratified.
Iron T-clamp with anchor-shaped head. Arms taper slightly

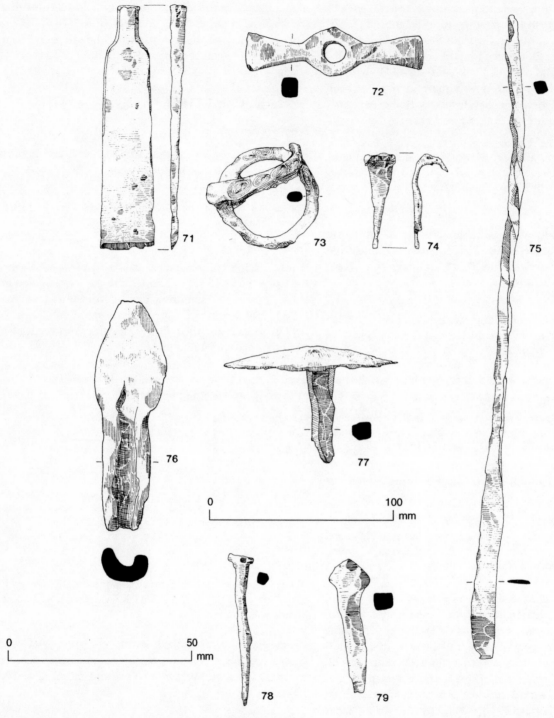

Fig. 58 Tools 71-75, Military Object 76, Fasteners and Fittings 77-79 Scale 1:2 (except 72 and 76, 1:1 and no. 75 approx. 3:8)

and are turned down. Shaft broken. Shaft length 29mm, width 7mm, thickness 9mm.

The T-clamp is a common structural fitting which would have fulfilled many functions. This form most likely held pieces of curved wood in place. A mid-first century parallel comes from Hod Hill, Dorset (Manning 1985, 131-2 and pl. 62).

84) Site 2, 1971.566 OC.
Iron T-clamp with slightly splayed arms. Length 263mm.

This is a form often used to hold vertical box-tiles in position. Similar examples come from Risingham, Northumberland (Manning 1985, 132) and Shakenoak Farm site A (Brodribb, Hands and Walker 1968, fig. 107).

Latch-lifter

85) Site 1 Unstratified.
Iron latch-lifter. Flat handle with loop at head. Strongly curved blade of circular section has a slightly upturned tip. Length 249mm.

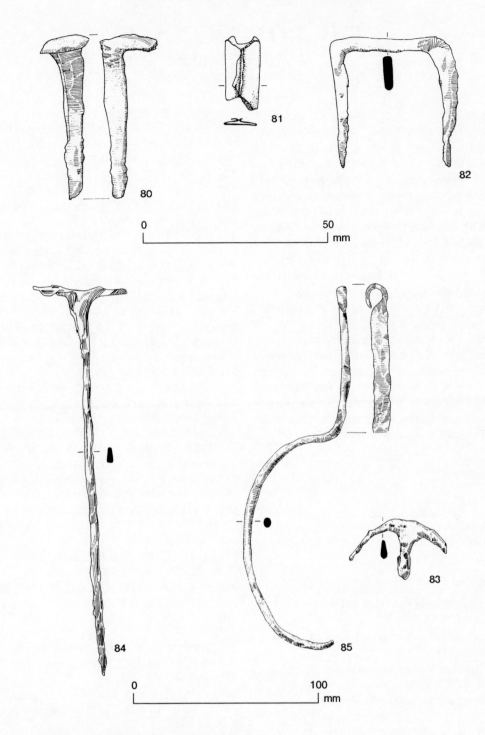

0   50
          mm

0   100
          mm

Fig. 59 Fasteners and Fittings 80-85 Scale 1:1 (except 84 and 85, 3:8)

This is a typical Roman form; good parallels come from Borough Hill, Northants. (Manning 1985, 89 and pls. 38-39).

Note:

A number of objects from Sites 1 to 5 have not been included here, mainly because positive identification was impossible. This body of material includes probable items of personal adornment, toilet instruments, fasteners and fittings, tools, metalworking offcuts, and material associated with amber, bone and glass working. A full catalogue is held in archive.

Acknowledgements

I am grateful to Graham Morgan for his time and encouragement. Patrick Clay, Nicholas Cooper, Yolanda Courtney, Nina Crummy, Anthony Gouldwell, Peter Liddle, and Deirdre O'Sullivan provided much appreciated advice and information, and Hilary Cool and Sian Davies carried out the initial glass identifications.

THE ROMAN COINS
Matthew Ponting

Introduction

A total of 62 coins from Site 1 and 2 are included in this report (32 from Site 1 and 30 from Site 2), of which only 57 were sufficiently clear to allow their attribution to one of the 21 issuing periods used. The methodology employed in this report is based on the work of Reece (summarised in Reece 1988) and is founded on the view that the pattern of coin loss on a given site reflects a variety of economic and social conditions. It is, however, important to understand that a straightforward interpretation of such data is misleading, and that the following factors need to be considered:

i) The volume of coinage produced at any one period.
ii) The length of the period analysed.
iii) The relative values of the coins between periods.

With the data from Sites 1 and 2, it is also important to appreciate the small size of the assemblages in question. Despite this however, it is felt that it is possible to detect certain important general trends within the two assemblages, especially when they are combined and treated as a single group.

The Catalogue

Site 1

1) ANTONINUS PIUS. AE *Sestertius*. Rome. AD 140-144. ANTONINVS.AVG.PIVS.P.P.TR.P.COS.III. laur bust r. PROVIDENTIAE. DEORVM.S.C. winged thunderbolt. 31mm. RIC 618.
EPR 70.310.

2) GALLIENUS.AE *Antoninianus*. Rome. AD 260-268. GALLIENVS.AVG. rad.bust.r. APOLLINI.CONS.AVG. z . Centaur.r. 19mm. H.95. EPR 70.307.

3) CLAUDIUS II. AE *Antoninianus*. AD 268-270. Corroded and illegible. 17mm. EPR 70.333.

4) DIOCLETIAN. Pre-reform *Antoninianus*. AD 284-296. 21mm. damaged. EPR 71.406.

5) Unidentifiable radiate, probably official. 15mm. EPR 71.419.

6) Unidentifiable radiate, probably official. 17mm. EPR 70.321.

7) Unidentifiable radiate, probably Claudius II. 20mm. EPR 70.334.

8) Radiate copy. Tetrician prototype-PAX type. (cut quarter of flattened regular coin?). 15mm. EPR 70.302.

9) Radiate copy. 'matchstick man'-type. 10mm. EPR 70.314.

10) CARAUSIUS. AE *Antoninianus*. AD 286-293. 'C' mint. IMP.C.CARAVSIVS.P.F.AVG. rad.bust.r. PAX.AVG. s p . Pax.stg.l. 23mm. H.131. EPR 71.410.

11) CONSTANTINE I. AE *Follis*. AD 312-313. London. IMP.CONSTANTINVS.P.F.AVG. Rev.SOL.INVICTO.COMITI. *PLN. RIC.279. 20mm. EPR 71.405.

12) CONSTANTINE I. AE *Follis*. AD 321-324. illegible mint. CONSTANTINVS.AVG.laur.hd.r. BEATA.TRANQVILLITAS. globe set on altar inscribed. VOTIS.XX. 19mm. corroded. EPR 71.400.

13) Urbs Roma. AD 330-337. illegible mint. wolf and twins. 17mm. worn. EPR 69.122.

14) House of Constantine. AE3. AD 330-335. illegible mint. GLORIA EXERCITVS. Two soldiers either side of two standards. 17mm. Corroded. EPR 69.181.

15) CONSTANTIUS II. AE3. AD 330-335. Lyon. FL.IVL.CONTANTIVS.NOB.C. laur.hd.l.rev as no.14 above. PLG. 18mm. LRBC 182. EPR 70.303.

16) House of Constantine. AE3. AD 335-337. Trier. GLORIA.EXERCITVS. .TRS. Two soldiers either side of one standard. 14mm. copy?. LRBC 87-91. EPR 69.133.

17) CONSTANS. AE3. AD 335-337. Rome (?). FL.CONSTANS.NOB.CAES.laur.hd.l.rev.as 16 above. 16mm. copy?
LRBC 561 (?). EPR 69.176.

18) CONSTANS. AE3. AD 337-341. Trier. CONSTANS.P.F.AVG.laur.hd.l.rev.as 16 above. TRPV. 14mm. copy? LRBC 131. EPR 69.182.

19) CONSTANS. AE3. AD 337-341. Trier(?). as 18. rev. as 16. .TR. not in RIC or LRBC. 15mm. EPR 69.180.

20) CONSTANS. AE3. AD 337-341. Trier. CONSTANS.P.F.AVG.laur.hd. rev.as.16. .TRP. LRBC 110. 13mm. copy?. EPR 71.308.

21) CONSTANS. AE3. AD 341-346. illegible mint. CONSTANS.P.F.AVG.laur.hd. rev. as Site 2 no.20. 13mm. copy? EPR 69.149.

22) CONSTANS. AE3. AD 341-346. Lyon (?). type as 21 above. 13mm. copy (?). EPR 69.172.

23) VALENTINIAN I. AE3. AD 364-375. illegible mint. SECVRITAS. REIPVBLICAE. victory adv.l. 17mm. very worn.
EPR 69.177.

24) THEODOSIUS I. AE3. AD 388-392. Aquilea. SALVS REIPVBLICAE. AQS. victory.l. LRBC 1106. 12mm. EPR 69.134.

25) ARCADIUS. AE3. AD 388-392. Aquilea. SALVS.REIPVBLICAE. AQS. victory.l. LRBC 1107. 12mm. EPR 70.306.

26) House of Theodosius. AE3. AD 388-402. type as Site 2 no.26. 12mm. very worn. EPR 70.309.

27) House of Theodosius. AE3. AD 388-402. uncertain types. 12mm EPR 70.305.

28) Uncertain AE4. possibly minim (?). 10mm. EPR 69.125.

29) Uncertain AE4. Late 4th century (?). 12mm. EPR 69.174.

30) Uncertain AE4. Late 4th century (?). 12mm. EPR 70.331.

31) Uncertain AE2. early 4th century (?). 23mm. EPR 71.403.

Additional Coin. This was identified in 1969 by an unknown individual and was subsequently lost.

ANTONINUS PIUS. AE Sestertius AD 138-161. 29mm? EPR 69.119.

Site 2

1) *GALLIENUS.AE.Antoninianus*. Rome. AD 260-268. GALLIENVS.AVG.rad.bust.r SECVRIT.PERPET. H .Securitas.stg. 20mm. H.78. EPN 71.519.

2) CLAUDIUS II. AE *Antoninianus*. AD 268-270. Corroded. 19mm. EPN 71.516.

3) CLAUDIUS II. AE *Antoninianus*. AD 268-270. Rome. IMP.CLAVDIVS.AVG. rad.bust.r. PROVIDENT.AVG. X . Providentia.stg. 19mm H.36 (var). EPN 71.537.

4) VICTORINIUS. AE *Antoninianus*. AD 268-270. Cologne (?). IMP.C.VICTORINIVS.P.F.AVG.rad.bust.r. PAX.AVG. V . Pax.stg.l. 20mm. H.11. EPN 71.574.

5) TETRICUS I. AE *Antoninianus*. AD 270-273. Trier (?). IMP.TETRICVS.P.F.AVG.rad.bust.r. HILARITAS.AVGG.Hilaritas.l. 18mm. H.17. EPN 71.551.

6) Unidentifiable radiate, probably a copy. 15mm. EPN 71.521

7) Radiate copy. Unclear Tetrician prototype. 15mm. EPN 71.546.

8) Radiate copy. corroded. 14mm. EPN 71.568.

9) Radiate copy. `matchstick man' type. 10mm. corroded. EPN 71.530.

10) Radiate copy. illegible. 8mm. EPN 71.572.

11) CONSTANTINE I. AE *Follis*. AD 318-319. Trier. IMP.CONSTANTINVS.laur. and helmeted hd.r. VICTORIAE.LAETAE.PRINCIPIV. PTR . two victories. similar to RIC.209. Crude style. 17mm. EPN 71.539.

12) CONSTANTINE I. AE *Follis*. AD 321. London. CONSTANTINVS.P.AVG.rad.bust.l.holding eagle-tipped sceptre. BEATA.TRANQVILLITAS. as Site 1 no.12 above. PLON . 19mm. RIC.201. corroded. EPN 71.541.

13) Constantinopolis. AD 330-337. illegible mint. victory on prow. 13mm. copy? corroded. EPN 71.503.

14) Urbs Roma. AD 330-337. illegible mint. wolf and twins. 13mm. copy?. EPN 71.500.

15) Urbs Roma. AD 330-335. Lyons. wolf and twins . PLG . 15mm. copy? LRBC.184. EPN 71.562.

16) Urbs Roma. AD 330-335. Lyons. wolf and twins. PLG . 15mm. LRBC 184. corroded. EPN 71.502.

17) CONSTANTIUS II. AE3. AD 330-335. Trier. FL.IVL.CONSTANTIVS.NOB.C.laur.hd.l.GLORIA.EXER CITVS. Two soldiers either side of two standards. TR.P. 17mm. LRBC 64. EPN 71.571.

18) CONSTANTIUS II. AE3. AD 330-335. Sisca. FL.IVL.CONSTANTIVS.NOB.C.rev.as Site 1 no.14. .ASIS. . 17mm LRBC 749. EPN 71.570.

19) House of Constantine. AE3. AD 330-341. type as Site 2 no.16. 13mm. copy? corroded. EPN 71.504.

20) CONSTANS or CONSTANTIUS. AE3. AD 341-346. Trier. VICTORAE.DD.AVGG.Q.NN. two victories. TRP . LRBC 139/140. 15mm. corroded. EPN 71.522.

21) CONSTANS. AE3. AD 341-346. Trier. as 20 abovebut TRP . LRBC 142. 16mm. EPN 71.528.

22) Fel.Temp Copy. AD 354-364. soldier spearing fallen horseman type. 13mm. EPN 71.533.

23) FEl.Temp Copy. AD 354-364. soldier dragging barbarian fron hut type. 10mm. very worn. EPN 71.307.

24) VALENS or VALENTINIAN I. AE3. AD 364-378. illegible mint. type as Site 2 no.23. 13mm. very worn. EPN 71.567.

25) VALENTINIAN II. AE4. AD 388-392. illegible mint. VICTORIA.AVGGG. victory adv.l. 11mm. EPN 71.501.

26) THEODOSIUS I. AE3. AD 388-392. Lyon. VICTORIA.AVGGG.PLG. victory.l. LRBC 391. 12mm. EPN 71.538.

27) House of Theodosius. AD 388-402. Aquilea. SALVS.REIPVBLICAE. AQS . victory.l. 12mm. EPN 71.531.

28) House of Theodosius. AE3. AD 388-402. Uncertain type. 12mm. EPN 70 (trial trench).

29) Clipped AR Siliqua. post 397 (?). VIRTVS.ROMANORVM. rev.type. 12mm. EPN 71.515.

30) Uncertain AE4. possibly minim(?). 9mm. EPN 71.534.

Abbreviated References used in the Catalogues.

H = Roman Imperial Coins in the Hunter Coin Cabinet, Vol.IV.

RIC = Roman Imperial Coinage (Mattingley and Sydenham 1925 etc.).

LRBC = Late Roman Bronze Coinage (Carson et al. 1965).

Discussion

The spread of coin loss across the issuing periods, is demonstrated in the form of histograms, firstly for each of the two assemblages, and secondly with the data from the two sites combined (fig.60). Despite the increased effects of the minor variations caused by the very small numbers of coins from each site, both show a comparable coin loss pattern. When the combined figures are compared with the pattern established by Reece for the 'British Background' (Reece 1987, 80), there are only slight differences. These may be due to the statistical variation caused by the still rather small number of coins. There are however, three areas exhibiting differences which may be due to other factors, and these are discussed below.

Reece (1988, 91) was the first to notice the tendency for specific types of Romano-British site to cluster when their coin loss figures are plotted. There is, in particular, a notable division between urban and non-urban settlements (Reece 1987, 93), and it is significant that Sites 1 and 2, fit into the lower mid-range non-urban area of Reece's graph along with most other small towns and rural settlements.

Looking at the individual coins from the combined assemblage, only the *sestertii* of Antoninus Pius (Site 1 no.1 and the additional coin from site 1, now lost) dates from before the middle of the third century, when coin use on both sites would appear to take off, and there is good reason to suspect that the degree of wear might indicate that it was not in fact lost until the mid-third century as well. Casey has stated (1988, 49) that the `...observation of finds...indicate that large numbers of second century *sestertii* circulated till the middle of the third...'.

The assemblages from both sites show a weighting towards the later years, and this is consistent with the majority of non-urban Romano-British sites. While this may be a reflection of the intensity of occupation on the

Date	Issue	Site 1	Site 2	Combi.
to AD41	1	0	0	0
41-54	2a	0	0	0
54-68	2b	0	0	0
69-96	3	0	0	0
96-117	4	0	0	0
117-38	5	0	0	0
138-61	6	7	0	2
161-80	7a	0	0	0
180-92	7b	0	0	0
193-222	8	0	0	0
222-38	9a	0	0	0
238-59	9b	0	0	0
259-75	10	24	36	31
275-96	11	7	0	3.5
296-317	12	4	0	2
317-30	13a	4	7	6
330-48	13b	35	32	33.5
348-64	14	0	7	3.5
364-78	15a	4	3	3.5
378-88	15b	0	0	0
388-402	16	15	15	15
		100	**100**	**100**

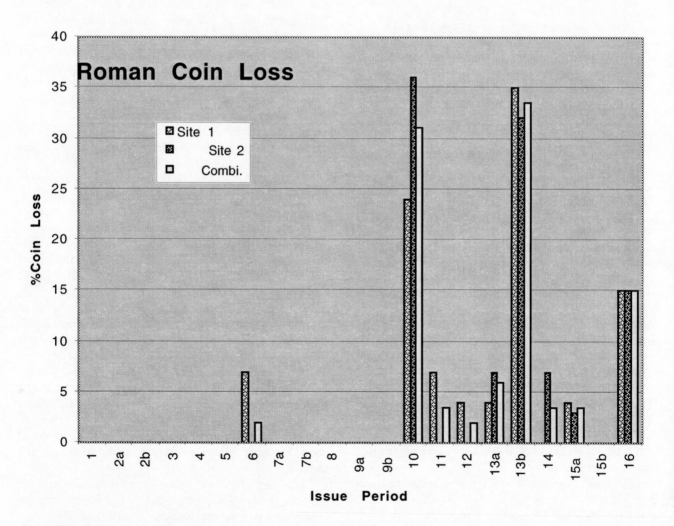

Fig. 60 Roman Coin loss at Empingham. A) Site 1 B) Site 2 C) Combined

two sites, or a number of local factors, it is important to remember that a lack of coinage does not necessarily reflect a lack of occupation, but more a lack of coin use.

In the case of Sites 1 and 2, the evidence would suggest that the use of coinage on any scale does not begin until the reign of Gallienus (AD 260-268). A total of 17 coins from both sites were recorded for the period AD 260-273, and they can be subdivided as follows: 5 'Central' Empire; 2 'Gallic' Empire; 3 Uncertain; and 7 copies; usually dated AD 270-286. All of the copies, where identifiable, are from Gallic prototypes, and have the following diameters: 3 at 15mm; 1 at 14mm; 2 at 10mm; and 1 at 8mm. This represents a fairly narrow range, and is at the lower end of the scale. The recovery of such small coins also provides evidence for the recovery standard of the excavation; some sites having a bias towards the larger copies because of their greater visibility (Hammerson. 1989.423).

One coin of Carausius and one pre-reform coin of Diocletian occur from the period 284-296. The coin of Diocletian is badly damaged, presumably in antiquity, and such coins tend to be rare as site finds in Britain. However, coins of this period in general are usually common on British sites, and the low number from Sites 1 and 2, is therefore rather unusual and may indicate a lower level of economic activity at this time.

The period AD 296-317 is represented by one well preserved coin of Constantine I. This gives a less anomalous figure than the previous period.

Four coins belong to the period AD 317-330. The earlier coin is relatively unworn, but is of a rather 'vernacular' style having no exact duplicate in RIC.

Coins of the period AD 330-348 are common on the majority of British sites, and so the number from Sites 1 and 2 is unexceptional. Recent work suggests that a high proportion of these coins are in fact contemporary copies, and although only three of the 19 from Empingham can be regarded as copies with certainty, it is probable that a greater percentage are in fact copies. Reece (1972, 274), classes up to 30% of coins from this period as copies, and as many as 60-70% of the issues from Richborough now appear to be copies (Hammerson 1989, 424). It is only by establishing the silver content of these coins that their origin can be established as only the official issues contain 1-2% of silver (King 1978, 45). Hammerson regards size as being a useful indicator: the official issues ranging from 16-18mm for the earlier coins, and 15-17mm for the later types. Taking 15mm therefore as our threshold for official coins, it emerges that at least nine out of the 19 coins are likely to be copies (47%). These copies were probably introduced as a supplementary coinage between AD 341, when official production appears to have stopped, and AD 348, when the coinage was reformed (upgraded).

The products of this reform (from AD 348-364), comprise large 25mm argentiferous bronze coins of high value, which are rarely excavated in Britain, and were immediately supplemented by a further spate of copying to remedy the lack of 'small change'. The two examples from the Empingham assemblage are both copies, now dated to AD 354-364. The module size of these copies varies considerably, and the two examples are both small, measuring 13mm and 10mm. Each coin represents a different prototype; the smaller is of the earlier type with a soldier dragging a barbarian from his hut. The larger of the two depicts a soldier spearing a fallen horseman. These coins are usually common site finds, especially on non-urban sites, and particularly associated with temple and oppida sites (Brickstock 1987, 85). It may be significant therefore that the two coins from the Empingham sites amount to around 40% below the 'norm' calculated by Reece (1987, 83).

The coins from Sites 1 and 2 belonging to the last 40 years of the Roman administration in Britain, AD 364-402, can be divided into two groups; those of the House of Valentinian (AD 364-378), and those of the House of Theodosius (AD 388-402). Only two very worn examples are present for the earlier period, which is usually a period of fairly considerable coin loss on most British sites. This fact may be significant at Empingham, especially as the degree of wear may indicate deposition sometime after their official issue slot.

In contrast the later period (AD 388-402) at Empingham is characterised by increasing activity, at a time when most British sites experience a gradual fall-off in coin finds, and presumably, coin use. This period yields nearly 16% of all coins, and is the third most prolific period, when both sites are viewed together.

Of particular interest is the clipped siliqua (Site 2 no.29). These coins have been seen as an official or semi-official issue or action, reducing the weight of the existing silver pieces to 1.3g in line with the issues produced after AD 397 (Boon 1988, 145). It may however, have been a purely fraudulent action. Nevertheless, it does suggest a late date for their loss, and if taken with the relatively large volume of Theodosian and later coins, it seems reasonable to suggest continued monetary economic activity until the very end of the fourth and even into the early fifth century.

THE ROMAN TILE

Idris Bowden

Introduction

A total of 781 fragments of tile weighing 170.133 kg was retrieved from all sites, the vast proportion of which derived from Sites 1 and 2, with smaller amounts from Sites 3 and 5. The on-site retention policy for the tile does make a comprehensive study difficult, since only material from stratified contexts was kept, but it was considered that this probably represented an accurate sample of the range of fabrics and forms present.

Classification

All the material was classified into the following form and fabric types and quantified by weight and numbers of fragments.

Types

Roof tile

Tegula: Flat roof tiles with flanges on two parallel sides.

Imbrex: Curved roof tile designed to span across the edges of adjacent *tegulae*.

Slates: Diamond-shaped sheets of stone with suspension hole at the top.

Hypocaust tile

Box Flue tile: Hollow rectangular tile

Voussoir: Tapering flue tile for vaulted roofs

Chimney: Rounded flue shape with arched cutouts

Structural tile

Wall tile: Large square bricks with thickness over 35mm. Used in levelling courses in walls or for *pilae* flooring supports.

Fabrics

Four tile fabrics were identified.

Fabric 1

Orange oxidised clay fabric with quartz sand inclusions, and often a reduced grey core. The degree of coarseness is variable but separate definable fabrics are not apparent.

Fabric 2

Clay fabric with abundant shell tempering, varying in colour from orange to grey brown.

Fabric 3

Stone roofing slates produced from a local limestone quarried in the area of Collyweston, five miles to the south east of Empingham, and known as Collyweston slate.

Fabric 4

Stone roofing slate produced from slate quarried from Swithland in the Charnwood area of north-west Leicestershire.

Analysis

The quantification by weight of the tile by fabric and form is summarised in Tables 21, 22, and 23. Weight is judged to be the most objective measure of the amount of tile since the weight discrepency between different fabrics and forms is not great, and it gives a more accurate estimate of the amount of unclassified material which by its very definition occurs in a larger number of fragments of small size.

	Fabric 1	Fabric 2	Fabric 3	Fabric 4	Total
Site 1	24815	914	20825	308	46862
Site 2	105232	9137	6392	–	120761
Site 3	1590	–	–	–	1590
Site 5	920	–	–	–	920
Total	132557	10051	27217	308	170133

Table 21: *The Occurrence of Tile Fabrics by Site, Quantified by Weight (g)*

	Site 1	Site 2	Site 3	Site 5	Total
Tegula	8036	35699	–	448	44183
Imbrex	1320	1172	–	–	2492
Slate	21133	6392	–	–	27525
Boxflue	6040	21045	1590	352	29027
Voussoir	–	1176	–	–	1176
Wall	3861	48853	–	–	52714
?Chimney	500	–	–	–	500
Unclass.	6472	5924	–	120	12516
Total	46862	120761	1590	920	170133

Table 22: *The Occurrence of Tile Types by Site, Quantified by Weight (g)*

	Fabric 1	Fabric 2	Fabric 3	Fabric 4	Total
Tegula	44183	–	–	–	44183
Imbrex	2492	–	–	–	2492
Slate	–	–	27217	308	27525
Boxflue	20304	8723	–	–	29027
Voussoir	1176	–	–	–	1176
Wall	52714	–	–	–	52714
Chimney	500	–	–	–	500
Unclass.	11188	1328	–	–	12516
Total	132557	10051	27217	308	170133

Table 23: *The Occurrence of Tile Type by Fabric, Quantified by Weight (g)*

Discussion

The above tables highlight a number of areas of interest. The assemblages from Sites 3 and 5 are too small for comment except to say that they possess only Fabric 1 which is the commonest of the four fabrics, and that in the case of Site 3, there is no structural evidence to suggest the use of tile, and so the material could well be rubbish deriving from Site 1.

The villa building on Site 2 with its hypocaust system not surprisingly possessed a wide range of tile types and fabrics including voussoirs, but the range from Site 1 is equally wide and includes a possible chimney fragment. One anomaly springing from this is the occurrence of so much box flue tile on Site 1, which presents no evidence for the existence of a hypocaust system, unless it lay in the badly damaged north-western part of Building 1. Roofing tile is very common on both sites, but what is slightly surprising is the low amount of *imbrices*, which cannot be explained just by their smaller size when compared with *tegulae*. *Imbrices* are inherently more breakable and this may have led to a retrieval bias during excavation. One contributing feature of tile use on Site 2 was that *tegulae* were used or possibly reused as *pilae* bases in the hypocaust.

Fabric 1 appears to have been used for all categories of tile, while in contrast the shell-tempered Fabric 2 was only used for the production of box flue tiles. There would not appear to be any technological reason for this, and it is probable that the workshop simply supplied that type of tile for a specific building project such as the insertion of a hypocaust system into an existing building. Evidence from excavations of Drayton II Roman villa, Leics., on the Welland, 12 miles to the south-east, indicates that the same shell-tempered tile

was used for all forms and a Northamptonshire source is likely (Cooper, Beavitt, O'Sullivan and Young 1989, 15).

Of the two stone fabrics 3 and 4, Fabric 3 is not surprisingly the most common, as the Collyweston quarries lie only a few miles from the Gwash Valley. However it is somewhat surprising that any Swithland slate reached the site at all, considering the distance of 25 miles, although it does appear to have been used to roof at least part of the villa building at Drayton II (Cooper *et al.* 1989, 14). The occurrence of different fabrics probably relates to different phases of building as supply patterns changed. On Site 1, Collyweston roofing slates appear to have been used specifically in the construction of Building 2 at some point in the fourth century. The large amount from Site 2 is exaggerated by the occurrence of a number of complete examples which were dumped down the well, sometime late in the fourth century at the earliest.

WALL PLASTER AND MORTAR

G. C. Morgan

Introduction

12.7kg of wall plaster was retrieved from the excavations, and the bulk of this came from the villa building on Site 2. The lack of above-ground structural survival dictated that no plaster was found *in situ*, and most was recovered from the rubble layers overlying the building and the fill of the well. While this material can be attributed to the villa building with confidence, the occurrence of wall plaster fragments from Sites 1 and 3 is more problematic, since none of the structures suggest a residential function, and it is therefore most likely that this material was introduced to the site perhaps in hardcore rubble during rebuilding.

The fragmentary nature of the wall plaster dictates that little structural information or detail of decorative schemes can be gained. However, information on materials employed in the production of plasters and mortars can be obtained, and changes in composition provide some evidence for phases of refurbishment. Representative samples were therefore selected for analysis with this aim in mind.

Examining the Layer Make-up of Wall Plaster

The macroscopic analysis of wall plaster samples established the following range of layer thicknesses.

Layer	Thickness (mm)		'Lime' content/Acid soluble
	Range	Average	
Paint	0.05-0.2	0.07	-
intonaco	0.1-0.6	0.2	-
upper	5-28	12	43% sand, 49% sand & tile
middle	15-30	16	-
lower	13-30	21	43%
single layer	23-40	33	43% tile
single layer	30-50	41	43% sand

Table 24: *Layer Make Up and 'Lime' Content of Wall Plasters.*

Painting Technique

Generally, the paint appeared to have been applied by the *buon fresco* method, although some of the over painting may have been in *fresco secco*. The use of pink on white *intonaco* is of note as it was used as a ground layer for cinnabar on occasion. The single occurrence of cinnabar (Site 1) was, however, on a white ground.

Pigments

The pigments used were predominantly those commonly found in Roman Britain, and comprised red ochre (haematite) or brick dust, yellow ochre (limonite), green earth (glauconite), white lime, black soot or charcoal, and crushed Egyptian blue which was manufactured and probably imported. However, the occurrence of red cinnabar which was also imported is of significance. In this instance, it is confined to use on the oolitic plasters.

Particle Size Analysis

Particle size analysis was carried out on 17 samples of plaster and mortar, one from Site 1 and 16 from Site 2. Five broad categories of plaster and mortar were identified as follows.

1) Fine buff plaster containing quantities of clay or silt.
2) Coarse sand plaster.
3) Tile, and sand or gravel plaster.
4) Tile only *opus signinum* plaster.
5) Oolitic limestone plaster.

The composition of the 17 samples is summarized in the following table.

Composition by % Weight

Sample		Gravel	Sand	Silt	'lime'	comments	Type
1	(Site 1)	0	2	98	29	mainly silt	1
	Site 2						
2	PL1 (middle)	42	30	28	44	tile	4
3	PL1 (lower)	34	40	26	46	tile	4
4	PL2	1	65	34	42	coarse sand	2
5	QQ1 Rm.8	29	49	22	50	tile and sand	3
6	QQ2(upper) Rm.8	2	63	35	44	coarse sand	2
7	QQ2(lower) Rm.8	1	70	29	43	coarse sand	2
8	QV1 Rm.8	29	46	25	48	tile and sand	3
9	QV2 Rm.8	29	45	26	48	tile and sand	3
10	QV3 Rm.8	3	64	33	42	coarse sand	2
11	RK3	1	66	33	43	coarse sand	2
12	RL1 Rm.8	58	29	13	42	tile	4
13	RL2 Rm.8	28	53	19	48	tile and sand	3
14	RS (middle)	38	30	32	50	tile	4
15	RS (lower)	31	43	26	42	tile	4
16	RZ1 Rm.8	63	19	18	36	tile	4
17	RZ2 Rm.8	2	58	40	45	coarse sand	2

Table 25: *Aggregate Particle Size Distribution Analysis of Plaster from Empingham Sites 1 and 2.*

The results of the aggregate particle size distribution analysis are summarised in the following graph (fig.61), in which the composition of one example of each of plaster types 1 to 4 is plotted. Type 5 is not plotted since the sample was comprised almost entirely of acid soluble material. The sample plotted are numbers 1, 2, 13 and 17.

Discussion

Figure 61 clearly illustrates the differences in particle size composition exhibited by the plasters and mortars examined due to the use of a variety of aggregate types. Ironstones ranging from ferruginous sandstones to fossiliferous haematite and ferruginous limestone were commonly present. Fossiliferous and oolitic limestones were also found, together with round to sub-angular quartz sand, crushed brick or tile and small amounts of flint and quartzite. This indicates the exploitation of a variety of local geological sources.

The sample from Site 1 is the only one falling into Type 1, with a remarkably high silt content of 98%. Of the samples from the villa building on Site 2 those from the rubble filling around the hypocaust of Room 8 are much coarser, falling into Types 2, 3, and 4, but particularly Type 4, the *opus signinum* plaster which is typically used for plaster in bath suites. The fact that three different types of plaster were present in the rubble filling of one room may indicate that refurbishment had taken place on more than one occasion but was not evident from the excavated structure.

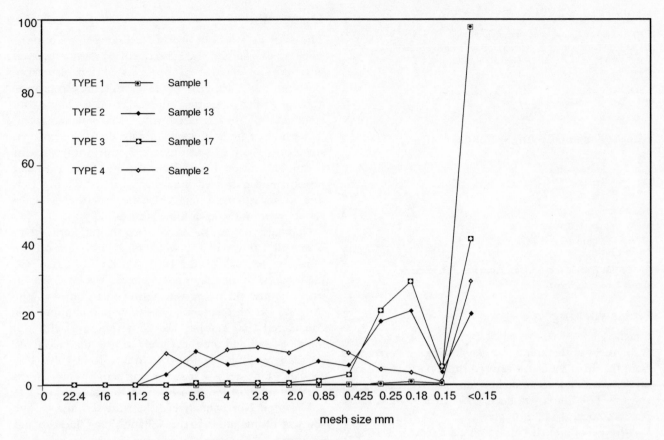

Fig. 61 Particle Size Analysis of Roman Wallplaster and Mortar Aggregates

METALWORKING AND GLASSWORKING RESIDUES

G. C. Morgan

Introduction

Industrial residues were recovered from all sites except Sites 5 and 6, and were examined in order to assess the range of activities undertaken on each. Analysis resulted in the following identifications summarised below.

Results

Site 1 (Roman)

Context		Material	Weight
69	AR	Tap slag	250g
69	EA	Fired clay possible mould fragments	35g
69	EH	Hearth slag	27g
69	u/s	Hearth residues	30g
70	GB	Tap slag	50g
70	GD	Tap slag	32g
71	DO	Vitrified clay and slag (furnace lining)	34g
71	DO	Tap slag	35g
71	u/s	iron slag	2g
71	EZ	roasted (prepared) ore	10g
71	AP	Hearth slag (incl. iron and charcoal)	53g
71	AS	Vitrified clay (?furnace lining)	9g
71	AS	Tap slag	6g
71	AU	Vitrified clay	9g
71	AS	Tap slag/furnace slag	108g
71	BA	Tap slag	86g
71	BJ	Hearth slag	139g
71	BK	Blast furnace slag ?modern	11g
71	BU	Tap slag	16g
71	DB	Tap slag	155g
71	DB	Furnace slag	63g
Total			**1160g**

Total Amount of Tap Slag   738g
Total Amount of Hearth Slag   219g
Total Amount of other residues   203g

Site 2 (Roman)

The Well

71	NQ	Hearth slag (forging residues)	18g
71	NZ	Hearth bottom	215g
71	OE	Hearth bottom (forging)	676g

Other contexts

71	SE	Tap slag	90g
71	OF	Tap slag	99g
Total			**1098g**

Total Amount of Tap slag   189g
Total Amount of Hearth slag   909g

Site 3 (Anglo-Saxon)

EMP 66 unstratified.	Tap slag	72g
EMP 66 unstratified.	Furnace slag	38g
EMP 67 unstratified	Tap slag	48g
EMP 67 unstratified	Furnace residues	40g
EMP 67 Grave 7 fill	Tap slag	251g
EMP 67 Grave 7 fill	Furnace residue (Fe stone)	13g
EPS 69 AA	Tap slag	56g
EPS 69 AG	Tap slag	59g
EPS 70 ZY (SFB 2).	Tap slag	177g
EPS 70 ZY (SFB 2).	3 Furnace bases	1234g
Total		**1998g**

Total Amount of Tap slag   663g
Total Amount of Furnace Residue   1325g

Site 4 (Anglo-Saxon)

EPW 72 AM	Tap slag	354g
EPW 72 AQ	Iron working hearth residue	12g
EPW 72 AX	Hearth residues	5g
EPW 72 BM	Hearth slag	189g
Total		**560g**
Total amount of tapslag		354g
Total amount of hearth residues		206g

Site 7 (Tickencote Anglo-Saxon)

(1)	100/160 Tap slag	58g
(2)	Furnace slag	105g
(2)	Tap slag	206g
(11)	Tap slag	86g
Total		**455g**
Total Amount of tap slag		350g
Total Amount of furnace slag		105g
Grand Total		**5261g**

Table 26: *Evidence of Metalworking Residues from Empingham.*

Glassworking

Site 3

A fragment of the lining of a glass furnace was retrieved from the fill of Sunken-Featured Building 1. It is of very fine clay with a layer of melted blue-green glass over the surface. The lining has been subsequently built up to partially cover the layer of glass.

A runnel of melted blue-green glass (35mm x 10mm) (Sf.no 54) was also retrieved from 3.0m east of Sunken-featured Building 1.

Discussion

The sites as a whole provide evidence for both the smelting of iron and the subsequent working of iron in hearths. The relative proportions of tap slag from smelting, and hearth residues from smithing can provide a guide to the processes undertaken at each site, but caution should be exercised with such a small amounts. The evidence must be coupled with that for associated structures such as hearths, which were only present within the aisled barn (Building 1) on Site 1, and possibly in the disused Sunken-Featured Building 2 on Site 3, although in the latter case the structural evidence is unclear from the excavation records.

Comparisons can be drawn with the adjacent site at Whitwell 1.0 km to the west, which also lies on the ironstone bedrock (Todd 1981, 15; fig.9), and so had ready access to the major raw material. Two oval-shaped iron-smelting furnaces were found in Room 4 of the Romano-British rectangular masonry building, but it is considered that neither are contemporary with the building itself and are most likely to post-date it, falling somewhere within the fourth century (Todd 1981, 19). Evidence for extensive iron working activity comes from the excavation of the Iron Age and Romano-British site at Wakerley, Northants. which lies just six miles to the south of Empingham, in the Welland Valley (Jackson and Ambrose 1978).

The evidence for glassworking is very slight, and the furnace fragment could well be residual from the Roman occupation of Site 3, rather than being Anglo-Saxon. However, the melting down of Roman glass for reuse as frit for beads is a possibility.

THE ANIMAL BONE

Anita Morrison*

*Integrating information from archive reports by R. Clark, M. Harman, and S. Hinds.

Introduction

This report considers a total of 4,388 stratified bone fragments from Sites 1, 2, 4, and 6. Due to small sample size and poor contextual information, material from Sites 3 and 5 was ignored. A total of 3,714 fragments was analysed by Anita Morrison in 1991. The remainder comprised two stratified late Roman well groups. The first, from Site 1 (Phase 3), contained (at least) 374 fragments analysed initially by Mary Harman soon after the excavation in 1970 and subsequently by Richard Clark in 1990, confirming the findings of the original report. The second, from Site 6, contained 300 fragments and was analysed by Sarah Hinds in 1991. The following report summarises the contents of the key stratified groups, the remainder of the information is in archive.

Preservation and Context

The preservation of bone at Empingham varied according to context and area but 49% was identifiable to species and bone type. The groups from the Romano-British farmstead on Site 1 produced much in the way of neonatal material and the small bones of wild birds, owing to the greater time available for retrieval and the more secure stratification of the deposits. With the exception of the Roman well deposit on Site 6, the material from the other sites was often more fragmentary by comparison. The occurrence of large groups of stratified bone coincides closely with that of the large groups of well-dated ceramic material, and so it has been possible to study the bone assemblage from the Iron Age to the Early Anglo-Saxon period in discrete chronological groups with a degree of confidence. Unfortunately, the amount of bone belonging to successive phases varies, and so comparison across groups has to be undertaken with caution.

Methodology

Identification

The identification of the material was undertaken with reference to the comparative skeletal collections of the University of Leicester and Leicestershire Museums. The identification of animal bone was assisted by reference to Schmidt's *Atlas of Animal Bones* (1972) and Cohen and Serjeantson's *Manual for the Identification of Bird Bones from Archaeological Sites* (1983). Neonatal bones and juvenile animal bones were identified with reference to Amorosi (1989), and an attempt was made to age this material using formulae given in Prummel (1988 & 1989). Amphibian material was identified using *An Atlas of Chordate Structure* (Bracegirdle and Miles 1979).

Age Determination

Two methods were used to determine the ages of the animals at death: epiphyseal fusion and mandible wear stages (some data held in archive). Fusion data were studied using Silver (1969) and Amorosi (1989), and for neonatal material, Prummel (1988; 1989). Cattle, sheep and pig mandibles were studied with reference to Grant (1982) and horse mandibles with reference to Levine (1982).

The Proportions of Animals Represented

The proportions of animals represented were determined by counting the total number of identified bone fragments. Counts for 'Epiphyses Only'; and 'Minimum Number of Individuals' (Grant 1975) were made when sample size was appropriate.

Unidentified Material

Material unidentifiable to species or bone type, which made up 51% of the bone recorded, was divided into 'unidentified fragments' and 'ribs' and further subdivided by size into small, medium, large and neonatal. The information concerning each site has been tabulated and is held in archive.

Arrangement of the Report

The material is presented in chronological order, beginning with stratified groups of Iron Age date from Site 4, followed by the Roman wells and other deposits from Sites 1, 2, and 6, and ending with the Anglo-Saxon assemblage from Site 4 (tables 27-35).

The Iron Age

Stratified material of this date derived from the fills of the pit and the eaves drip gully associated with Iron Age Building 3 and are presented below (table 27).

Species	MNI	%MNI	Frags	%Frags	Epiph	%Epiph
Cattle	2	25	7	22	2	30
Sheep	3	37.5	14	44	3	40
Pig	3	37.5	11	34	2	30
Totals	8	100	32	100	7	100

Table 27: *Species Represented at Site 4 (Iron Age)*

The Roman Period

Site 1

Material from Phases 2A, 2B, and 3 is tabulated below.

Species	Frags	%Frags
Cattle	10	43
Sheep	7	30
Pig	3	13
Horse	2	9
Dog	1	5
Totals	23	100

Table 28: *Species Represented at Site 1, Phase 2A (Feature 50) Later 1st Century*

Phase 2A

Material comprised a small sample from Feature 50, a ditch running across the south end of the site dating to the later first or early second century AD (table 28).

Phase 2B

Data are derived from a combination of material from contexts sealed by the Phase 3 masonry aisled barn (Building 1) including Features 1, 2, 4, and 26 (table 29), and dating to the later second century AD.

Species	Frags	%Frags	Epiph.	%Epiph	MNI	%MNI
Cattle	54	7	16	9	9	12
Sheep*	719	88	152	84	51	66
Pig	22	3	5	3	6	8
Dog	3	0.5	4	2	1	1
Chicken	8	1	1	<1	3	4
Goose	3	<1	2	1	2	3
Duck	2	<1	0	0	2	3
Crow	1	<1	0	0	1	1
?Pheasant	1	<1	0	0	1	1
Thrush	1	<1	2	1	1	1
Totals	814	100	182	100	77	100

Table 29: *Species Represented at Site 1, Phase 2B Later 2nd Century*

* Includes 28 neonatal sheep totalling 519 bone fragments.

Phase 3

Material derived from the well on the south side of Building 1, dated by pottery to the late third or early fourth century AD (table 30). The material from below 1.2m depth was considered to form a single coherent group comprising mostly complete and excellently preserved bones with very few unidentifiable fragments.

The group included bones from at least six cattle. Fusion data suggested that they ranged in age from 15 months to possibly in excess of four years with most being at of least 24-30 months. The predominance of lower limb and skull bones as well as knife and chopping marks indicates that the remains represent butchery waste (further details of butchery are held in archive).

At least twenty sheep were represented, at least fourteen (but probably seventeen) were represented by their butchery waste bones alone, whilst three were deposited whole, two as lambs and one as a three and a half year old adult. In all, seventeen skulls were represented. A combination of fusion data, tooth eruption and mandible wear stage analysis indicated that five of the sheep were between 20-28 months old with twelve younger than this.

The pig bones included those from two adults, one of two and a half to three years, the other over three years old. The skeletons of four piglets were also identified, one between one and four weeks, two between one and two weeks and one possibly foetal or neo-natal.

The group also included the near-complete skeletons of two dogs, one an adult male of 18 months, the other a puppy of five to twelve weeks. Numerous small rodents including two shrews, two voles and a mouse were identified as well as amphibians such as frogs or toads during the original analysis by Mary Harman.

Species	MNI	%MNI	Frags
Cattle	6	14	92
Sheep	20	45	221
Pig*	6	14	0
Horse	1	2	1
Dog*	2	5	0
Chicken	5	12	52
Swallow	1	2	2
Kite	1	2	1
Water Rail	1	2	1
Ho. Sparrow	1	2	5
Totals	44	100	374

Table 30: *Proportions of Species Represented from Site 1, Phase 3: the Well*

* Fragment data not calculated for all domesticated mammals.

Site 2

All the material derives from the destruction deposits of the villa building which date to the later fourth century at the earliest and may belong to the early fifth century. The material has been split into two groups; that deriving from deposits sealed by the masonry rubble of the building (table 31), and that deriving from the well, the most securely stratified material from the site (table 32).

Species	Frags	%Frags
Cattle	31	22
Sheep	64	46
Pig	15	11
Horse	2	1
Red Deer	1	1
Cat	2	1
Chicken	16	12
Goose	4	3
Mistle Thrush	1	1
Song Thrush	1	1
Pigeon	1	1
Totals	138	100

Table 31: *Species Represented at Site 2*

Species	MNI	%MNI	Frags	%Frags	Epiph.	%Epiph
Cattle	2	9	15	9	1	1
Sheep	6	27	77	44	58	41
Pig	5	23	51	29	62	44
Horse	1	5	2	1	0	0
Cat	1	5	1	1	0	0
Chicken	2	9	9	5	7	5
Goose	2	9	12	7	5	4
Thrush	1	5	1	1	2	1
Woodcock	1	5	1	1	2	1
Crow?	1	5	3	2	4	3
Totals	22	100	172	100	141	100

Table 32 *Species Represented at Site 2 : The Well*

Site 6

Context

Material from this site derives from the fill of the well, and immediately overlies a dump of pottery of fourth century date (table 33). The well appeared to have been filled over a short period with the lowest 0.75m occupied by a large pivot stone and a dump of pottery (see p.89) but little bone. The animal bone was confined to the metre of deposits above this from 1.75m to 0.75m from the base. The three metres of deposits above this were graded away but it was observed that the fill contained very little bone.

Summary

The animal bone within the main deposit was exceptionally well preserved, comprising almost complete skeletons of a horse and an immature ox indicating deposition soon after death. There were bones from several other horses and oxen including three more well-preserved ox skulls and a number of horn cores. As with the Phase 3 well deposit on Site 1, the sheep were mainly represented by skull and foot bones showing signs of butchery and gnawing. The pig bones comprised two adults and two piglets. The red deer were represented by fragments of sawn antler which may have been imported to the site. The fact that no birds or small mammals were represented could have been due either to the short and deliberate nature of the deposition or, most likely, the lack of opportunity for retrieval under rescue conditions. The fragment counts for species represented are tabulated below. The summary of complete bone measurements for ox, horse and sheep are given in table 34 (see von den Driesch 1976).

Species	Frags	%Frags
Cattle	129	43
Sheep	36	12
Pig	11	4
Horse	122	40
Red Deer*	2	1
Total	**300**	**100**

Table 33: *Species represented at Site 6: The Well*

* Antler only

Species	Bone	Measurement *	Range (mm)	mean (mm)	N
Ox	Horn core	Max. basal diam.	54.7-67.5	61.2	8
	Scapula	GLP	65.0 – 86.7	70.8	6
		SLC	45.8 – 62.9	54.8	6
	Humerus	GL	> 278		1
	Metacarpal	GL	181 – 205	193	2
		Bp	52.6 – 76.3	64.5	2
		Bd	55.4		1
	Tibia	GL	405		1
		Bd	80.8 – 80.9	80.9	2
	Metarsal	GL	214 – 261	234	4
		Bp	46.7 – 64 .0	56.5	4
		Bd	57.0 – 77.3	64.9	3
	Astragalus	GB	91.2 – 91.5	91.4	2
	Ist Phalange	GL	72.4 – 73.1	72.8	2
Horse	Scapula	GLP	90.1 – 92.3	91.5	2
		SLC	56.3 – 67.0	61.6	4
	Humerus	GL	282 – 289	285.5	2
	Metacapal	GL	227 – 229	228	2
		Bp	47.0 – 50.0	48.5	2
		Bd	49.3 – 50.0	49.7	2
	Femur	GL	385 – 394	389.7	3
	Tibia	GL	355 – 357	356	2
		Bd	72.4 – 73.4	72.9	2
	Metatarsal	GL	229 – 276	258.7	3
		Bp	49.8 – 54.9	52.1	4
		Bd	48.3 – 52.2	49.8	3
	Astragalus	GB	62.1 – 63.2	62.7	2
	1st Phalange	GL	82.3 – 87.5	84.8	4
Sheep	Horn core	Max. basal diam.	21.0 – 27.5	24.5	6
	Metacarpal	Bp	15.4 – 23.3	20	6
	Metatarsal	Bp	18.0 – 19.5	18.9	5

Table 34 *Summary of Bone Measurements at Site 6: The Well* * see von den Driesch 1976

Oxen

From the bone evidence at least four individuals are represented, whilst the horn cores indicate at least seven, showing no evidence of butchery or gnawing. Fifty-nine of the bones came from a single, large (table 33), immature individual aged from fusion data between one year and 18 months (Silver 1969). The fused bones of the other individuals indicated that, although smaller, they were all adult. The fifteen horncores were all down-curving and appear to have come from sub-adult and adult males (Armitage 1982, 43).

Horse

Of the 122 fragments, over 90% came from a single, near-complete individual, the remainder coming from two others. In common with those of the oxen, the bones showed no signs of butchery or gnawing. The near-complete horse was aged by fusion data and tooth wear to between five and six years (Silver 1969) and was between 136cm and 144cm high at the shoulder (about 14 hands). This is somewhat larger than ponies from contemporary settlements in southern England (Maltby 1985) but is comparable with a complete horse buried at the Romano-British site at Maddle Farm, Berkshire (Brown 1989).

Sheep

In contrast, the remains of sheep from the well, of which four individuals are represented, indicate butchery waste. From fusion data and mandible wear stage analysis (Grant 1982) all appear to have been no more that a year old.

The Early Anglo-Saxon Period

Material of Early Anglo-Saxon date derived from Pit C, Pit J, Sunken-Featured Building 1, and gully FG on Site 4 and has been treated as a single group (table 35).

Species	Frags	%Frags
Cattle	128	50
Sheep	96	37
Pig	25	10
Horse	2	1
Fox	1	0.5
Chicken	3	2
Goose	1	0.5
Totals	**256**	**100**

Table 35: *Species Represented at Site 4 (Early Anglo-Saxon)*

Discussion of the Domesticated Species

Although the material from the sites is well-dated by its association with contemporary ceramics, the small assemblage size precludes the accurate detection of trends across time. When assemblages are larger, such as the well fills on Site 1 and especially Site 6, their content is probably atypical.

Proportions of Species

Table 36 summarises the fragment count data for the three major domesticated species, cattle, sheep and pigs from the above groups

Site/Period	% Cattle	% Sheep	% Pig	Tot. Frags
Site 4 Iron Age	22	44	34	32
Site 1 R-B Ph.1	50	35	15	20
Site 1 R-B Ph.2	7	90	3	795
Site 1 R-B Well	19	62	19	32 MNI *
Site 2 R-B Well	10	54	36	143
Site 2 R-B Villa	28	58	14	110
Site 6 R-B Well	73	21	6	176
Site 4 E.Saxon	51	39	10	249
Total Frags	384	1013	138	1535

Table 36: *Relative Proportions of Cattle, Sheep and Pig from each group* .

MNI figures used as pig fragments not calculated for this group.

The above table indicates that from the Middle to Late Iron Age through to the Early Anglo-Saxon period, sheep are generally the most common livestock species with cattle second and pig third. However, allowing for the greater meat yield of cattle it is likely that this species represented the greatest proportion of the diet. This profile, with a lower but still significant proportion of pig, is consistent with the gradually Romanising picture of production and consumption painted by King, with cattle gradually becoming more important (1991, 17). The sample for the Iron Age is too small to warrant detailed analysis but the presence of pig in such a small group might be seen as notable given that it only becomes a significant part of the diet in the Gallicised areas of the South East in the very Late Iron Age (King 1991, 16). The Early Anglo-Saxon group with a high proportion of cattle appears to continue the late Roman pattern and this would appear to be broadly consistent with other sites (King 1991, 18)

Phases 2 and 3 of Site 1, Site 2 and the Anglo-Saxon phase on Site 4 produced a total of 134 identified fragments of bird bone of which 108 belong to domesticated species of chicken and goose. This is a very small amount of material, which may be due to poor survival and lack of sieving during on-site retrieval. However, some tentative comments can be made. Chicken is generally better represented than goose by all of the three quantitative methods. It is interesting to note the occurence of immature chickens which may have been young cocks, while the hens were presumably kept for egg laying. The low occurrence of goose in the Roman period has also been noted at Exeter where the species 'was rarely found in the deposits. It became a more common resource in the medieval period, reflecting the greater importance of domestic poultry at that time...' (Maltby 1979, 74).

Age at Death
Age at death patterns were recorded for all the groups (data in archive), but sample size for groups other than those described above were consisdered too small to be statisitically valid. The following statements are therefore tentative. While examples of cattle under two and a half years occurred on Site 1 (Phase 2), the majority across the sites appear to have been over two years with one over five years. Whilst this would tend to indicate milk production rather than meat, it is likely young bullocks were taken away to market on the hoof rather than being butchered on site.

Excluding the neonatal material from Site 1, fifty-three sheep bones could be aged. Across all the groups, very few animals were younger than 13 months or older than three years; the majority of sheep on Site 1 appearing to have been killed between 18 and 21 months. This might tend to indicate a strategy aimed toward meat rather than wool production. However, if the waste represents the consumption patterns of the inhabitants then they may have been rich enough, or free enough, to choose younger, tender meat. In contrast it appears that those on less Romanised sites lacked this freedom and that their consumption matches more closely that of the wool economy on which they may have been dependant (King 1991, 18; Grant 1989, 136). Site 1 also produced a group of twenty-eight neonatal lambs sealed beneath the masonry Building 1. Given the problems of comparing modern and ancient material it is considered that these represent neonatal rather than foetal deaths resulting from a widespread infection soon after birth.

Butchery
The details of butchery evidence for each group is held in archive, and although clear changes across the period could not be detected, probably due to small sample size, features of Roman practice such as filleting (Maltby 1979, 81) and the preparation of chops indicated by two transverse knife cuts on vertebrae were identified (Grant 1984, 392;). The horn cores from the Site 6 well had all been removed from the skull using a saw indicating that they were intended for secondary use.

A common breakage pattern for poultry bones was observed across the Empingham sites. Femora and humeri tended to be represented by their proximal or distal ends, with no evidence for knife cutting, and this could indicate that it reflects breakage after cooking, during consumption of the meal, when the bones are softer.

Ritual Practice?
The atypicality of the Late Roman well group from Site 6 which contained complete horse and cattle carcasses may indicate ritual practice in the closing of a well through deliberate filling over a short time rather than gradual silting and rubbish accumulation as recorded from many of the wells at Portchester (Grant 1975). The carcasses lay immediately above a discrete group of eight largely complete, narrow-mouthed ceramic vessels. As stratigraphically earlier it might simply be assumed that the jars were lost during water collection and have no association with the animals deposited once the well had gone dry or foul. However, given the narrowness of the well (0.68m by 0.57m), it would not appear such an obvious place to dump complete carcasses of large animals. Such deposits have not been widely recognised on Roman sites, although complete burial of a horse is known from Winnall Down, Winchester (Maltby 1985, 108) and of a pony with a human at Maddle Farm, Berkshire (Brown

1989, 183). Ritual or structured deposits are however now widely recognised during the Iron Age at sites like Danebury and other sites in the Wessex area where domestic animals and humans are buried in pits formerly used for grain storage (Grant 1984, 540 pit 321 and pit 909).

Discussion of Wild Species

The occurrence of wild species of animals and birds will reflect the nature of the surrounding habitat, and their small numbers and lack of butchery would indicate that they rarely formed part of the diet of the inhabitants. The range would tend to support the idea of an open farmland landscape. Evidence for fox came from an Anglo-Saxon context on Site 4, while frog or toad was found in the wells of both Sites 1 and 2.

Amongst the wild birds the occurrence of immature crow (*Corvus corone corone*), red kite (*Milvus milvus*), pigeon (*Columba oenas*), swallow (*Hirundo rustica*), house sparrow (*Passer domesticus*), song thrush (*Turdus philomelos*), mistle thrush (*Turdus viscivorus*), and woodcock (*Scolopax rusticola*)would also indicate open land with woodland, while duck; (*Anas platyrhynchos*), and water rail (*Rallus aquaticus*) would correlate with the river valley situation.

Acknowledgements
Thanks are due to Anthony Gouldwell and Annie Grant for assistance, advice, and encouragement throughout the writing of this report, and for access to the reference collection at Leicester University. Thanks also to Jan Dawson for giving me access to the avian reference collection at the New Walk Museum in Leicester.

THE INSECT FAUNA
P. C. Buckland*

Introduction

The permanently waterlogged nature of the lower part of the deposits in the third-century well on Site 1 (EPR 70 EY) provided ideal conditions for the preservation of fossil insects and many fragments were recovered during the sorting of samples for identifiable plant remains reported on separately here. Although the material was washed out over a 300 micron sieve, no attempt was made to separate the arthropod remains by any flotation technique (cf Coope and Osborne 1968) and recovery is therefore biased towards the larger, more evident individuals, resulting in a preponderance of Carabids and a paucity of the smaller taxa, including many of the phytophages (Table 37).

Results

Despite the restrictions imposed by such an assemblage, several tentative conclusions may be drawn. Some plant hosts are indicated by the insect fauna (Table 38) and the overall impression provided by the more peripatetic elements in the fauna, particularly the ground beetles, is of a cleared and cultivated landscape. Timber is indicated by the ubiquitous and predominantly synanthropic furniture beetle, *Anobium punctatum*,

perhaps from the structure of the building that may have enclosed the well, the stag beetle, *Lucanus cervus*, and the click beetle, *Melanotus erythropus*. The latter species is recorded from most types of tree (Palm 1959) and the four individuals could have been introduced in any piece of rotten wood, perhaps faggots intended for the fire. The stag beetle, *L. cervus*, most frequently breeds in large stumps of old oaks, although it is also recorded from beech (Palm 1959), and is probably more common in parkland with old trees than in old woodland. The beetle is a strong flier and could be wholly adventitious in this assemblage. There are, however, no recent published records from the East Midlands (Clark 1966) and, whilst there may be small relict populations of the species in the less disturbed parts of Sherwood Forest, the principal headquarters are now concentrated around London and in south-east Essex, about 100km to the south of the Gwash Valley. It is probable that the human disruption of woodland and old parkland habitats has resulted in the disjunct distribution of this and many other *Urwald* insects (Buckland 1979) at the present day.

Three other species from this sample also tend to be rather southern in their present distribution and these are not associated with timber. Both *Zabrus tenebrioides* and *Brachinus crepitans*, the bombardier beetle, reach their northward limit at about the latitude of south Leicestershire (Lindroth 1974) and there are few recent records for the snail-feeding Silphid, *Silpha laevigata*,

*This report has been previously published (Buckland 1986). This version incorporates some more recent references.

outside the South-East. Other elements in the fauna have, however, only become widespread since forest clearance and the inhabitants of the 'cultursteppe', the man-made landscape (Hammond 1974), are well represented. With many of the species of *Amara* and *Harpalus* and several dung beetles; *Zabrus tenebrioides* may be a late anthropochorous, perhaps Roman immigrant to Britain from the Continent. The adults of *Z. tenebrioides*, although omnivorous, feed principally on seeds, usually the unripe grains of cereals in the ear, and the beetle has long been known as a serious pest of cereal crops in Western and Central Europe (Curtis 1862; Jeannel 1942; Lindroth 1945). The insect is rarely found far away from arable land and the larvae are also corn-field pests, devouring the young green shoots (Jeannel 1942). The species provides tenuous evidence for the cultivation of cereals on the villa estate. The syn-anthropic element, of insects associated with stored products, principally grain (Buckland 1981), however, is absent from this assemblage.

Indicators of livestock are provided by the Scarabaeoid beetles, *Geotrupes*, *Colobopterus* and *Aphodius* spp., whose normal habitat is dung, and this group is second only to ground beetles in frequency. These species are supplemented by several Hydrophilids and Staphylinids usually associated with dung or related habitats and the impression of a mixed farming economy is strongly reinforced. The dung fauna gives no indication of the species of herbivore involved and the majority of coprophiles from this deposit are eurytopic. *Colobopterus fossor* and *Aphodius obliteratus*, however, prefer open, exposed pasture (Landin 1961), the habitat of the rootfeeders, *Phyllopertha horticola*, *Athous haemorrhoidalis* and *Agriotes* sp., and these support the picture provided by the ground beetles, of an open landscape not dissimilar from that of the present day.

Several elements in the fauna can be associated with the immediate environment of the farmyard, as distinct from those which reflect a sample of the more active ground-living animals which fell accidentally into the well. Both spider beetles, *Ptinus fur* and *Tipnus unicolor*, are flightless and, whilst there are outdoor records from birds' nests and 'old wood' (Hunter *et al.* 1973), their present cosmopolitan distribution must reflect accidental transport by humans. With *Typhaea stercorea* and the large number of individuals of earwig, *Forficula* prob. *auricularia*, they may be associated with hay stored in the immediate vicinity. The few phyto-phages in the assemblage (Table 41) include feeders upon nettles and knotgrass, probable elements in the more neglected corners of the farmyard. Surprisingly, the carrion element, which might be expected from the sheep bones in the well is poorly developed and the probability is that these were devoid of flesh before deposition.

Discussion

Despite several studies of insect faunas from Roman sites, there is still insufficient evidence to suggest that the assemblage from Site 1 is typical of any type of settle-ment and Amsden and Boon's (1975) criticism that the 'endless lists can but signal the severely restricted utility of the work from an archaeological standpoint' is wholly unjustified. Faunas from two other villa wells have been published, from Barnsley Park, Glos., (Coope and Osborne 1968) and Rudston in East Yorkshire (Buckland 1980). In addition, three urban wells, at Chichester (Girling 1989), Alcester, Warks., (Osborne 1971) and in the Colonia at York (Hall *et al.* 1980), are relevant. All the wells clearly acted as pit fall traps for the active ground fauna, as well as receiving other debris, either deliberately or otherwise, and Kenward (1975) has rightly argued for caution in interpretation. Yet, even allowing for the stochastic element in any pit fall trapping exercise (Adis 1979), the similarity of the Empingham assemblage to that from Barnsley Park is remarkable and Coope and Osborne's (1968) comment that 'All the species in the faunal list might be found today in any settled rural area in the southern part of England' is equally apposite. Allowing for its more northerly position, Rudston is also very similar and it is perhaps possible to identify a generalised open ground background fauna distinct from the urban assemblage of Alcester (Osborne 1971) and York (Hall *et al.* 1980). Whether it will eventually be possible to take this further and differentiate between variations in land exploitation between villas and lesser settlements remains to be seen, although Robinson (1983) has recently suggested that it is possible to derive arable to pastoral ratios from insect assemblages. The similarity to modern associations does suggest that the fauna of our 'cultursteppe' had come together by the Roman period; on the Chalk of Wiltshire, Osborne's (1969) work on the Wilsford shaft has shown that several elements, assembled from their refuges in the continuous forest of the mid-Holocene, had been brought together by the Late Bronze Age. Much more research is necessary, however, before the detail can be added.

Although the small size of the fauna and sorting bias of the sample impose strict limitations on the environ-mental reconstruction, the insect fauna provides a picture of a farm practising a mixed farming economy in a cleared landscape, not dissimilar from that of the present day.

Acknowledgements

The initial study of the Empingham sample was carried out in 1974 in Doncaster Museum and the author is grateful to P. Skidmore for his assistance and the identification of Dipterous remains. The woodlouse, *Porcellio scaber* was kindly identified by the late Dr M.Girling of the Ancient Monuments Laboratory. R. C. Alvey of Nottingham University Museum sorted and made available the original sample and the comments of P. J. Osborne and Dr C. C. Hayfield are gratefully acknowledged.

Isopoda	
Oniscoidea	
Porcellionidae	
Porcellio scaber Lat.	1
Insecta	
Dermaptera	
Forficulidae	
Forficula prob. *auricularia* L.	40
Hemiptera	
Lygaeidae	
Heterogaster urticae F.	3
Jassidae	
Aphrodes sp.	1
Trichoptera	
indet.	1
Coleoptera	
Carabidae	
Carabus monilis F.	1
C. violaceus L.	5
Leistus spinibarbis (F.)	3
Nebria brevicollis (F.)	16
Clivina collaris (Hbst.)	4
Trechus obtusus Erich.	1
T. obtusus Erich./*quadristriatus* Schr.	3
T. micros (Hbst.)	1
Bembidion lampros (Hbst.)	1
B. quadrimaculatum (L.)	1
Pterostichus madidus (F.)	5
P. melanarius (Ill.)	32
P. nigrita (F.)	1
P. versicolor (Sturm.)	1
Pterostichus spp.	20+
Calathus fuscipes (Goez.)	19
Calathus sp.	1
Synuchus nivalis (Panz.)	3
Agonum dorsale (Pont.)	2
Amara aulica (Panz.)	4
Amara spp.	23
Zabrus tenebrioides (Goez.)	3
Harpalus rufipes (Deg.)	9
H. (Ophonus) spp.	8
Dromius linearis (Ol.)	1
Brachinus crepitans (L.)	1
Dytiscidae	
Agabus bipustulatus (L.)	1
Hydrophilidae	
Helophorus spp.	2
Sphaeridium bipustulatum F.	1
S. scarabaeoides (L.)	1
Cercyon sp.	2
Megasternum obscurum (Marsh.)	2
Leiodidae	
Catops / Choleva spp.	23
Silphidae	
Silpha laevigata (F.)	1
S. obscura L.	4
Staphylinidae	
Lesteva longoelytrata (Goez.)	1
Omalium sp.	1
Coprophilus striatulus (F.)	1
Platystethus capito Heer / *nodifrons* (Mann.)	2
Lathrobium sp.	1
Othius punctulatus (Goez.)	1
Gyrohypnus fracticornis (Muell.)	4
Xantholinus linearis (Ol.) / *longiventris* Heer	4
Philonthus nigrita (Grav.)	1
Philonthus sp.	1
Staphylinus ater Grav.	1
S. olens (Muell.)	5
Quedius tristis (Grav.)	1
Quedius spp.	2
Tachinus signatus Grav.	1

Lucanidae	
Lucanus cervus (L.)	1
Geotrupidae	
Geotrupes stercorosus (Scrib.)	1
Scarabaeidae	
Colobopterus fossor (L.)	1
Aphodius ater (Deg.)	2
A. contaminatus (Hbst.)	2
A. granarius (L.)	22
A. lividus (F.)	1
A. obliteratus Panz.	2
A. rufipes (L.)	1
Aphodius spp.	5
Oxyomus sylvestris (Scop.)	5
Phyllopertha horticola (L.)	1
Cetonia aurata (L.)	1
Elateridae	
Melanotus erythropus (Gmel.)	4
Athous haemorrhoidalis (F.)	1
Agriotes lineatus (L.) / *obscurus* (L.)	1
Anobiidae	
Anobium punctatum (Deg.)	15
Ptinidae	
Tipnus unicolor (Pill. @ Mitt.)	6
Ptinus fur (L.)	12
Cryptophagidae	
Cryptophagus sp.	1
Lathridiidae	
Lathridius sp. (*minutus* (L.) group)	2
Cortinicara gibbosa (Hbst.)	1
Corticaria / Corticarina sp.	1
Mycetophagidae	
Typhaea stercorea (L.)	1
Chrysomelidae	
Phyllotreta nigripes (F.)	1
Longitarsus sp.	1
Crepidodera ferriginea (Scop.)	1
Chaetocnema concinna (Marsh.)	2
Apionidae	
Apion pomonae (F.)	1
Apion sp.	1
Curculionidae	
Barynotus obscurus (F.)	3
Sitona sulcifrons (Thun.)	1
Sitona sp.	1
Hypera nigrirostris (F.)	2
Cidnorhinus quadrimaculatus (L.)	2
Ceutorhynchus litura (F.)	1
Ceutorhynchus sp.	1
Rhinoncus / Phytobius sp.	1
Scolytidae	
Leperisinus varius (F.)	1
Hymenoptera	
Formicidae	
Lasius fuliginosus (Lat.)	1
Chrysididae	
Chrysis ignita (L.)	1
	Parasitica
indet.	1
Diptera	
Larvaevoridae	
indet.	1
Calliphoridae	
Calliphora sp.	1
indet.	1
Muscidae	
Muscina sp.	1
Anthomyiidae	
Paragle cinerella (Fall.)	1
indet. puparia	5

Table 37: *Arthropod Remains from the Well*
Taxonomy follows Kloet and Hincks (1945) with revisions.

Cruciferae	*Phyllotreta nemorum*
Papilionaceae	*Sitona sulcifrons*
	Apion pomonae
Trifolium spp.(clover), *Ononis*	
spinosa (restharrow)	*Phytonomus nigrirostris*
Polygonaceae	*Rhinoncus* sp.
Polygonaceae esp. *P.aviculare* (knotgrass)	*Chaetocnema concinna*
Urtica dioica (greater stinging nettle)	*Heterogaster urticae*
	Cidnorrhinus
	quadrimaculatus
Fraxinus excelsior (ash)	*Leperisinus varius*
Carduus, Cirsium spp. (thistles)	*Ceutorhynchus litura*
Cereals	*Zabrus tenebrioides*
Cereals and other low vegetation	*Crepidodera ferruginea*

Table 38: *Plants Indicated by the Insect Remains*
(Data from Dieckman 1972; Hoffmann 1954, 1958; Lindroth 1945; Mohr 1966; Osborne 1969; Palm 1959).

CHARRED PLANT REMAINS

R. C. Alvey and Angela Monckton

Introduction

This report was undertaken in 1970, following the first two seasons of work on Site 1, when three features presenting favourable preservation conditions were identified and, during excavation, samples were extracted for wet sieving. The samples came from the fill of Phase 2B ditch Feature 1, dating to the later second century, the primary fill of the phase 3 well dating to the later third century, and the lower fill of the corn drier Phase 4.5, dating to the fourth century. Subsequently a further sample was retrieved from the H-shaped corn drier on Site 6 excavated in 1973.

The material was extracted by washing over a 300 micron sieve, and no other flotation technique was employed. The material was then examined microscopically, and the following results obtained (Table 39). Dimensions of measurable complete seeds were also recorded (Table 40).

Summary

Four cereal species were represented in the samples, the most common being spelt wheat (*Triticum spelta*), although emmer wheat (*Triticum dicoccum*) is also present as is barley (*Hordeum* sp) and oats (*Avena* sp). The presence of the grass (*Bromus* sp) indicates weed contamination.

There is a lack of comparable data from other published Leicestershire sites, but samples from corn driers excavated at Milton Keynes (Jones 1987) demonstrate that all species represented are commonly found on Romano-British sites. The presence of germinated seeds in both studies may be of significance since the process of drying was intended to halt this prior to storage. It may lend support to the idea that corn driers were in fact used as malting floors during the process of brewing ale.

Discussion

Angela Monckton

Site 1, F1 Ditch, Phase 2B, Mid-Late Second Century

A sample from a black layer (EPR 69 AR) contained grains of spelt with some emmer present and the sample was dominated by wheat chaff fragments. In hulled wheat such as emmer and spelt the grains are held firmly in the chaff even after threshing, which breaks the cereal ear into spikelets so that additional processing is needed to free the grains. This involves parching and pounding the cereal, breaking each spikelet into two parts (glumes) and two grains, the chaff is then removed by fine sieving (Hillman 1981). This sample represents these cleanings from dehusking mainly spelt wheat, the chaff being burnt possibly as fuel and then dumped in the ditch. The waste contains a few grains included with the waste and a seed of brome grass, a common weed of the cereal fields in the past, the oat may be wild oat which was also an arable weed. The sample shows the processing of wheat for consumption in this phase.

Site 1, Well, Phase 3, Later Third Century

This sample was dominated by grains, mainly of spelt with a little wheat chaff and occasional grains of barley and oat. This sample consists mainly cereal product and may therefore represent waste from food preparation, including accidentally burnt grains and a little waste sorted from the cereal. This probably is domestic waste removed from a hearth and dumped in the well.

Phase Century AD Feature type	2B 2nd Ditch	3 3rd Well	4-5 4th Corndrier	Site 6 4th Corn drier	
CHAFF					
Triticum dicoccum Schubl (sf)	–	1	–	–	Emmer spikelet fork
Triticum spelta L. (sf)	–	2	–	–	Spelt spikelet fork
Triticum dicoccum/spelta (gl)	440	–	8	–	Emmer/Spelt glume
GRAINS					
Triticum dicoccum Schubl.	1	–	–	–	Emmer
Triticum spelta L.	13	46	39	–	Spelt
Triticum sp. (germinated)	–	–	–	27	Wheat
Hordeum sp. (hulled)	–	1	–	1	Barley
Avena sp.	1	4	–	–	Oat
Cereal embryo shoots	9	–	–	–	Cereal
SEEDS					
Bromus sp	1	–	–	–	Brome grass
TOTAL	465	54	47	28	(Items)
Sample size	–	–	200	60	(g)
PROPORTIONS OF REMAINS					
GLUMES	96	11	17	0	%
GRAINS	3	89	83	100	%
SEEDS	< 1	0	0	0	%

Key: Chaff: (sf) = spikelet fork, (gl) = glume base/spikelet part.

Table 39: *Charred Plant Remains from Empingham*

Site 1, Corn Drier, Phase 4-5, Fourth Century

This sample from the phase 4/5 corn drier was from a layer of black soil which was the lower fill at the west end of the corn drier, it was dominated by spelt grains and contained a little chaff. This may be the remains of the cereal being processed in the feature, it possible represents grains being parched, some of which have fallen into the fuel. Grain was sometimes parched to facilitate milling or for storage. However, it could represent spelt in spikelet form which was being parched for dehusking, the chaff may have been lost because chaff does not survive burning as well as grains (Boardman and Jones 1990). There is evidence that features known as corn driers had a number of uses (van der Veen 1989) and *in situ* remains from them provide evidence of only the last use of the feature.

Site 6, Corn Drier, Fourth Century

The second sample was from the west side of a H-shaped corn drier and contained only grains, mainly of germinated wheat. This was thought to be possible evidence of malting because germinated grain was roasted before extraction of the malt for brewing, there is evidence of spelt being used for malting at Catsgore

(Hillman 1982). However there is also evidence of partly sprouted crops being processed in corn driers, probably to parch or dry them for use or storage (Monckton 1999). Although this is a small sample, most of the grains were germinated, this may therefore suggest that malted grain was being processed for brewing.

This material was some of the first charred plant remains identified from the area and the first analysed from a corn drier in Rutland and Leicestershire. Samples from a corn drier at Norfolk Street Roman villa in Leicester were analysed (Jones 1982) and reported as containing wheat chaff used as fuel (van der Veen 1989). Chaff was a favoured fuel for malting and cereal processing using dehusking waste to process further cereal. Although charred plant remains have now been found at many sites in the area (Monckton 1995) other corn driers have been found and sampled only recently. These are at Ridlington in Rutland, Appleby Magna in Leicestershire and Crown Hills in Leicester by the University of Leicester Archaeological Services, and at Ketton in Rutland by Northamptonshire Archaeology, all contain evidence of cereals and analysis is in progress at the present time.

Sample	Remains	Length	Width	Thickness	Number measured
Ditch, phase 2B	Spelt grains	5.71	3.73	3.26	(maximum)
		4.9	2.85	2.15	(minimum)
		5.23	2.65	2.56	Average of 5 grains
	Emmer grain	5.94	1.98	2.22	1 grain
	Oat grain	4.45	1.55	1.47	1 grain
	Brome grass	4.33	1.57	1.07	1 grain
Well, phase 3	Spelt grains	6.88	4.09	3.08	(maximum)
		4.90	2.38	2.00	(minimum)
		5.58	3.23	2.62	Average of 10 grains
	Barley grain	4.70	2.57	1.97	1 grain
	Oat grain	5.50	1.73	1.60	1 grain
	Spelt spikelet forks	-	2.73	1.50	
		-	2.37	1.20	2 forks
	Emmer spikelet fork	-	1.62	1.15	1 fork
Corn drier, phase 4.5	Spelt grains	7.61	4.09	3.20	(maximum)
		5.18	3.18	2.52	(minimum)
		5.55	3.54	2.91	Average of 10 grains
Corn drier, site 6	Wheat grains	5.93	3.26	2.73	
	(all germinated)	6.15	3.59	2.94	
		6.44	3.14	2.55	
		5.93	3.20	2.99	4 examples of grains

Table 40: *Dimensions of Plant Remains (mm)*

CHARCOAL

G. C. Morgan

The charcoal, retrieved by hand collection, was examined microscopically and the identifications are summarised in the following table.

A total of six species were identified from the charcoal samples retrieved, the most common of which was oak.

Site	Context	Species	Diameter	No.Rings	Est.Age (yrs)
ROMAN					
1	69EH	oak(axe cut)	50mm	18	25
1	69EH	ash	25mm	3	8
1	69EH	field maple	25mm	12	18
2	71NQ	elder	10mm	3	3
2	71NQ	broom	30mm	15	20
2	71OC	hazel	15mm	15	15
2	71PN	ash	15mm	12	12
2	71QP	field maple	>50mm	10	>20
2	71RK	oak	15mm	6	8
2	71SE	oak	20mm	12	15
EARLY ANGLO-SAXON					
3	EMP 67	oak	-	-	-
7	(2)	oak	>50mm	-	-
7	(4)	field maple	>50mm	-	-
7	(11)	oak	>80mm	9	50

Table 41: *Tree Species identified from Charcoal Samples*

SETTLEMENT IN THE GWASH VALLEY
TO THE NORMAN CONQUEST

Nicholas J. Cooper

Introduction (Fig. 62)

This chapter aims to combine the findings of the foregoing excavation reports with archaeological evidence from the Gwash Valley as a whole. The additional evidence comes from four sources, the first of which is the existing Sites and Monuments Record for Rutland, into which information from the other three sources is being incorporated. During the last decade in particular, our knowledge of settlement in the valley has grown rapidly due to the work of professional contractors (primarily University of Leicester Archaeological Services), local amateurs and staff and students of Leicester University's School of Archaeology. Professional work has been largely in response to small scale developments in the medieval village cores, in accordance with PPG16 (the Governments's planning and policy guidance note). In contrast, the work of the amateur and student groups has involved systematic fieldwalking survey of targeted areas. The Archaeological Committee of the Rutland Local History and Record Society (RLHRS, formerly the Rutland Field Research Group) has undertaken invaluable work in recent years, including the systematic field walking surveys of Oakham, Egleton and Martinsthorpe parishes in the upper part of the valley (Jones 1999, 407-410). Additionally, fieldwalking survey of 25 fields in Empingham and Hambleton parishes was undertaken by the University between 1990 and 1994 (Cooper 1998, 189). The findings of all these bodies are documented annually in both the *Transactions of the Leicestershire Archaeological and Historical Society* and *Rutland Record*, the Journal of the RLHRS.

Placing the excavations within the wider context of what is known of settlement in the Gwash Valley as a whole, will allow a fuller appreciation of the evolving pattern and identify elements of continuity and change (fig. 62). A numbered list of all sites is provided at the end of the chapter together with a series of period maps showing their distribution (figs. 63-66). The site numbering sequence established for the excavated sites **(1-7)** is continued on, with the site name followed by a number in bold text.

The Earliest Inhabitants:
the Mesolithic, Neolithic and
Bronze Ages in the Valley (Fig. 63)

Although evidence for Upper Palaeolithic occupation dating to more than 30,000 years ago has recently been discovered at nearby Glaston, the earliest settlement evidence in the Gwash Valley dates to the Mesolithic, probably about 7,000 years ago. With the exception of the two pits containing worked flint on **Site 3**, the period of Prehistory in the area of the Gwash Valley around Empingham itself is largely devoid of excavated evidence until the Iron Age (**Site 4**, **Site 9** Whitwell, and the holloway on **Site 8** Empingham II), with the bulk of the information coming in the form of unstratified flint scatters detected during excavation and fieldwalking. However, elsewhere in the valley, and particularly in its upper reaches, structural evidence has been recorded during both excavation and aerial survey.

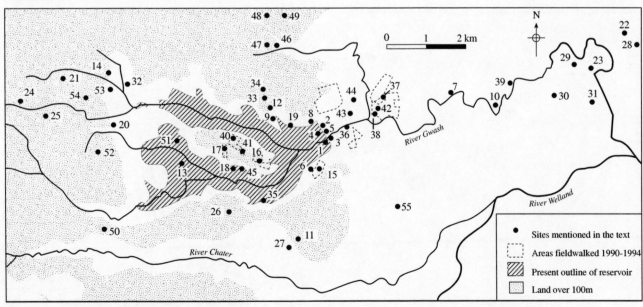

Fig. 62 Settlement in the Gwash Valley: All Periods

Structural Evidence

The only excavated evidence comes from a site at Burley Road, Oakham (Clay 1998) **(14)**, lying to the northeast of the town in the uppermost part of the valley (SK 867 096). The site was originally identified from a cropmark in the form of a sub-circular post-hole structure (Pickering and Hartley 1985, 60 no.18). Fieldwalking, undertaken by the Rutland Field Research Group in 1985 , identified two concentrations of surface flint, the smaller of the two lying over the cropmark, and the larger, to the east (Clay and Graf 1986, 82). Both foci included an earlier industry dominated by blade-type implements, and a later flake tool element including knives and scrapers. Excavation in advance of development took place in 1986 and examined an area of 2500 m sq; identifying three phases of Neolithic pit circle, and a Late Neolithic barrow burial (Clay 1987, 87-90). Further fieldwalking in 1988 demonstrated that the eastern flint scatter extended south-eastwards across the Burley Road towards the Gwash (Clay 1989, 108).

Additional evidence from the upper part of the valley comes in the form of four separate cropmarks, the first of which is located southeast of Oakham, towards Egleton (SK 870 081). A triple-ditched boundary **(20)** runs northwards for 300m to hit the Gwash at right angles and appears to continue for a further 400m north of the river in the form of a pit alignment, noted in the SMR to the north of the Stamford road (SK 869 086). To the west of the triple ditch are two ring ditches, which may be barrows, the southerly of the two having a conspicuous causeway across the western circumference (Pickering and Hartley 1985, 60 no.17). Fieldwalking in 1992, by the Rutland Local History and Record Society group as part of their Egleton Parish Survey, detected a substantial Early Bronze flint scatter of 455 pieces associated with the triple ditch and ring ditches **(20)** (Jones 1996, 282). Further evidence of barrows is indicated by a cropmark lying between Oakham and Barleythorpe (SK 852 095) on the south bank of the Gwash **(21)**, where two ring-ditches adjoin, one of which is double-ditched and appears to partly overlap the other (Pickering and Hartley 1985, 60 no.14). A second pit alignment **(53)** is known to the south of Burley Road (SK 869 092) .

Evidence from the lower part of the Valley is also derived from cropmarks in the area of Ryhall. An interesting, but truncated, arrangement of pit-alignments **(22)** lies outside the north bend of the Gwash (TF 043 113), close to the double-ditched Iron Age enclosure described below **(28)**, while on the inside of the bend (TF 034 102), a pit-alignment **(23)**, paralleled by a ditch, follows the line of the floodplain, along which is evidence for six round barrows and related pits (Pickering and Hartley 1985, 68 nos. 1 and 4). A further pit alignment **(31)**, 250m in length lies close to the county boundary (TF 033 089) (Pickering and Hartley 1985, 68 no.6).

Pottery and Flint

Besides the artefactual material from the excavations and fieldwalking at Oakham mentioned above which included occasional sherds of Late Neolithic and Early Bronze Age pottery including Grimston and Peterborough wares, the only other occurrence of non-lithic material earlier than the Iron Age is that of the Bronze Age collared urn fragment from the excavations at Whitwell **(9)** (Todd 1981, 21 and fig. 12, 1A). The evidence for the use of flint is, however, more substantial.

At the time of the excavations in the late sixties and early seventies, a total of 769 pieces of worked flint was retrieved during excavation and random surface collection (Head and Young, above p.60), and a further 1317 pieces including 69 implements have been collected and reported on from the 19 fields during the systematic fieldwalking programme undertaken by

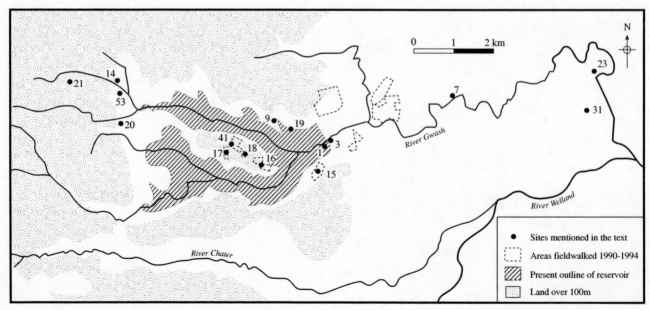

Fig. 63 Settlement in the Gwash Valley: The Neolithic and Bronze Age

Leicester University from 1990 to 1992 (Herepath 1993 unpublished MA dissertation, University of Leicester). Additional material has come from the six fields subsequently walked up to 1994 as well as from random collection along the north shore of the reservoir **(19)** between Whitwell and Sykes Lane (immediately south of Empingham II Early Anglo-Saxon cemetery). This area of the reservoir west of Sykes Lane (i.e. away from the immediate area of the dam) was not graded by machinery, leaving the topsoil intact. The action of waves on the shore has sorted this topsoil, separating the heavier pebbles amongst which the worked flint has been found (along the 84m contour). A high proportion of blades, in particular, have been found, suggesting Mesolithic or Early Neolithic activity.

Prior to the current programme of fieldwalking, the evidence comprised a substantial scatter detected in the area of Sites 1 and 3 and the contents of two pit features on Site 3 which are not closely dated. Smaller scatters had been discovered on Sites 2, 4, and 5, and in 1990 on Site 7 at Tickencote. Fieldwalking undertaken since 1990 has identified substantial scatters on Field 8 at Normanton **(15)**, immediately east of the Romano-British **Site 6**, and Field 11 on the Hambleton Peninsula **(16)**, with minor scatters from Fields 12, 13 and 14 and 25 also on the Peninsula **(17 and 18)**. Field 8 produced a total of 773 pieces of flint, including 31 implements from an area of 0.125 km sq. Field 11 **(16)**, the site of an Iron Age rectangular enclosure shown as a cropmark produced 104 pieces including three implements from a traverse and stint survey (10m by 30m), and a subsequent intensive gridwalk (10m by 10m) confined to the area of the enclosure yielded 113 pieces including three implements.

Defining the types of activity represented by these scatters is problematic given the area's restricted access to good quality flint (confined to flint pebbles in the boulder clay), and the difficulties of measuring the duration that the term 'occupation' represents. However, a simple threefold division between dispersed activity (1-20 flints/ha), transient activity (?ritual) (20-80 flints/ha), and occupation activity (80+flints/ha), has been devised for Leicestershire and can be applied here (Clay 1989, 112). The densities represented on Fields 8 and 11 would appear to represent occupation sites, whilst the minor scatters probably represent dispersed or transient activity.

The occurrence of substantial amounts of worked flint on top of the Hambleton Peninsula above 100m and high on the valley side at Normanton above 90m is significant when compared to the negligible amounts (0-30 pieces per field) from the valley side north west and north east of Empingham (Fields 1 – 7, and 16 -24 respectively), all of which lie on the Lincolnshire Limestone, and away from the boulder clay which appears to be the source of the raw material (fig.3). The Peninsula is predominantly underlain by ironstone with boulder clay overlying it on the north edge, while Field 8 lies over the junction of an area of boulder clay and the lime-

stone. The material from the north shore, while overlying the ironstone is not close to the boulder clay. Evidence from the Medbourne Area Survey (P. Liddle pers. comm.) indicates a relationship between underlying geology and the distribution of flint scatters, with a correlation between ironstone bedrock and early flint scatters. Whether this is also true of the Gwash Valley is at present unclear. Initial work on the relationship between flint scatters and underlying geology, indicates that the glacially derived clay soils covering over 60% of Leicestershire and Rutland were not actively avoided (Clay 1989, figs. 8.1 and 8.2), and this would appear to be supported by the evidence of the Gwash Valley.

In summary, the presence of blade industries on the south facing side of the Gwash Valley indicates that, by the later Mesolithic or Early Neolithic, clearings in the post-glacial forest were already being exploited. The more widespread occurrence of flint scatters of Late Neolithic or Early Bronze Age date indicates that exploitation became progressively more intense, and this is complemented by a growing range of ritual and occupation sites from the valley as a whole. Clay has recently suggested a model for Neolithic and Early Bronze Age developments in Leicestershire and Rutland, in which 'core areas' established during the Mesolithic, close to the headwaters of rivers and streams, continue, coupled with expansion downstream. Oakham represents one of three major 'core areas' detected on liassic or boulder clay areas through systematic survey along with Medbourne and Misterton. It would appear that the original core areas take on a ceremonial function as settlement expands downstream during the Neolithic and Bronze Age (1999, 14).

Significantly the later Bronze Age does not appear to be represented in the archaeology of the valley and this must be mainly due to a problem of visibility and the difficulties of dating site and artefact types during the preceding Early Bronze Age and subsequent Iron Age. The continued use of flint through the Bronze Age and into the Iron Age is an area of current debate (Young and Humphrey 1999) and the dating of ceramics and enclosure sites remains tentative due to a lack of excavation.

The Valley Fills Up: The Iron Age (Fig. 64)

The excavated evidence for the middle or later part of this period, confined to the central part of the valley, comprises three round house structures and associated pits on **Site 4**, a portion of enclosure ditch and associated gullies and pits at Whitwell (SK 924 082) **(9)** (Todd 1981, 7), and a holloway and associated features forming the south western boundary of the Anglo-Saxon cemetery at Empingham II **(8)** (Timby 1996, 9). The only evidence of earlier Iron Age activity comes from the single large, shouldered jar occupying Pit D on **Site 4**.

Aerial survey has provided the bulk of the additional evidence for Iron Age settlement which comprises a number of enclosed farmsteads of rectangular or sub-rectangular form distributed along the length of the

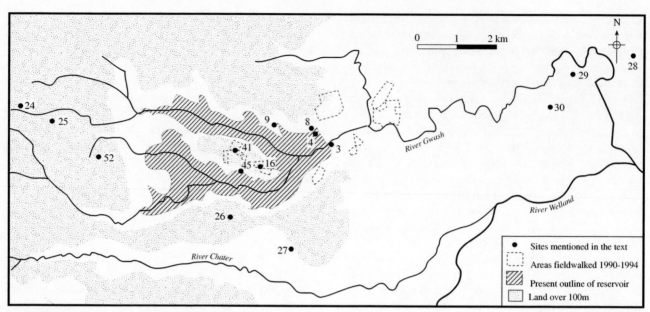

Fig. 64 Settlement in the Gwash Valley: The Iron Age

valley. Two such sites are located in the upper reaches of the valley, immediately west of Oakham and close to the source of the Gwash. The first of these **(24)** (SK 835 087), comprises a substantial rectangular enclosure with signs of a larger sub-rectangular enclosure on its west side. The second **(25)**, (SK 846 083) comprises a sub-rectangular, almost square, enclosure with three sides of a similar-sized enclosure immediately north east (Pickering and Hartley 1985, 60 nos.15 and 16). Fieldwalking survey by the Rutland Local History and Record Society group has detected Iron Age, Roman and Anglo-Saxon occupation **(52)** at The Grange Farm, to the west of Egleton (SK 864 072, E. Jones pers. comm.).

Further enclosures have been detected by aerial survey on the south side of the valley at Edith Weston (SK 908 054) and on the watershed of the Gwash and Chater at North Luffenham (SK 931 042). The example at Edith Weston **(26)**, is high up on the valley side at 115m and sub-rectangular in plan whilst that at North Luffenham **(27)** comprises two sub-rectangular enclosures, between which runs a double-ditch boundary or trackway (Pickering and Hartley 1985, 64 nos. 2 and 3). The North Luffenham Anglo-Saxon cemetery lies less than 200m to the east along the watershed.

The last example of an enclosure in the upper part of the valley comes from the Hambleton Peninsula **(16)**, (SK 919 069) (Pickering and Hartley 1985, 64 no.1). A large sub-rectangular enclosure, measuring 80m north-south by 120m east-west, is located at the eastern end of the Peninsula above the 100m contour and overlooks the lower part of the valley (pl. 11). There is a distinct entrance at the east end, and a possible entrance at the west end appearing to be incorporated into a rectangular internal entrance way. There are two circular structures internally, indicated by penannular ditches. The smaller of the two, presumably a building, is about 10m in diameter, comparing in size with those from the Iron Age occupation on Site 4, while the larger is up to 30m

in diameter, and may be a stock enclosure. Externally there are linear ditches leading away to the south and west, which may be traces of an associated field system.

Fieldwalking of the site in 1992 produced only two abraded sherds of scored ware, amongst an abundance of Romano-British pottery, and while it is possible that the inexperience of some of the fieldwalking team may have affected this figure, it is also likely that ploughing has not yet disturbed the lower fills of the enclosure ditch and internal features. Where fieldwalking or excavation has occurred on rectangular enclosures of the kind found in this upper part of the valley, scored ware, dating from the fourth to the first century BC confirms an Iron Age attribution and, in the case of Hambleton and Whitwell, subsequent activity during the Roman period. Two further sherds of scored ware came from Field 25 on the peninsula close to the Romano-British pottery scatter **(40)**. A Later Iron Age and Early Roman site has recently been identified on the southern shore of the peninsula, south east of Hambleton Wood (SK 912 067) **(45)** (Jones 1997, 320). The structural evidence comprised a length of linear ditch and part of a curvilinear ditch probably relating to a roundhouse with two internal postholes. The small amount of pottery retrieved indicated dates in the first century AD.

Further settlement evidence for the Iron Age occurs in the form of cropmarks from the lower part of the Gwash Valley in the area of Ryhall and Little Casterton. On the north side of the Gwash (TF 048 109) east of Ryhall, lies a double-ditched sub-rectangular enclosure **(28)** with traces of a possibly associated field system immediately north and west. Scored ware recovered during the laying of a pipeline trench in 1983 indicated a Late Iron Age date. On the opposite side of the river, enclosed by its large bend, further traces of a rectangular enclosure with an entrance on the east side have been recorded **(29)** (TF 028 103). The entrance faces a larger, faintly defined subrectangular enclosure, and a

Plate 11 Cropmark of Iron Age enclosure on the Hambleton Peninsula Site 16 (SK919 069) looking north

further small enclosure lies to the south (Pickering and Hartley 1985, 68 nos. 2 and 3). Two overlapping rectangular enclosures lie on the crest of a low ridge on the south side of the valley at Little Casterton **(30)** (TL 020 092) (Pickering and Hartley 1985, 68 no.5).

From Iron Age to Roman (Fig. 65)

By the Late Iron Age the impression is of a densely settled valley, with enclosed farmsteads spaced evenly along its sides, probably not dissimilar to other valleys in the Corieltauvian territory. However, the question of the continuity of rural settlement from the Iron Age to the Roman Period is not easily answered on present evidence, due to the lack of excavation or fieldwalking on the enclosed farmsteads detected by aerial survey. In the case of Whitwell **(9)** there are clearly phases of later Iron Age and Roman occupation but a break in occupation between the two phases has been argued for (Todd, 1981). The Roman pottery derived from fieldwalking on the enclosed Iron Age farmstead **(16)** on the Hambleton Peninsula, while spanning the Roman period, is predominantly late Roman and so continuity cannot be assumed. However, it would be interesting to see how many characteristically Iron Age cropmarks also produced Roman material, without any apparent Romanisation of buildings indicated by aerial photographs or tile scatters.

Meanwhile, it is unclear whether the early enclosure ditches on **Sites 1** and **3** are immediately pre- or post-conquest in origin, but certainly neither produced the distinctive scored ware pottery characteristic of Whitwell,

Hambleton or Empingham **Site 4**, the last of which did not produce any evidence for subsequent Roman occupation. The pattern that is likely to emerge, as further field survey is undertaken, might be similar to that observed in the Medbourne area (Liddle 1994), where most sites of Iron Age occupation also produce Roman material, but that the transition also led to the abandonment of some sites and the establishment of new ones.

The immediate impact of the Roman invasion on the lives of those inhabiting the valley is difficult to assess, but the river was clearly considered to be of enough strategic importance to warrant the construction of a fort above the crossing point of Ermine Street, at Great Casterton **(10)**. The first fort, enclosing 2.4 ha (5.9 acres), was constructed in the AD 40s soon after the invasion and was occupied in its original form until c. 70 AD, at which point it was reduced in size to 2.1 ha (5 acres) by the construction of a new south-eastern ditch and rampart inside the line of the original (Burnham and Wacher 1990, 130). The modified fort was probably evacuated by the late 70s AD, but occupation had been sufficiently long to allow a civilian settlement or *vicus* to develop in the area outside the south-western rampart and the crossing point, enclosed in a loop of the river.

From the evidence of limited excavation, the timber buildings that comprised the early settlement focused on the street frontage leading from the fort gate to Ermine Street (Ryhall Road), a perfect position from which to sell local produce to the military and tap into the exotic range of goods travelling along this major northward bound thoroughfare. However, with the evacuation of

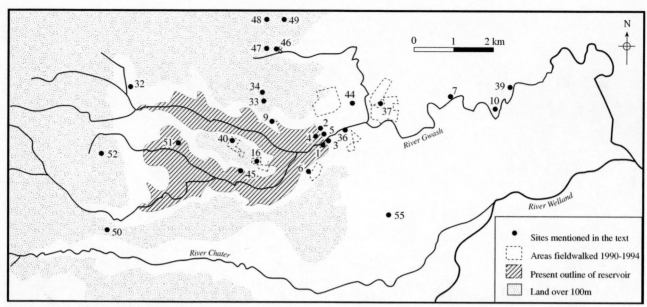

Fig. 65 Settlement in the Gwash Valley: The Roman Period

the fort it is likely that the focus of the settlement may have shifted to Ermine Street itself alongside which an official *mansio* was constructed in the later first century, lying in the southwest corner of the area eventually surrounded by the defensive circuit in the later second century (Burnham and Wacher 1991, 133).

The native inhabitants of the Gwash Valley were therefore exposed to an unprecedented range of cosmopolitan influences but the detailed chronology of their sites is not sufficiently known to gauge the speed of their reactions. Examination of the excavated pottery assemblages (p.72) suggests that only Whitwell (9) was enjoying a range of wares comparable to that gracing the tables of the local fort during the mid-to late first century (Todd 1981).

The excavations in the central part of the valley at Empingham and Whitwell (1,2,3,5,6 and 9) as well as those lower down at Great Casterton villa (39) provide the bulk of evidence for Romano-British rural settlement. The fourth century structure at Great Casterton (Corder 1954) is the most luxurious of the masonry buildings recognised, and in addition to Site 2, is the only establishment that might be traditionally termed a villa. The structures on both these sites and the other recognisable masonry structures on Site 1 and at Whitwell, are based on an aisled plan or, in the latter case, succeed an aisled building. Sites 5 and 6 both possessed masonry buildings but neither plan was preserved.

Early Roman occupation of first and second century date was recognised on the south side of the river, at Sites 1 and 3, and on the north side at Whitwell (9). Sites 1 and 3 lying only 150m apart, appear to have been linked by a stone trackway (SK 943 077 and SK 944 077 respectively). The enclosure ditch on Site 3 appears to have gone out of use by the second century, and although Roman pottery of fourth century date occurs residually in Early Anglo-Saxon features there is no recognisable intervening occupation. The timber build-

ings and associated features on Site 1 appear to have been levelled, possibly after a fire, in the 150s AD or slightly later, and there may have been a break in occupation until the early third century. At Whitwell, no building structures accompanied the relatively rich assemblage of mid-late first century pottery deposited in the large ditch that formed part of a system of enclosures (Todd 1981, 8), and it is likely that further early evidence still lies in the areas unavailable for excavation.

The Later Roman Landscape: Farmsteads, Villas and Towns

The Later Roman picture is more coherent. On **Site 1**, the masonry aisled building was constructed probably in the early third century, with alterations and additions being made to the complex over the next century. Both agricultural and iron-working functions are indicated by the presence of corn driers and hearths. At some point, probably later in the third century, occupation began 400m to the north, directly across the valley on **Site 2** (SK 941 081), where the final phase of construction comprised a masonry villa building of rectangular plan, comprising at least eight rooms arranged into two aisles each side of a large hall. At least one of the rooms had a hypocaust and, in contrast to Site 1, the structure appears to have been purely residential, lacking the evidence for industrial hearths found in the aisled building on Site 1. The point at which an aisled building becomes a villa is rather arbitrary as both buildings lie along a continuum between the undeveloped and developed form, with Site 2 displaying more 'Romanised' features or overt elements of private space than Site 1. Consequently, it is tempting to view the Later Roman occupation of these two sites as the residential and productive halves of a single farming establishment, straddling the valley, and the detection of associated contemporary structures between them (**Site 5**), including iron furnaces and corn driers, illustrates the dispersed nature of its constituent elements. The two stone coffin burials of fourth century date (see p.14 and 19 burials 5R and 7R), associated with Sites 1 and 2, which appear to face each other across the valley contribute a more personal piece of evidence in support of the idea that the two sites were linked in some way, but the existence of separate cemeteries for each probably indicates that they were self-contained establishments.

At Whitwell (9), a timber aisled building of similar proportions to the masonry example on Site 1, was constructed in the later second century and was replaced by a stone-founded rectangular building by the later third (Todd, 1981). The lack of coinage and pottery dating to the second half of the fourth century led Todd to conclude that the site, and its associated field system and industrial enclosure, had been abandoned by the mid-fourth century. While this is quite possibly the case, it contrasts with the evidence from the neighbouring Sites 1 and 2 and the villa at Great Casterton where pottery and coins indicate that occupation continued right up to the end of the fourth century, and probably into the early fifth. Only nine Roman coins were retrieved from Whitwell, which was not surprising considering the difficult conditions of excavation, and the five of mid-fourth century date came from the upper filling of a single isolated post pit feature 10 (Clough 1981, 34). It may therefore be the case that later fourth century coins were missed during excavation, and that the 'early' date of abandonment may require revision.

While the Roman coin assemblages from Sites 1 and 2 are not that much larger, they both suggest that the period AD 388-402 was one of increasing activity, at a time when most sites were experiencing a gradual fall-off in coin finds, and the generally worn nature of the Theodosian and later coins may indicate a late date of loss conceivably extending into the fifth century (Ponting above p.00). This evidence can be coupled with the late fourth century deposits from Great Casterton Villa which dated its destruction to 'certainly after AD 388 and probably after AD 395' (Corder 1961, 76) and which remain, even after 40 years, the most securely dated late contexts in the region.

The remaining excavated site belonging to this late Roman period was a masonry farmstead (Site 6) lying 1km south-west of Site 1, (SK 936 067) slightly higher up the valley side near Normanton Church. Little of the masonry building itself was preserved, and while the pottery in the fills of the associated corn drier and well indicate that it in use during the fourth century, the date of abandonment cannot be pinpointed with any further accuracy.

The late Roman evidence from the town of Great Casterton (10) on Ermine Street, the only 'urban' settlement positively identified in the Gwash Valley (but see below), is rather sketchy as only limited excavation has taken place inside the walled area. Knowledge is confined to the reorganisation of the defences, including the addition of bastions, in the mid-fourth century, and to the inhumation cemetery identified outside the north gate. The cemetery was first excavated in 1959 and revealed rows of burials with feet pointing to the east, dated by associated pottery to the later third to mid-fourth century (Burnham and Wacher 1991, 135). Additional later burials were excavated from the counterscarp bank of the modified defences near Ryhall road in 1966, demonstrating that the use of the cemetery continued well into the fifth century (Grainger and Mahany forthcoming). These burials are discussed in further detail below in relation to the succeeding Early Anglo-Saxon cemetery.

Settlement Throughout the Valley

A number of Roman sites additional to those excavated have been identified. Moving down the valley, work carried out by the Rutland Field Research Group has identified a site in the area of Dog Kennel Spinney (32), east of Oakham (SK 874 094, Jones 1995, 241). The scatter comprised pottery, tile and wall plaster and may be indicative of a villa building.

At Whitwell, about 1km north of the Iron Age and Roman site excavated in 1976-77 and immediately north west of the village itself (SK 921 090), a second site (33) is indicated by the discovery, in 1990, of a substantial coin hoard including *siliquae* extending into the early fifth century, which is associated with a coin scatter of fourth century date. On the northern edge of this scatter, inhumation burials without grave goods were previously discovered in the 19th century and are probably Roman in date (34). More recent metal detection survey has indicated that this site is much larger, possibly up to 20 acres (P. Liddle pers. comm), and establishing the nature of the site must be seen as a priority for further research in the area.

On the south side of the valley an associated settlement site is indicated by the discovery of two Roman burials (35) accompanied by pottery vessels on the slipway of the sailing club at Edith Weston (SK 922 057) in 1991. A complete pot had previously been discovered in 1990 (Lucas 1993, 144). Along the Hambleton Peninsula, in addition to the fieldwalked scatters of Romano-British pottery mentioned above in relation to Iron Age settlement (16) and (40), further evidence is known to the west of Middle Hambleton in an area now submerged (51) (SK 894 073, E. Jones pers.comm.).

In the vicinity of Empingham itself, there is evidence for three further sites. Fieldwalking undertaken by Anthea Diver in the late 1960s located a scatter of Roman pottery including colour-coated ware and iron slag south of the village, on the south bank of the river (36) at SK 949 082. Immediately east of Empingham, a Roman coin and brooch were discovered in Chapel Spinney (37), and the site would appear to extend across the field to the south (Field 16 on the survey) where a number of coins were metal detected. Fieldwalking undertaken in 1992 indicated a fairly even scatter of Roman pottery of 1-2 sherds per 60m stint, which may represent intensive in-field manuring rather than settlement itself. Survey of the field to the north of the Spinney (Field 17), did not indicate that the site extended in this direction. Within Empingham village, a site, indicated by unabraded pottery, was recently discovered in Loves Lane **(44)** (SK 953 090, Jones 1997, 320).

Fieldwalking undertaken in 1990 in the area immediately north west of Empingham (Fields 1-7) failed to provide evidence for further sites of Roman date or manuring activity, which would tend to indicate that the focus of settlement sites was largely confined to the valley bottom, with the sides being utilised predominantly as pasture or woodland. The existence of a spring line between the limestone (ironstone) and the underlying liassic clay running along the valley side would appear to have acted as an important factor in the location of settlement.

Lack of fieldwork in the lower part of the Gwash Valley between Empingham and Great Casterton distorts the likely distribution of Roman settlement. In addition to the limited evidence for occupation indicated by unstratified Roman pottery from the excavation of the Anglo-Saxon settlement site at Tickencote (Site 7) in 1990, one, or possibly two, villa sites have also been recognised there, one of which is listed by Todd (1973, 78) amongst his Class III villa establishments. It may be of significance that the Petrofina pipeline along which Site 7 was discovered did not encounter any Roman sites as it continued southwards up the valley side towards Ketton and Tixover. The watershed between the Gwash and Chater has, however, yielded substantial cropmark evidence in the quarry area north of Ketton, and recent excavations in advance of quarrying (SK 969 056) have revealed a late Iron Age and Romano-British farmstead and a previously unknown late Saxon church and settlement **(55)** (Meadows 1999, 119-121).

The pattern as it appears gives the impression of a very much valley-based distribution with a distinct increase in activity in the later Roman period. This would tend to corroborate the findings of the Medbourne Area Survey in the Welland Valley where there is evidence for a retreat from the margins in the Later Roman period as occupation and manuring scatters disappear from the higher ground and nucleation around a number of long-lived, valley-based villas appears to occur, with the higher ground presumably continuing as pasture or woodland. This would appear to indicate the existence of a 'Vale and Wold' landscape and the insect evidence form the well on Site 1 (p.36) would certainly support the idea that the valley at least was open and cultivated. In the Gwash Valley, the majority of Roman sites recognised are those which have been excavated and so consequently, due to the location of the development, have produced or exaggerated this valley-based pattern. However, apart from the two sites on the Hambleton Peninsula **(16 and 40)**, and the four metal-detected sites near Exton **(46-49)** (SK 92 11, P. Liddle pers. comm.) and to the north of Whitwell **(34)**, fieldwalking has not so far contradicted this pattern. Evidence for iron smelting in the form of scatters of tap slag detected from fieldwalking which are located higher up the valley sides (Fields 8, 22, 24 and 25), would support the idea that these were maintained as areas of woodland (J. Cowgill pers. comm.).

The Early Anglo-Saxon Transition: Continuity or Change? (Fig. 66)

Overall, the Roman evidence from the valley points to the continuity of activity into the fifth century and it is therefore necessary to ask what significance can be placed on the location of the Early Anglo-Saxon settlement and cemetery **(Site 3)** just 150m east of Site 1 ? The aisled barn and associated structures could potentially have continued intact throughout the fifth century at least since there was no need to rob their masonry, and while it is reasonable to suggest that the

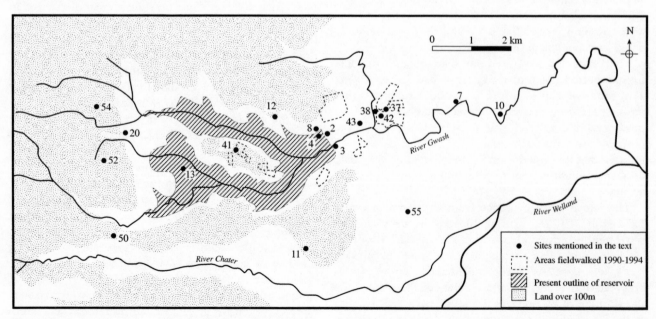

Fig. 66 Settlement in the Gwash Valley: The Anglo-Saxon Period

buildings may have been made use of by the new focus of settlement immediately to the east, the small amount of Anglo-Saxon pottery found on the site would not really support the idea. The evidence of domestic pottery and grave-finds suggests that the Anglo-Saxon occupation of Site 3 does not begin before the later fifth century, and so there is difficulty in suggesting any form of direct continuity between the two periods. The evidence at Empingham forces comparison with the scenario put forward by David Miles for Barton Court Farm, Oxon. (Miles 1984, 52), in which Saxon settlement moves on to a Roman site abandoned in the second or third decade of the fifth century (20 to 30 years previously), as the result of the collapse of the economic system into which it was integrated. The relationship between the two occupations would thus be seen as butt-jointed, as suggested by Brown (1974), and would thus make untenable Rodwell's assertion that the 'Romano-British farming economy.....was no more destroyed by the departure of the Roman Imperial government than was Iron Age farming by its arrival' (1985, 75). However, the presumed lack of any form of continuity at all also causes difficulties, since we have to explain what happens to the substantial post-Roman population inhabiting the valley. The situation at Orton Hall Farm, Cambs. (Mackreth 1996), at least sees the necessity for the post-Roman farm to be still operational at the time of the Anglo-Saxon settlement with Phase 4 of the Roman occupation ending c.AD 375, followed by a period of decline during Phase 5 which overlaps with Anglo-Saxon occupation beginning c.AD 420, but perhaps as early as c.AD 390 or as late as c.AD430/440 (D.Mackreth pers.comm).

While there is no problem in accepting that the Late pre-Roman Iron Age population of Britain took on the material culture of the Roman Empire, there is a reluctance to accept that a substantial native population could possibly be hiding behind the entirely different material culture of the Anglo-Saxons. The reason for this is that the transition from Iron Age to Roman is far more easily understood as the Romans took advantage of a trend towards early state formation which was already established (if only in the Lowland Zone) prior to the invasion while, in contrast, the Anglo-Saxons moved into the vacuum caused by the collapse of that system (Miles 1984, 52). The collapse appears to have largely removed the material culture of the Romano-British population, without much attempt at introducing an archaeologically visible replacement. Therefore we can rarely see where or how they lived during those intervening decades, unless they continued to occupy the same sites and used the ageing products of late fourth century specialists, replacing them with organic alternatives or products which are simply not being recognised (Cooper 1996a). Esmonde Cleary sees this disappearance and lack of renewal as an expression of a social crisis as profound as the economic and material ones which cleared the ground for the evolution of a new order (1989, 173). If we accept that at least the lower orders of

post-Roman society, lacking a distinctive material culture remained to farm the land at subsistence level as indicated by the pollen record (Turner 1981), then the transition is explicable and perhaps the descendants of that population occupy the (?unfurnished) graves of the Early Anglo-Saxon cemetery on Site 3.

Establishing an Early Anglo-Saxon Settlement Pattern

The Early Anglo-Saxon sites discussed in this volume are vital components in starting to understand the chronology and character of such settlement in Leicestershire and Rutland because of the paucity of excavated evidence. While excavations in 1996 to 97 at Eye Kettleby near Melton Mowbray revealed a settlement of much larger extent (Finn 1997, 88), the sites excavated between 1967 and 75; **Sites 3, 4,** and Empingham II **(8)**, represent the only examples of cemeteries occurring alongside contemporary settlement in Rutland, and very few others are known in Leicestershire (Liddle 1996). The existence of likely Roman period antecedents for the settlements is also not as clear as it appears for the Empingham sites.

The evidence from **Site 3** comprised three sunken-featured buildings and associated pits, cut into the southern edge of the stone trackway which, it is conjectured, linked Sites 1 and 3. **Site 4** lay on the north side of the valley (SK 936 079), 300m west of Site 2, and 750m north west of Site 3. It partly overlay the Iron Age settlement described above, with no apparent structural evidence for occupation during the Roman period. The excavated evidence comprises two sunken-featured buildings and associated pits and gullies, lying immediately north west of the Iron Age round houses (SK 937 079). Pottery from both sites indicates occupation in the fifth and early sixth century contemporary with the earliest phases of the two associated cemeteries, and it is likely that the excavated areas represent small parts of larger settlements which gradually shifted over time as demonstrated at Mucking (Hamerow 1989).

On Site 3, the later phase of burials overlies the eastern-most building excavated, indicating that the settlement was shifting westwards, while on Site 4 there are indications that the Anglo-Saxon features lay within or to the edge of a much larger settlement possibly shifting northwards. Observations made during 1973 by Bill Thomas, a dedicated local amateur, prior to the discovery of Empingham II Anglo-Saxon cemetery, indicate that the settlement may have spread northwards, lying between Sykes Lane and the cemetery itself. He observed at least 20 possible sunken-featured buildings, as well as hearth features and pottery in the area, but unfortunately the evidence was destroyed immediately without any photographic or written record being made. Such observations must be treated with caution, but if correct, would certainly provide evidence of a settlement capable of generating the Empingham II cemetery immediately to the north.

The last of the three settlements **(Site 7)** was recently discovered 3 miles downstream of Site 3 on the north side of the river at Tickencote (SK 985 093). Two sunken-featured buildings of irregular plan with associated hearths and pits were excavated by the Leicestershire Archaeological Unit during construction of the Petrofina pipeline. The pottery from the site indicates a sixth century date. From the upper part of the valley, a possible sunken-featured building **(54)** with fifth to sixth-century pottery, was partly excavated at South Street, Oakham (SK 8591 0869, Jones 1995, 241). Most recently, fieldwork by Rutland Local History and Record Society has produced new evidence in the area of Martinsthorpe (SK 867 044) in the upper reaches of the southern tributary **(50)**, with a scatter of 122 sherds of Early Anglo-Saxon pottery, associated with Roman material (Jones 1999, 407). A smaller scatter was also detected at Egleton **(20)** within the substantial Early Bronze Age flint scatter.

A further possible site of Early Anglo-Saxon occupation has been identified from a thin scatter of pottery detected during fieldwalking of Field 15/25 **(41)**. The sites and monuments record also refers to the discovery of two sunken featured buildings in Mowmires Spinney (SK 941 073), but this is probably erroneous, and is more likely to be a reference to a post pad building excavated by Bill Thomas in 1973, but for which no dating evidence was retrieved.

Turning to the detail of the burial evidence associated with the two Early Anglo-Saxon settlements identified on Sites 3 and 4, fourteen inhumations were excavated from what may have been only part of a larger Anglo-Saxon cemetery, in the north and east part of Site 3, the later phase of which cut into the sunken-feature building 1.

The cemetery evidence from Site 3 is coupled with that from the much larger cemetery excavated on the opposite side of the Valley at Empingham II **(8)** (SK 936 082, Timby 1996). The cemetery was discovered in 1974, on the north side of Sykes Lane, during the construction of a car park for the Sykes Lane leisure area. The site was excavated initially by Sam Gorin, and in 1975 by N.M.Reynolds, and yielded 136 inhumation burials and a single cremation, with a total of 153 individuals of all ages and both sexes. There were several instances of double burials with one multiple burial of four individuals. Analysis of the bones and teeth suggests that the cemetery comprised 96 adults (18 years and over), and 54 juveniles (1-18 years), with an average age at death of 28.4 years (Mays 1996, 25-26).

Some 78% of the individuals were accompanied by some form of object ranging from single knives or buckles to in excess of 10 individual items. Women were accompanied by an array of brooch types, sleeve clasps, girdle hangers, and beads, while adult men were generally accompanied by spearheads, shields and knives, but no decorative ornament. Bronze buckets, cauldrons and pottery were also represented. From the artefactual evidence the cemetery would appear to have been in use from the early fifth century to the early seventh century.

The internal arrangement of the cemetery appears haphazard with no clearly defined linear or radial patterning or chronological progression apparent within the overall linear form which uses an earlier Iron Age and Roman holloway as its south western boundary. However, in no instance does one grave cut another, which either suggests that they were clearly marked above ground, or that the cemetery was only in use for a relatively short period of time (Timby 1996). The latter suggestion is supported by Reynolds' original observation, based on the occurrence of cruciform brooches of the florid art-style, that the main period of use for the cemetery lay in the later sixth and early seventh century (Adams *et al.* 1982).

Additional Early Anglo-Saxon cemetery evidence comes from the lower part of the valley at Great Casterton **(10)** where excavations by Christine Mahany in 1966 discovered a number of Early Anglo-Saxon burials cut into the counterscarp bank of the town defences. The bank had been created from the spoil generated by the recutting of the town ditch during the reorganisation of the defences in the mid-fourth century or slightly later (after 354 and before 370) (Corder 1961, 12-13, Grainger and Mahany, forthcoming). Of the 79 burials excavated in 1966, 29 are late Roman inhumations (Grainger and Mahany, forthcoming, Group I), 35 are Anglo-Saxon cremations (Group II), and 15 are Anglo-Saxon inhumations (Group III).

Precise dating of the burials is unfortunately impossible. It is likely that the sequence of late Roman inhumations continues into the fifth century and, allowing 20 years between intercutting graves, the latest could theoretically be as late as c.460 *(ibid.)*. On the whole, the Anglo-Saxon inhumations appear to post-date the cremations which are thought to belong to span the period 475-550. Finds from the inhumations would indicate continued use of the cemetery until at least the last quarter of the sixth century *(ibid.)*.

The three cemeteries so far considered all lie along the bottom of the Gwash Valley alongside associated settlement, and are of broadly similar status. However, consideration of a fourth early Anglo-Saxon cemetery, at North Luffenham **(11)**, may shed light on the wider regional significance of the Gwash Valley area. In contrast to the other three, it lies along the watershed between the Gwash and the Chater to the south (SK 932 045). The small area of the cemetery recorded during sand extraction in 1855 and early in the twentieth century yielded at least ten swords, the unusually high number of which was remarked upon at the time (Crowther-Beynon 1903, 91). The location and richness of the cemetery at least place it among other outstanding cemeteries such as the sixth century inhumation cemetery at Spong Hill, Norfolk which appear to have been catering for an elite group at a regional level rather than the local population, and in this respect, the royal associations of the Rutland area discussed below are of particular relevance.

No Christian burials were identified either from the Empingham II cemetery, or conclusively from **Site 3**

(Empingham I cemetery), and there is nothing to suggest the continued use of these areas beyond the early seventh century. The evidence from the associated settlements is less precise due to the difficulties in dating undecorated pottery, but it does not contradict this picture, which is one of an essentially dispersed settlement pattern beginning to undergo a process of nucleation.

Fieldwalking in a number of areas of Leicestershire is beginning to support this picture of dispersed Early Anglo-Saxon settlement, and a review of the present state of knowledge has recently been published (Liddle 1996). In the Medbourne area of the Welland Valley, a survey of six contiguous parishes has revealed some 16 certain, or likely, Early Anglo-Saxon settlements, only one of which, at Blaston, has been confirmed by excavation. A similar pattern is known in the Langtons (Bowman 1996), and is hinted at in a number of smaller surveys at Brooksby and Lockington/Kegworth. The discovery of settlement and associated cemetery evidence, although only demonstrated conclusively at Empingham, is likely to become a gradually more common phenomenon as co-operation between metal detectorists and fieldwalkers grows. Fieldwalking by the Birstall Fieldwork Group has already indicated the existence of a settlement site next to the cemetery at Wanlip, burials from which were salvage excavated in 1958 (Liddle 1980).

The Middle and Late Anglo-Saxon Periods (Fig. 66)

The process of nucleation indicated by the abandonment of early Anglo-Saxon settlements and cemeteries in the valley during the seventh century is likely to have been a complex and gradual one, involving a complete reorganisation of the landscape, and there is very little detailed archaeological evidence for the steps involved. The Roman villa on **Site 2** was reused in the middle to late seventh century as a Christian cemetery, and possibly as an early church, the detailed arguments for which have been outlined above (p.21) and separately (Cooper 1996b), but evidence for an associated settlement of Middle Anglo-Saxon date is lacking.

However, documentary evidence helps to flesh out the meagre evidence for the Middle and Late Anglo-Saxon period, and places the valley within its regional context. Cutting west to east, the Gwash Valley bisects the modern district of Rutland, the origins of which have been most recently considered by Phythian Adams (1977 and 1980). The Domesday Book reveals that in 1086, the area described as *Roteland* comprised only the north-westerly two-thirds of the modern district of Rutland, and was made up of two wapentakes (Alstoe and Martinsley) formerly within the territory of the Five Boroughs (the area of Danish settlement) (Thorn 1980), and formed a detached portion of Nottinghamshire (Phythian-Adams 1980, 5 and fig.1). The upper part of the valley, above Empingham, lay within *Roteland* and predominantly in the wapentake of Martinsley with the northern tributary of the Gwash

forming part of the southern boundary of the wapentake of Alstoe. The lower part of the valley including Empingham lies in the south-easterly strip of modern Rutland formerly belonging to Northamptonshire, and known as the double Hundred of Witchley (Phythian-Adams 1980, 5).

Phythian-Adams argues (1980, 6-8) that the original extent of *Roteland* did include the Northamptonshire portion as well as the area of Stamford, (the town lying at the confluence of the Gwash and Welland which had been severed from the district by 894, and incorporated into Lincolnshire by the time of the Conquest), and that it probably existed as a discrete unit within the Middle Anglian territory before its subjugation to Mercia in the early seventh century, belonging at some point to the individual known as *Rota*. The survival of this administrative area is attributed to the fact that it was probably, by this time, a Middle Anglian *regio*, the royal centre of which has been placed by Phythian-Adams (1980, 8) at Hambleton, on the peninsula separating the twin tributaries of the Gwash, and which then became a possession of the Mercian kings. As such the area survived the Scandinavian invasions and the creation of the Five Boroughs, a point amplified by the fact that although it lay in the heart of the Danelaw, there is remarkably little evidence for the adoption of Danish placenames. By the mid-tenth century at the latest Rutland had become the dower lands of the Late Anglo-Saxon queens, and Phythian-Adams argues that this tradition may have extended backwards to include the queens of Mercia well before the Danish Invasion (1980, 9-11). At the time of the Norman Conquest therefore, the area of the valley above Empingham (the wapentake of Martinsley) belonged to Queen Eadgyth, wife of Eadward the Confessor, while Empingham itself would appear to be the location of the seven and a half hides one bovate of 'the King's soc of *Roteland* in Empingham' which appear as part of the lands held by Gilbert of Ghent in Domesday.

The conjectured long survival of the area as a royal estate as far back as the seventh century would be supported by the existence of the high-status inhumation cemetery at North Luffenham which lies close to the south boundary of the wapentake of Martinsley, and about 1km south of the village of Edith Weston (after Queen Eadgyth). The cemetery is therefore some distance from the proposed site of the royal residence across the valley at Hambleton, which may support the idea of an alternative location for the *caput*, perhaps near Edith Weston, unless the boundary location of the cemetery is significant.

Long before the Conquest then, the dispersed pattern of Early Anglo-Saxon settlement along the valley, nucleated into the villages of Hambleton, Whitwell, Empingham, Tickencote, Casterton, and Ryhall, with Oakham at its head, probably acting as the administrative centre after Stamford's detachment. Presumably the process of village formation took place during the later seventh, eighth, and ninth centuries, but there is very little archaeological evidence to demonstrate it. The major barrier is the lack of a distinctive Middle Anglo-Saxon pottery tradition in the East Midlands compounded the lack of imported Ipswich ware from East Anglia. Therefore a ceramic gap exists between the end of the pagan Anglo-Saxon tradition *c*.650 and the earliest products of the Stamford ware industry dated *c*.850. The reason for this gap is unclear; either people stopped using pottery in favour of other materials such as metal or wood, or we have simply failed to recognise middle Anglo-Saxon material. This may be due to its similarity to the earlier tradition or the fact that we have not been looking in the right places. Much of it must remain hidden beneath modern building or beneath the deserted parts of those medieval villages which suffered shrinkage. The opportunity to excavate such sites has occurred both at the time of the Rutland Water's construction and more recently during small scale developments within the village cores of Whitwell and Empingham for example (Meek 1998, 368 and Thomas 1998, 368 respectively). At the time of construction, excavations were undertaken by the Rutland Field Research Group (now the Rutland Local History and Record Society) initially at Nether Hambleton (13) (SK 894 067) between 1973 and 1976, and latterly at Whitwell (12) from 1976 onwards (SK 924 086). Interim reports have been produced (Adams *et al*. 1982 and Jones 1999, 408), and the chronological information relating to origin is summarised below.

At Nether Hambleton, a substantial building and associated street was excavated, dating to between the 11th and 15th centuries (Adams *et al*. 1982, 64). Detailed examination of the pottery (Woodland unpublished) identified a probable vessel of Ipswich Ware dating to *c*. 650-850, and a possible sherd of Pingsdorf/Badorf ware dating from 650-1000. The bulk of the assemblage was, however, supplied from the nearby industry at Stamford, operating between *c*. 850 and 1250, with most products on the site dating to the 11th and 12th century. At Whitwell the earliest medieval pottery from structures excavated comprise the early products of Stamford (Adams *et al*. 1982, 65), but precise dating is lacking. Most recently, excavations at Ketton quarry (55) have shown the potential of large-scale open area excavations in the valley by revealing a previously unknown late Saxon settlement with a timber church, graveyard and timber halls occupied for a limited period between 900 and 1100 before total abandonment (Meadows 1999, 121).

Turning to the evidence for the earliest origins of the village of Empingham itself, a group of Saxo-Norman Stamford Ware vessels was discovered by Hilary Healey in 1965, under the floor of a barn forming part of Church Farm, next to the parish church (43). In addition to this, a number of burials were discovered in the village in the 19th century from the Prebendal House on the east side of the church, and again in 1969 which may derive from earlier areas of graveyard covered by later street modification (43).

Other evidence may suggest that Empingham originally had two centres, the other lying to the east of the modern village possibly focusing on the chapel of St Botolph located in Chapel Spinney (37), which has already been identified as the centre of a possible Roman site. Earthwork evidence demonstrates the existence of plots for crofts along the line of Mill Lane (38) (Hartley 1983). Fieldwalking of the area adjoining the east side of these crofts (Fields 16 and 20) (42) identified a dense scatter of early medieval pottery (including Saxo-Norman Stamford Ware), indicating intensive in-field manuring or settlement which may well have been deserted by the 13th century.

Conclusion

Fieldwork in the Gwash Valley spanning a period of thirty years has provided evidence for a dense pattern of continuous settlement from the later Mesolithic to the Norman Conquest. Much of the settlement evidence prior to the Late Saxon period (the Domesday pattern) would have been thought unlikely to exist at all by landscape historians of the late 1950s such as Hoskins, who believed that the heavy clay soils would have 'attracted early man only in small numbers' to the extent that 'even the Romans made comparatively little impression' (1957, 2). With regard to the prehistory of Leicestershire and Rutland especially, this view was difficult to refute even by the late 1970s, due to a lack of fieldwork (Clay 1989, 111). However, the partial removal of the barrier of archaeological invisibility through increased ploughing and the concerted efforts of both amateur and professional archaeologists, through both fieldwalking and aerial survey, have helped to change this picture totally.

The increase in ploughing in Leicestershire and Rutland since the Second World War, while eroding that fossilised Medieval landscape which so dominated Hoskins' view, has brought to light the evidence for a much longer heritage. The Domesday landscape (which has itself continued to evolve since) can therefore be viewed as the end product of a long term process of gradual intensification of landuse, probably punctuated with periods of regression as indicated by the later Roman evidence from the Medbourne Area Survey in south-east Leicestershire (Liddle 1994).

The gradually increasing level of exploitation indicated from the Later Mesolithic or Early Neolithic appears to accelerate during the Later Neolithic and Early Bronze Age. It becomes more coherent in terms of definable occupation sites during the Iron Age (following an archaeological blindspot in the Later Bronze Age), with at least fourteen settlement sites being identified, on a mix of valley bottom and watershed locations. The extent to which the Iron Age settlement pattern forms the foundation for that in the Roman period is, however, still unclear from the sites excavated, although fieldwalking survey has indicated the potential for Iron Age enclosure cropmarks to produce Roman material, and this should be considered as a priority for future work.

The Roman period does appear to represent a further intensification of settlement, although the increased visibility of sites through use of building stone must be borne in mind. The apparently valley-based concentration of the pattern needs to be tested with a more extensive survey of the upper valley sides and watersheds required. This may help to confirm the nature of settlement and landuse there and any relationship with those in the valley bottom. In particular, further fieldwork must be directed towards the site north of Whitwell (34), which would appear to be a potential local centre. If this could be confirmed then it would call into question the present assumption that these rural settlements looked only to the small town of Great Casterton as a market with access to destinations north and south via Ermine Street.

The question of continuity from Roman to Early Anglo-Saxon will continue to be hotly debated (Cooper 1996), but the increasing coincidence of Roman and Early Anglo-Saxon pottery scatters encountered during fieldwalking survey promotes the contribution of the post-Roman population to the dispersed pattern of settlement which emerges. The evidence from the Gwash Valley, at least in the area of the excavations, indicates an Early Anglo-Saxon population density at least equal to that in the Roman period, and further fieldwork indicates that this pattern is repeated along the valley.

The least understood part of the Anglo-Saxon period concerns the process of nucleation which transforms this dispersed pattern into the Domesday landscape, the basis of the pattern of villages we see today. The Middle Anglo-Saxon represents a considerable gap in the picture filled at present only by a meagre collection of burials at a former villa site (2). If, as suggested by Liddle (1996, 5), the Middle Anglo-Saxon settlements lie beneath the medieval villages, this would, in part, explain their elusiveness. A concerted campaign of garden walking within these villages, coupled with excavation within the village cores, whenever development opportunities arise, may begin to provide some answers. However, unless distinctive cultural markers such as pottery can be identified for the period, this step in the landscape development process is likely to remain the subject of conjecture.

At present the potential for further fieldwork in the Gwash Valley lies in the hands of professional contractors and local amateurs, and no doubt the picture presented here will increase its resolution. The valley joins a growing list of intensively surveyed landscape 'parcels' in Leicestershire and Rutland which includes the Medbourne area (Liddle 1994), the Langtons (Bowman 1996), and the Swift Valley (Clay 1999). These areas present a broadly consistent picture of how the Midland landscape develops, and provide benchmarks of archaeological potential in less intensively surveyed areas facing development threats. They also provide a huge dataset for future works of synthesis across the region. This process of synthesis has already begun for the prehistoric evidence with Clay's overview of the East Midlands claylands (Clay 1996 and forthcoming), and a major contribution to understanding the reorganisation of the landscape during the Anglo-Saxon period has also been made (Bowman 1996). However, despite the increasing wealth of evidence, little headway has been made toward understanding the evolution of the Romano-British landscape and particularly its relationship with the Iron Age pattern which preceded it or the Anglo-Saxon which followed.

The evidence from the Gwash Valley coupled with that from Medbourne in the Welland Valley, as well as the large number of parish-based surveys currently underway in Leicestershire and Rutland, could provide the foundation for such a study. While it is unlikely that the further collection and synthesis of fieldwalking data alone will begin to answer detailed questions concerning continuity, it would enable an informed selection of sites on which further survey and excavation might yield answers. At present, developer-led archaeology rarely provides the opportunity to target such sites and so research funding must be sought. Only then will we begin to convert the dots on the map into a better understanding of how people actually lived within these landscapes and appreciate the physical, economic, social and political factors which shaped their lives.

List of Sites Discussed in the Text (Figs. 62-66)

1) Empingham Romano-British farmstead (SK 943 077)
2) Empingham North Romano-British villa (SK 941 081)
3) Empingham I Early Anglo-Saxon settlement and cemetery (SK 944 077)
4) Empingham West Iron Age and Early Anglo-Saxon settlement (SK 936 079)
5) Empingham 1968 Romano-British site (SK 942 080)
6) Renners Park Romano-British site (SK 936 067)
7) Tickencote Early Anglo-Saxon settlement (SK 985 093)
8) Empingham II Early Anglo-Saxon cemetery (SK 936 082)
9) Whitwell Iron Age and Romano-British settlement (SK 924 082)
10) Great Casterton Romano-British Town and Early Anglo-Saxon cemetery (TF 002 090)
11) North Luffenham Early Anglo-Saxon cemetery (SK 932 045)
12) Whitwell deserted medieval village (SK 924 086)
13) Nether Hambleton deserted medieval village (SK 894 067)
14) Oakham, Burley Road pit circle (SK 867 096)
15) Flint Scatter Field 8 (SK 938 066)
16) Iron Age enclosed farmstead cropmark with fieldwalked scatters of flint, Iron Age and Roman pottery (Field 11) (SK 919 069).

17) Field 13 Hambleton Peninsula flint scatter (SK 907 073)

18) Field 14 Hambleton Peninsula flint scatter (SK 914 072)

19) North shoreline of Rutland Water between Sykes Lane and Whitwell, flint scatter (SK 930 081)

20) Egleton, Bronze Age triple ditch cropmark and flint scatter (SK 870 081 to SK 869 086)

21) Barleythorpe, Neolithic or Early Bronze Age ring-ditch cropmarks (SK 852 095)

22) Ryhall, pit alignment cropmark (TF 043 113)

23) Ryhall, pit alignment and ring-ditch cropmarks (TF 034 102)

24) Oakham, Iron Age enclosure cropmark (SK 835 087)

25) Oakham, Iron Age enclosure cropmark (SK 846 083)

26) Edith Weston Iron Age enclosure cropmark (SK 908 054)

27) North Luffenham Iron Age enclosure cropmark (SK 931 042)

28) Ryhall, Iron Age double-ditched enclosure cropmark (TF 048 109)

29) Ryhall, Iron Age enclosure cropmark (TF 028 103)

30) Little Casterton, Iron Age enclosure cropmark (TF 020 092)

31) Ryhall, pit alignment cropmark (TF 033 089)

32) Dog Kennel Spinney, fieldwalked Romano-British pottery scatter (SK 874 094)

33) Whitwell, Roman coin hoard (SK 921 090)

34) Whitwell ?Romano-British burials found in 19th century (SK 921 091)

35) Edith Weston, Romano-British burial at sailing club (SK 922 057)

36) Empingham, Romano-British site discovered by Anthea Diver (SK 949 082)

37) Empingham, Romano-British finds in Chapel Spinney (SK 961 089)

38) Empingham, medieval croft earthworks in Mill Lane (SK 959 086)

39) Great Casterton Romano-British villa (TF 007 097)

40) Hambleton Peninsula, Field 25 Romano-British pottery scatter (SK 910 077)

41) Hambleton Peninsula, Field 15 Early Anglo-Saxon Pottery scatter (SK 918 076)

42) Empingham, Field 16/20 Saxo-Norman pottery scatter adjacent to crofts 38 (SK 959 086)

43) Empingham, medieval burials in village (SK 952 085)

44) Empingham, Romano-British site in Loves Lane (SK 953 090)

45) Hambleton Peninsula, Iron Age/Romano-British ditch and round house (SK 912 067)

46) Exton Romano-British site 1 (SK 92 10)

47) Exton Romano-British site 2 (SK 92 10)

48) Exton Romano-British site 3 (SK 92 11)

49) Exton Romano-British site 4 (SK 92 11)

50) Martinsthorpe, Romano-British and Early Anglo-Saxon site, and deserted medieval village (SK 867 044)

51) Middle Hambleton, Romano-British site (SK 894 073, E. Jones pers. comm.)

52) The Grange Farm, Egleton, Iron Age, Romano-British, and Anglo-Saxon occupation. (SK 864 072, E.Jones pers. comm.)

53) Oakham, Bronze Age pit alignment to the south of Burley Road (SK 869 092)

54) Oakham, Early Anglo-Saxon sunken-featured building in South Street (SK 8591 0869).

55) Ketton Quarry, late Iron Age and Romano-British farmstead and late Saxon church and settlement (SK 969 056)

BIBLIOGRAPHY

Aberg, N., 1926 *The Anglo-Saxons in England during the early centuries after the invasion.* Cambridge.

Adams, A. W., Clough, T. H. McK., Gorin, M. S., Reynolds, N. M. and Todd, M., 1982 'Archaeological discoveries at Rutland Water', *Hydrobiologica* **88**, 56-77.

Adis, J., 1979 'Problems of interpreting arthropoid sampling with pitfall traps', *Zoologischer Anzieger* **202**, 177-184.

Akerman, J.Y., 1855 *Remains of Pagan Saxondum.* London.

Allason-Jones, L. and Miket, R., 1984 *The Catalogue of Small Finds from South Shields Roman Fort.* Gloucester.

Allen, J. R. L. and Fulford, M. G., 1996 'The distribution of South-East Dorset Black Burnished Ware Category 1 pottery in South-West Britain' *Britannia* **27**, 223-285.

Allsop, J., 1998 'Ab Kettleby church', *Trans. Leicestershire Arch. and Hist. Soc.* **72**, 162.

Amorosi, T., 1989 *A Postcranial Guide to Domestic Neonatal and Juvenile Animals: The identification and ageing of Old World Species,* BAR (International Series) **533**. Oxford.

Amsden, A. F. and Boon, G. C., 1975 'C. O. Waterhouse's list of insects from Silchester (with a note on early identifications of insects in archaeological contexts)', *J. Arch.Science* **2**, 129-136.

Anderson, A., 1980 *A Guide to Roman Fine Wares.* Vorda Research Series **1**, Highworth, Swindon.

Armitage, P., 1982 'A system for ageing and sexing the horn cores of cattle from British post-medieval sites (17th to early 18th century) with special reference to unimproved British longhorn cattle' *in* B.Wilson, C. Grigson and S. Payne (eds.) *Ageing and Sexing Animal Bones From Archaeological Sites .* BAR (British Series) **109**, 37-54. Oxford.

Barnatt, J. and Myers, A., 1988 'Excavations at the Bull Ring Henge, Dove Holes, Derbyshire, 1984-5', *Derbyshire Archaeological Journal* **108**, 5-20.

Bass, W. M., 1987 *Human Osteology – A Laboratory and Field Manual,* 3rd Ed. Missouri Archaeological Society Inc.

Bateman, T., 1848 *Vestiges of the Antiquities of Derbyshire, and the Sepulchral Usages of its Inhabitants, from the Most Remote Ages to the Reformation.* London.

Bird, J., 1981 'The samian ware' *in* Todd 1981, 25-26.

Birley, R., 1977 *Vindolanda:A Roman Frontier Post on Hadrian's Wall.* London. Thames and Hudson.

Boardman S., and Jones G., 1990 'Experiments on the effect of charring on cereal plant components', *J. Archaeological Science* **17**, 1-11.

Boddington, A., 1996 *Raunds Furnells:The Anglo-Saxon Church and Church Yard.* English Heritage Archaeological Report 7. London.

Boon, G., 1988 'Counterfeit coins in Roman Britain', *in* R. Reece and J. Casey (eds.) *Coins and the Archaeologist* , 102-189. London.

Booth, P., and Green, S., 1989 'The nature and distribution of certain pink, grog-tempered vessels', *Journal of Roman Pottery Studies* **2**, 77-84.

Bourne, J., 1996 *Anglo-Saxon Landscapes in the East Midlands.* Leicestershire Museums, Leicester.

Bowman, P., 1996 'Contrasting *pays:* Anglo-Saxon Settlement and Landscape in the Langton Hundred' *in* Bourne 1996, 121-146.

Bracegirdle, B. and Miles, P. H., 1979 *An Atlas of Chordate Structure* London: Heinemann.

Bradley, R. J., 1970 'The excavation of a beaker settlement at Belle Tout, East Sussex, England', *Proc. Prehist. Soc.* **36**, 312-379.

Brailsford, J. W., 1949 'Excavations at Little Woodbury, Wilts.' *Proc. Prehist.Soc.*, **12**, 156-68.

Brickstock, R. J., 1987 *Copies of Fel. Temp. Reparatio coinage in Britain,* BAR (British Series) **176**. Oxford.

Brodribb, A. C. C., Hands, A. R. and Walker, D. R., 1968, *Excavations at Shakenoak Farm, Near Wilcote, Oxfordshire Part 1: Sites A and D .* Oxford.

Brothwell, D. R., 1959 'Teeth in earlier human populations', *Proc. Nutritional Society* **18**, 59-65.

Brothwell, D.R., 1972 'Palaeodemography and earlier British Populations', *World Archaeology* **4**, 75-87.

Brothwell, D.R., 1981 *Digging Up Bones* 3rd Edn. OUP, Oxford.

Brown, S., 1989 'Report on the animal bone' *in* V. Gaffney and M. Tingle, *The Maddle Farm Project: and Integratd Survey of Prehistoric and Roman Landscapes on the Berkshire Downs.* BAR (British Series) 200, 183-92. Oxford.

Brown, A. E., 1994 'A Romano-British shell-tempered pottery and tile manufacturing site at Harrold, Bedfordshire', *Bedfordshire Archaeol. Journ.* **21**, 19-107.

Brown, D., 1974 'Problems in continuity', *in* R. T. Rowley (ed.) *Anglo-Saxon Settlement and the Landscape,* 16-19.

Buckland, P. C., 1979 *Thorne Moors: A Palaeoecological Study of a Bronze Age Site,* University of Birmingham, Department of Geography Occ. Paper **8**.

Buckland, P. C., 1980 'Insect remains from the well', *in* I. M. Stead, *Rudston Roman Villa,* 162-167. Yorks. Arch. Soc., Leeds.

Buckland, P. C., 1981 'The early dispersal of insect pests of stored products as indicated by the archaeological record' *J. Stored Products Research,* **17**, 1-12.

Buckland, P. C., 1986 'An insect fauna from a Roman well at Empingham, Rutland', *Trans. Leicestershire Archaeol. and Hist. Soc.* **60**, 1-6.

Burnham, B. and Wacher, J. S., 1990 *The Small Towns of Roman Britain.* Batsford, London.

Bush, H., and Zvelebil, M. (eds.), 1991 *Health in Past Societies.* Tempus Reparatum. Gloucester.

Bushe-Fox, J. P., 1928 *Second Report on the Excavation of the Roman Fort at Richborough, Kent.* Oxford.

Carter, R., 1996 'Dental report' *in* L. Cooper, 'A Roman cemetery at Newarke St, Leicester', *Trans. Leicestershire Archaeol. and Hist. Soc.* **70**, 44-51.

Casey, J., 1988 'The interpretation of Romano-British site finds' *in* R. Reece and J. Casey 1988, 39-57.

Charlesworth, D., 1974 'The glass' *in* Neal 1974, 203-207.

Clark, J. G. D., Higgs, E. S. and Longworth, I. H., 1960 'Excavations of the prehistoric site at Hurst Fen, Mildenhall, Suffolk, 1954, 1957, and 1958', *Proc. Prehist. Soc.* **11**, 202-246.

Clark, J. T., 1966 'The distribution of Lucanus cervus (L.) (Col., Lucanidae) in Britain', *Entomologists' Monthly Magazine,* **102**, 199-204.

Clark, R., 1999 'The Roman pottery' *in* A.Connor and R. Buckley *Roman and Medieval Occupation at Causeway Lane, Leicester.* Leicester Archaeology Monograph 5, 95-164. Leicester.

Clay, P., 1987 'An excavation at Burley Road, Oakham', *in* P. Liddle (ed.), 'Archaeology in Leicestershire and Rutland

1986', *Trans. Leicestershire Archaeol. and Hist. Soc.* **61**, 87-90.

Clay, P., 1989a 'Oakham, Burley Road' *in* P. Liddle (ed.), 'Archaeology in Leicestershire and Rutland 1988', *Trans. Leicestershire Archaeol. and Hist. Soc.* **63**, 108.

Clay, P., 1989b 'Out of the unknown: approaches to prehistoric archaeology in Leicestershire', *in* A. M. Gibson (ed.) *Midlands Prehistory*, 111-121. BAR (British Series) 201. Oxford.

Clay, P., 1992 'An Iron Age farmstead at Grove Farm, Enderby, Leicestershire', *Trans. Leicestershire Archaeol. and Hist. Soc.* **66**, 1-82.

Clay, P., 1996 *The Exploitation of the East Midlands Claylands in Later Prehistory: Aspects of Settlement and Landuse from the Mesolithic to the Iron Age.* University of Leicester unpublished Ph.D thesis.

Clay, P., 1998 ' Neolithic-Early Bronze Age pit circles and their environs at Burley Road, Oakham' *Proc.Prehist.Soc.* **64** , 293-330.

Clay, P., 1999 'The Neolithic and Bronze Ages of Leicestershire and Rutland', *Trans. Leicestershire Archaeol. and Hist. Soc.* **73**, 1-17.

Clay, P., forthcoming *The East Midlands Claylands in Prehistory* Leicester Archaeology Monograph Series. Leicester.

Clay, P. and Graf, A., 1986 'Fieldwork at a prehistoric site at Oakham' , *in* P. Liddle (ed.), 'Archaeology in Leicestershire and Rutland 1985', *Trans. Leicestershire Archaeol. and Hist. Soc.* **60**, 82.

Clough, T. H. McK., 1981 'The coins' *in* Todd 1981, 34.

Cohen, A. and Serjeantson, D., 1983 *A Manual for the Identification of Bird Bones from Archaeological Sites.*

Coles, J.M., 1987 *Meare Village East: The Excavations of A. Bulleid and H. St George Gray 1932-1956* Somerset Levels Papers **13**.

Connor, A., 1993 'Excavations at Drayton II Roman Villa, Leicestershire, 1992', *Trans. Leicestershire Archaeol. and Hist. Soc.* **67** , 79-83.

Cook, A. M. and Dacre, M. W., 1985 *Excavations at Portwey, Andover 1973-75.* Oxford University Committee for Archaeology Monograph **4**.

Cool, H. E. M. and Price, J., 1993 *The Roman Glass from Excavations in Colchester, 1971-1985.* Colchester Archaeological Reports 5.

Cool, H. E. M., and Price, J., forthcoming 'The Roman vessel glass' *in* P. Woodward, *Excavations at Greyhound Yard and the Old Methodist Chapel, Dorchester, Dorset.*

Coope, G. R. and Osbourne, P. J., 1968 'Report on the coleopterous fauna of the Roman Well at Barnsley Park, Gloucestershire', *Trans. Bristol and Gloucestershire Arch. Soc.* **86**, 84-87.

Cooper, L., forthcoming a *The Lithics from Launde, Leicestershire.*

Cooper, L., forthcoming b 'The lithics' *in* N. Finn *A Multi-period site at Eye Kettleby, Melton, Leicestershire.*

Cooper, L. and Humphrey, J., 1998 'The lithics' *in* M. Beamish 'A Middle Iron Age site at Wanlip, Leicestershire' *Trans. Leicestershire Archaeol. and Hist. Soc.* **72**, 63-74.

Cooper, N.J., 1989 'A Study of Roman pottery from the Lower Nene Valley kiln site at Park Farm, Stanground, Peterborough. *Journal of Roman Pottery Studies* **2**, 59-65.

Cooper, N. J., 1996a 'Searching for the blank generation: consumer choice in Roman and post-Roman Britain' in J. Webster and N. J. Cooper (eds.) *Roman Imperialism: Post-Colonial Perspectives*, 85-98. Leicester Archaeology

Monographs **3**. University of Leicester. School of Archaeology.

Cooper, N. J., 1996b 'Anglo-Saxon Settlement in the Gwash Valley, Rutland' *in* Bourne 1996, 165-180.

Cooper, N. J., 1998a 'Rutland Water Fieldwalking Survey, 1990-94',*Trans. Leicestershire Archaeol. and Hist. Soc.* **72**, 189-90.

Cooper, N. J., 1998b 'The supply of pottery to Roman Cirencester' *in* N. Holbrook (ed.) *Cirencester: The Roman Town Defences, Public Buildings and Shops.* Cirencester Excavations 5, 324-350. Cotswold Archaeological Trust.

Cooper, N. J., forthcoming 'The Early Anglo-Saxon pottery' *in* N. Finn *A Multi-period site at Eye Kettleby, Melton, Leicestershire.*

Cooper, N. J., Beavitt, P., O'Sullivan, D. M. and Young, R., 1989 'A report on geophysical survey and trial excavations at the site of the Roman villa near Drayton, Leicestershire, 1988', *Trans. Leicestershire Archaeol. and Hist. Soc.* **63**, 7-17.

Corder, P., 1951 *The Roman Town and Villa at Great Casterton, Rutland, First Report.* University of Nottingham.

Corder, P., 1954 *The Roman Town and Villa at Great Casterton, Rutland, Second Report.* University of Nottingham.

Corder, P., 1961 *The Roman Town and Villa at Great Casterton, Rutland, Third Report for the years 1954-8.* University of Nottingham.

Crowther-Beynon, V. B., 1903 'A Rutland Anglian Cemetery' *The Rutland Magazine* **1**, 87-92.

Crummy, N., 1979 'A chronology of Romano-British bone pins', *Britannia* **10**, 157-163.

Crummy, N., 1983 *The Roman Small Finds from Excavations in Colchester 1971-9.* Colchester Archaeological Report **2**.

Curtis, J., 1862, *British Entomology; being illustrations and descriptions of the Genera of Insects found in Great Britain and Ireland. Coleoptera Part 1.* Lovell Reeve and Co., London.

Cunliffe, B. W., 1971 *Excavations at Fishbourne, 1961-1969,Vol 2: The Finds.* Leeds.

Cunliffe, B. W., 1974 *Iron Age Communities in Britain.* RKP, London.

Dannel, G. B., Hartley, B. R.,Wild, J. P., and Perrin, R. J., 1993 'Excavations on a Romano-British pottery production site at Park Farm, Stanground, Peterborough, 1965-67', *Journal of Roman Pottery Studies* **6**, 51-94. Oxbow Books, Oxford.

de la Bedoyere, G., 1991 *The Buildings of Roman Britain* Batsford. London.

de Bethune, M., 1981 'The Roman pottery: the fine wares and common pottery', *in* Todd 1981, 26-32.

Dechelette, J., 1904 *Les Vases Ceramiques ornes de la Gaule Romaine* . Paris.

D of E., 1968 *Archaeological Excavations 1967* H.M.S.O.

D of E., 1970 *Archaeological Excavations 1969* H.M.S.O.

Dieckmann, L., 1972 'Ceutorhynchus-Studien (Coleoptera: Curculionidae)', *Beitrage Ent.* **21**, 585-593.

Dobney, K., and Goodman, A., 1991 'Epidemiological studies of dental enamel hypoplasias in Mexico and Bradford: their relevance to archaeological skeletal studies' *in* Bush and Zvelebil 1991, 81-100.

Driesch, A. von den, 1976 *A Guide to the Measurement of Animal Bones from Archaeological Sites.* University Press, Cambridge, Massachussets.

Duncan, C., 1998 'Sex determination using tooth measurements' *in* S. Anderson and K. Boyle (eds.) *Current and Recent Research in Osteoarchaeology.* Oxbow Books, Oxford.

Dutour, O., 1986 'Enthesopathies (lesions of muscular insertion) as indicators of the activities of Neolithic Saharan

Populations', *American Journal of Physical Anthropology* **71**, 221-224.

Elsdon, S. M., 1979 'Baked clay objects' *in* H. Wheeler, 'Excavations at Willington, Derbyshire', *Derbyshire Archaeological Journal* **99**, 197-210.

Elsdon, S. M., 1992a 'East Midlands Scored Ware' *Trans. Leicestershire Archaeol. and Hist. Soc.* **66,** 83-91.

Elsdon, S. M., 1992b 'The Iron Age pottery' *in* Clay 1992, 38-52.

Elsdon, S. M., forthcoming 'Iron Age pottery' *in* M. Beamish, *Pipeline Excavations in Rutland and East Leicestershire.*

Esmonde Cleary, A. S., 1989 *The Ending of Roman Britain.* Batsford, London.

Evison, V. I., 1977 'Supporting-arm brooches and equal-armed brooches in England', *Studien zur Sachsenforshung.*

Evison, V. I., 1987 *Dover: The Buckland Anglo-Saxon Cemetery.* HBMC(E) Arch. Report 3, London.

Farwell, D. E. and Molleson, T. I., 1993 *Poundbury Volume 2: The Cemeteries.* Dorset Natural History and Archaeology Society Monograph **11.**

Faussett, B., 1856 *Inventorium Sepulchrale: An Account of Some Antiquities Dug Up at Gilton, Kingston, Sibertswold, Barfriston, Beakesbourne, Chartham, and Crundale, in the County of Kent, from AD 1757 to AD 1773 .* London.

Finn, N., 1997 'Excavations at Eye Kettleby, Melton Mowbray' *Trans. Leicestershire Archaeol. and Hist. Soc.* **71,** 88.

Fowler, E., 1960 'The origins and development of the penannular brooch in Europe', *Proc.Prehist.Soc.* **26,** 149-177.

Fox, C., 1923 *The Archaeology of the Cambridge Region.* Cambridge.

Frere, S. S., 1972 *Verulamium Excavations 1.* Oxford.

Garton, D., and Beswick, P., 1983 'The survey and excavation of a Neolithic settlement area at Mount Pleasant, Kenslow', *Derbyshire Archaeological Journal* **103,** 7-40.

Gilbert Jr. R. I. and Mielke, J. H. (eds.), 1985 *The Analysis of Prehistoric Diets.* Academic Press Inc., Florida.

Girling, M. A., 1989 'The insect fauna of the Roman well at the cattlemarket' *in* A. Down, *Chichester Excavations* **6,** 234-241. Philimore, Chichester.

Going, C. J., 1987 *The Mansio and other sites in the South Eastern sector of Caesaromagus: The Roman Pottery.* Chelmsford Archaeological Report. CBA Res. Rep. **66.**

Going, C. J. 1992 'Economic long waves in the Roman period: a reconaissance of the ceramic evidence', *Oxford Journal of Archaeology* **11,** 93-117.

Going, C. J., and Ford, B., 1988 'The Romano-British pottery' *in* N. P. Wickenden, *Excavations at Great Dunmow, Essex.* East Anglian Archaeology Report **41,** Chelmsford Archaeological Trust Report 7, 61-76.

Grainger, G. and Mahany, C., forthcoming *Roman and Anglo-Saxon Burials, and a Roman Kiln, Excavated at Great Casterton in 1966.*

Grant, A., 1975 'The animal bones' in B. W. Cunliffe *Excavations at Portchester Castle, Volume 1,* 378-408. Oxford.

Grant, A., 1982. 'The uses of tooth wear as a guide to the age of domestic ungulates', *in* B. Wilson, C. Grigson and S. Payne (eds.) *Ageing and Sexing Animal Bones From Archaeological Sites.* BAR (British Series) **109,** 91-108. Oxford.

Grant, A., 1984 'Animal husbandry' *in* B. W. Cunliffe *Danebury: an Iron Age Hillfort in Hampshire.* CBA Res. Rep. **52,** 496-548. London.

Grant, A., 1989 'Animals in Roman Britain' *in* M. Todd (ed.) *Research on Roman Britain 1960-89* Britannia Monograph Series **11,** 131-142. London.

Green, B., and Rogerson, A., 1978 *The Anglo-Saxon Cemetery at Bergh Apton, Norfolk,* East Anglian Archaeology Report 7, Norfolk.

Green, S., 1980 *The Flint Arrowheads of the British Isles,* BAR (British Series) 75, 2 vols. Oxford.

Green, S., 1985 'Flint arrowheads: typology and interpretation', *Lithics* 5, 19-39.

Grew, F., and de Neergaard, M., 1988 *Shoes and Pattens, Medieval Finds from Excavations in London* 2. HMSO, London.

Guido, M., 1978 *The Glass Beads of the Prehistoric and Roman Periods in Britain and Ireland,* London.

Hadman, J., 1978 'Aisled buildings in Roman Britain', *in* Todd 1978, 187-95.

Hadman, J., and Upex, S., 1975 'A Roman pottery kiln at Sulehay, near Yarwell' *Durobrivae* 3, 16-18.

Haley, G., 1993 *Fieldwalked Flint from Oakham, Rutland.* MA dissertation in Post-excavation Skills. University of Leicester Library.

Hall, A.R., Kenward, H. K. and Williams, D., 1980 *Environmental Evidence from Roman deposits in Skeldergate,* Archaeology of York, fasc. **14/3** CBA, London.

Hall, M., 1992 'The prehistoric pottery' *in* J. Moore and D. Jennings *Reading Business Park: A Bronze Age Landscape,* 63-82. Thames Valley Landscapes: The Kennet Valley vol. 1.

Hamerow, H., 1989 'Anglo-Saxon Pottery and Spatial Development at Mucking, Essex', *Berichten. R.O.B ,* 245-273.

Hammerson, M., 1989. 'The Roman Coins from Southwark', *in Southwark Excavations 1989 ,* 417-426. Southwark and Lambeth Excavation Committee.

Hammond, P. M., 1974 'Changes in the British Coleopterus fauna' *in* D.L. Hawksworth (ed.) *The Changing Flora and Fauna of Britain,* Systematics Association Special Volume **6,** 323-370. Academic Press.

Harden, D. and Price, J., 1971, 'The glass', *in* Cunliffe 1971, Vol 2, 317-68.

Harke, H. 1989 'Early Saxon weapon burials: frequencies, distributions and weapon combinations' in S. C. Hawkes (ed.) *Weapons and Warfare in Anglo-Saxon England,* Oxford University Committee for Archaeology monograph **21,** Oxford, 49-62.

Hartley, R. F., 1983 *The Medieval Earthworks of Rutland, a Survey,* Leicestershire Museums Archaeological Report 7.

Hattatt, R., 1985 *Iron Age and Roman Brooches, a Second Selection of Brooches from the Author's Collection.* Oxford.

Hawkes, S. C. and Dunning, G. C., 1962 'Soldiers and settlers in Britain, fourth to fifth Century, with a catalogue of animal-ornamented buckles and related belt-fittings', *Med. Archaeol* 5 (1961), 1-70.

Hawkes, S. C., and Grove, L. R. A., 1963 'Finds from a seventh century Anglo-Saxon cemetery at Milton Regis'. *Arch .Cant . 78,* 22-38.

Henderson, A. M., 1949 'Small objects in metal, bone, glass, etc.' *in* J.P. Bushe-Fox, *Fourth Report on the Excavations of the Roman Fort at Richborough, Kent,* 106-160. Oxford.

Herepath, N., 1993 *Fieldwalked Flint from the Gwash Valley, Leicestershire.* Unpublished dissertation for the MA in Post-excavation Skills. University of Leicester Library.

Hermet, F., 1934 *La Graufesenque (Condatomago) .* Paris.

Hillam, J., 1985 'Excavations at Fiskerton, Lincs.' *Current Archaeology* **96,** 21-27.

Hillman G., 1981 'Reconstruction of crop husbandry practices from charred remains of crops' *in* R. Mercer *Farming Practices in British Prehistory.* Edinburgh University Press.

Hillman G., 1982 'Evidence for malting spelt', *in* R. Leech (ed.) *Excavations at Catsgore 1970-73. A Romano-British Village,* 137-41. Western Archaeological Trust Excavation Monograph 2. Bristol.

Hines, J., 1984 *The Scandinavian Character of Anglian England in the pre-Viking Period,* BAR (British Series) 124. Oxford.

Hines, J., 1989 'The military context of the adventus Saxonum' *in* S. C. Hawkes (ed.) *Weapons and Warfare in Anglo-Saxon England,* Oxford University Committee for Archaeology monograph 21, Oxford, 25-48.

Hingley, R., 1989 *Rural Settlement in Roman Britain.* Seaby, London.

Hirst, S. M., 1985 *An Anglo-Saxon Inhumation Cemetery at Sewerby, East Yorkshire,* University of York Archaeological Publications 4.

Hoffman, A., 1958 *Faune de France,* 52, 59, 62. Coleopteres Curculionides, Lechevalier, Paris.

Hoskins, W. G., 1957 *Leicestershire: and Illustrated Essay on the History of the Landscape.* Hodder and Stoughton, London.

Howe, M. D., Perrin, R.J. and Mackreth, D. F., 1980 *Roman Pottery from the Nene Valley: a Guide.* Peterborough City Museum Occasional Paper 2.

Hull, M. R., 1968 'The brooches' *in* B.W. Cunliffe (ed.)*Fifth Report on the Excavations of the Roman Fort at Richborough, Kent,* 74-93. Oxford.

Hunt, E. E. and Gleser, I., 1955 'The estimation of age and sex of preadolescent children from bones and teeth', *American Journal of Physical Anthropology* 13, 479-488.

Hunter, F. A., *et al.* 1973 'Insects and mites of maltings in the East Midlands of England', *J .Stored Products Research,* 9, 119-141. Pergamon Press, Oxford.

Hunter, R. H. F, 1982 *Reproduction of Farm Animals.* Longman Handbooks in Agriculture, London

Hyslop, M., 1964 'Two Anglo-Saxon cemeteries at Chamberlains Barn, Leighton Buzzard, Bedfordshire', *Archaeol. J.* 120 (1963), 161-200.

Isings, C., 1957 *Roman Glass from Dated Finds.* Groningen.

Jackson, D. A and Ambrose, T. M., 1978 'Excavations at Wakerly, Northants., 1972-75', *Britannia* 9, 115-242.

Jackson, D. and Dix, B., 1987 ' Late Iron Age and Roman Settlement at Weekley, Northants.', *Northants. Archaeology* 21 , 41-93.

Jackson, D. A. and Knight, D., 1985 'An Early Iron Age and Beaker site near Gretton, Northants.', *Northants. Archaeol.* 20, 67-86.

Jeannel, R., 1942 'Coleopteres Carabiques', *Faune de France* 40, 572-1173.

Jones, E., 1995 'Report of the RLHRS Archaeological Committee' *Rutland Record* 15, 240-242.

Jones, E., 1997 'Report of the RLHRS Archaeological sub-Committee' *Rutland Record* 17, 319-322.

Jones, E., 1999 'Report of the RLHRS Archaeological sub-Committee' *Rutland Record* 19, 407-410.

Jones, G., 1982 *Plant remains from the Roman villa at Norfolk Street, Leicester.* Ancient Monuments Laboratory Report 4973 English Heritage 1982.

Jones, G., 1987 'Carbonized grain' *in* D. C. Mynard (ed.) *Roman Milton Keynes: Excavations and Fieldwork 1971-82.* Bucks. Arch. Soc. Monograph 1, 192-3.

Keevil, G. D., 1996 'The reconstruction of the Romano-British villa at Redlands Farm, Stanwick, Northants.' *in*

P. Johnson and I. Haynes (eds.) *Roman Architecture in Roman Britain.* CBA Res.Rep. 94, 44-55.

Kennet, D. H., 1983 'The earliest male grave at Kempston', *Beds.Arch .J.* 16, 88-91.

Kenward, H. K., 1975 'Pitfalls in the environmental interpretation of insect death assemblages', *J .Arch. Science* 2, 85-94.

Kenyon, K., 1948 *Excavations at the Jewry Wall Site, Leicester.* Oxford: Rep. Res. Comm. Soc. Antiq. London 15.

King, A. C., 1991 'Food production and consumption – meat', *in* R. F. J. Jones (ed.) *Roman Britain: Recent Trends ,* 15-20. Recent Trends 5, J .R. Collis Publications, University of Sheffield.

King, C. E., 1978 'The Woodeaton hoard and the problem of Constantinian imitation, AD 330-341', *Numismatic Chronicle* 88, 38-65.

Kleot, G. S., and Hincks, W. D., 1977 *A Check List of British Insects,* 2nd Ed. (Completely Revised) Part 3: *Coleoptera and Strepsiptera* (rev. R.D. Pope). Roy. Ent. Soc. of London.

Knight, D., 1984 *Late Bronze Age and Iron Age settlement in the Nene and Great Ouse Basins.* BAR (British Series) 130, Oxford.

Landin, B. O., 1961 'Ecological studies of dung beetles', *Opuscula Entomologica* Suppl. 19.

Le Cheminant, R., 1978 'The development of the pipeclay hair curler – a preliminary study', *London Archaeol .* 3 (1976-1980), 187-191.

Leeds, E. T., 1945 'The distribution of the Anglo-Saxons archaeologically considered', *Archaeologia* 91, 1-106.

Levine, M. A., 1982 'The use of crown height measurements and eruption-wear sequences to age horse teeth' *in* B. Wilson, C. Grigson and S. Payne (eds.) *Ageing and Sexing Animal Bones from Archaeological Sites.* BAR (British Series) 109, 223-250. Oxford.

Liddle, P., 1980 'An Anglo-Saxon cemetery at Wanlip, Leicestershire', *Trans. Leicestershire Archaeol. and Hist. Soc.* 55, 11-21.

Liddle, P., 1994 'The Medbourne Area Survey' *in* M. Parker-Pearson and T. Schadla-Hall (eds.) *Looking at the Land: Archaeological Landscapes in Eastern England,* 34-36. Leicester.

Liddle, P., 1996 'The Archaeology of Anglo-Saxon Leicestershire', *in* Bourne 1996, 1-10.

Liddle, P. forthcoming *The Anglo-Saxon Cemetery at Glen Parva.*

Lindroth, C. H., 1945; 1949 *Die Fennoskandischen Carabidae Eine Tiergeographische Studie,* Meddelander fran Gotebords Musei Zologiska Avdelsing (3 vols).

Lindroth, C. H., 1974 Carabidae, *Handbooks for the Identification of British Insects,* 4, 2. Roy. Ent. Soc., London.

Lucas, J., 1993 'Roman burial at Edith Weston', *Rutland Record* 13, 144.

MacGregor, A., 1977 'Bone skates: a review of the evidence', *Archaeol .J .* 133 (1976): 57-74.

MacGregor, A., 1985 *Bone, Antler, Ivory and Horn: The Technology of Skeletal Materials since the Roman period.* London.

Mackreth, D. F., 1973 *Roman Brooches.* Salisbury.

Mackreth, D. F., 1996 *Orton Hall Farm: A Roman and Early Anglo-Saxon Farmstead.* East Anglian Archaeology Report 76.

Maltby, J. M., 1979 *The Animal Bones from Exeter, 1971-1975 .* Exeter Archaeological Reports 2.

Maltby, J. M., 1985 'The animal bones' *in* P. J. Fasham *The Prehistoric Settlement at Winnal Down, Winchester.* Trust for

Wessex Archaeology Monograph, 97-112.

Manchester, K. and Elmhirst, 1980 *The Anglo-Saxon Cemetery at Eccles, Kent.* Unpublished. University of Bradford.

Manley, 1985 'The archer and the army in the Late Anglo-Saxon period' in S. C. Hawkes, J. Campbell and D. Brown, *Anglo-Saxon studies in Archaeology and History* **4**. Oxford University Committee for Archaeology, Oxford.

Manning, W. H., 1972 'The iron objects' *in* Frere 1972, 163-195.

Manning, W. H., 1976 *Romano-British Ironwork in the Museum of Antiquities, Newcastle-Upon-Tyne.* Newcastle-Upon-Tyne.

Manning, W. H., 1985 *Catalogue of the Romano-British Iron Tools, Fittings, and Weapons in the British Museum.* London.

Marney, P.T., 1989 *Belgic and Roman Pottery from Milton Keynes.* Buckinghamshire Archaelogical Society Report **2**.

Marsden, P., 1998 ' The Prehistoric pottery' *in* M. Beamish 'A Middle Iron Age site at Wanlip, Leicestershire' *Trans. Leicestershire Archaeol. and Hist. Soc.* **72**, 44-63.

Marsden, P., 2000 'The Prehistoric pottery' *in* B. M. Charles, A. Parkinson and S. Foreman 'A Bronze Age ditch and Iron Age settlement at Elms Farm, Humberstone, Leicester' *Trans. Leicestershire Archaeol. and Hist. Soc.* **74**, 170-186.

Marsden, P., forthcoming *The Roman Pottery in Excavations at Melton Mowbray,* Leicestershire Museums Archive Report.

Martin, D. L., Armelagos, G. J. and King, J. R., 1979 'Degenerative joint disease of the long bones in Dickson Mounds', *Henry Ford Hospital Medical Journal* **27/1**, 60-63.

Martin, D. L., Goodman, A. H. and Armelagos, G. J., 1985 'Skeletal pathologies as indicators of quality and quantity of diet', *in* Gilbert *et al.* 1985.

Mays, S. A., 1996 'Human skeletal remains' *in* Timby 1996, 21-34.

Meadows, I., 1999 'Excavations at Ketton', *Trans. Leicestershire Archaeol. and Hist. Soc.* **73**, 119-121.

Meaney, A. L., 1981 *Anglo-Saxon Amulets and Curing Stones.* BAR British Series **96**. Oxford.

Meaney, A. L. and Hawkes, S. C., 1970 *Two Anglo-Saxon Cemeteries at Winnal, Winchester, Hampshire.* London.

Meek, J., 1998 'Whitwell, Main Street' *Rutland Record* **18**, 368.

Meindl, R. S. and Lovejoy, C. O., 1985 'Ectocranial suture closure: a revised method for the determination of skeletal age at death based on the lateral-anterior sutures' *American Journal of Physical Anthropology* **68**, 57-66.

Merbs, C. F., 1983 *Patterns of activity induced pathology in a Canadian Inuit Population,* National Museum of Canada, Ontario.

Miles, A. E. W., 1969 'The dentition of the Anglo-Saxons', *Proc. Royal Society of Medicine* **62**, 1311-1315.

Miles, A. E. W., 1989 *An Early Christian chapel and burial ground on the Isle of Ensay, Outer Hebrides, Scotland with a study of skeletal remains,* BAR (British Series), **212** Oxford.

Miles, D., 1984 *Archaeology at Barton Court Farm, Abingdon, Oxon.* Oxford Archaeological Unit Report **3**, CBA Research Report **50**.

Mohr, K. H., 1966 'Familie Chrysomelidae' *in* H. Freude, K. W. Harde and G. A. Lohse (eds.) *Die Kafer Mitteleuropas* **9**, 95-280 Goecke and Evers, Krefeld.

Molleson, T., 1989 'Social implications of mortality patterns of juveniles from Poundbury Camp Romano-British cemetery', *Anthropologisches Anzeiger* **47** (**1**), 27-38.

Monckton, A., 1995 'Environmental archaeology in Leicestershire', *Trans. Leicestershire Archaeol. and Hist. Soc.,* **69**, 32-41.

Monckton, A., 1999 *Charred plant remains from corn driers and other contexts of a Romano-British settlement site at Billesley*

Manor Farm, Warwickshire. Ancient Monuments Laboratory Report 25/99 English Heritage 1999.

Moore, K., 1985 *Clinically Orientated Anatomy,* 2nd edn. Williams and Wilkins, Baltimore.

Moore, W. R. G. and Williams, J. H., 1975 'A Later Neolithic Site at Ecton, Northampton', *Northamptonshire Archaeology* **10**, 3-30.

Morris, R. and Roxan, J., 1980 'Churches on Roman buildings' *in* W. Rodwell (ed.) *Temples, Churches, and Religion in Roman Britain.* BAR (British Series) **77**, 175-210. Oxford.

Myres, J. N. L., 1969 *Anglo-Saxon Pottery and the Settlement of England.* Oxford.

Myres, J. N. L, 1977 *A Corpus of Anglo-Saxon Pottery of the Pagan Period.* Oxford.

Myres, J. N. L. and Green, B., 1973 *The Anglo-Saxon Cemeteries of Caistor-by-Norwich and Markshall, Norfolk.* Soc. Antiqs. London.

Neal, D. S, 1974 *The Excavation of the Roman Villa in Gadebridge Park, Hemel Hempstead, 1963-8.* London.

Neal, D. S. and Butcher, S .A., 1974 'Miscellaneous objects of bronze' *in* Neal 1974, 157-187.

Ortner, D. J. and Putschar, W. G. J., 1985 *Identification of Pathological Conditions in Human Skeletal Remains.* Smithsonian Contributions to Anthropology **28**. Smithsonian Institution Press, Washington DC.

Osborne, P. J., 1969 'An insect fauna of Late Bronze Age date from Wilsford, Wiltshire', *J . Animal Ecology* **38**, 555-556.

Osborne, P .J., 1971 An insect fauna from the Roman site at Alcester, Warwickshire, *Britannia* **2**, 156-165.

Oswald, F., 1936-7 *Index of Figure-Types on Terre Sigillata ("Samian Ware").* Liverpool.

Oswald, F., and Davies Price, T., 1920 *An Introduction to the Study of Terra Sigillata.* London.

Palm, T., 1959 'Die Holz-und Rindenkafer der sud-und mittelschwedischen Laubbaume', *Opuscula Entomologica,* suppl. **16**.

Parsons, D., 1996 'Introduction: Leicestershire in the Anglo-Saxon period' *in* Bourne 1996, xix-xxiii.

Percival, J., 1976 *The Roman Villa: An Historical Introduction.* Batsford, London.

Perrin, R. J., 1980 'London ware' *Durobrivae* **8**, 10.

Perrin, R. J., 1981 'The Late Roman pottery of Great Casterton – thirty years on', *in* A. C. Anderson and A. S. Anderson (eds.) *Roman Pottery Research in Britain and North-West Europe.* BAR (International Series) **123**. Oxford.

Perrin, R.J., 1999 'Roman pottery from excavations at or near to the Roman small town of Durobrivae, Water newton, Cambridgeshire, 1956-58', *Journal of Roman Pottery Studies* **8**, 1-141.

Phythian-Adams, C., 1977 'Rutland reconsidered' *in* A. Dornier (ed.), *Mercian Studies,* 63-84. Leicester University Press, Leicester.

Phythian-Adams, C., 1980 'The emergence of Rutland and the making of the realm', *Rutland Record* **1**, 5-12.

Pickering, J., and Hartley, R. F., 1985 *Past Worlds in a Landscape: Archaeological Cropmarks in Leicestershire.* Leicestershire Museums Archaeological Report **11**, Leicester.

Pitt Rivers, A., 1888, *Excavations in Cranbourne Chase, near Rushmore, on the Borders of Dorset and Wilts., 1880-1888.* Vol. 2. London.

Pitts, M., 1978 'On the shape of waste flakes as an index of technological change in lithic industries', *J. Archaeol. Sci.* **5**, 17-37.

Pollard, R. J., 1991 'Drayton II Roman Villa' *Trans.*

Leicestershire Archaeol. and Hist. Soc. **65,** 85-88.

Pollard, R. J., 1994 'The Late Iron Age and Roman pottery' in P. N. Clay and R. J. Pollard, *Iron Age and Roman Occupation in the West Bridge Area, Leicester. Excavations 1962-71,* 51-114. Leicester, Leicestershire Museums, Arts and Records Service.

Pollard, R. J., 1999 *Roman Pottery Fabrics from Leicestershire: a Concordance.* Unpublished document. Leicestershire Museums.

Powlesland, D., 1998 'West Heslerton Assessment', *Internet Archaeology* **5.**

Powell, F., 1996 'The human remains' in Boddington 1996, 113-124.

Price, J., 1982 'The glass' *in* Webster and Smith 1982, 174-185

Price, J., and Cool, H. E. M., 1983 'Glass from the excavations of 1974-76' *in* A. E. Brown and C. Woodfield 'Excavations at Towcester, Northamptonshire: The Alchester Road suburb', 115-124, *Northamptonshire Archaeology* **118,** 43-140.

Prummel, W., 1988 *Atlas for Identification of Foetal Skeletal Elements of Cattle, Horse, Sheep and Pig. Archaeozoologia,* **II/1, 2,** Part 3, 13-26.

Prummel, W., 1989, Appendix to *Atlas for Identification of Foetal Elements of Cattle, Horse, Sheep and Pig. Archaeozoologia,* **III/1, 2,** 71-78.

Reece, R., 1972, 'A short survey of the Roman coins on fourteen sites in Britain', *Britannia* **3,** 269-276.

Reece, R., 1987 *Coinage in Roman Britain.* Seaby, London.

Reece, R., 1988 'Clustering of coin finds in Britain, France and Italy, *in* Reece and Casey 1988, 73-86.

Reece, R. and Casey, J. (eds), 1988 *Coins and the Archaeologist.* London.

Richmond, I. A., and Gillam, J. P., 1951 'The Temple of Mithras at Carrawburgh', *Arch. Ael.* **29,** 1-92.

Ripoll, G. and Arce, J., 2001 'The transformation and end of Roman *villae* in the west (fourth-seventh centuries): problems and perspectives' *in* G. P. Brogiolo, N. Gauthier and N.J. Christie (eds.) *Towns and their Territories between Late Antiquity and the Early Middle Ages* . Brill, Leiden.

Roberts, C. A. and Manchester, K., 1995 *The Archaeology of Disease* (2nd edn.). Alan Sutton, Stroud.

Robinson, M. A, 1983 'Arable/Pastoral Ratios from Insects', *in* M. Jones (ed.) *Integrating the Subsistence Economy,* 19-47, BAR (International Series) **181.** Oxford.

Rodwell, W. J. and Rodwell, K. A., 1985 *Rivenhall: Investigations of a villa, church and village, 1950-1977.* Chelmsford Archaeological Trust Report **4,** CBA Research Report 55.

Rogers, G. B., 1974 *Poteries sigillees de la Gaule centrale, Gallia* Suppl. **28.**

Rogers, J., Dieppe, I., and Dieppe, J., 1981 'Arthritis in Saxon and medieval skeletons', *British Medical Journal* **283,** 1668-70.

Rook, T., 1988 Proposal for the Reconstruction of Welwyn Roman Baths. Herts. Unpublished document.

Rose, J. C., Condon, K. W. and Goodman, A. H., 1985 'Diet and Dentition: Developmental disturbances' *in* Gilbert *et al.* 1985.

Saville, A., 1973 'A reconstruction of the prehistoric flint assemblage from Bourne Pool, Aldridge, Staffordshire', *Staffs. Arch. Hist. Soc.* **14** , 6-28.

Saville, A., 1981 'Honey Hill, Elkington: A Northamptonshire Mesolithic Site, *Northamptonshire Archaeology* **16,** 1-13.

Scmidt, E., 1972. *Atlas of Animal Bones.* Elsevier Publishing Company, Amsterdam.

Sills, J. and Kinsley, G., forthcoming *Excavations at Weelsby Ave. Grimsby* .

Silver, I. A., 1969. 'The ageing of domestic animals', *in* D. R. Brothwell and E. Higgs (eds.) *Science in Archaeology* , 289-295. Thames and Hudson, London.

Smith, J .T., 1964 'Romano-British aisled houses', *Archaeol. J.* **120,** 1-30.

Smith, J .T., 1978a 'Halls or yards? A problem of villa interpretation', *Britannia* **9,** 351-358.

Smith, J .T., 1978b Villas as a key to social structure *in* Todd 1978, 149-85.

Stanfield, J. A. and Simpson, G., 1958 *Central Gaulish Potters.* London.

Stead, I. M., 1976 *Excavations at Winterton Roman Villa 1958-67.* DoE Archaeological Report 9.

Stead, I. M. and Rigby, V., 1986 *Baldock: The Excavation of a Roman and Pre-Roman Settlement, 1968-72* . London.

Stewart, T. D., 1958 'The rate of development of osteoarthritis in American whites and its significance in skeletal age identification', *The Leech* (Johannesburg) **28,** 144-151.

Stirland, A., 1991 'Diagnosis of occupationally related palaeo-pathology: can it be done?' *in* D. J. Ortner and A. C. Aufterheide (eds.) *Human Palaeopathology: Current Syntheses and Future Options,* 40-47. Smithsonian Institution Press, Washington D.C.

Stuart-Macadam, P., 1987 'Porotic hyperostosis, more evidence to support the anaemia theory', *American Journal of Physical Anthropology* **74,** 521-6.

Stuart-Macadam, P., 1991 'Anaemia in Roman Britain: Poundbury Camp', *in* H. Bush and M. Zvelebil 1991, 101-114.

Swanton, M. J., 1973 *The Spearheads of the Anglo-Saxon Settlements.* Royal Archaeological Institute.

Symonds, R., forthcoming a *Roman Pottery from Excavations at Thistleton, Leicestershire.*

Taylor, J., forthcoming a 'Rural society in Roman Britain' *in* S. James and M. Millett (eds.) *Research Agendas for Roman Britain* . CBA Res. Rep. Series.

Taylor, J., forthcoming b '*Houses, tradition and social discourse: some thoughts on rural architecture in Roman Britain'.*

Thomas, J., 1998 'Empingham, Main Street' *Rutland Record* **18,** 368.

Thorn, F., 1980 *Domesday Book: Rutland,* Phillimore Chichester

Timby, J. R., 1996 *The Anglo-Saxon Cemetery at Empingham II, Rutland.* Oxbow Monograph 70. Oxford.

Tixier, J., 1974 *Glossary for the description of stone tools, with specific reference to the Epipalaeolithic of the Maghreb,* Translated by M. H. Newcomer, Washington State University Press.

Todd, M., 1968a 'The commoner Late Roman coarse wares of the East Midlands', *Antiq. J.* **48,** 192-209.

Todd, M., 1968b *The Roman Fort at Great Casterton, Rutland.* Nottingham University.

Todd, M., 1973 *The Coritani.* London

Todd, M. (ed.), 1978 *Studies in the Romano-British Villa.* Leicester University Press, Leicester.

Todd, M., 1981 *The Iron Age and Roman Settlement at Whitwell.* Leicestershire Museums Archaeological Report Series **1**

Tomber, R. and Dore, J. N., 1998 *The National Roman Fabric Reference Collection: a Handbook.* MoLAS Monograph 2. London.

Turner, J., 1981 'The vegetation' *in* M. Jones and G. Dimbleby (eds.), *The Environment of Man: The Iron Age to the Anglo-*

Saxon Period. BAR (British Series) **87**, 67-73, Oxford.

Ubelaker, D. H., 1978 *Human Skeletal Remains: Excavation, analysis and interpretation*. Aldine, Chicago.

Veen van der M., 1989 'Charred grain assemblages from Roman-period corn driers in Britain'. *Archaeol. J.* **146** (1989), 302-319.

Vince, A. G. and Young, J., 1992 *The East Midlands Anglo-Saxon Pottery Project: Fourth Annual Report*. City of Lincoln Archaeology Unit Arch. Rep. 86.

Wakely, J., 1996 'Skeletal analysis' *in* L. Cooper 'A Roman cemetery at Newarke St., Leicester', *Trans. Leicestershire Archaeol. and Hist. Soc.* **70**, 33-44.

Wakely, J., Manchester, K. and Roberts, C. A., 1991 'Scanning electron microscopy of rib lesions', *International Journal of Osteoarchaeology*, **1**, 185-189.

Waldron, A., 1993 'The health of the adults' *in* T. Molleson and M.Cox, *Spitalfields Volume 2: the Middling Sort*, 67-87. CBA Res. Rep. **86**.

Waldron, A., 1994 'The human remains' *in* V. Evison, *An Anglo-Saxon Cemetery at Great Chesterford, Essex*, 52-66. CBA Res. Rep. 91.

Waldron, T., 1989 'The effects of urbanisation on human health: The evidence from skeletal remains' *in* D. Serjeantson and T. Waldron (eds.) *Diet and Crafts in Towns – the evidence of animal remains from the Roman to the Post-Medieval periods*, , BAR (British Series) **199**, Oxford.

Walker, P. L., Johnson, J. R., and Lambert, P. M., 1988 'Age and Sex biases in the preservation of human skeletal remains', *American Journal of Physical Anthropology* **76**, 183-188.

Wardle, A., 1990 'The artefacts other than coins, pottery and glass vessels' *in* D. S. Neal, A. Wardle and J. Hunn (eds) *Excavation of the Iron Age, Roman, and Medieval Settlement at Gorhambury, St Albans*, 113-169. London.

Webster, G., 1982, 'The small finds', *in* G.Webster and L. Smith, 'The excavation of a Romano-British rural establishment at Barnsley Park, Gloucestershire, 1961-1979, Part 2: *c.* AD 360-400+, 107-139. *Trans Bristol and Gloucestershire Archaeological Society* **100**, 65-189.

Weiss, K. M., 1972 'On the systematic bias in skeletal sexing', *American Journal of Physical Anthropology* **37**, 239-250.

Wenham, L. P., 1968 *The Romano-British Cemetery at Trentholme Drive, York*, DoE Archaeol Rep, HMSO, London.

West, S., 1985 *West Stow: The Anglo-Saxon Village*, 2 vols. East Anglian Archaeology Report **24**, Ipswich.

Wheeler, R. E. M, 1943 *Maiden Castle, Dorset*. Oxford.

Wheeler, R. E. M. and Wheeler, T. V., 1936 *Verulamium, a Belgic and two Roman Cities*. London.

White, R. H., 1988 *Roman and Celtic Objects from Anglo-Saxon Graves: A Catalogue and an Interpretation of their Use*. Oxford.

Whitwell, J .B., 1982 *The Coritani: Some Aspects of the Iron Age Tribe and the Roman Civitas*. BAR (British Series) **99**, Oxford.

Whitwell, J .B. and Dean, M. J, 1966 'Great Casterton', *East Midlands Archaeological Bulletin* **8**, 4-6.

Wickham-Jones, C. R., 1991 *Rhum: Mesolithic and later sites at Kinloch, Excavations 1984-86*. Society of Antiquaries for Scotland Report 7.

Wild, J. P., 1973 'A fourth century potter's workshop and kilns at Stibbington, Peterborough' *in* A. P. Detsicas (ed.) *Recent Research in Romano-British Coarse Pottery* CBA Report **10**, 135-38.

Wild, J. P., 1975 'The pottery' *in* Hadman and Upex 1975, 16.

Wild, J. P. and Dannel, G. B., 1973 'Lynch Farm' *Durobrivae* **1**, 20.

Wilson, D. R., 1970 'Roman Britain in 1969', *Britannia* **1**, 269-305.

Wilson, D. R., 1971 'Roman Britain in 1970', *Britannia* **2**, 243-288.

Wilson, D. R., 1972 'Roman Britain in 1971', *Britannia* **3**, 299-351.

Woodland, R., 1982 *Pottery from Nether Hambleton*. Unpublished Archive Report, Leicestershire Museums.

Woods, P.J., 1970 *Excavations at Brixworth, Northants, 1965-70 The Romano-British Villa*. Northampton.

Young, R., 1987 *Lithics and Subsistence in North-Eastern England*. BAR (British Series) **161**, Oxford.

Young, R. and Humphrey, J., 1999 'Flint use in England after the Bronze Age: time for a re-evaluation?' *Proc. Prehist. Soc.* **65**, 231-242

Young, R. and Kay, D., 1989 'Discriminant function analysis (DFA) of mixed lithic scatters in the north-east of England: a case of misclassified identity.' *Lithics.* **9**, 9-14.

Youngs, S., (ed.) 1989 *The Work of Angels: Masterpieces of Celtic Metalwork, 6th-9th Centuries AD*, London.